The abc of Fishing

A complete guide to angling for coarse, sea and game fish

Books by Colin Willock

HAZANDA

THE ANIMAL CATCHERS

KENZIE : THE WILD-GOOSE MAN

THE BEDSIDE WILDFOWLER (ED.)

Roach

Rutilus rutilus (page 119)
Specimens 2 lb and over
Record 3 lb 14 oz

Rudd

Scardinius erythrophthalmus (page 135)
Specimens 2 lb and over
Record 4 lb 8 oz

The abc of Fishing

A complete guide to angling for coarse, sea and game fish by Eric Tenney

Edited by Colin Willock

ANDRE DEUTSCH

FIRST PUBLISHED NOVEMBER 1964 BY
ANDRE DEUTSCH LIMITED
105 GREAT RUSSELL STREET
LONDON WC1

SECOND IMPRESSION MAY 1967
THIRD IMPRESSION FEBRUARY 1968
DE LUXE EDITION JUNE 1969

PRINTED IN GREAT BRITAIN BY
HAZELL WATSON & VINEY LTD
AYLESBURY BUCKS
SBN 233 95921 1

For Francis Butterfield,
the good friend who first took me fishing

Contents

List of Colour Plates

A NOTE ON THE COLOUR PLATES

The colour plates illustrate virtually every species that the angler is likely to encounter, either as a quarry species or as an accidental catch. Several species are therefore illustrated which are not likely to be deliberately fished for, and are not referred to in the text.

*Denotes record quoted on colour plate no longer recognised by British Record Fish Committee. Open to new claims since December 1968.

Contributors

HARRY BROTHERTON: Died while this book was being prepared. He was a fine all-round angler who nevertheless specialized in tench during the tenchy months of June to September. He wrote a good deal in the angling press about his favourite quarry and contributed the tench volume to the 'How to Catch Them Series'.

DEREK FLETCHER: Lives five minutes from the sea at Mudeford, Hampshire. Has written two books on sea fishing and is a regular contributor to the *Angling Times*. Covers angling events for regional television, and has arranged a number of programmes for sound radio in the past. Has fished abroad in several international sea angling tournaments and won a number of awards.

CLIVE GAMMON: Born 1929. First fish (a whiting) caught in 1933. Has written seven fishing books to date, and is at present angling correspondent for the *Daily Express* and writes the salt-water column in *Creel* magazine. In intervals between fishing lectures in English at a Teachers' Training College.

F. W. HOLIDAY: Has written books on game fishing. Angling correspondent and reviewer of *Western Mail*. Has fished in every area of the British Isles and also in N. America, Europe, Africa, and the East. Believes that fly-fishing for big sea-trout offers more than any angler has a right to expect from his sport.

WILLIAM HOWES: An all-round angler who has fished for coarse, game, and sea fish in many waters in England and abroad. Contributes regularly to the angling Press, writes a weekly column for the *Middlesex Chronicle*, runs L.C.C. evening classes, and broadcasts on radio and TV. He is the author of six books on fishing.

S. NORTON-BRACY: Chairman of European Federation of Sea Anglers. Has written three sea-fishing books. Winner of the European Sea Fishing Championships 1962, has also won the Norwegian, Danish, Welsh, Scottish, and French International Championship.

RAYMOND PERRETT: Fishing tackle dealer, fish breeder. Has written two coarse-fishing books and hundreds of articles on angling. Hon. Secretary, Bridgwater Angling Association; Hon. Secretary, South, East, and West Somerset Federation of Angling Clubs; Fisheries Representative on the Somerset Rivers Board.

HARVEY TORBETT: Broadcaster and commentator on angling – has also televized on the sport. He teaches biology and is author of *Techniques of Legering*, *Freshwater Fishes*, *Coarse Fishing*, and *Sea Fishing*. His recent film *A Boy Goes Angling* won the Isabel Elder trophy at the 1963 Edinburgh Festival.

Editorial Foreword

Every week-end more people go fishing than watch professional football. Fishing is the greatest recreational revolution Britain has seen since leisure became common property and in one way at least this is rather odd. Despite the fact that angling wins hundreds of thousands of new recruits each year, fishing remains a difficult thing to start if you know nothing about it. To the newcomer, angling of any sort appears a baffling conglomeration of strange technicalities and stranger mystiques. The would-be fisherman's reaction is often: 'How can I ever come to understand it all?' It speaks a good deal for the lure of fishing that new anglers do continue to pour into the sport. Just the same, it isn't easy to cast your first line. To make it considerably easier is one of the purposes of this book.

Of course, if you, as a novice, have a devoted friend who will take you to the waterside and instruct you in these arts, then you are more than half-way there. But my experience of devoted angler friends who escort novices to the water is that patience and time to instruct shrink very quickly at the first dip of the teacher's float. He wants to be catching fish himself, not telling the newcomer how to do it. There may be exceptions. If so they must be saintly men. Alas, even in angling, there are probably fewer saints at large than fifty-pound pike.

My own theory is that a good many new anglers come to the sport almost casually and without really believing that it will get a hold on them. It may be a summer holiday that makes them buy a (usually quite unsuitable) rod to catch bass from the beach or perch from the river. Naturally, they do not know how to go about things, what tackle to buy, what bait to use, what is the best time of the tide, or which is the most likely swim in the river. There is no one to tell them. Just the same, some of them manage to hook a fish or two and with the first bend of the rod find themselves hooked for life. They are lucky if this happens and their stroke of luck may drive them to find out more about this business of fishing. But by then the holiday and perhaps the opportunity to try for mullet, or bream, or trout will have gone by for another year. They will certainly have wasted time and made elementary mistakes that a really devoted fishing friend could have helped them to avoid. I hope this *Companion* will replace that friend on the beach, by the slow-running bream river, and by the salmon and trout stream, too.

For a book of this sort, it takes, perhaps, an unusual form. It has a number of contributors, all well-known angling experts and all in their highly individual ways working to the same brief. Their brief was simply this: 'Tell the readers how to catch fish. Tell them so that the absolute novice who looks up PERCH in this book knows how to go about catching the animal. Tell them so that the experts, too, will find in each entry the complete distillation of your own expertise. Give us your theories, even your personal experiences where the reader can learn something from them. But leave us in no doubt how to go about the business of catching roach, bream, pike, sea-trout, tope, and all the rest of these exciting creatures.'

So you will find that the longer sections especially are spiced with the writer's own views. This, I am certain, is right and proper for very little about angling is definitely proved. There is always room for disproof and counter-theory. Anglers thrive on argument and there is plenty here to provoke the expert as well as excite and instruct the novice.

The entries conform to the same basic plan, which will, I am certain, make the book easy to use as a work of reference. Fish are treated alphabetically within the three sections COARSE FISHING, GAME FISHING, SEA FISHING. Each section starts with a brief outline of suitable tackle and a glossary of basic terms. Each individual entry follows the same pattern: a description of the fish concerned and its haunts and habits at different seasons of the year; the bait and tackle needed to outwit it; how to use that tackle; and a general section of miscellaneous information about record fish and so on.

I have kept cross-referencing to a minimum. Where a word (usually the name of a fish) occurs in capital letters, it means that it is more fully dealt with under its own separate heading There is, in addition, a most comprehensive index which should enable the reader to find, for example, what bait to use for bass on a Pembrokeshire storm beach in August.

Though I have said a great deal about this book's value to the novice there are certainly some general things he will want to know which he will not find by consulting individual entries. The first is the question of what tackle to buy.

I wish there was an easy answer to this one in the form of a general-purpose rod that would see you through for all coarse fishing, all sea fishing, all salmon and trout fishing. Unfortunately, this is far from the case. Rods have a number of different purposes: to get the bait to the fish, to work the bait once it has been cast to the fish, and finally, one hopes, to play the fish. Plainly the first question is: what fish? A forty-pound tope will require something very different from a one-pound school bass; what can a rod to cast a fly to a trout have in common with the weapon a match angler uses to flick out four-ounce roach, one after the other? I'm afraid the answer is – nothing. Nor does it end there. Not only the size of the quarry but the nature of the bait affects the choice of rod. Granted, a skilful angler could play, and might land, a thirty-pound pike on a roach rod (though he'd have to be lucky as well as skilful to get away with it), but such a rod could never get the bait to the pike in the first place. A single maggot or a piece of crust used to lure a two-pound roach weighs virtually nothing and therefore imposes no strain on the rod in casting. The live-bait or dead-bait necessary to catch the thirty-pound pike could easily itself weigh half a pound, and what kind of rod do you need to cast *that* thirty or forty yards? Thus practically every kind of fish and fishing demands a different rod.

If you are new to the game don't despair entirely. There are a number of different fish in each category that can be caught with the same rod. The most important thing is to buy sparingly and buy well. Get one good rod for one purpose for a start. Add another good rod for a quite different purpose when you feel ready for it. I repeat: there is no such thing as an all-purpose rod and don't let anyone tell you differently.

To some extent the same applies to reels, though here the choice is more limited. Because of the apparent complexity of choice of tackle each of the three main sections starts with a short note on the gear that you have at your disposal with some suggestions about basic requirements.

For the beginner, too, I would like to say something about another issue which he often finds confusing; this concerns the right to fish, and the permits and licences necessary.

If you except the sea (for which, by the way, there are no close seasons), there are very few free fisheries in Britain. It might be as well to add that you may even get caught out in sea fishing. Though the foreshore below the mean high-tide mark is almost invariably public property, the right of access to it may not be. The same applies if you are fishing from a harbour wall or jetty. These belong to somebody, and though the sea itself is free-fishing, the right to fish from that particular spot probably isn't and you may have to pay someone a small sum or at least ask permission.

Inland, practically every piece of running and still water belongs to, and is administered by, someone who has a right to collect a due from you. The one great exception is the River Thames below the Town Stone at Staines, which was presented to the citizens of London as a free fishery for all time by Richard II. The whole of the Thames is an exception in another way, for though above Staines you will have to pay the land or riparian, owner a due, the Thames Conservancy Board demands no licence fee from you along the river's entire course. However, as a recent Court case ruled, this freedom from licence buying does not entitle you to fish from a tow-path on the upper Thames. Even though a tow-path exists, the fishing rights still belong to the landowner across whose fields the path runs.

When fishing all other rivers in England you may take it that you need a River Board licence. There are, therefore, usually *two* fees to be paid. The first goes to the River Board, and varies from a few shillings a year for coarse fishing to several pounds for salmon and trout. The second is paid in the form of day ticket or annual subscription, or club rental, to the owner of the banks. By law he owns the fishing in the river to its middle line. These days he will probably have let his water to a fishing club, in which case you must either buy a day ticket (if they issue them) or join the club. The same, of course, applies to lakes and gravel pits. Somebody invariably owns the fishing rights. Generally speaking you don't have to have a River Board licence to fish still waters, but you must still pay the riparian owner or his tenant. The safe rule is: ask before you start fishing.

Close seasons are broadly speaking the same throughout Britain, though each River Board can name its own dates and make its own by-laws. In an appendix you will find some examples of the sort of by-laws you will be expected to conform to and also a note on some of the main variations in close seasons for freshwater fish from area to area.

Finally, it is one of my personal contentions that one cannot get the most out of an elemental sport like this unless one has some feeling for and understanding of one's quarry. This understanding adds a great deal both to one's pleasure in the sport and to one's success in it. For this reason the book starts off with a section by Harvey Torbett, who is a lecturer on fish as well as a fisherman, on the subject of fish anatomy and fish behaviour in general. And now, good reading and good fishing.

Note

Undoubtedly there will be some things the reader will want to know which this book does not precisely tell him. This *Companion* has a long life ahead of it and there will be in the future opportunities to add to and revise it. So I, the editor, would appreciate readers' reactions and suggestions. The publishers will always forward your letters to me, and I assure you that their contents will be considered and gratefully acknowledged.

Colin Willock

Introduction

Externally, fishes look much alike, the shapes being fundamentally spindle-like, with various modifications according to the particular species and its way of life. The EEL, for example, is elongated and cylindrical, but the PLAICE is compressed or flattened from above, while the BREAM is flattened from the side. Further minor modifications are seen in the bottom-feeding BARBEL, which is flattened lightly along the belly, with the head depressed from the medial line to give it its typical wedge shape. The opposite occurs in the surface-feeding BLEAK, which has its dorsal surface less curved than the belly, and the mouth and head tilting strongly upwards.

Colour

The basic colour pattern is almost universal, with the back and upper body shades dark, those of the belly bright, and the flanks shading intermediately between the two extremes. This much alone gives effective camouflage from above and below, irrespective of the colours involved. Obviously such protective coloration is considerably improved if the predominant hues match the environment in some way, either by obliterative colouring, or by direct matching. To this end some fishes are laterally striped (MULLET and GRAYLING), and others are transversely barred (PERCH). Some are marbled or mottled (father lasher or goby), and some bear large or small spots (SALMON, TROUT, BASS, shad). Beneath the basic colour pattern the colours themselves are surprisingly restricted in most fishes of temperate zones, the great majority being predominantly silvery, brassy or golden, green or brown.

With so much restriction in shape and colour, the differences between the various species are small, and the angler's attention is often focused on details, such as the head, mouth, eyes, fins, tail, and scales, which have a variety of character sufficient for recognition.

The Head

This extends to the edges of the gill-covers and bears the major sense organs: eyes, nose, and mouth. The mouth may be oblique (RUDD and BLEAK), or almost horizontal (ROACH and BREAM). It may be superior, with the lower jaw extending beyond the upper (RUDD and PIKE), or the opposite, with the lower jaw well underslung (BARBEL, Sturgeon). The lips may be fat (CHUB), thin, or absent, and may bear feelers known as barbules or barbels (CARP). Barbels may also be attached to the corners of the mouth (BARBEL and CARP), or to the snout (Burbot, Catfish).

In some fishes the scales extend on to the cheeks (BASS and PIKE-PERCH) and even on to the snout between the eyes

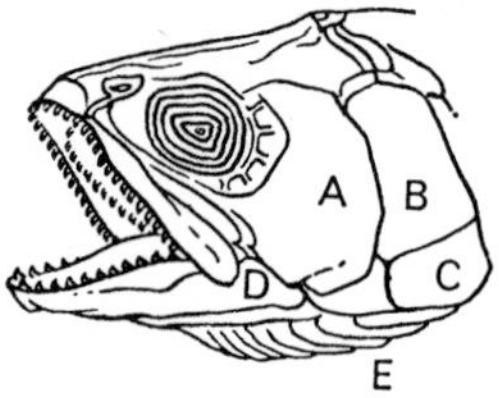

Jaw structure of a predatory fish. (A) fore gill-cover or *operculum*; (B) gill-cover proper; (C) under gill-cover; (D) intermediate gill-cover; (E) gill-rays.

(MULLET), or they may be absent from the head altogether (ROACH, RUDD, DACE, CHUB, etc.). The mouth may lack teeth, as in CARP-family fishes, or bear only small bristle-like teeth (PERCH, shad), or may have many rows of sharp strong teeth (SALMON, PIKE, COD).

In some fishes the maxillary (jaw) bone is easily observable along the lower jaw line; it may be short or long according to species. The nostrils are not normally conspicuous, and the eyes, although varying in size and position, are set either on the side of the head or towards the upper surface. (See further 'The Senses and Sense Organs', below.)

The Trunk In the interests of streamlining there is no neck, the head being joined directly to the trunk. The body is normally covered completely from head to tail with a layer of separate overlapping scales which give protection without impairing body movement. The scales may be fairly soft as in the CARP family of fishes (Cyprinidae), hard and rough-textured as in the PERCHES, or large, projecting, and bony as in sturgeon and SKATE. A few fish are scaleless, and the skin is then tough and leathery to compensate (bullhead).

In most fishes a lateral line is visible along the centre row of scales on the flanks. This consists of a series of tiny pores found only on centre flank scales, one to each. This line may extend to the head as in PIKE and TENCH.

Fins All true fishes have fins, the paired fins representing the forerunners of the limbs in other animals, and the unpaired ones lying on the medial line and being extensions of the vertebral processes.

The *dorsal* fins are set sail-like on the ridge of the back, and the *anal* fin keel-like beneath. There may be one dorsal (CARP), two (PERCH), or even three (COD). In some fishes there are two anal fins on the underside. These fins work in

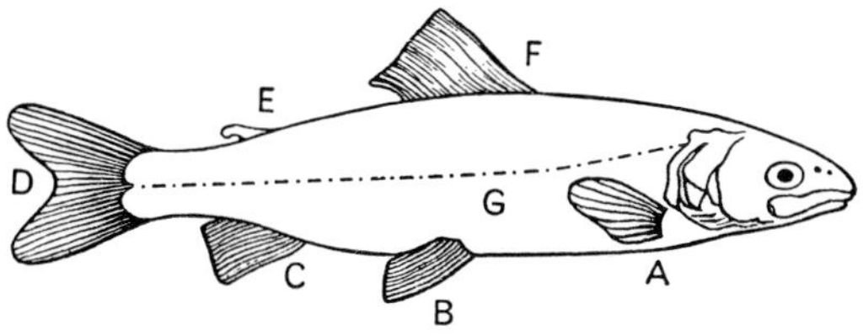

Fin diagram. (A) pectorals; (B) ventrals; (C) anal; (D) caudal (tail); (E) adipose (in salmon family only); (F) dorsal; (G) denotes the lateral line.

conjunction with each other as stabilizers and also have some function in swimming.

The paired fins, pectoral and pelvic, are attached to the lower body, the *pectorals* being just behind the gill-covers, on the lower flank. Sometimes the *pelvic* fins are set on the underside just below the pectorals (PERCH, BASS), but in the CARP family of fishes and the salmonoids they are attached roughly level with the dorsal fin, but on the underside of the body. These are of great importance in starting, stopping, reversing, turning, and maintaining a position.

All fins consist of a fairly thin membrane supported by bones or rays. In PERCH or BASS the first dorsal fin bears stout spines, but the second bears mostly finer flexible branched rays similar to those which support the fins of the CARP family of fishes. In the bullhead, the rays are also flexible, being jointed and unbranched. A further kind of fin is found in salmonoid fishes. This is simply a fatty finger of flesh protruding from the back near the tail, and totally unsupported by bones of any kind. It is called the adipose and its function is not really known.

The tail fin is perhaps the most obvious and variable. It may be steeply forked and symmetrical as in BLEAK and PERCH, or asymmetrical, with the lower lobe rounded (BARBEL and BREAM). In TENCH and adult SALMON, the tail fin is unforked, being almost square-ended, or very lightly concave at the trailing edge.

A description of the trunk would be incomplete without mention of the smooth layer of slime which covers the bodies of fish. This slime in fact protects the fine layer of live skin cells superimposed over the scales and acts as a barrier to infection by bacteria and parasites, as well as lubricating the surface and preventing water from soaking through the body of the fish. (See p. 24.)

The Senses and Sense Organs

Sight: The eyes of fish are lidless and have a muscular control within a limited range which permits them to move up and down or sideways within the orbit. The pupil is not adjustable, and the sight is normally of short range. Long sight would be of no advantage to a creature living even in clear water, which itself considerably restricts the range of vision. Scientists are not entirely agreed as to whether fish have colour vision or not, but the eye is known to be associated with colour changes in the appearance of the fish, which is continually adjusted to camouflage with changes of surroundings. Blind fish lose this capacity and become evenly dark coloured.

Shoal fishes which are non-predatory bear eyes set to the sides of the head, giving a very wide radius of simple monocular vision on both sides of the body, with only a very narrow radius 'blind' in the region of the tail. Binocular vision is of little importance to these fishes and is possible only over a very small radius in front of the head. All-round visual alertness to attack is their primary need. Predatory fishes, on the other hand, have eyes set forward and on the upper surface of the head to give them a good overall view of the surface above them, and a wide radius of binocular vision which is essential for judging distances, so that they may accurately grasp their fleeing prey. The radius of monocular vision on either side is correspondingly limited.

The angler is often concerned with how far, and how well, the fish is able to see objects above the surface. Vision is modified by refraction, familiar enough to the fisherman who sees his landing-net handle *appear* to bend when he puts it in the water

If the handle is held vertically, no distortion is apparent, but as it is tilted away from the vertical the amount of bending increases. If the angler sighted along his net handle at an angle of about seventy degrees he would find himself unable to see through the surface because of dazzle from reflection. Anyone studying fish below the surface knows that his line of sight must be close to the vertical to prevent dazzle obscuring the view.

From the fishes' viewpoint much the same is true, since there comes a point at which total reflection occurs because the line of sight of the fish reaching the surface at an angle of fifty degrees or more is bent horizontally along the surface itself.

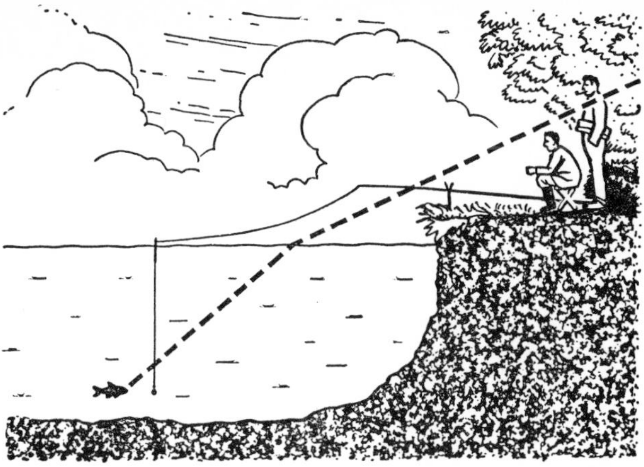

How refraction affects the vision of a fish from water to air. The light rays are bent downward at the surface. Note how the angler standing up is brought within the fish's view by refraction, whereas the sitting man escapes. A lesson here in taking cover.

This means that a fish at any given point can see through the surface only so long as the line of sight strikes the water at an angle smaller than fifty degrees to the vertical. The fish, therefore, views the outside world through a circular 'window', the size of which is determined by its own depth in the water.

This can best be represented by the roof of an inverted cone, the apex angle being about 100 degrees, and resting upon the eye of the fish. The cone 'widens' above the surface because rays of light coming from above are bent towards the vertical. The fish's 'window' is thus filled with images of the objects outside the water which actually occupy the visible horizon, but which appear compressed into the space of the 'window'. In many respects this would account for the shyness of the fish when bank objects are moved suddenly, because these always appear to be more directly over its head than they are in fact. Obviously too, the size of the window varies with the depth of the fish. A fish lying sunning itself in six inches of water would have only a small window about a foot or so in diameter. Conversely, a fish in ten feet of water would have a window of twenty feet across. Other factors also operate here, otherwise a fish really deep in the water would be practically unapproachable. First, the colour and nature of the water tend to obscure images as the light diminishes with increasing depth, and secondly, the near-sightedness of the fish prevents really effective vision beyond ten or twelve feet. Nevertheless, at this range the fish is still capable of discerning movements and these are sufficient to frighten it. In the last resort, much depends on the water and particularly whether it is at all coloured. The angler has only to recall swimming a few feet below the surface in clouded water to have a very good idea of how limited above-water vision is, and how little light penetrates well below the surface. Fortunately for him, most of these factors operate to the angler's advantage.

Hearing: Fishes do not possess external ears, which would interfere with streamlining. They do not require them in any case, since the internal ear structure is in direct contact with the water through the skin and is therefore capable of conveying vibrations and sounds to the central nervous system. The ear is also equipped with semicircular canals which are responsible for balance and kinetic sense. This is also aided by the functioning of the lateral line, which picks up information about pressure variations necessary for station keeping and body control in swift-surging and variable currents of water. The lateral line is also capable of detecting vibrations of certain frequencies which are transmitted to the brain. The swim-bladder too is associated with hearing in some fishes, being taut like a drum and capable of receiving vibrations of low frequencies. In some fishes this is linked to the ear by means of a series of tiny articulated bones.

Undoubtedly this complex and efficient hearing mechanism is of the utmost importance to fish in detecting the presence of danger as well as in seeking prey, avoiding attackers, and making accurate movements in turbulent waters.

Taste and Smell: Taste and smell are almost indistinguishable in aquatic creatures, which receive impulses of this kind through the agency of the water in which they live and must be capable of detecting minute concentrations of substances in solution. The mouth and barbels bear taste cells, and the nostrils, each of which consists of a pair of openings, are also equipped with sensory organ cells. Water is continually flowing into the first opening through the connecting canal, and out of the other. In doing so it passes over the sensory cells which obtain information from it, detecting food flavours and such things as chemical pollution. The salmon probably homes by detecting the taste-smell of a river estuary while cruising along the coast.

Barbelled fishes are usually bottom-feeders. The barbels serve as additional sense organs in helping them to locate concentrations of micro-organisms in the bottom layers which are often dark or muddy enough to prevent them searching for food by purely visual means.

The Skeleton

Fishes are the earliest of the vertebrates so it is to be expected that the skeleton is less complex than that of land animals. Some fishes, such as the SKATES, SHARKS, and RAYS, have purely cartilaginous (i.e. gristly) bones, but the majority (the 'true fishes') have bones which contain calcium.

In most animals, the function of the skeleton is bound up with body support as well as articulation and protection. In fishes, support is largely unnecessary, since the fish is borne up chiefly by the water in which it lives and is weightless for all practical purposes. Rigidity is achieved with simple, thin, needle-like bones, which at the same time give protection to the brain, vital organs, and spinal chord. Articulation is comparatively simple since the limbs bear no complicated joints. Body movement is indeed confined to the undulatory movements of the body in swimming, the moving of the paddle-like fins, and movements of the eyes, jaws, and tail.

To this end bones require to have little weight or strength, although the muscular system which operates upon them in movement comprises the greater part of the total body mass.

The Blood System

The function of the circulatory system is to transport food and oxygen to the tissues and remove waste matter for disposal. It is also important in combating bacterial invasions and controlling body temperatures.

In fish the task is simplified because they are cold-blooded, and, within a degree or two, maintain the temperature of the water around them. The heart is therefore a simple three-chambered muscular organ situated in the throat quite close to the gills where blood is re-oxygenated. Blood flows sluggishly from the heart to the gills; thence to the head and body, collecting food from the digestive system and liver, getting rid of waste via the kidneys and intestines.

The Gills

These are provided with fine, feather-like tissues richly endowed with tiny blood vessels. These are the gill filaments. They have a wide surface area over which water flows so that the oxygen can be extracted. For protection from gritty particles which might damage these delicate tissues, the gills are supplied with rakers or comb-like appendages which filter off solids in suspension and also serve to collect or strain out tiny food particles, which are directed to the gullet. Oxygen and carbon dioxide are exchanged in the blood stream at the gills. The gills are very delicate and in danger from attack by parasites, as well as being easily damaged by the angler's hook.

Osmosis and the Slime Barrier

Paradoxically, the fish, which lives in water throughout its life, requires a slime layer to keep its body watertight, because of the process of osmosis. This is essentially a physical phenomenon which operates when two liquids of different concentrations or strengths are separated by a semi-permeable membrane – such as the skin of the fish. The liquid from the weaker solution tends to pass through the separating layer, diluting the stronger solution until equilibrium is achieved.

In freshwater fishes, the blood and vital liquids of the fish are stronger than the fresh water surrounding the body. The water therefore tends to soak through the skin and gills, diluting the body solutions and blood-stream of the fish. Freshwater fishes cope with this continual dilution by not drinking and by the efficient and hard-working action of their kidneys, which continually throw out the excess water. The slime barrier effectively prevents osmosis taking place through the skin to any marked degree, although the gills still absorb considerable amounts of water.

In sea fishes the effect is the opposite, since the salt water in which the fish live is actually stronger than the vital liquids of the fish. The fish is, therefore, continually losing water through the gills and in constant danger of dehydration. To counteract this tendency, sea fishes drink considerable amounts of water, and produce very strong waste liquids which are disposed of through the kidneys. In both sea and freshwater fishes, damage to the slime layer increases the burden of osmotic pressures by increasing the areas through which liquids can pass one way or the other. In freshwater fishes this throws a great burden on the kidneys, and in sea fishes the danger of dehydration is very much increased.

Damage of this sort is probably more serious because of the possibility of bacterial attack or infection occurring at the same time through the damaged areas of skin.

The Digestive System

Non-predatory fishes feed largely upon small articles which require little chewing and absorption by the system. Vegetable matter forms a large part of their diet. Chewing is performed by the pharyngeal teeth, which are attached to the fifth gill arch and set behind the gills so as not to interfere with the ordinary business of respiration. These teeth are often the only certain means of identifying such oddities as possible hybrids. Non-predatory fishes have no separate stomach, the gullet merging into the gut and intestines, which may fold twice or several times within the body cavity before ending at

Pharyngeal, or throat teeth, of fish from members of the carp family. From left to right these belong to: carp, tench, roach, barbel. These are crushing teeth of non-predatory fishes. Only one half of each set of teeth is shown here.

the anus where waste is expelled. Digestion occurs throughout the length of the tract where digestive juices and enzymes break down and extract from the food the substances required by the body. Nourishment is obtained from vegetable substances containing cellulose by the action of bacteria in the lower intestines.

In predatory fishes the teeth in the mouth are used not to chew, but simply to grasp the prey. Once swallowed this is received by a pouch-like stomach where powerful digestive juices act upon it. The rhythmic movements of the stomach assist in breaking it down into a sludge-like consistency capable of being dealt with by the intestines, where it is finally absorbed by enzymes and juices from the pancreas. Undigested food and waste products from the kidneys are passed to the vent where they are expelled.

The Reproductive System

The 'roes' of fishes require little description. The hard roes consist of the female ovaries which, during the breeding season, are packed with ripening eggs ready for expulsion through the narrow tract which leads from the ovaries to the vent. In the male fish soft roes are packed with ripe sperms which are shed when the fish mate.

During the breeding season these organs of reproduction take up considerable space within the body cavity and are responsible for the plump appearance of the belly. Once spawning has occurred the fish appear lean and out of condition. Often, too, they are exhausted by the rigours of spawning and make for the streamy well-oxygenated reaches where they can scour and recover. Associated with spawning in many fishes is the formation of tiny wart-like protuberances which appear on the head or scales of the male. These give the flanks a rough, raspy texture. This undoubtedly secondary sexual characteristic, found only in the male fish, has some value in assisting the shedding of spawn when the fish rub against each other. It is probably also significant in shoal fishes, which cannot distinguish each other in the densely packed shoals except by touch, enabling the females to recognize male fish in close proximity and vice versa.

Eggs are shed amongst the weed, where they may sink or float according to the type. The sinking kinds become attached to weed stems where some of them at least are hidden from the attentions of the innumerable creatures which feast on the many millions of eggs produced by any single shoal. Some fishes cover their eggs with gravel to protect them, but the great majority simply leave them to chance.

The young fry hatch within a few days or several weeks according to species, and take shelter amongst the weeds or stones during early life. Within a year or two, their numbers very much reduced, they make up shoals and undertake the instinctive pattern of life for their particular species. As the years pass the shoals become smaller and smaller until the older and larger fish are few and far between, when they may continue to live socially in small groups or, in some species, adopt solitary habits and become more predatory.

Hybridism, uncommon in the sea, but fairly common in fresh water, occurs when two shoals of different but closely allied species happen to be spawning simultaneously in close proximity to each other. Fishes on the fringes of both shoals tend to intermingle accidentally and eggs from one species are fertilized by sperms from the other. The resulting hybrids are intermediate between the species, and in most cases are quite infertile, although in laboratory experiments it has been shown that one or two species can produce fertile hybrids.

Special Organs

The swim-bladder and lateral line have already received mention in certain contexts, but both have particular functions of great importance. The swim-bladder is undoubtedly of immense value as a hydrostatic organ enabling the fish to make small adjustments to its specific gravity as it moves from deeper waters into shallow zones or vice versa. The lateral line is important, not only as a 'hearing aid', but as a gauge of changing pressure on the flanks. It enables the fish to interpret vagaries of current and properly control itself in very turbulent waters. It probably also has some function in shoal behaviour, which is little understood but is nevertheless of great importance in the survival of the species, particularly among the non-predatory fishes.

Harvey Torbett

Coarse Fishing*

* The term 'coarse fish' is applied to all British freshwater fish other than members of the Salmonidae family (which includes the trout and the grayling as well as the salmon).

Glossary

Anti-kink device	A gadget, either a small celluloid vane or a weight, that prevents a rotating spinning bait, such as a spoon, from putting twist into the line. Usually used with a swivel and attached between this and the reel line.
Arlesey Bomb	A special kind of pear-shaped weight with swivel attached. Used for legering. The line passes through the swivel eye.
Balanced bait	A bread bait made up so that it will just sink. This is achieved by making it part of dough paste and part of crumb or crust. When the bottom is covered with weed the bait will settle on top of it.
Bite alarms	Buzzer apparatus, often part of a rod rest and powered by a torch battery. Used to indicate a bite when night fishing, usually for carp.
Breaking strain	The maker's estimate of the dry strength of his line. This is usually lower when the line is wet and is lowered still further by the addition of knots and, of course, by use.
Bubble float	A round, plastic float into which water can be put. Water gives weight for casting. Even when nearly full, the float won't sink.
Bung	A large, cork, live-bait float for pike.
Check	Ratchet to stop a reel rotating too freely. Coarse-fishing reels are made with an optional check that can be removed by movement of a button or catch.
Coffin lead	Bored lead for legering, shaped as the name implies.
Controller	Celluloid quill, or wooden float device whose main purpose is to give weight for casting a light bait, such as a fly.
Dap	To lower from a concealed position either a live or imitation bait, usually an insect, to a surface-feeding fish.
Dough bobbin	A lump of bread paste pinched on the line between reel and bottom rod ring, or between rod tip and water. Its sudden movement indicates a bite. Used when legering.
Disgorger	Device for easing the hook out of a fish's mouth.
Ferrule	Brass male and female joint between sections of rod.

Fixed-spool reel Casting reel in which the spool is set at right angles to the axis of the rod. Such reels are fitted with a pick-up for retrieving line and slipping clutch for slowing and tiring a powerful fish.

Flake Bread bait made by slightly compressing the crumb of a new loaf.

Flight A tackle designed to make a small natural bait spin and wobble.

Float Device, usually of celluloid, quill, or a combination of these with cork. Its main job is to indicate bites. In running water, floats are used to carry bait naturally to where the fish are feeding. There are many varieties, including: antenna, a float for windy days, with a long stem, designed to be fished with only this stem showing above the surface; self-cocking, a float that carries its own weights in the base; sliding, a float designed for use where the water depth is greater than the length of the rod in use. The slider surfaces after the cast and rests against a stop on the line.

Gaff A large barbless hook attached to a handle and used for landing heavy fish. Its use is to be discouraged in coarse fishing, where fish are normally returned to the water alive. It is perhaps permissible for landing pike, but only when the gaffing is done through the angle of the lower jawbone, where it does not harm the fish.

Gentles Another name for the maggots of bluebottle or housefly.

Ground-baiting Putting into the water a substance similar to the bait used on the hook, but preferably less appetizing, the object being to attract fish into the angler's swim.

Keep-net A large sleeve-like net, closed at the bottom end, used for keeping the catch until the end of the day's fishing. Small keep-nets should never be used; they damage fish. In fishing matches, the content of the net is weighed to decide the winner.

Laying-on Fishing with a float but with bait and at least some of the weights on the bottom.

Leger Fishing on the bottom with a weight through which the line passes. The weight is stopped from running down to the hook by a split-shot pinched on to the line. When a fish takes, it draws the line through the weight without feeling resistance.

Long-trotting A technique for 'swimming' float tackle as far as fifty or sixty yards downstream to where the fish are feeding. This allows the angler to remain unseen. The float must be allowed to 'trot' naturally at the pace of the river.

Margin fishing A technique used in carp fishing, usually at night. The angler sits with the wind in his face (so that surface food will be blown under his bank). He rests his rod with the tip just out over the water. He uses no weights, simply a large (8–4) hook stuck through a substantial lump of crust. Matchbox size is not too big. The crust is allowed to hang from the rod top, just touching the water. Carp and other fish will often take this.

Match fishing Competition fishing. Each competitor's catch is kept in his keep-net and the bag weighed at the end of, usually, five hours' fishing.

Otter Device for recovering tackle caught on an underwater obstruction.

Paternoster Tackle designed for fishing a bait, often a small live-bait, at one precise spot, perhaps a small hole in a weed bed where a pike is known to lurk. The tackle ends in a weight. Above this, set at right angles to the line, are celluloid booms, or, more simply, lengths of fine wire or nylon. The bait is attached to a hook at the end of these and can thus only move round the axis of the vertical line running down to the weight.

Pick-up The rotating arm of a fixed-spool reel. This is disengaged for casting but snaps back into position at the first half-turn of the reel handle on the retriever. The pick-up then connects with the line and pays it back on to the spool.

Pilot float Small circular float used when live-baiting to keep the reel line between main float and rod on the surface.

Plug Imitation of a small fish, usually of plastic, which wobbles and darts when retrieved. Plugs are made as floaters, slow-sinkers, and sinkers. In addition they have a diving-plate attached below the nose which makes them plunge and wobble. Used mainly for pike.

Plummet Cone-shaped weight with a metal loop in the top and cork set into the base. The hook is passed through the loop and stuck lightly into the cork. When the whole tackle is lowered into the water, the plummet will take the float under if it is not set high enough for the depth; the float will lie flat if it is set too high. By adjustment of the float and use of plummet the angler can gauge the exact depth of his swim throughout its length.

Technique used with small dead-bait such as a minnow, and sometimes a worm, for perch or pike. The weighted fish is allowed to plunge to the bottom and is then retrieved in a sink-and-draw movement that often proves irresistible. *Sink-and-draw*

Tackle used in fishing live-bait for pike and consisting of two treble hooks, one of which is adjustable to size of bait. The hooks are mounted on wire. *Snap-tackle*

To cast and retrieve an artificial bait or dead-bait in order to catch a predatory fish. *Spin*

Small lead shot (sizes vary) slit so that it can be squeezed on to the line as weight. *Split-shot*

Spinning bait whose body is roughly spoon-shaped. *Spoon*

A form of laying-on, sometimes known as tight-corking, in which a float is used and the line is kept taut between float and rod top. The bait and weights are fished on the bottom. The weights often consist of a small bored circular bullet placed between two split-shot which are pinched on to the line. These weights are allowed to move down the swim a little at a time. The line from bait to rod is kept straight at all times. *Stret-pegging*

The act of raising or flicking the rod tip in response to a bite in order to drive the hook point and barb home. *Strike*

The piece of river or lake bed over which the angler is fishing. *Swim*

A perforated plastic cylinder attached to the line and acting as a leger weight. The cylinder is packed with ground-bait which is released slowly by action of the water, close to the hook-bait. *Swim-feeder*

Trotting a bait at the pace of the current through your own swim. *Swimming the stream*

A 'false' tip attached to the rod top and made of floppy nylon so that it hangs loosely down. The line is threaded through the rings on this. When legering, this acts as a most sensitive bite-indicator since it swings at the slightest touch. *Swing-tip*

A small metal device to prevent the line becoming twisted. It has an eye at each end, each eye being free to rotate independently on a central mounting, often called the barrel. The most satisfactory kind are ball-bearing swivels. *Swivel*

An out-of-date term for a fixed-spool reel. *Threadline reel*

To let out float gear freely for a long distance downstream. *Trot*

Tackle for Coarse Fishing

I shall list seven possible basic rods in this category. You would be a happy man to own them all. You would certainly be over-equipped. You could be both happy and very adequately equipped with half the number. You could get by comfortably with two rods (most anglers do) and you could have a great deal of fun with one. The only question is: which one? To my mind the choice is clear and easy. First, however, the possible starters.

Rod	*Purpose*	*Reel*
1. 12 foot Avon-type rod with at least top (third) section made of split-cane	Roach, chub, dace, rudd, bream, tench, perch, medium-sized barbel	Centre-pin or fixed-spool
2. Mark IV Avon 9 foot, 2-piece of split-cane	Similar species to above. Very suitable rod for fishing from boat	Centre-pin or fixed-spool
3. Mark IV carp rod	Carp, barbel, big pike	Fixed-spool
4. Light spinner, 7–8 foot, probably fibre-glass throughout	Perch, pike, chub when caught with spinning baits	Fixed-spool
5. Match rod, 11–13 foot, two lower joints of hollow cane or Spanish reed; tip of split-cane or fibre-glass	Expressly for match fishing where quick striking of smallish fish and no prolonged playing of heavyweights is called for	Fixed-spool or centre-pin
6. Roach pole, 14 foot	Going out of fashion but ideal for fishing over reeds where a quick strike for roach, chub, or dace is needed	No reel used
7. Pike, live-baiting rod, 9–10 foot, fibre-glass, steel or split cane	Needs plenty of backbone for casting live-baits of up to ½ lb.	Fixed-spool

This list does not, of course, conclude the possibilities but it is fairly comprehensive. To take the simplest item first. You will see that there are only two kinds of reels mentioned – centre-pin and fixed-spool. The centre-pin is a free-running drum reel. The drum diameter should be four inches and the drum should be enclosed in a cage to avoid line tangles. Ideally, the spindle should be so perfectly machined that the drum will rotate at a breath. This is necessary because in some forms of fishing, such as long-trotting (see page 42), the action of the float riding downstream on the current must be enough to turn the drum freely and allow line to pay off without check.

A fixed-spool reel is the type in which the spool does not rotate in casting. On the contrary, it lies at right angles to the axis of the rod, the line spilling over the edge without hindrance when the cast is made. The main function of a fixed-spool reel is to make long-distance casting easy. It is not so sensitive in playing a big fish as a drum reel, though it can be made so in the hands of an expert. These reels are increasingly used for float-fishing.

There is no doubt that before many months are out the newcomer to angling will want both these types of reel. My advice is that he should get himself a centre-pin first and learn to use that before graduating to a fixed-spool. By then he will know which reel is right for each sort of fishing he does. To learn fishing with a fixed-spool straight away is rather like learning to drive on a car with an automatic-change gearbox.

First choice for a reel then is a centre-pin of the kind described. Good reels are not cheap. A first-class centre-pin reel costs (1964) between £3 and £8. The same is true of a fixed-spool reel, of which there are many excellent patterns. Go for one with left- and right-hand wind and a slow and lengthy in-and-out action of the spool on recovery (this prevents line piling up), and two spools of different holding capacity.

A third type of reel is the multiplier. This is in essence a drum reel though the drum is replaced by a thin, free-running spindle. The reel is fished on top of the rod and the speed at which the spindle holding the line rotates is checked by the angler's thumb. The handles give a highly geared retrieve, every turn rotating the spindle between four and five times. Most multipliers have an adjustable brake for playing a powerful fish. They are used in coarse fishing mainly when plug spinning for pike with a short bait-casting rod. This rod is usually about 5 ft long, is made of steel or fibre-glass, and has a recessed reel seating which enables the reel to be used on top of the rod and brings the top of the line, when fully loaded on

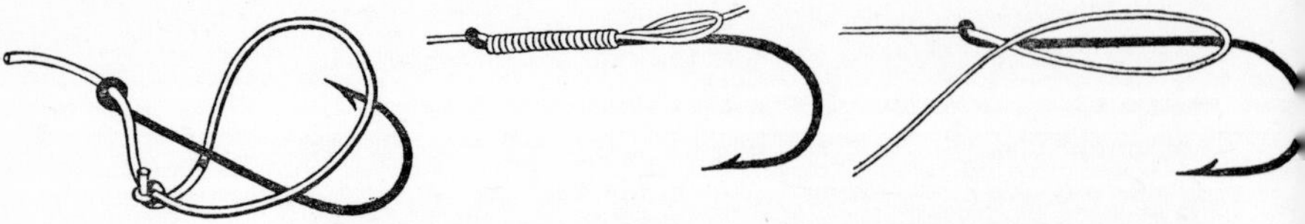

Two knots for tying hooks to nylon: Left, the turle knot, used with eyed hooks and for flies. The hook is threaded on the nylon and slipped out of the way. A slip-knot is then tied in the end and the hook brought back, as here, and passed through the slip which is tightened against the eye. Centre, a whipping knot for tying hooks to nylon. In the right-hand diagram a loose loop of line is laid against the hook-shank. Then, starting from the eye, eight or more turns are taken round this loop and shank and the end of the nylon slipped through the end of the loop. The nylon above the eye is then pulled tight. Any spare nylon towards the bend of the hook is cut off when the whipping has been tightened.

the spindle, level with the thumb of the caster's right hand. Most anglers would consider this rig a last addition to their complete armoury.

First choice for a rod is also quite clear in my view. Unless you intend to do nothing but match fishing, then a three-piece Avon rod will catch you everything from a quick-biting DACE that requires rapid striking to a big TENCH or medium-sized BARBEL. The trouble about the latter is that if you are fishing a barbel river like the Hampshire Avon or Dorset Stour you can't really be sure that the barbel will be so obliging as to come in small sizes. Hook anything from an 8-pounder upwards and you will be lucky not to have your line broken.

Note that I say *line*. There should never be any question of having your rod broken, for the most important principle where all tackle is concerned is that line strength and rod should match.

Here, perhaps, I had better say a word about 'test curves'. A rod is designed to exert maximum pressure on a fish when the line running through the bent tip is at right angles to the butt. The pull required to do this is known as the 'test-curve loading'. The importance of this factor is that the pull in pounds required to put this curve into the rod is about one-fifth of the breaking strain of the line normally used with the rod in question. Thus, if the test-curve loading of the rod is 1½ lb., the correct average line strength for that rod will be about 8 lb. In skilled hands the rod can safely handle lines with a latitude of about thirty per cent in either direction. This means that you can fish as low as 5 lb. or as high as 11 or 12 lb. I say skilled hands because a clumsy angler may break a fine line at the cast, particularly if using a heavy bait. If the angler uses a line above the top level indicated by the test curve (i.e. about 12 lb. in the case of a 1½ lb. rod) he could easily strain, or even smash, his rod. The point is that when rod and line are properly matched it is the line that will go first in moments of excessive strain. However, these moments should never arise. There is a reel, remember, with which the angler can give the line under pressure to a powerful fish and the rod itself is a spring and buffer to the struggles of the fish.

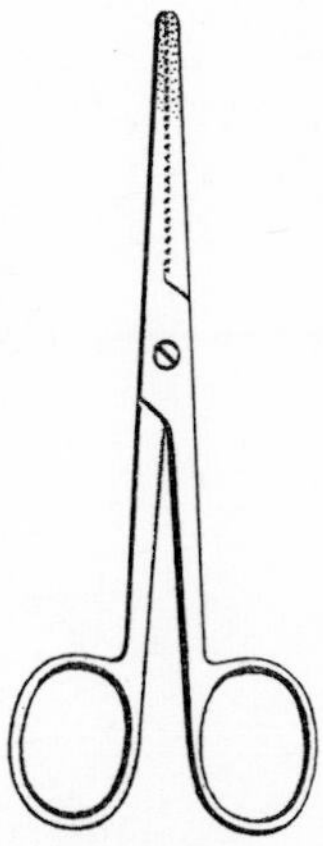

A simple pair of angler's scissors. More elaborate ones include disgorgers, screwdrivers, and shot-pinching and splitting devices.

Now for the second-choice rod. This lies, I think, between a Mark IV and a light or medium spinning rod. The Mark IV is an ideal rod for powerful fish such as CARP, but its action is heavyish for casting light spinning baits.

For serious PIKE anglers who really go for monsters and fish such waters as the Broads with large live-baits, a specialist rod such as the Dennis Pye pike rod is essential.

It is hard to give exact prices for rods. As with reels, quality costs money. A good rod in most classes can be bought for between £8 and £12, but it will last half a lifetime if well looked after.

Finally, some other essentials: a landing-net (£1–£2); a keep-net for retaining fish alive before returning them to the water at the end of the day (£1–£2); a seat basket or patent canvas seat cum tackle holdall (£3–£4); floats, hooks, shots, leger weights, plummet, disgorger, angler's scissors etc. (£1 10*s.* should cover these).

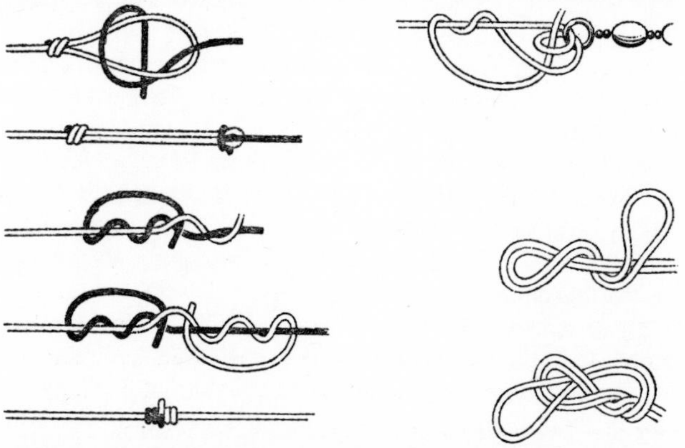

Basic knots. Top left, figure of eight for securing reel line to cast (two diagrams). Below, three stages in tying a blood-knot; the finished knot with loose ends cut off is shown at bottom; invaluable for joining sections of tapered lasts of varying diameter. Top right, a sound knot for fixing line to swivel eye. Below right, unslippable loop in nylon.

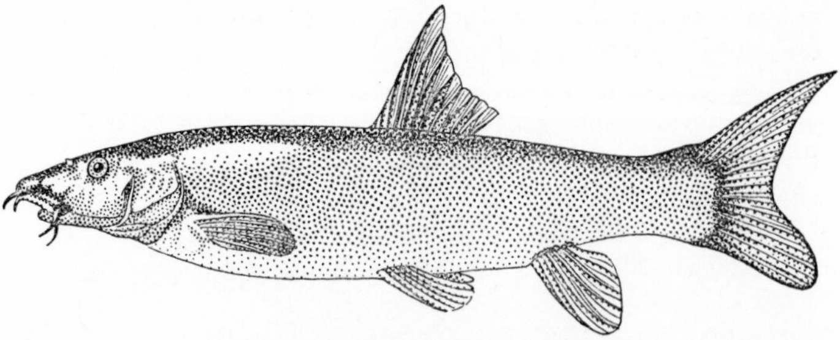

Barbel

BARBEEL

The barbel (*Barbus barbus*) has a grey-brown or green-brown back, varying in shade in different districts, and the flanks are paler, being bronzed or straw-coloured with a distinct metallic lustre. The belly is cream or buff, the metallic appearance giving way to a pearly sheen. The dorsal fin is brownish, toning to the colours of the back, and the abdominal fins are grey or off-white, sometimes with brown streaks. The leading spine of the dorsal fin is very tough and serrated on its rearward edge. The paired fins are large and spade-shaped. The body is almost cylindrical at the shoulder, but flattened underneath, and is laterally compressed towards the tail. In profile the shape is wedge-like at the head, tapering smoothly to the tail, and flattens underneath. The snout is sharp and the mouth distinctly underslung, with thick leathery lips. Two barbels are situated on the middle of the upper lip and one in each corner of the mouth. The tail is asymmetrical, the lower lobe being rounded and the upper one pointed. For the size of the body, the scales are very small.

Very young fish are silvery in appearance and lightly speckled with tiny black spots. The fins are not speckled and can therefore be easily distinguished from those of the similar shaped GUDGEON. In fish up to six or seven inches long the barbels are often very small and underdeveloped, and may indeed be difficult to find. For all this, the young fish is rounder in the belly than a similar-sized gudgeon, and the speckling on the flanks fades in the second year.

Much evidence has still to be collected on the subject of growth rates, but in waters like the Kennet and Avon the rate is fairly fast, a year-old fish attaining a length of 6 ins. by the end of its first season, and reaching a weight of about ½ lb. during the second year (about 9–10 ins.). At the end of the third year the fish may be 10–14 ins. long and weigh between 1 and 1½ lb. A 5 lb. fish may be anything between six and eight years old, and a 10-pounder may be eleven or twelve. Fish of record class and weighing 14–15 lb. are usually twelve to fifteen years old, and in Britain this must be considered fairly close to the maximum age. *Barbel*

Barbel are useless for eating – around spawning time in fact they are nearly poisonous – and should always be returned to the water for the benefit of other anglers.

Barbel are indigenous to the eastern counties of England, and were formerly found only in rivers in that area. They have, however, been introduced in many other rivers over the past fifty years or so, are now commoni n the Hampshire Avon and the Dorset Stour, and are becoming settled in many other western-county rivers. They belong essentially to fast clean waters where hard bottoms predominate, and when introduced to fresh waters habitually seek out the gravelly reaches somewhat below the main TROUT zones, taking up residence permanently at points where the flow is suitable. Failing suitable conditions they do not often flourish.

They show a marked preference for mill-tails, weir pools, and the swift scours and runs, even to the extent of taking to quite shallow water if necessary. Here they feed on the bottom, grubbing about among the gravel for food, using their barbels to locate it and their tube-like mouths, in a sucking manner, to shift small stones or gravel. They are especially fond of the weed of the fast waters and often stay in the very thick of it, sometimes among islands of reed or weed which the swift water has isolated by washing away softer soils.

Barbel spawn in early summer amongst the swift gravelly shallows, leaving their eggs on the gravel and sometimes covering them with scooping movements of their large tails. Once spawned they immediately move into fast shallow water or into the weir-pool scours where they may often be observed right under the sill of the pool lying behind the tumble of water and close to the masonry. By August they have scoured themselves and work into deeper water and among the DACE and ROACH swims.

In winter, when the weeds have rotted, the fish work into open water, where they can be found on the margins of fast water but with cover which compensates for the loss of the weed. Once the first frosts come, the fish seem to go off feed and become semi-hibernatory, feeding only when warm sunny spells break the winter weather.

Baits

Like CHUB, barbel are voracious and will eat almost anything which is brought down by the stream, ranging from silkweed and small insects to minnows, crayfish, and frogs. In between these extremes they like sausage, bacon, bread, cheese, elderberries, and a wide variety of foodstuffs which come their way. During the early part of the season (mid-June–mid-July) they show marked predatory tendencies and are often caught on minnows or crayfish. They are also partial to worms and maggots.

The angler often gets the impression that the fish feed only occasionally, but this may be because they are preoccupied with items too small for the angler to present as bait. Gathering as they do in quite large shoals, usually of similar sizes, they can dispose of very large amounts of ground-bait when on the feed.

Almost any ROACH bait may be successful for barbel, but for serious angling there are a number of baits which stand apart. *Bread* in the form of flakes, cubes, crusts, or paste is a well-proven barbel bait, and in most cases a fairly large bait presented on a No. 6–4 hook will produce the best results. However barbel are sometimes very fastidious feeders and when preoccupied with small items of food may be taken on very small bait. Then the angler must try morsels of the selected bread bait and fish with suitably sized hooks, say 10–12s. The danger always present is that these smaller baits will be grabbed first by impatient and hungry roach or dace. For a bait of bread flake, a large piece of new bread is squeezed in the middle to make a compact firm nucleus. The hook is then inserted through the hard centre. Alternatively, the bread flake may simply be pressed on the bend of the hook so that the softer and flakier edges obscure the appearance of the hook without preventing swift penetration.

Cheese is an excellent bait, and has the advantage of definitely attracting the fish towards it as a result of its smell. The highly smelling cheeses are particularly good, but, being soft, tend to come off the hook too easily in some of the faster waters. A slab of cheese of the cheddar type is very good, but flaky-textured cheeses are best avoided as they crumble too quickly. The cheese can be used in cubes, in which case the hook is pushed into the cube with the point close to the surface, or as a paste, in which case the cheese is first kneaded into a soft consistency and then moulded about the hook. Cheese paste is good on very foul bottoms such as are often found in weir pools. For baits which are trotted, tripped, or rolled along the bottom, cheese pastes have much to recommend them, since they seldom permit the hook point to catch up in bottom debris.

Almost any kind of *worm* is useful, but, owing to their size and toughness when properly scoured, lobworms are probably the best. The whole worm (or even two worms) is used and the hook must be scaled to the bait size. A difficulty with worm baits is that the hook point must invariably be left protruding and is liable to get caught on the bottom more easily than with other baits, in which it is masked. Some anglers prefer to hook the worms twice to make sure they don't come off easily, others believe that hooking only once makes the worm appear a more natural bait.

Barbel have often been taken on a single *gentle* (maggot) on a No. 12 hook, intended for roach, but to set out to hook big fish with hooks this size is somewhat unrealistic except in very special conditions. The problem is not merely one of hooking such a large-mouthed fish with so small a hook, but also one has to consider the strength of the smaller hooks, which are of necessity made up of fairly fine wire. Barbel can straighten out quite large hooks.

A bunch of maggots on a No. 6 is a reasonable compromise on size and strength and some anglers like to use twenty or thirty maggots on a sharp No. 4 or 2. A swim-feeder used in conjunction with maggot bait helps. There is no doubt that a trickle of maggots drifting down the stream is often sufficient to bring the fish up to the hook-bait. In shallow waters the angler may see his swim-feeder picked up and shaken to remove the maggots. Certainly this does happen when barbel are feeding well. Beyond incorporating a hook in the swim-feeder there is little he can do.

When using a *crayfish* as a bait, you should first kill it with a sharp blow on the back of the shell at the head and then hook it through the tail with a No. 4 or 6 hook. It is not necessary to remove the large pincers, although some anglers prefer to do so. With crayfish baits (usually on leger tackle) it is unwise to be *too* fast on the strike because the fish often mouth the bait somewhat before taking. Often the fish crushes the shell with its pharyngeal teeth before pushing the bait back into the mouth to suck at it. The hook in the tail is usually free of the hard carapace of the shell and can get a clean hold in the mouth only if the angler doesn't pull it out by striking too soon. He should wait for a definite 'run'.

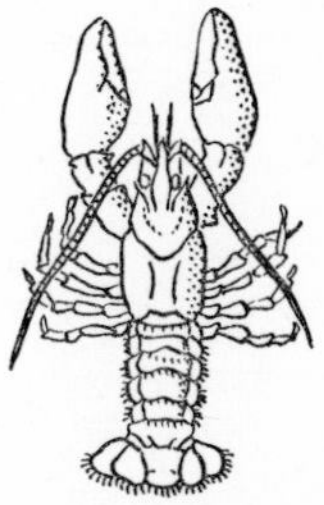

Freshwater crayfish, *astacus*. Found in clear, pure streams, lives in holes in bank, can be caught by baiting drop-net with dead fish. Olive green is its natural colour.

Minnows make a very good early season bait and may be lip-hooked and trotted through the swim, or presented as dead-baits, sink-and-draw style, or on a leger tackle, or even simply float-fished through the swim. Preferably the bait should be presented so as to give a semblance of life; a swivel (a small metal device to prevent the line becoming twisted) a foot or two above the hook enables a dead minnow to flutter attractively in the water and makes it a very killing bait.

Loaches, elvers, small lampreys, and even GUDGEON should be tried as dead-baits and live-baits when the barbel are feeding, especially during the early season. Many big barbel have succumbed to spinning baits, even tolerably large ones, and the angler may well find such a bait very effective.

Frogs are best presented dead. Kill the frog with a sharp blow on the head or neck, and hook it through the body and out at the vent. A small frog on a No. 6 or No. 4 will sometimes take barbel when other baits fail. This can be trotted or legered and often accounts for CHUB as well.

Hooks can be baited with silkweed simply by dragging them through this growth.

During the early season, and when you are fishing weir pools, a large piece of *silkweed,* the green, cottonwool-like weed found on weir sills and elsewhere, wound around the bend of the hook is sometimes effective. The hook should be a No. 8. This bait sometimes tempts fish lying under the sill to move out and take the offering. Other good baits are wheat, hemp, swan mussels, caddis, sausage, and bacon. Anglers experimenting with liver or fresh meat are also sometimes rewarded with an occasional fish.

Tackle

It cannot be sufficiently emphasized that to catch barbel the angler must be prepared to come properly equipped or have his tackle ruined. It is true that barbel are sometimes taken on ROACH rods, but reports of this kind of thing seldom mention the condition of the rod afterwards. Far better use a rod suited to the task. There can be no doubt that in view of the speed of barbel waters and the stubborn, powerful nature of the fish, the task is indeed a tough one.

An all-through action is essential for a barbel rod, which should preferably be made of built-cane throughout. The Avon type of rod is useful, but few rods today are specifically designed for barbel fishing, the Bill Howes 'leger and barbel' rod being a notable exception. Power is essential for any rod intended either to combat the fast water during legering, or to cope effectively with striking at a range of several yards against the current.

Since the rod must also be capable of handling a really tough, fighting fish in a very fast current, it is wise to have it fitted with rod rings of stainless steel and a tip and butt ring suitably lined with agate such as the Aqualite or Sapphrite patterns.

The reel may be either of centre-pin or of fixed-spool type according to preference. It must be a strong one, however, and should carry up to one hundred yards of line. Centre-pins are very pleasant to use when fishing long-trotting methods since they are suited to the style and give a continual and effective contact with the fish throughout the fight. For legering tactics, however, or where longer casting is necessary, the fixed-spool reel takes a lot of beating.

Floats are necessary too, and for long-trotting they must be realistically large. Good shotting is essential to get the bait down in the fast water quickly, and the float must be capable of carrying this kind of weight. An Avon or Thames type of float carrying about a dozen medium shots or six large ones is very suitable. The shots are often best arranged in groups evenly along the line to get the bait down and to prevent line belly between float and hook.

The line should be of about 6 lb. breaking strain. Where heavy fish are expected or waters are particularly weedy this could be increased to 8 lb. b.s. with advantage. If this weight of line is used, the angler must consider buying braided lines instead of monofilament because these are far more supple in the heavier weights, as well as being less elastic.

The plummet should be a fairly heavy one to give an accurate indication of depth in fast water. An ounce is reasonable, but many people prefer one twice as heavy. A disgorger is essential because of the very tough nature of the barbel's mouth. A pair of Spenser-Wells artery forceps is an excellent buy, and one that the versatile angler will find useful for many other purposes.

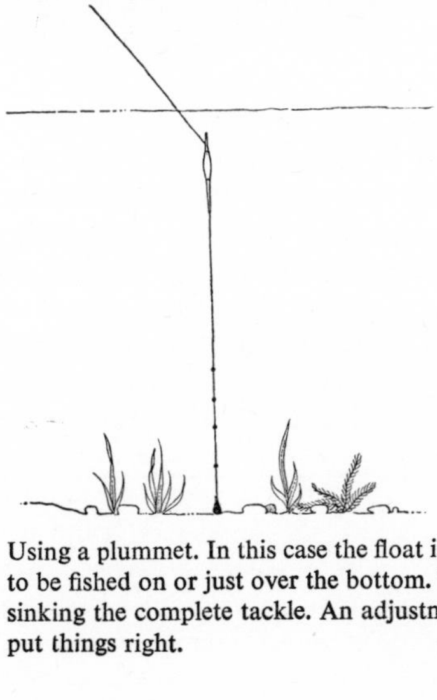

Using a plummet. In this case the float is set slightly too low for the bait to be fished on or just over the bottom. The plummet has shown this by sinking the complete tackle. An adjustment of the float up the line will put things right.

Fishing Methods Ground-baiting is an important preliminary to serious barbel fishing; the results are often well worth while. Bucketsful of worms were once used as the staple ground-bait; and if time and money permit the method is still a good one. Today it is more usual to use bread made up into a good 'duff' sprinkled liberally with maggots, worms, chrysalids, etc., and thrown into the swim each morning for several days in advance of the fishing. Then the swim is left unbaited for twenty-four hours immediately prior to fishing it. In view of the speed and variable nature of many barbel waters it is a good plan to try several swims downstream of the baited one lest the bait should have travelled farther than was intended.

The chief methods used on most barbel waters are legering, long-trotting, and stret-pegging. Which is adopted will depend on conditions. *Legering* has become more of a necessity in recent years owing to the continual overcrowding of

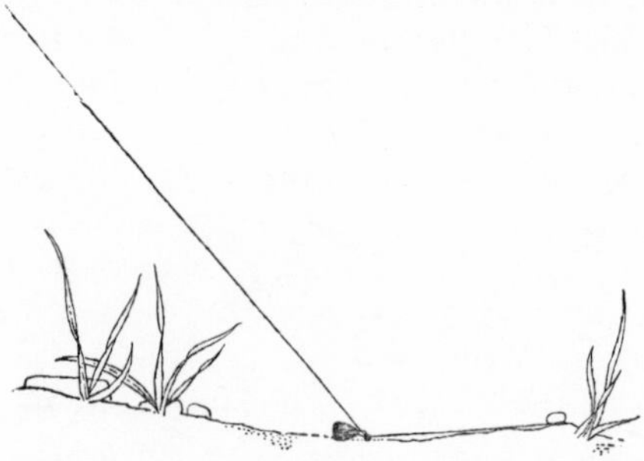

Legering with paste when using a pear-shaped lead stopped by a shot. When a fish picks up the bait, it will pull the line freely through the loop or swivel attached to the leger and flip the rod top to show a bite.

fisheries where good barbel are likely to be taken, since barbel water is often good DACE, CHUB, and ROACH water. Overcrowding often means that the angler anxious to float-fish may not do so with any chance of success because he cannot find several yards of bank free downstream of him. This obliges him to use the leger.

Long-trotting is excellent where the angler has a large undisturbed length of bank immediately downstream of him. The length of bank necessary depends on the water in question and the kind of bank, but for good fishing some twenty to fifty yards is about right. On many Thames swims, the shorter distance may be adequate, but on the Kennet or Avon the larger distance is preferable. This is chiefly because barbel waters are usually so fast that by the time the float has been cast into position and the tackle is correctly set it has travelled

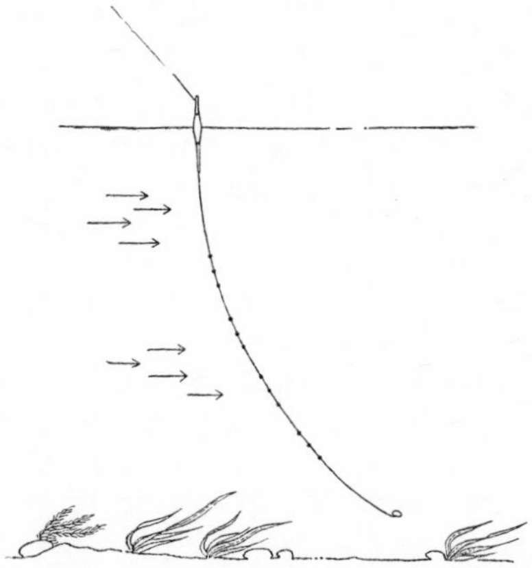

Avon-type rig. The bait is possibly being swept too far ahead by the current. Perhaps more shot should have been added low down.

several yards downstream. To give a reasonable chance of its being effective it should remain in the water for at least a few seconds after this. On the Avon this short time is sufficient to carry the tackle fifty yards or so from the angler.

The float should be selected so that it is large enough to carry several shots, sits high enough in the water to give visibility at some distance, and is heavy enough to withstand the pull of current or wind movement which may cause a bight of line between it and the rod tip. At the same time, shotting must be sufficient to make the float reasonably sensitive. This combination of terminal tackle must also allow the angler to 'mend his line' (see p. 73) at intervals without interfering with the conduct of the float.

Depth must be accurately gauged with the plummet, preferably at selected distances throughout the swim. The float is then set at a depth which will carry the bait near the bottom in deeper runs, and touching bottom in shallower ones. When the tackle passes through shallow spots or over denser weed patches, the bait is lifted off bottom by retarding the float momentarily.

The float must in any event be preceded by the bait, and allowance must be made for the 'tilt' of the line under such conditions so that the bait is not pulled too far off the bottom layers. The float should be lightly checked by line control to give the bait precedence through the swim. If a centre-pin reel is used this can be allowed to run freely, the current pulling line off the reel. This is usually sufficient to give the necessary amount of check to the running line. If a fixed-spool reel is used, the line has to be checked manually by holding the free hand close to the spool so that line brushes against it as it runs off. Striking is sometimes a problem when fishing in this way, and the usual procedure is to snap the finger across the lip of the spool, so trapping the line on its next revolution as it falls from the spool. Striking from a fixed-spool reel is by no means as instantaneous as from a stopped centre-pin. However, barbel take very definitely as a rule, and the very swift strike of the ROACH angler is not so necessary.

Stret-pegging is a style very similar to long-trotting, but the line is arranged with the float a foot or so higher than the depth. The tackle is made up with a single drilled bullet at the lower end of the cast. This is stopped about eighteen inches from the hook with a single split-shot, and a similar stop is fitted a foot or so above it also. The tackle is cast into position and the float is held back until the bullet drags upon it, when it is released, either by following it with the rod tip or by paying out a short length of line. In this way the float is allowed to pass slowly through the swim, the bait being tripped over the uneven bottom and through patches of weed until the swim has been thoroughly searched. Bites are usually quite swift and distinct and they are often felt on the rod tip as quickly as they are seen by the float. In some waters it is best to lower the rod tip to allow the bite to develop; in others it is necessary to strike right away. When the tackle swings in under the bank it is withdrawn and re-cast. The method is useful for searching out the whole of a swim from one bank to the other, the tackle swinging in a semicircular path around to the near bank at varying distances from the angler according to choice at each successive cast.

The tight-line *leger* is at its best for barbel, bites being signified by a sharp knock or tug at the rod tip. The weight is a drilled or perforated one suitable to the stream and conditions. If a static bait is wanted, a coin lead or Capta-type, flat-bottomed lead is best, but if the tackle is required to roll the bottom a pear-shaped lead with a swivel incorporated or attached is essential to prevent line twist as the lead rolls through the swim. Usually a lead just heavy enough to hold bottom is used. It is shifted at intervals by raising the rod tip and lifting the weight off the bottom, when the current carries it further downstream.

The weight is, of course, stopped with a split-shot or split-ring attached to the line about eighteen inches or so from the hook below the weight. However, the length of the 'trail' depends on conditions and may be varied from eight inches or so to five or six feet. The angler should try both extremes to find which is best. Sometimes fish will only take baits from a short trail, but on another day, even in the same spot, they will accept only a long trail.

On leger gear, the only signal the angler gets as a rule is a sharp knock or tug at the line. Sometimes this is a very gentle tap, sometimes it is a vicious thump. Sometimes fish tap the bait before taking and follow this with a thump. There is no knowing beforehand, except by studying the water and the fish. The angler must then decide whether to strike immediately at the taps or await the thumps. One day he will be correct, another day the same tactics may be entirely wrong. When barbel are really feeding in earnest they often hook themselves. Then, at least, there is no doubt about it.

Whatever the method, once the fish is on, the fisherman may well be amazed at the sheer power and endurance of this magnificent fighter. A good fish will give him many uneasy moments before it is safely netted. Usually it is as well to let the fish have its head and run for the opening moments of the fight. However, where dangerous obstacles or thick weed jungles have to be avoided, it may be necessary to haul the fish in immediately after striking, before it has time to collect its wits.

Mere ribbon weed fringes need not worry the barbel fisherman who is confident of his tackle, but water-lilies or reed beds are a different matter and must be avoided if at all possible. If the fish heads for such a sanctuary, it must be turned by applying side-strain until it is well clear. This isn't so easy in a narrow river because the angler is restricted in his choice of position and there is often no open water into which he can lead the fish. Sometimes he must run upstream or downstream to get above or below the fish to head it off. Sometimes the fish becomes weeded in apparently insignificant weed and nothing will budge it. In these circumstances the fisherman should always apply slack-line tactics, hoping that when it feels resistance gone the fish will clear itself. Then the angler can resume the battle as soon as he sees the tell-tale line running away again. Once the fish is seen, the worst of the battle is over, but these last-moment dives can be a great source of danger unless the angler is ready to give line or drop the rod to soften their effect. Once the fish is beaten he shows it clearly by turning on his side. The net is ready and the fish is drawn over it. Sometimes on seeing it he dives straight in, thinking it offers a retreat. Then he is soon on the bank.

But this is in a way the most difficult moment of all, because a barbel fights so hard that he is usually quite exhausted when he comes ashore. If he is not quickly unhooked and returned, there is a very good chance that he may never recover. This is where the artery forceps are so useful, because they expedite the removal of the hook and enable a quick return to be made. If the fish must be kept in a keep-net, it is essential that he is placed there with his head *upstream;* otherwise he may well die in the net. On returning the fish, support it in the water for a minute or so until it has recovered sufficiently to swim away under its own steam. If a fish gives a lot of bother and seems to be wasting time, *never, never* attempt to pump the offending excess air from the swim-bladder by pressing or stroking at the lower flanks. More fish are killed than saved by this expedient.

General The British record fish weighed 14 lb. 6 oz., this honour being shared by three fish taken at different times and from two different rivers. The first was taken from the Thames in 1888 by T. Wheeler, and the second from the Avon by H. Tryon, in 1934. A further fish of the same weight was also taken from the Hampshire Avon during 1937, by F. W. Wallis.

Many reports of even larger fish have been substantiated, but since these fish were taken out of season, or found dead on the banks, they are not acceptable as records. They indicate that a future record may well be one or two pounds heavier than the present record weight. The best such fish was a 16 lb. 8 oz. specimen hooked by Mr Parkinson on the Royalty fishery during 1948, when he was spinning for salmon. Roy Beddington's 16 lb. 4 oz. fish was taken from the same water in 1943, although this fish was foul-hooked in similar circumstances. Other fish include a 15 lb. 12 oz. specimen taken by an otter and left dead on the banks and several near-15 lb. fish taken by salmon anglers out of the coarse season and therefore not eligible.

On the Continent barbel grow to far greater sizes than in England. For big fish in England the Thames, Kennet, Hampshire Avon, and Dorset Stour probably offer the best chances. Other important barbel rivers are the Great Ouse, Wye, Yorkshire Ouse, Nidd, Swale, Dove, Wharfe, Derwent, and Trent. Recent introductions in the Medway and Severn must await the passage of time before reliable comment can be made.

H. T.

Bleak

ELVER

The bleak (*Alburnus alburnus*), often described as a freshwater sprat, is a member of the carp family. When fully grown it has a length of about 7 ins., but the average size is more like 4 to 5 ins. In colouring it is green, blue-green, or grey-green along the back, silvery on the flanks. A bleak closely resembles a small DACE in shape and general colouring, but its identity can be checked by comparing the anal fins, that of the bleak being much longer.

Bleak

Bleak spawn in early summer as do the other members of the CARP family and, as with them, the eggs adhere to the stems of water plants. They are not widely distributed in the British Isles, being found only in certain parts of England and Wales; the Thames and some other rivers are teeming with them. They much prefer the quiet, easy-flowing water of rivers, but they can exist in still water. They seem to do well, in fact, in disused gravel pits, where some large specimens around the 2 oz. mark are occasionally taken.

Baits

During the summer months, when most other species are disinclined to feed, bleak swim in large shoals feeding and sporting around on the surface, constantly dimpling the surface as they rise to flies. Fly-fishing for bleak can be lively and any artificial fly will take them. A change to a maggot (a plastic imitation will often do), fished on a small hook and cast in the fly-fishing manner, will bring some fun. (See 217 ff.) Bleak will take other baits – bread, cheese, hempseed, etc. – but maggots are favourite.

Tackle

A very light rod with a fine nylon line is best. The smallest of floats (a match-stick float will do admirably), a tiny split-shot, and a No. 14 or 16 hook complete the tackle necessary.

Fishing Methods

It is best, following usual coarse-fishing tactics, to throw in some loose maggots beforehand. The bleak will soon be attracted to within a few inches of the surface, and the float must then be set accordingly. Once the shoal are in the swim they take loose maggots – and the hook-bait – as soon as they touch the water, splashing and dimpling the surface as they do so. In winter bleak desert the surface layer, and the bait must then be fished near the bottom to catch them.

General

On some rivers, bleak are important to match-anglers because they take a bait so readily and help to fill out the catch. Several big competitions have been won on bleak – but casting, striking, unhooking, and re-baiting must be done at high speed to pile up a winning weight of 15 lb. or more.

Bleak make good quarry for young anglers and beginners before they go on to larger quarry. They are easily caught and, if light tackle and the right tactics are employed, will provide a few hours of active and enjoyable sport.

The British record is held by a 3¼ oz. fish caught in 1958 by J. Oliver from the Thames at Kingston. However, there is a 5¼ oz. specimen on record, caught in the Trent about 1890.

William Howes

Bream

BRASEM

1. The Common Bream (*Abramis brama*). Other names include: bronze bream, bronzed bream, black bream, carp bream, bream carp, etc.

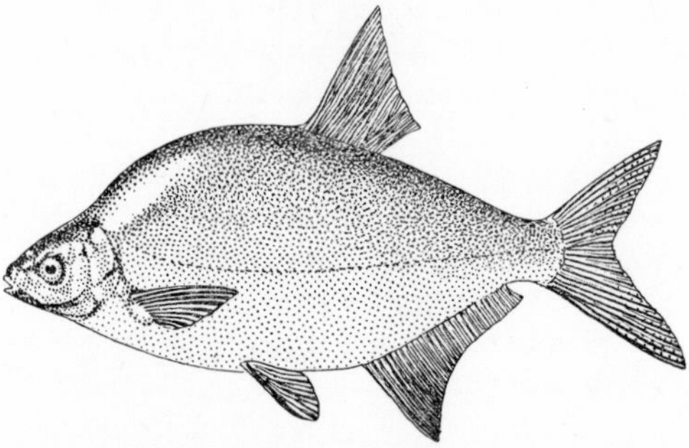

Common bream

The back is green-brown, grey-brown, brown, slate-coloured, or even black in old age. The flanks are paler, being olive-coloured or green-brown with metallic bronze tints. Young fish are silvery flanked with a touch of pale green and develop the brassy or bronze hues in maturity, becoming darker with increased age. The underside is buff, white, or cream, with scarlet streaks and pink tints.

The body is deep-bellied, hump-backed, and thin in section. The total depth of the body is often about a third of the length or even more and the width across the body is a third of the depth. The abdomen is rounded, with the scales lapping evenly over each other. The tail is deeply forked, but asymmetrical, being pointed on the upper lobe and rounded on the lower one. The body is covered with a very thick layer of slime, and the anal fin is very long, reaching from the mid point of the belly almost to the tail.

2. The Silver Bream (*Blicca bjoernka*). This species differs from the bronzed or common bream chiefly in being considerably smaller and in having predominantly silvery flanks, which it retains into full maturity. It is sometimes known as the white bream or 'tinplate'. Because of similarity in colour, young

Barbel

Barbus barbus (page 36)
Record 14 lb 6 oz*

Common Bream

Abramis brama (page 48)
Specimen fish 4 lb—8 lb
Record 13 lb 8 oz*

Silver Bream

Blicca bjoernka (page 48 and following)
Average weight $\frac{1}{2}$ lb – 1 lb
Record 4 lb 8 oz*

Common Carp

Cyprinus carpio (page 57)
Record 44 lb

Mirror Carp

Cyprinus carpio (page 59)
As for Common Carp

Crucian Carp

Carassius carassius (page 57)
2 lb is a fair fish
Record 4 lb 11 oz*

Leather Carp

Cyprinus carpio (page 59)
No separate record for this species
As for Common Carp

common bream are often confused with mature silver bream, but identity can be established by scale and fin ray counts. The main differences are tabulated here for quick comparison and reference:

Character	*Common bream*	*Silver bream*
Anal fin: branched rays	23–29	19–23
Dorsal fin: branched rays	8–10	7–9
Lateral line: scales	49–57	44–50
Rows above lateral line (scales)	11–15	8–11
Rows below lateral line (scales)	6–8	4–6
Pharyngeal teeth	A single row of 5 teeth on each side	Two rows on each side, with 5 in one and 2 in the other
Abdomen section beneath	'U' shaped, with scales overlapping	'V' shaped, scaled edge to edge
Colour	Predominantly brassy	Predominantly silver

During the first year, young common bream attain a length of 3–4 ins. when they weigh less than an ounce, being very thin in body section. During the second year they may more than double their weight and length and by the end of this season may be 6–7 ins. long and weigh two or more ounces. In three years they are about 9 ins. long, filling out in the body, and may become sizeable (12 ins.) during the fourth year, when they may weigh up to twelve ounces.

Considerable variation in growth rates occurs from one water to another, and the figures given are for good waters such as the Thames. In reservoirs or suitable still waters these may be improved upon.

In rivers bream prefer the muddier reaches, where there is plenty of slow-water weed, and the deeper sluggish stretches. They are occasionally taken in gravelly places where ROACH are found, but this is largely due to their moving from one suitable reach to another and feeding spasmodically en route. They move in large shoals comprised of fish of about the same size and age. Owing to the large numbers in a shoal the fish find it necessary to move about considerably, both in rivers and still waters, to visit fresh pastures.

They patrol the banks, and also the deeps, hugging the bottom in the search for food. Betweer feeding they often play on the surface, diving and splashing about in a manner which many anglers believe means sport. Unfortunately the sport is often just for the bream

Their food consists of worms, molluscs, small crustaceans, and insects, as well as microscopic animal organisms found in the bottom muds and silts. Much of theii feeding is done by sucking at the bottom detritus, or by blowing water upon it to bring food to light. When a shoal is feeding in this manner it displaces a great deal of mud and discolours the water for some distance. In shallow lakes or rivers this discoloration is fairly easy to see, and when it is accompanied by the release of gas bubbles trapped in the bottom mud the colour is brought to the surface even in fairly deep waters. A good angler knows by these signs that the bream are feeding and selects his swim accordingly. In rivers the colouring is not so marked because the current is continually washing it away. Because of this, the angler must present his baits somewhat upstream of the coloured water if he is to locate the shoal.

Bream spawn between early May and June. After a cold spring they may still be busy spawning after the opening of the season in mid-June. Their condition is then easily recognizable by the wart-like growths which form on the scales of the male fish at this time, by their roughness to the touch, and their having rather less slime on their bodies. Female fish are recognized by the swollen abdomen.

Spawning occurs in the shallows, often right in the middle of quite thick reed beds, or among marginal bottom weed. The newly hatched fish remain in the weed for the first few months of their lives. Soon after spawning the older fish make for deeper waters where they remain during the summer months, becoming more and more mobile as the season lengthens. When frost kills off the weed, the fish drop into deeper holes; in still waters they cease to feed except in warmer periods during the winter. In rivers the continual forage for food is maintained except in the coldest weather. Winter fish frequently feed at night when the water temperature is higher than that of the air around it.

Baits Most ROACH baits will take an occasional bream, but the really exceptional baits are bread derivatives, worms, freshwater mussels. and maggots, in roughly that order of efficiency.

Flake from the inside of a new loaf can be pressed on the bend of the hook (No. 8 or 10) or the flake can be firmly pressed in the centre and the hook passed through the compact nucleus. *Bread* cubes of about ¾ in. size can be used on a No. 6 or 8 hook. Crust is a good bait and remains on the hook well if damped and pressed between boards overnight. Bread paste is probably the best of the bread baits; it may be made with white or wholemeal bread and thickened with flour or custard powder, or by teasing cotton wool into it. It can also be flavoured with aniseed, pilchard oil, or icing sugar, or by working in a little slime from a freshly caught bream according to preference. Flavoured baits should certainly be made with clean hands, not even with hands smelling of soap.

Bream

Worms are another highly successful bait. The larger the mouthful, the better the bream like it, and in spite of their comparatively small mouths they have little difficulty in managing quite large lobworms which are presented on hooks suited to the bait size (6–8). Any worms will do. Brandlings and redworms are also useful, but these require smaller hooks (10–8). When worm baits are used, bread ground-baits are often useful. Many anglers like to wrap the hook-bait in a lump of bread ground-bait prior to casting, on the principle that this soon crumbles and helps attract fish to the hook-bait.

There is no doubt that *maggots* are good baits in many parts of the country, especially in those regions where maggot baits are practically ritualistic in use. Opinions vary about hook sizes. Single maggots are used on 16–12 hooks, and bunches on 8–10 hooks. In one district the angler with his single maggot can work havoc amongst a bream shoal; in another region, such as the upper Thames, twenty maggots on a No. 8 can be every bit as effective.

In waters where freshwater *mussels* are found they make excellent baits. The mussel is removed from its shell and hooked through the toughest part of the body, then tied in place with a piece of cotton.

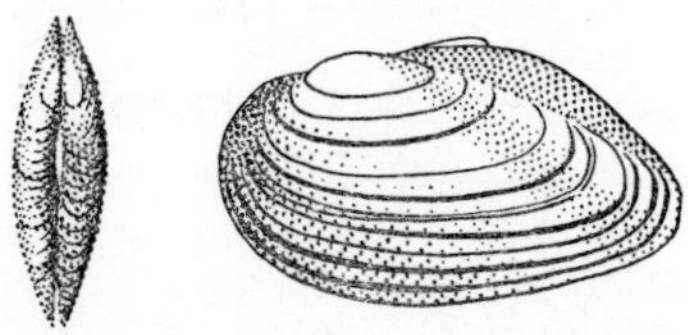

Swan mussel. To bait with this, open the mussel, remove body, hook this through the toughest part, and tie on the hook with cotton.

Tackle The match-type rod (see p. 32) is not the best for bream fishing although it can obviously take medium-sized fish if the angler can spare time to land them on this delicate tackle. The average weight of specimens in many waters is generally such as to strain light rods and a far stronger rod is preferable. A rod with action in the tip and middle joints such as the Avon-type rod is ideal. The butt may be of whole-cane with the tip and middle of built-cane or fibre-glass. Length is often important in waters where deep reed fringes border the margins, or where the deeper holes are well out in midstream. The longer rod (12 ft) enables the angler to control 'laying-on' tackles (for fishing with float but with bait on the bottom and line between float and rod top tight) well out in the brisker currents which are often found at the surface, because the bream may well lie in sluggish waters amongst the bottom holes and beneath the fast surface layers.

In still waters the rod may usefully be shorter (10 ft) because the bait is more easily controlled at a distance; for canals and sluggish drains also this length may suffice. Choice of reel depends on the angler's preferences, many bream anglers preferring the centre-pin because this permits fishing direct from the reel in a very sensitive manner. On the other hand, where long casting is required, the fixed-spool reel has much to recommend it. Ease of casting is its main advantage.

The line is usually of 3 or 4 lb. breaking strain, which gives the fisherman a fair chance of dealing with medium-sized fish. Where weed growth or fish sizes warrant it, somewhat stronger lines are used. When conditions demand ultra-light tackles, a cast of lower b.s. than the main line can be used to improve the presentation.

Float-fishing is a much used method of taking good bream and the angler will require a variety of floats for varying conditions on different kinds of water. For still waters, the small porcupine quills from 4 to 8 ins. in length may be ideal, but for running waters the bait often needs heavier shotting than such floats would carry. Here a cork-bodied quill or Thames-type float is more suitable.

Apart from the normal range of split shots and half-moon leads carried by every angler, weights will also be required for legering and laying-on. Much depends on the water, but as a general guide the drilled bullets are useful for float tackles requiring heavy shotting, and the Arlesey Bomb types are better for leger work. A variety ranging from a ¼ oz. to 1 oz. should cover every eventuality.

Ground-baiting is vital in bream fishing because the large shoals take so much food that if the angler is to get a share of the fish before they move elsewhere he must keep them in the vicinity by continual ground-baiting. Bread is the staple ground-bait, but manufactured packet ground-baits are also very good. The ground-bait for serious bream fishing can be reckoned in buckets. The bait is mixed with rusk, bran, maggots, and chopped worms. To begin the session, several large balls are thrown in, and a lump is added to the swim from time to time as soon as the fish begin to feed. Consistency must of course vary with the type of water, in brisker waters being fairly stiff, in still waters somewhat thinner.

Bream are essentially bottom-feeders and most successful fishing methods require the hook-bait to be placed on the bottom. For this reason, swimming-the-stream and trotting tactics are seldom employed except where the bait is presented by tripping the bottom or stret-pegging. The main methods are therefore laying-on, float legering, and legering.

For ordinary tripping the bottom, the float tackle is arranged as if for swimming the stream, but the float is set higher to keep the bait well down. Few fish are taken by this expedient.

Laying-on, sometimes known as 'tight corking', is the standard method of bream fishing. It requires the float to be set about 18 ins. or a yard further from the hook than the

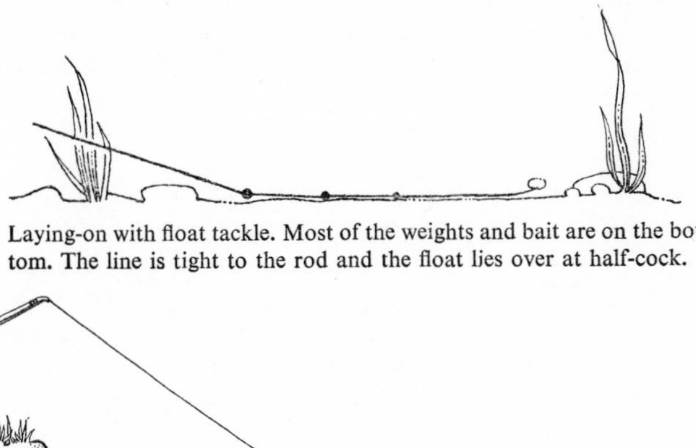

Laying-on with float tackle. Most of the weights and bait are on the bottom. The line is tight to the rod and the float lies over at half-cock.

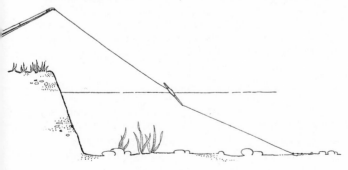

depth as indicated by the plummet. The shots are arranged on the lower part of the cast so that they actually lie on the bottom when the float is cocked slightly sideways. Usually the float is shotted to balance it with slightly positive buoyancy, but in some circles an additional shot is added a foot or so higher up the line so that the float is negatively buoyant and will sink the moment the bottom shots are lifted by a taking fish. Bream bites can be deceptive to the point of frustration; the fish often seem to nibble at the bait for an eternity before making a positive move off with it. During this time the float may sink slightly, rise slightly, or even keel over and lie flat on the surface. When a definite run occurs, the float usually submerges distinctly enough. Opinions are divided as to how such bites should be dealt with, some anglers preferring to strike when the float lies flat, others insisting on awaiting a real ducking of the float.

When laying-on in a brisker current, the angler can select a suitable combination of floats and weights capable of working properly without being continually submerged by the pull of the current. Often the rod must be arranged to exert a light pull on the float from the rod tip in order to balance the tackle between current and rod tip. When a knock occurs it is sometimes necessary to lower the rod tip momentarily to prevent the fish feeling any resistance and allow the bite to develop.

In such a water the float can be allowed to swing down and towards the bank at intervals, so searching out a considerable area of water. These tactics are valuable in locating the fish. The tackle is re-cast when it swings right under the near bank.

In still waters, the tackle might consist of a small quill weighted with one or two shots, especially when fishing within a reasonable distance of the bank. For longer casting, however, the terminal tackle must be slightly heavier to give good casting, and also to allow the angler to control the tackle in light winds or surface drift. Sometimes it is a good plan to attach the float by the lower ring only so that line between the float and rod tip can be sunk. This can give very sensitive fishing, but in running water it requires considerable practice. For sluggish waters, light tackle can be used for close range laying-on; in brisker water a Thames-type float weighted with several shots may be necessary.

Innumerable variations on float, shotting, and tackle will suggest themselves and the float can even be fitted to the line temporarily after the cast has been made. Carefully positioned on the line near the rod tip, and free to slide down the line when a fish is taken, the float can be used as a sort of swing tip indicating bites by bobbing on the surface, or on the line. Slider floats are also valuable in still waters where the depth is greater than the length of the rod.

Leger tackle is set up with an Arlesey Bomb slipped on the line and stopped with a single shot below it about 18 ins. from the hook, although the distance varies with conditions; sometimes a long trail of up to 4 or 5 ft can usefully be employed. On other occasions a very short trail may be more efficient. A pear lead and swivel can be used instead of the bomb, with the advantage that if a spring-link swivel is employed the weight can be changed at a moment's notice with little trouble.

In waters where the bottom is exceptionally soft the problem is that the lead tends to become buried in the mud, so stifling bites and muffling the strike. This is overcome by attaching a short nylon 'leg' to the weight, with a swivel at the end. The running line is then passed through the free eye of the swivel and stopped in the usual way. This makes a smooth resistance-free tackle which is often most effective. If the bait itself is thought to be sinking in mud, or beneath soft flannel weed where it is obscured, this can often be overcome by flattening the bait on the hook to dispose its weight over a larger area. Alternatively, the balanced bread bait developed for carp fishing by Richard Walker (see CARP, pp. 62–3) may be adopted. This consists of a piece of crust moulded to paste so that the buoyancy of one cancels the weight of the other when it lies on the bottom.

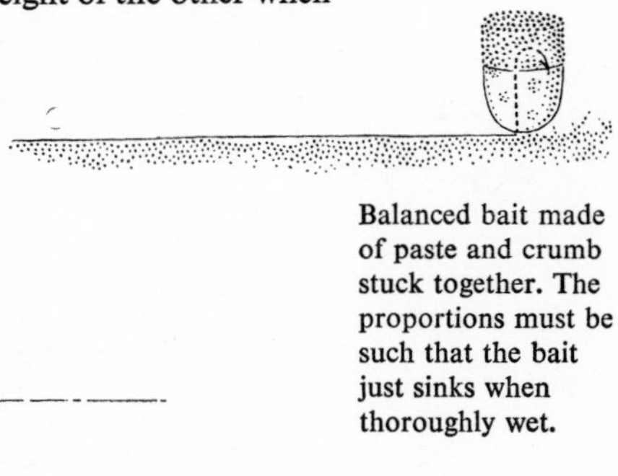

Balanced bait made of paste and crumb stuck together. The proportions must be such that the bait just sinks when thoroughly wet.

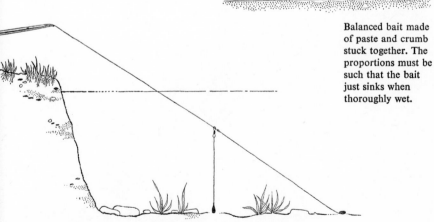

Leger weight on a separate 'leg' to prevent it becoming buried in soft bottom and setting up resistance to a fish.

Detecting the bite is always a problem for leger anglers but there are several ways of providing for the accurate and sensitive detection of the bites. The simplest is to use a dough bobbin, a small ball of paste, attached to the line somewhere between the butt and the reel. A little slack line is allowed to give free movement and bites are usually indicated by a definite movement of the bobbin as line runs out. Some anglers prefer to attach the dough close to the rod tip, hanging a foot or so below it. This is the principle of the 'swing tip', the dough swinging as the line is tightened when bites occur.

The angler can of course fish directly off the reel. If a centre-pin reel is used it must be free-running and the rod must be arranged to point in the same direction as the line so that runs will not cause the tip to vibrate before the reel begins revolving and so put off a taking fish. The angler strikes at the running of the reel, stopping it as he does so. If a fixed-spool reel is used, this can be left with the pick-up open so that line is quite free to run. A small piece of silver paper attached to the line gives easy visibility when the line does run, and the angler simply closes the pick-up and strikes simultaneously.

In fairly brisk waters, the angler must fish with a tight line, depending on movements of the rod tip or the feel of the line between his fingers to inform him of bites. Often it is necessary to lower the rod tip at once to give the fish enough line to 'run'.

Fixed-spool reel. Screw at front of drum controls slipping clutch. Behind this can be seen pick-up arm. Handles are often interchangeable for left- or right-hand wind.

Bream

Probably the best method of all is the slack-line style but this is suitable only for still and very slow waters and requires a windless day. The cast is made, the line drawn tight to rod tip, and then a little slack is eased back through the rings so that the line lies in a natural curve from rod tip to water. The angler watches the line at the water's surface, and when this runs out, he strikes.

All the methods described here are suitable for silver as well as common bream fishing. Note that the silver species is very slightly more inclined to take baits fished just off the bottom.

General

The British record bream is a 13 lb. 8 oz. specimen caught in Chiddingstone Castle Lake by E. Costin, in 1945. Several fish over 12 lb. are recorded from waters like the Tring Reservoirs. Other excellent bream waters include the Queen Mary Reservoir at Staines, Walthamstow Reservoirs, Startops Reservoir, and Marsworth Reservoir. Generally the larger fish are found in still waters. River fish are, however, usually considered to be better fighters. Amongst the exceptional bream waters must be included the many Lincolnshire drains, the Norfolk Broads, and the Fens. The Thames (the upper reaches round Pangbourne), Medway, Arun, Witham, Nene, Welland, and Great Ouse are also noteworthy.

Bream are found in all parts of Great Britain except the most northern and western parts; they are very common in Ireland.

H. T.

Carp

KARPER

1. The Crucian Carp (*Carassius carassius*). This is something of a poor relation of the common carp (see below) and is rarely caught intentionally because of its small size, the British record fish being only 4 lb. 11 oz. It may be recognized immediately by its lack of barbels at the mouth. In the normal form the crucian is deep-bodied and reminiscent of the BREAM in shape, and, even without searching for barbels, the angler would be aware that this is no ordinary carp. However, a variety exists which has a body shape similar to that of the common carp; in this event the lack of barbels is sufficient to distinguish it.

Crucians are good aquarium fish when taken young, being attractive and easily tamed. They may be caught by most carp methods, most successfully by float-fishing with ROACH bait.

2. The Common Carp (*Cyprinus carpio*). The back is dark in

colour, varying between a grey-green and a slaty-blue. The flanks are paler and may be straw-coloured or olive-green with a hint of pink; they have a metallic appearance. The belly is yellow, orange, cream, or buff with a pearl-like lustre to the scales.

The body shape is broad, but laterally compressed to give an oval body section, and the back is humped as it rises in a strong curve from the head to the leading edge of the dorsal fin. The dorsal fin is long, extending from about halfway along the body almost to the tail. It is concave along the top edge with the leading spines conspicuous, and lightly serrated at the rearward edge.

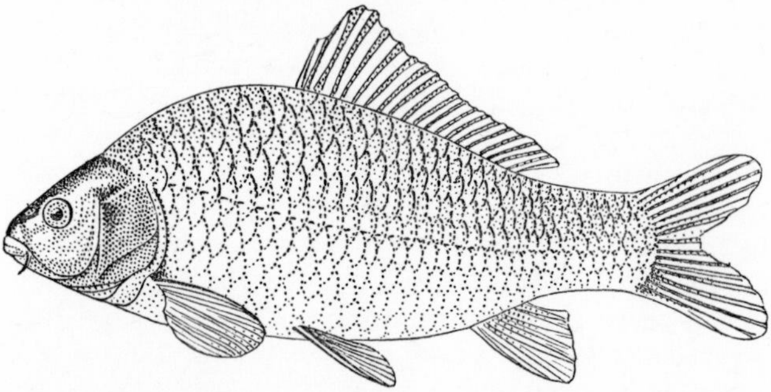

Common carp

The abdominal and paired fins are light-coloured to blend with the belly and may be pink, red-tinted, or streaked. The anal fin is short and the paired fins are large and powerful.

The mouth is terminal and slightly inferior, with thick leathery lips. The barbels, of which there are four, are quite conspicuous, two of them on the upper lip, and the others at the corners of the mouth. In wild fish the body is fully scaled, but scaling is subject to considerable variation in the domesticated varieties, which are usually deeper in the flanks, fuller in the body, and generally heavier.

Other Carp Varieties

Fundamentally the possession of a long dorsal fin and four barbels indicates the common carp, but the varieties, although bearing these characteristics, occur in several forms.

The first is an albinotic and gold-coloured form of decorative origins which is called the *hi-goi*, or *golden carp*. Apart from its colour it is exactly similar to the wild fish, although under extremely good conditions it may also be fuller bodied.

The other varieties are collectively known as *king carps* because of their larger sizes in maturity and their greater growth rate capacities. These are of two main kinds, one being scaled or partially so, the other being virtually unscaled.

The leather carp is almost entirely devoid of scales except for a few, stunted and irregular, at the fin roots. To compensate for the lack of scales the skin is tough and leathery. In this form the dorsal fin is usually shorter than that of wild or scaled fish. The leather carp is also very much less resistant to poor climatic conditions and is found in warmer places, becoming less common in colder regions. It is, for example, common in Israel where it is bred for food, but scarcer in eastern Europe. The farther east the less common it becomes, and the farther south the more likely it is to succeed.

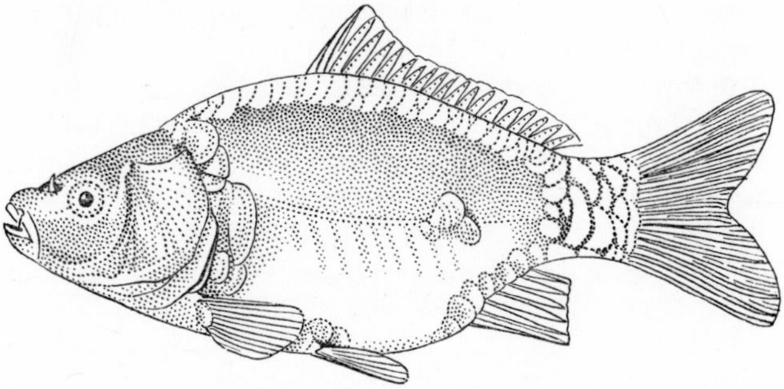

Mirror carp

The body of the *mirror carp* is partially scaled, the scales often being distorted and extra large, in scattered patches or in even rows. The dorsal fin is normal. The mirror and leather carps are biologically the same fish, being simply genetic variations from the same brood or batch of fish, and often of the same parentage. The mirror, however, is very much hardier than the leather carp, and even in fairly good conditions, where unpredictable percentages of each kind result from a given spawning, the leathers die off younger and in larger numbers than the mirrors, many more of whom survive to maturity.

A third type of carp also occurs. This is the more normal fish, having the appearance of the wild variety, but sharing the fuller body and higher growth rates of the cultivated ones. It is fully scaled and may either be scaled evenly like the wild fish, or possess the larger, distorted and irregularly shaped scales of the mirror carp. It is usually quite distinguishable from the wild variety by its greater depth of body.

Distinctions of this kind are considered by some to be pedantic but they are necessary if the background of the various carp varieties is to be understood. This also involves a consideration of the history of the carp, as it spread during the Middle Ages from unknown sources in the Far East into the countries of Europe.

Carp are not indigenous to Great Britain; although the exact date of their introduction is obscure, it can be fixed with some certainty between the years 1300 and 1400. The fish were obviously imported for food purposes and traditionally belong in monastic or manorial ponds and lakes. Being highly fertile and capable of surviving out of water for some time, the species soon spread fairly evenly throughout the southern counties of England, where its value as a food during Lent could hardly be over-estimated. Furthermore, the arts of husbandry were soon put to work on it to produce bigger and better strains.

In Britain, however, carp breeding became neglected during the Industrial Revolution, when the rapid spread of steam transport made sea fish easily transportable to the larger cities. So naturalized stocks of carp, neglected in their unused stew-ponds, acclimatized themselves to wild conditions and became the forbears of the fish we now call the 'wild carp', which is to be found in lakes and ponds all over Britain.

In Europe, however, stronger religious traditions and the considerably greater distances involved, together with the rather slower spread of steam transport, meant not only that the carp survived to compete successfully with sea fish as food, but also that the art of farming them improved considerably. This resulted in highly successful carp strains being evolved. These showed a tremendous growth rate far in excess of that of the wild fish, as well as an ability to attain far greater general proportions and maximum sizes.

From time to time since about 1920 numbers of highly cultivated fish were brought into Britain and stocked in various waters. These were often of the carp varieties, and are today known (with their progeny) as the king carps.

Not only are these fish larger and faster growers than the now naturalized wild carp but, being of the same species, are capable of interbreeding with them. This has resulted in intermediate forms of fish at almost every possible level between the fully domesticated fish and the wild fish. It has most certainly produced an improvement in the wild fish where the two kinds are mixed and the different characteristics are reproduced in the progeny. Now it is possible to see fish which by their scaling are mirror carp, yet by their depth of body are wild carp; the possible permutations to be found are practically endless. Provided fresh importations are continued, and as long as anglers are eager to catch big carp, the chances are that the average standard of carp caught will progressively improve. If, however, such importation ceased altogether, the once-cultivated fish would, over generations, revert to the size and growth capacities of their own wild forbears.

In view of what has been said about carp varieties it would be surprising if growth rates were not highly variable. The figures given here, therefore, while based on work performed on actual fish, can by no means be taken as averages since the growth rates of carp almost certainly vary from lake to lake.

The domestic fish can attain a weight of 5 lb. during their third year, but the wild fish may take five or six years to grow to this size. In fifteen years, domestic fish can achieve 30 lb. in weight, while the wild ones rarely exceed 14 lb. In ideal conditions, domestic fish surpass these rates, as the capture of Richard Walker's British record carp in 1952 indicates. This fish weighed 44 lb. when caught, and was calculated to be fifteen years old. It remains to be seen how long this fish will continue to live in the London Zoo aquarium, where it has now reached the age of twenty-five years.

Obviously, interbreeding between domesticated and wild fish will reflect growth rates somewhere between the extremes mentioned and, to be safe, keen carp anglers must study their own local fish and calculate for themselves the growth rates applicable to their own waters. This is by no means a difficult task, provided anglers are willing to collect scales and take careful measurements over a period of several years.

Carp are found in rivers, but are far more at home in still waters, where the conditions of life suit them and the tempo of life is slower. Lake fish are usually larger than river fish, and their food is very varied, consisting of insects, micro-organisms of the bottom detritus, worms and crustaceans, plankton and algae, and various kinds of weed. In waters which are much fished these ratios are undoubtedly supplemented by angler's baits – usually eaten long after the anglers in question have left for home.

Carp shoal, but even the younger ones show some individuality and wander off independently at intervals. Older and larger fish tend to become more solitary except during the breeding season in May and June, when the fish gather among the weed, forming small groups comprising a single female and several males. The eggs are shed on the weed and sink to stick upon the stems.

Carp soon resume their normal behaviour patterns after spawning, shoaling and patrolling the water as they grub about the bottom for food, being assisted in the search by the taste buds on their barbels which enable them to locate concentrations of food in the bottom mud.

Feeding occurs in temperatures roughly between 56° and 69°F. During the early season, the fish may feed at any time of day or night as temperature and water conditions become suitable. Towards September, when the cold creeps over the water, they feed in the shallows which first receive the early morning sun and warmth, but as soon as the colder weather sets in between October and November, they become torpid until the approach of spring again. They may feed on exceptional days when winter sun suitably warms the waters, but they are generally in a condition of semi-hibernation and may indeed actually bury themselves in the bottom layers of fine soft detritus or mud. In rivers they seek out the warmer reaches during winter and may be taken at intervals throughout the year, although it would require considerable optimism on the part of the angler to fish specifically for them in winter.

In the very hot weather when carp are not feeding they can be seen basking in the shallows or surface waters and come on to feed towards sunset or as the temperature falls as a result of cooling winds on the surface. A great deal depends on both the size of fish and the depth of water in question. Carp behaviour in deeper waters is much affected by wind, feeding being induced in one region when others are totally unsuited.

Baits There are innumerable baits which will on occasion take carp, but those mentioned are time-honoured baits which the serious carp angler relies on.

A piece of *bread crust* the size of a golf ball is by no means too big, and crumb or flake baits should also be large. Large baits require a large hook, and Nos. 2, 4, and 6 are favoured by many.

Whole *lobworms*, or bunches of smaller *redworms* or *brandlings* should be presented on appropriately sized hooks.

The golfball-sized *new potatoes* are employed and must be parboiled in order to make them soft enough for the fish to eat, yet stiff enough not to be flung from the hook by the action of casting. The potato is boiled in its skin and baited with a baiting needle, the hook being tied to the end of the line and the bait slid down to it. The potato is then partially skinned.

Balanced bread is a bait designed to enable the bottom-feeding carp to annex a bait without feeling the nylon attached to it. It has the virtue of settling on the bottom, perhaps above silkweed or soft mud, with the softer crusty part upwards and the heavier pasty part down. If the hook is inserted through the paste and into the crust this keeps the bend upwards, the point down, and the line well underneath the bait. A piece of paste is moulded to a lump of crust so that the whole bait has a very light negative buoyancy and sinks very slowly, settling as described.

Tackle

Carp are tough, artful, fighting fish, and since they may weigh anything between 3 and 30 lb. the rod must be fairly heavily built, with an 'all-through' action extending down to the end of the butt. Built-cane is the ideal material and two possibilities may be considered. The Avon type of rod is suitable for ordinary carp fishing where the quarry is not expected to be larger than 8 or 9 lb., but for specimen hunting and where big fish are expected the rod specially designed by Richard Walker, known as the Mark IV carp rod, is essential.

The choice of reel is a very personal matter. Frequently carp fishing requires long casting and for this the fixed-spool reel is ideal, although anglers really expert at casting from centre-pin reels often prefer these for the more satisfactory contact which they give with a fighting fish. For many forms of carp fishing involving leger methods. however, special methods of bite detection are employed, and these are generally more easily applied with fixed-spool reels which allow a wider choice of method, especially when fishing direct from the reel with nothing but a baited hook on the line.

The line should be of about 6–8 lb. breaking strain for ordinary carp fishing, but where big fish are sought it can be increased to about 10 or 12 lb. b.s. For the lighter weights monofilament is very suitable, but for the heavier sizes the braided lines are more flexible, less elastic, and therefore more suited to long range work.

Most carp anglers prefer to tie the hook directly to the end of the line without having separately attached casts between hook and reel. To this end the line is often stained in various colours to camouflage it against the bottom weed. When this is necessary the line is bunched in coils and inserted in suitable dyes for half of the diameter, the other half being later stained with some different shade. Brown and green are the favoured colours, but conditions in various waters must be considered.

Weights are used only when essential, anglers usually preferring to cast baits under their own weight. When weights are used they must be swivelled to prevent fouling about the line during the cast or when sinking. The Arlesey Bomb is ideal when so fitted, and can be used in weights varying from ¼ oz. to 1 oz. Alternatively a pear-shaped lead with a clip-on link swivel attached enables a change of weights to be carried out with considerable convenience. For float-fishing, split-shots are used, but transparent glass beads find favour with some anglers.

Carp have big mouths and the hook must in any case be big enough to accommodate a bait large enough not to be spoiled by the frequent attentions of small fish. Hooks of size 6 to 2 are usual. Eyed hooks are recommended and may be of any reliable pattern, although most anglers agree that a short shank is preferable. The hook must be kept razor sharp. A small stone is carried by many successful carp anglers so that the point can be touched up.

When floats are employed they are intended to indicate the bite rather than to support the bait and they must therefore be as light as possible within the given conditions. Some anglers prefer small PERCH floats when surface drift interferes with the surface line. Many like to leave the float flat on the surface, where it will not produce vibrations at the bait end and can be drawn well clear of the bait.

An electric bite alarm is essential for the serious carp angler. Several types are now available. The indicator is used in conjunction with a rod rest which is normally incorporated with it.

Keep-nets and landing-nets must be as large as possible in order to accommodate the size of fish sought. A reasonable size for the landing-net is about two feet in diameter with a depth of mesh of about four feet. The Y pattern with a supporting cord carrying the mesh between the arms is very popular, since it is so easy to stow.

Keep-nets are not often used for carp fishing because anglers like to photograph and return their fish immediately after capture. Where they are used they must be of about three feet in diameter and six feet or so in length.

Fishing Methods

More than any other kind of angling, successful carp fishing demands careful preparation, and this, quite apart from the selection and preparation of suitable tackle, involves prebaiting, observation, and a careful study of the water in question and the habits of the fish sought. Many anglers do manage to catch odd carp without any preparation at all, but they would often be the first to admit that the catch was in the nature of a pleasant and welcome surprise which no doubt focused the angler's attention on the thrills and skills of this kind of fishing. Such a catch is often the first step towards becoming a keen and dedicated carp fisherman.

It is necessary to visit the water beforehand solely for the purpose of discovering the regular patrolling routes of the feeding fish and, if possible, to notice their feeding places. Then the water must be studied with a view to locating suitable places from which to fish and several swims must be earmarked for attention later. Any angler looking over his carp swim seeks first a place which will give him reasonable cover from the suspicious fish. Then he wants the spot to be one where he can expect the fish to take a bait, and one from which he can reasonably cast to such a place. Finally he wants the swim to be one which gives him a fair chance of landing the fish, and this means that he must note major hazards in the form of lily beds, brambles under the bank, or any other obstacle which any worth-while carp will immediately make for when it finds itself in trouble. This doesn't mean that the presence of such risks will prevent his using a particular swim altogether, but that he will survey the spot to understand how best to cope with those risks when the time comes.

Once this much is decided the angler must decide what bait to use. If the water is also stocked with RUDD and other small fish it may be expedient to use a bait such as potato, which is tolerably free from attacks by these fishes. This is important because it is essential that, whatever bait is used, it should not first be snatched up by other less important fishes before the carp have had a fair chance to see it.

The swim is then pre-baited with the selected bait for several days in advance. This gets the carp into the habit of feeding confidently in the selected areas, educates them (should they require it) to take a bait hitherto unfamiliar to them, and ensures that they will regularly visit the spot in search of food.

Some anglers like a two-day interval between each pre-baiting, others like to tackle the job regularly every day. Obviously several such visits are necessary to establish the routine the angler wishes the carp to adopt. Then the spot is left completely unbaited for twenty-four hours before the day chosen for fishing. On the day itself little or no baiting is done, except when the hook is inside the bait presented.

Actual fishing techniques can reasonably be divided into those which seek carp feeding at the surface, and those which seek the bottom-feeders. Float-fishing can be tried, but few successful carp anglers have any real faith in float methods. If floats are used they should be as far from the bait as possible, and are best left uncocked, simply lying on the surface where they act chiefly as bite indicators. The angler must be in no hurry to strike until a well-developed run occurs.

Legering is better performed *without* the use of any weights at all other than the bait itself, which, being of about golfball size, provides sufficient casting weight, and sinks easily enough to hold bottom naturally.

The bait is cast into position and the line is left quite slack and lying on the bottom. If a considerable distance is involved it may be taken up slightly to ensure that there are no bellies or unnecessary slacks. The rod is fished from rests, preferably two of them, one at the butt, and the other at the butt ring. For this kind of fishing a fixed-spool reel is probably most effective.

The rod is set up more or less horizontally on the rests with the top pointing towards the water and in the same direction as the line itself. This ensures that when a run develops there is no lateral or vertical 'rod wag' at the tip, which might alarm a taking fish by transmitting vibrations along the line. The reel pick-up is left open so that line may fall freely from it when a fish takes, but if the line tends to spring off the spool of its own accord a small piece of dough or paper may be attached to the line just below the spool, or the line may be slipped under a matchbox to hold it steady. The dough bobbin, suitably shaped to run through the butt and second rings, can itself be the bite detector, or alternatively an electric bite alarm may be used.

The electric alarm is usually incorporated in a rod rest which is set up at the butt of the rod, close to the butt ring. The antenna of the alarm is adjusted to prevailing conditions by a few turns of the adjuster screw, and the line from the reel is led first to the side of the antenna and thence through the butt ring. Any tightening of the line, temporary or otherwise, is sufficient to move the antenna and so close the delicate contact points and set off the buzzer. Bites are usually signalled by an intermittent or continuous buzzing, at which the angler closes the pick-up and strikes with a sweeping swing of the rod to take up all slack line and set the hook fast in the mouth of the fish. The spool of the reel is fitted with an adjustable clutch mechanism which allows the fish to take off line under tension when the rod is fully bowed to its test curve.

Once the carp is well hooked it is played by using side-strain to turn it from weed beds or other refuges into which it will certainly dive if given the chance. Line is recovered at intervals by 'pumping' the rod down to the fish, the spool of the reel being operated with a finger control across it to prevent the clutch slipping as the angler hauls back on the rod to regain line, yard by yard. Only when the fish shows definite signs of tiring should the net be slipped into the water in readiness for landing.

Surface fishing is usually employed when a known fish is being stalked and then lured by placing a floating crust in its path, either by casting this into position, or by arranging it under the rod tip among the margins. Margin surface fishing is an expedient practised towards evening, when most anglers have left the pond, and in those waters where the fish show a tendency to patrol the surface margins, taking the floating remnants of the departed angler's baits. This is opportunist fishing. The angler requires good cover and his rod must be correctly set up, with the pick-up open and the crust lying unsuspiciously still. If other fish nibble repeatedly at the bait, it can even be suspended a few inches from the surface where the carp have no difficulty in taking it.

Anglers margin fishing in this way must be prepared to hold a tough carp within a few yards of the bank, and control it there until it is ready for the net. The method is both exciting and rewarding.

General

The record carp was a 44 lb. fish caught by Richard Walker in 1952. In his many writings on the subject, Walker has stated with considerable conviction his view that carp over 60 lb. exist in British waters. Together with other members of the Carp Catchers Club of Great Britain he has accounted for several fish over 30 lb. in weight by rod and line. Certainly the 20 lb. carp is now far more likely to fall to the angler's rod than at any time in history, and with so many introductions of good stocks now taking place it is simply a matter of time before many more such fish are taken.

It is extremely difficult to list waters containing large carp. The essentials today are simply that the water be alkaline, carry a good weed growth and full insect and plant life, and be of a temperature conducive to good breeding and survival, as well as food production. Experiments in Palestine over recent years show that immense carp can be obtained in comparatively short periods of time by scientific farming methods. Any angling club possessing suitable waters and funds can work on these principles.

H. T.

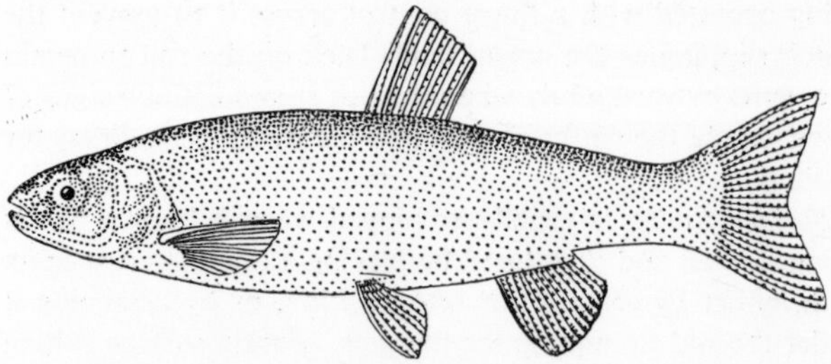

Chub

KoPvooRN

The chub (*Squalius cephalus*) is also known as loggerhead, chavender, chevin, alderman, skelly.

The back is grey-green, grey-brown, or grey-blue and the flanks are silvery when young, becoming yellower and finally bronzed in maturity. The belly is cream or buff and occasionally pink-tinted or streaked. The dorsal and tail fins are grey or almost black, and the fins on the underside are yellow, orange, or pinkish with grey tints. Both dorsal and anal fins are convex-edged. The body is spindle-shaped and almost circular in section at the shoulder, where it is very thick-set.

The head is large with a terminal, large, thick-lipped mouth. The body scales are large, with a metallic appearance.

In suitable waters a year-old fish may be 4 to 6 ins. in length, attaining 8 or 10 ins. within the next year. At the age of about seven the fish may weigh 3 lb. or so and under exceptional conditions more.

The chub is quite easily confused with the ROACH, and a ray and scale count is sometimes necessary. The chub's anal and dorsal fins both bear from seven to nine branched rays and the lateral line consists of from forty-two to forty-nine scales. There are seven or eight rows of scales above this, and three or four rows beneath to the roots of the pelvic fin. The pharyngeal teeth are large and hooked and are arranged in two rows on each side, with five teeth in one and two in the other.

The chub is common in most of England and Wales, unusual in Devonshire, and absent in Cornwall. In Scotland it occurs south of the river Forth. Until fairly recently it was not found in any part of Ireland. It is now reported in scattered colonies in the river Blackwater and undoubtedly exists elsewhere as a result of recent introductions.

Chub are essentially river fish and do not occur naturally in still waters except where they have somehow become isolated there by earthworks and river improvement schemes which cut off areas of backwater to form unconnected lakes.

When introduced into lakes and ponds the fish thrive and reach good proportions, in many cases making a very worthwhile contribution to the coarse fishery.

Under natural conditions chub love the stream and are almost always to be found close to moving water. When young they congregate in large shoals and inhabit the surface layers, but as they grow older they tend to become more solitary and predatory. They are fond of gravelly reaches and hard bottoms, but in muddy rivers they make the best of conditions and achieve good living standards over the mud and harder clays. The older fish tend to take up residence in particular places where they make foraging expeditions along the reach, returning regularly to their holes under the bank or beneath tree roots. Throughout their seasonal wanderings they return repeatedly to such a stronghold, whether it is behind cut campsheathing, alongside isolated piles, or in the lee of bridge buttresses beneath the undercut below the masonry. They love to hang about near bridges but always lie on the edge of the faster water which brings food down to them. They also like the streamy shallows and can often be seen moving upstream and downstream in an apparently aimless manner, returning over the same beat again and again. Even quite small rivers and streams support surprisingly good chub, which seem most adept at making the best of whatever conditions they find there.

Their diet consists of practically anything edible, especially as the fish get older and become semi-predatory. They will eat slugs, silkweed, worms, insects, shrimps, snails, flies, minnows, frogs, tadpoles, crayfish, and elvers as well as the fry of their own and other species. They are by no means above rooting about in the bottom when on short commons.

Chub are less conservative than most species and feed in temperatures which would put other fish down. In very hot weather they feed close to the surface, and during colder spells drop into middle-water habits, searching the stream for young fry or anything else which is brought down by the current. They are very much less inclined to be fussy about baits than other fishes and do not seem to become preoccupied with particular foods to the exclusion of all others. Anything floating down which might be edible is enough to evoke interest provided the fish are in a feeding mood, as they almost invariably are.

Spawning occurs on sandy or gravelly shallows among the weed, during April or May, or even as late as June when the early season has been cold. Once spawning is over, the fish soon leave the weed, working into swifter waters to recover. During this time they are often to be seen near the surface, in mill-tails and weir pools and on the fast gravelly stickles or scours. By August they tend to move into deeper water but always on the fringe of the stream, taking up residence in selected holes. In the winter they patrol the reach, searching for food, but continually returning to their holes at intervals. When floods arrive they take to the eddies and more sheltered places, but remain in the stream rather than in the slacks. Towards spawning time they become gregarious again and can be seen in pairs or small groups. The smaller fish spawn communally, but older ones work in small groups comprising one or two females and several males.

Growth rates vary considerably according to the water, although chub in poor waters probably make better progress than most other fish because of their non-selective appetites, which enable them to make the best of things. Winter growth is also better than in many fishes to judge by the condition of the scales when examined with a microscope. The winter marks are less easily distinguishable from the summer ones than might be expected.

Baits In view of the omnivorous habits of the species there is hardly a creature which lives in water which, provided it is of a suitable size, would not make a good chub bait. The angler has thus a very wide choice.

Several baits stand apart, however, and among these are cheese, crayfish, elvers, worms, frogs, and minnows. Chub baits should generally be large ones, presented on hooks of suitable size, which may range from Nos. 8 to 4. For good-sized chub, a golfball-sized bait is not too large, but a great deal depends on conditions; in certain circumstances, chub will willingly take very small baits. Presentation is probably far more important than choice of bait, and in view of this fish's reputation for wariness the silence, caution, and stillness of the angler are paramount.

During the early season, live-baits such as a lip-hooked minnow or GUDGEON can be very effective, and small spinning baits often have a fatal attraction for the fish at this time. Fly spoons, large flies, and small spinners will sometimes tempt the apparently uninterested fish. The angler must use all his ingenuity to experiment with various baits and presentations.

Tackle The rod must be sturdy enough to hold and handle a fish of several pounds. For this a tip-and-middle or all-through action is essential, perhaps particularly because chub are often taken by long-trotting or leger methods. For legering a good Avon-type rod is useful, or one specifically designed for legering in fairly fast water such as the Bill Howes 'barbel and leger' rod.

The reel may be a centre-pin or fixed-spool according to choice and the methods chiefly used. Line should be of 4–5 lb. breaking strain, but where conditions are especially snaggy or big fish are confidently expected this may be increased to 5–6 lb. or even more.

Many anglers still tend to fish for chub with ROACH hooks, which are far too small for the fish. A glance at the mouth of even a 1½ lb. chub is surely sufficient to convince the doubtful that something realistically large is required. Look at the mouth of a 5 or 6 lb. fish and there can be no disputing that a 4–6 hook is, comparatively speaking, a small one. For general purposes a No. 8 or No. 6 will be suitable, but circumstances do arise when a No. 4 or 2 would be better.

Hooks should preferably be eyed, since chub give a very powerful resistance during the early stages of the battle, which can often be protracted for some time. Spade-ended hooks are liable to come adrift in these conditions, but a four-turn half-blood knot on a No. 4 eyed hook is a very suitable combination and can be relied upon to cope in waters where snags make it necessary to hold the fish very hard.

Fishing Methods

Ground-baiting is important for chub, not so much in the matter of quantity but in its being accurately and sparingly placed. The old dodge of throwing in a sample of the hook-bait at intervals will often bring the fish out of their holes to await the next donation. If this carries a hook, it should be as naturally presented as possible, or the chub will not touch it.

Chub can be taken on float, leger, fly, or spinning tackles according to their situation in the water and the time of year. Whichever method is employed, however, it is important to stay out of sight of the fish, which has a wholly justified reputation for disappearing the moment it spots the angler. This means approaching the water with considerable caution, and necessitates methods which enable a bait to be presented from a distance. For this reason, long-trotting and leger methods are very successful.

When *long-trotting*, the angler first surveys the water to locate likely-looking chub holes. Overhanging trees, ancient piles, sunken barges, bridge buttresses, and high clay banks undercut by current are often very suitable. Having chosen his spot, he settles himself down some twenty yards or so upstream, taking good advantage of any natural cover available. After ground-baiting the swim with some of the hook-bait, tossing this well downstream so that morsels trickle along in the stream to cover several such holes, he sets up his tackle.

A cork-bodied float capable of carrying several shots is used. This is set to cock with about a quarter of an inch of the float showing to give good visibility at a distance. If the swim is a particularly long one, the float is capped with a Richard Walker float vane which, being cut like the wings of a dart, gives excellent visibility and very little extra weight or resistance when the float is submerged. The vane should, of course, be cut down to the size which is suitable. You will probably have to make up one yourself.

Fairly heavy shotting is employed to get the bait well down in the fairly fast water into which the chub sally from their points of vantage. The bait can be cast down and across so that during its passage through the swim it passes close to the various chub lies. During the trot down, the float must be preceded by the bait, and this is effected by means of a continual but light check on the line from the reel. A good centre-pin reel normally allows the stream to draw line from the reel, the angler having a light finger control on the drum in readiness for striking and to prevent over-run. A few morsels of the hook-bait, aimed at the float during its passage, will often bring maurading chub into the stream, where they will inspect the bait and, with good fortune, take it. Once the swim is covered, the angler retrieves his tackle quickly but gently, possibly by 'batting' the drum (i.e. by spinning it, with the check released, with quick strokes of the palm). It is a wise expedient to bring the rod tip around during retrieve so that the float returns across the middle of the stream and away from the bank being fished.

Where the nature of the bottom is known, gravelly runs can be fished in this manner also, the float being checked at intervals to raise the bait momentarily in the water. The gentle way in which a bait so manoeuvred settles again is often very tempting to the fish, which perceives an item of food sinking very naturally past its 'window'. Chub will sometimes simply mouth the bait, causing only the very lightest tremble of the float. It requires considerable self-control not to strike immediately at touches of this kind. More often an interested fish will bolt the bait definitely and turn away with it, giving the float a quite sudden plunge which must be met by a firm strike.

In long-trotting, the bait should be presented at varying depths, the surface and middle waters being searched as well as the bottom because fish often move into these upper layers and take mid-water baits. If the angler is casting to near swims, lighter tackle must be employed. Where conditions permit, a slowly sinking, long-trotted bait is sometimes very effective.

Whatever the depth or the method used, it certainly pays to check the float at intervals to make the bait waver attractively near the surface before slowly sinking it again. This expedient is invaluable when fishing an uneven bottom, since it enables the fisherman to swing his bait over the shallower portions of the swim before settling it down among the deep runs again.

If the float is set a foot or so higher than the actual depth, the bait can be trickled along the very bottom by a careful manipulation of the tackle.

Fixed-spool reels are also employed for long-trotting techniques. The angler fishes with the pick-up open, allowing the line to run off freely as the float moves through the swim. To check the float so that the bait precedes it, the palm of the hand can be held poised lightly about the spool so that the coils of line slipping off brush lightly against it. Sufficient friction can thus be applied to check the float through the swim. Another effective method is to hold the finger across the spool and apply friction to the running line, or the finger may be used to trap the line against the rim of the spool at intervals. In any event the finger must be ready to stop the line in readiness for an instant strike. There is seldom time to close the pick-up before striking, but a finger across the spool can be just as effective, the pick-up being closed immediately the strike has been completed.

All float-fishing methods for chub require that the line should be well greased to keep it on the surface. Sometimes bights of line occur on the surface as a result of the swing of the current, or of wind at the surface. These should be 'mended' at intervals by raising the rod tip, lifting the line, and laying it back on the surface straight without disturbing the passage of the float. Long-trotting in this way is a most effective and killing method, and may be performed with worm, bread, maggot, and cheese. Suitably arranged, the tackle can be modified to present a live minnow or elver passing through the swim.

Stret-pegging is used in fast waters where thick weed growth or uneven bottoms prevent a clean long-trot. The float is much the same as for long-trotting, but should preferably be slightly heavier. The weight is a single drilled bullet which will not ordinarily submerge the float when clipped in position with a single shot about eighteen inches or so from the hook. A further shot is clipped on the line a foot or two above the bullet, and the tackle is fished from a tight line, the bait and weight resting on the bottom and controlled from the rod tip so that the float cocks sideways, pointing downstream. By carefully checking the line at intervals, and then occasionally letting out a further foot or two, the angler can make the bait trip along the uneven bottom and can control it throughout the swim. Bites are usually felt or spotted at the rod tip as quickly as at the float, and every touch is struck. If this fails to connect, the angler must try lowering the rod tip as soon as a touch is felt, striking at the more pronounced bite which often follows.

In sluggish waters the *laying-on* method is excellent; with it the bait can be presented from a suitable distance with accuracy and ease. The float is set up a foot or so higher on the line than the depth requires, and cast down and across so that the line extends out in front of the float at the cast. The bait then settles well in front of the float, which the weights cause to cock slantwise. It may be necessary to withdraw or give a few inches of line to cock the float satisfactorily. The rod is then fished from a rest. Bites are normally quite definite, the float plunging in a slow, deliberate, and dignified manner.

Very often the angler when laying-on finds that the stream shifts the terminal tackle, swinging the bait slowly downstream and in towards the bank at intervals. If he cares to let out a little line on each occasion the tackle can be made to search out a considerable area in this way. Where the stream is insufficient to shift the tackle of its own accord the angler helps by lifting the rod tip at intervals, shifting the bait momentarily, and allowing the stream to do the rest.

For surface fishing, baits can be presented by long-trotting methods, using an unshotted light float, or with a controller or a bubble float. If the bait drags badly the chub will not look at it, and it may then be better to sink it somewhat below the surface, either by using a heavy bait, or by adding a shot or two just below the float.

Fly-fishing (see p. 151 ff.) for chub is very effective when hot weather brings the fish near the surface and the usual methods are hopeless. It is every bit as difficult as fly-fishing for trout, and if anything the angler must be even more careful to obtain good cover. Casting a big buzzy fly to a rising fish is frequently worth while, and a No. 8 hook on fly tackle, baited with a single lobworm, will sometimes take a good fish. The presentation must however be very delicate if the worm is to stay on the hook; a light TROUT outfit is suitable for the task.

In known chub holes the same expedient may be used with a fixed-spool reel and ordinary bottom tackle. The worm is left to sink simply by its own weight, without float or shots. Sometimes too, this tackle is good enough for presenting small fly spoons, which are worked through the swim.

A fixed-spool reel with an ordinary bottom rod is a very suitable piece of equipment for surface baits. Paste, crust, crayfish, or small frogs may be presented in this way. Often the fish will take the bait immediately it strikes the water, but should nevertheless be allowed to sink to the bottom before being retrieved.

Dapping is a traditional way of taking chub at the surface, usually when stalking a known fish. Such a fish often has a hole in a pretty impregnable position to which it is almost impossible for the angler to cast his bait by normal methods. He must then try an attack from immediately above the fish, taking great care to avoid being spotted, and preparing his bait and tackle before approaching the banks.

The bait can be a large dragonfly or bluebottle, hooked so that it is alive and struggling, or even a worm or crust. The hook, about a No. 8, is tied directly to the end of the line, which must be tough enough to hold the fish at close quarters, because often the brunt of the battle will take place close by, and the angler may not have very much space to make full use of the power and suppleness of his rod.

The angler must locate a suitable hole in the bank-side foliage to put the rod through. He can either bring the bait up to the rod tip, put the rod out over the spot, and then pay out line to get the bait on to the surface, or he can first arrange the bait at a suitable distance from the rod tip, and then wind the line around the rod tip several times to get the clearance for poking the rod through the foliage. In either case he will probably need a single split-shot close to the bait to get the line out when the rod is in position.

Once the rod is out, the bait is lowered to the surface, where, if an insect, it struggles in a lively manner. If the angler has successfully avoided being seen or heard, the bait is often taken immediately. Then he must strike and play the fish as well as conditions permit. This can be a very effective method of taking really big chub, although landing them through a hole in the brambles is often a tricky business.

Legering is by far the most productive method of taking good-quality chub, especially perhaps because the other methods often take ROACH or other fish before the chub has a good chance to get at the bait.

Some anglers advocate legering upstream, but most prefer to fish down and across. Upstream legering is a highly skilled business. It is suitable only for certain kinds of water and requires considerable experience, especially in detecting bites. It also requires the tackle to be carefully balanced so that the weight just holds bottom against the flow of the current. It is wise to strike at any suspicious movement of the rod tip or the line.

For the more orthodox forms of legering the weight will vary according to the bottom, the stream, and the presentation desired. If a static bait is desired, and the water is at all fast, a flat-bottomed Capta weight or a coin lead is probably best. Both are designed to hold bottom. Coin leads are particularly suitable on the Hampshire Avon and Kennet for this technique. On the other hand, if a rolling leger presentation is wanted, an Arlesey Bomb or pear lead and swivel is essential both to make the lead roll easily on the bottom and to prevent kinks arising from line twist.

The length of 'trail' (distance between the weight and the hook) must also be varied according to conditions. It is not possible to stipulate rules for this, and the angler must experiment to find the most taking method in each case. Sometimes a very short trail of only a few inches will get fish taking madly; on other occasions, even in the very same swim, a length of four or five feet may be required before the fish will take the bait confidently.

The main thing is to get the bait into the edge of the stream off the likely-looking holes and bays, or beneath overhanging trees which frequently shelter big fish. Once the bait is in position it can be fished with a tight line in fast water, but where the stream permits, other tactics can be employed.

When fishing a tight line it is extremely difficult to decide when to strike. Sometimes the merest touch must be 'hit' and sometimes the angler must patiently avoid touching these and await the really hefty thump which most big chub give when they confidently take the bait. This must be decided as a result of experience. When the angler finds that striking at small bites fails to hook the fish, or alternatively shows that the fish are small ROACH or DACE, he must turn to the other expedient.

In slow or sluggish waters the leger can be fished from a slack line, or, if a fixed-spool reel is used, even directly from the reel. For this, the bait is cast into position and the line is first tightened, then slackened off to allow it to hang in a gentle curve. Bites are signified by a distinct tightening of the line, easily visible where the line meets the surface. If the leger is fished directly from the reel, a spindle-shaped piece of dough, small enough to run easily through the butt and second rings, is fitted to the line where it hangs below the spool with the pick-up open. The dough prevents the line slipping off the spool, but runs freely through the rod rings when a fish takes. The angler then closes the pick-up, watches the line tighten, and strikes firmly.

Chub

Other legering devices include the use of a dough bobbin between the reel and butt ring, hanging with a foot or so of loose line, or a swing tip. In very sluggish waters, and where the adjustment permits, an electric bite detector can be used with considerable success.

General

The British record chub was taken from the river Annan by Dr D. Cameron and weighed 10 lb. 8 oz., a truly remarkable fish for British waters, although on the Continent chub are reported to attain 12 lb.

The only comparable fish from British waters was a fish of 10½ lb., claimed to have been taken from the Middlesex Crane in 1875. The present runner-up, a fish of 8 lb. 8 oz., was taken from the Sussex Rother by D. Deeks, in 1951. Other 8 lb. specimens are reported from the Hampshire Avon and the Dorset Stour.

Seven-pound fish are found in some waters. The Great Ouse, Kennet, Thames, and Wissey (Norfolk) are amongst those likely to produce big fish. Other good chub waters are the Wye, Severn, Trent, Derwent, and Border Esk, and many south Scottish game waters probably contain specimen chub.

Although large chub are probably far more common than the average angler might suppose, their proverbial shyness is such that they are very hard fish to catch once they have the experience and strength that go with size.

Certainly there is no shortage of good chub waters. Besides those mentioned here, many smaller rivers are capable of producing surprisingly good chub.

H. T.

Dace

The dace (*Leuciscus leuciscus*), sometimes called the dart or dare, is a slim fish, predominantly silvery in colour but olive-green to brown along the back. Its pectoral, ventral, and anal

SERPELING

fins are generally yellowish but sometimes have a slight tinge of pale pink. The caudal, or tail, fin is forked; the dorsal and anal fins are concave. The dace has a comparatively small head, with a brilliantly coloured eye. The scales are medium to small in size, and there are forty-seven to fifty-four of them along the fish's lateral line. A dace may easily be mistaken for

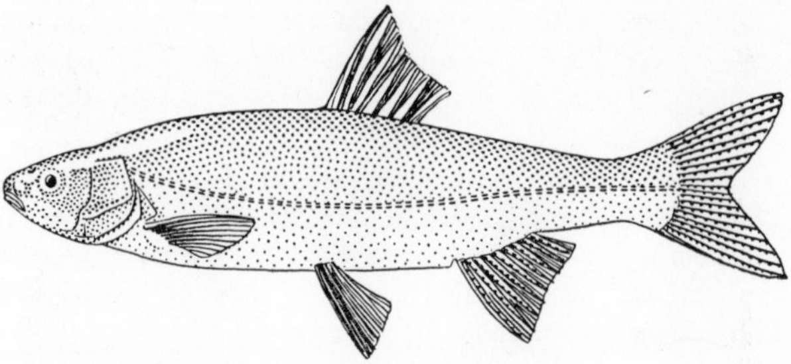

Dace

a small CHUB, and vice versa, but they may be identified one from the other by the dorsal and anal fins which are concave in the dace and convex in the chub.

The angler might catch a dace/bleak or a dace/chub hybrid. Hybrids of bleak/chub *have* been recorded, but Dr Tate Regan in his standard work on British fish states that these recorded hybrids may possibly be bleak/dace. If you do catch a fish which you think may be a cross between these species, keep it for further examination.

The dace is a member of the Cyprinidae family of fishes and like most species in the group is almost always to be found in shoals. Dace shoals in general prefer the swifter currents of the stream, particularly the clean, gravelly shallows. Yet many large shoals inhabit some deep, slow-flowing rivers and may also be found in still waters.

In April and May dace gather for spawning. Each adult female deposits an enormous number of eggs in the weedy shallows. These eggs are small and sticky, which enables them to adhere to stones and aquatic plants. The males fertilize the eggs, which are then left to hatch. This takes only a few days. Once hatched the young fry have to fend for themselves. During the first few days, they live on the yolk-sac, which is a small reserve of food, and when this has been used up they start feeding on minute water insects. The natural food of dace consists of flies, fly larvae, and other aquatic insects, snails and worms, and silkweed and similar water plants.

Because they prefer well-aerated water, dace are among the

first of the coarse fishes to recover from the efforts of spawning. Fish exhausted by spawning undoubtedly need a good deal of oxygen. Even on the first day of a new season, they are fit, in good condition, and ready to put up a game fight.

Dace

Baits

Most of the anglers' baits will take dace, at any time of the season; it is the presentation of the bait which is the most important consideration. Care should always be taken when putting a bait on to the hook.

Clean, lively *maggots* are the best all-round dace bait. More dace are taken on them than on any other bait. For presenting a maggot correctly the hook must be as sharp as a needle, since a blunt hook will tear the maggot's skin, allowing the white inside to ooze out. If that happens the maggot is practically useless as a bait. Nick the sharp point of the hook into the skin of the thick end. If this is done carefully the maggot will not be punctured and will wriggle alluringly.

Earthworms are a popular dace bait on some waters, with the small redworm as first favourite. A brandling worm, recognized by the yellow rings down its body, is also useful. The tail of a lobworm is effective for big dace, particularly the larger specimens which may be found in strong-flowing weir streams. The dace which live in these weir-pool swims are usually also fond of silkweed. This is to be found growing on the submerged wood pilings, steps, and stonework of weirs. As bait, silkweed is best used on a No. 12 to 14 hook trotted down the fast, clear swims on float tackle.

Bread baits, paste, crust, and flake may be used to good effect at any time during the season. The best of these is undoubtedly flake-crumb from a white loaf. The popularity of this bait is due not only to its effectiveness, but to its requiring no previous preparation. All that is needed is an absolutely new loaf, which will have quite enough moisture in it to make it ready for use without further attention. When baiting the hook, a No. 10 or 12, simply take a small pinch from the spongy white crumb and squeeze it on to the hook. It is best left ragged and natural; the smaller particles which break off and drift down with the current will help to attract fish.

Hempseed on hook. Bend of hook is stuck into white kernel.

Hempseed is used as bait on some rivers, notably the Thames where some large bags of fish are taken by the regular anglers. Before it can be used as bait it must be prepared by simmering it in water until the seeds split and expose the white germ. The bend of a No. 12 or 14 hook is pressed into the opening where the seed has split. The fish are fond of the white kernel which protrudes from the cooked seed, and for this reason many anglers paint the shanks of their hemp hooks white. This is supposed to disguise the hook and improve the appearance of the bait.

Ground-baiting with hempseed can easily be overdone; you should use only small and diminishing quantities. Start sensibly by using two or three grains at a time, and continue to do so at frequent intervals throughout the day. Don't throw in handfuls, since this will only spoil your chances of catching good fish and ruin the prospects of other anglers near by.

When fishing a regularly hemped swim I find a bait of crushed hemp mixed with bread paste a successful lure for the extra big dace. This bait is fished on the bottom.

An angler who finds that the dace are too fast for him to hook would do well to change the hook-bait from hemp to elderberry. Apart from those mentioned, many other baits take dace, including caterpillars, earwigs, woodlice, mealworms, caddis grubs, wasp grubs, freshwater shrimps, bloodworms, pearl-barley, and wheat.

Tackle

For dace fishing, a light rod with a fast action, especially in the top joint, is ideal. A 12 ft match-type rod, with built-cane top, is suitable for fishing swimming-the-stream style. A Nottingham-type reel, with large drum, optional check, and free-running action is best, but a fixed-spool reel will do. The reel should be loaded with fine line. As a guide I would suggest 1½ to 3 lb. breaking strain nylon monofil.

The hook should be sharp and of smallish size, varying of course with the type of bait to be used. I normally favour hook sizes 12 and 14. Since a large float requires many split-shot to balance it correctly, always use the smallest float possible. Almost any small float will do, provided it is not too thick at the middle, because the resistance this causes is certainly felt by a taking fish; in any case it generally spoils bite registration. Correctly loaded and adjusted, the float will be extremely sensitive and give warning of the slightest touch.

Fishing Methods

The depth at which dace are to be caught depends on the nature of the swim. If it is free of weeds the fish are to be found either around mid-water facing upstream, or searching the gravel for insects. In swims containing much weed, however, they are often found near the surface. Where weeds fringe narrow, fast-flowing runs, the dace will be found in the runs ready to intercept any items of food which come down with the stream.

Chub

Squalius cephalus (page 68)
Specimens 4 lb and over
Record 10 lb 8 oz*

Dace

Leuciscus leuciscus (page 77)
Specimens 14 oz and over
Record 1 lb 8 oz 5 drams*

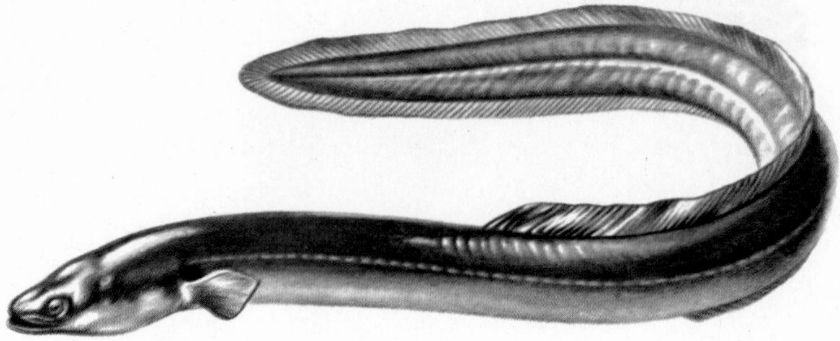

Eel

Anguilla anguilla (page 85)
Specimens 4 lb and upward
Record 8 lb 8 oz*

Brook Lamprey

Lampetra planeri
Not a sporting quarry

Gudgeon

Gobio gobio (page 91)
Seldom grows over 3 oz*

Minnow

Phoxinus phoxinus
Only grows to bait size

Bullhead

Cottus gobio
Only grows to bait size

Stone Loach

Nemecheilus barbatula (page 93)
Only grows to bait size

Spined Loach

Cobitis taenia (page 93)
Only grows to bait size

The best way of fishing with a maggot is by swimming the stream with float tackle. However, before tackling-up, consider what the conditions are, the level of the river, strength of flow, colour, and so on. Then choose the line strength and size of float, and decide on the shotting arrangement. If it is a deep swim, use a float capable of supporting sufficient split-shot to take the bait down to the fish. Don't put the shot all in one bunch but spread them out along the cast, placing the larger shot nearer the float, and making the lower one near the bait a tiny dust shot.

Dace

I prefer to start fishing deep. First of all it is necessary to use a plummet to ascertain the depth of the swim. The float can then be set so that the bait, in this case a maggot, will swim just clear of the bottom. It is possible to experiment by pushing the float down the line periodically and thus raising the hook until a taking depth is found.

The dace's nature compels it to dart and grab at almost everything resembling food that comes down with the current. So if you present your bait so that it travels as naturally and unhindered as possible it should entice a fish to take it.

With maggots as hook-bait, it is essential also to use them as ground-bait. They can either be thrown in loose to attract the dace, or mixed with some softish ground-bait mixture and tossed in at the head of the swim. If the stream is fast, calculate just how far upstream this must be put in for it to reach the swim at the right level along the path over which the maggot-baited hook will travel.

As quietly as possible, cast the tackle in slightly upstream, and, as the float rides through the swim, follow its journey by

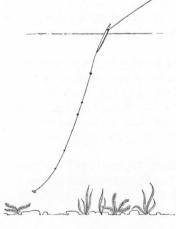

Dace rig for swimming the stream.

pointing the rod tip at it, avoiding slack line between float and rod tip. In this way you will get a quick and direct strike. Since a dace can eject a bait instantly, it takes a sharp strike to hook your fish.

I normally start by putting two maggots on the hook, and delay baiting with single maggots until the dace begin to bite short, nipping the ends of the bait. This is a sure sign that their appetites are becoming satisfied. You can also try nicking the point of the hook carefully in the skin at the maggot's middle, which should bring more definite bites. Occasionally, let the tackle trot a few feet below the normal limits of the swim and then hold the float back. This causes the bait to rise in the water and waver around attractively with the current.

On some rivers, notably the Thames, it is essential to get the bait down past the bleak shoals if you want to catch a sizeable dace. A typical Thames matchman's tackle arrangement consists of a quill float, shotted immediately below the ring and shotted again about 12 ins. from the hook. Some anglers add an extra dust shot 2 or 3 ins. from the hook to assist the bait in getting quickly down past the small fish. The hook size favoured by some is 16 or 18 with single maggot bait, though I prefer a larger size (14 to 16) with a single maggot.

As well as correct spacing of split-shots, correct weighting is needed to sink the float so that only about half an inch is showing above the surface. This rig, used with a long rod, can yield a good bag of fish, but you will need to strike smartly. With the longer rod the line can be kept fairly taut between float and rod tip, so that as the float dips the rod can be given a quick flick to hook the dace.

Stret-pegging is a method worth trying in swims which have fair depth with a medium to slow current close to the bank, and one with which you are likely to pick up the bigger fish, because you can manoeuvre the float and search thoroughly all over the swim.

A large quill float capable of carrying four to six medium-sized split-shot is fitted to the line. Again, the shot are best spread out along the cast and not bunched in one place. The lowest split-shot should be 12 to 18 ins. from the hook. The exact shotting arrangement depends largely on the type of swim and river conditions, and adjustments should be made after a trial cast or two.

The plummet is used to check the depth, and the float adjusted so as to allow some 12 to 18 ins. more than the depth of water in the swim. Once this has been done, and just before starting to fish, take up a position at the head of the swim, and then throw in a little ground-bait. This mixture should have a base of well-mashed bread, which will sink fairly quickly. Maggots thrown in loose should be thrown some way above the swim if they are to be of use. The ground-baiting rule to observe throughout the day's fishing is 'little and often'.

The hook may be baited with a redworm, the tail of a lob-worm, maggots, or the white crumb from the inside of a loaf.

Long casting isn't necessary, so cast in with an underhand swing. With the rod held directly in front of the body allow the tackle to trot a few yards down the swim. Then, holding the baited tackle there, let the flow of water raise the bait off the bottom and waver it about alluringly. If, after a moment or two, no bite is registered, work the float tackle a little further down the swim and hold it still again. The tackle can be worked all over the swim in this manner, and you should pick up a few of the bigger dace.

If the dace in the swim are of good quality, I have sometimes found it pays to use a slightly larger bait than usual and not to hurry the strike.

When using hempseed as a bait, *swimming the stream* is the best method. It is a mistake to use split-shot on the tackle when hemp fishing, since dace often bite at the split-shot in mistake for the hempseed. A thin lead wire coiled neatly on the cast will be more satisfactory, though you'll have to use one small split-shot to prevent the coil from slipping down the line.

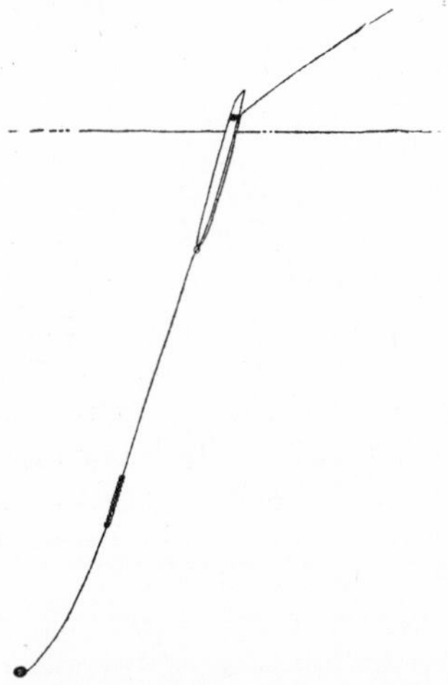

Lead wire is often used as a weight when hemp fishing. Fish sometimes mistake lead shot for the bait.

Coarse Fishing

Using hemp you will almost certainly get bites which, although numerous, will be very quick. It takes great skill and concentration to strike them, so every sizeable dace caught on hempseed is well-deserved.

Legering a bait on the bottom often catches the larger dace, but the bait should have movement to attract the fish. Redworms are lively bait here, but maggots are also effective especially when they have been put in the swim for some time.

For legering, the best terminal tackle is as follows: a small leger weight, bullet, flat lead, pear-shaped lead, or Arlesey Bomb. The weight is stopped from sliding right down to the end of the line by pinching on a split-shot.

During the summer, dace may be seen rising freely to take flies from the surface. This is the time to take a fly-fishing rod with you (see pp. 153–4) and fish the rises. But if you want a couple of hours *fly-fishing*, then fish the water whether the dace are rising or not. Fished dry or wet, an artificial fly will account for grand dace – but sometimes they take with lightning speed and you will need sharp reflexes to match them.

The selection of fly pattern is not so important as size. Use tiny hooks at first, but as the sun goes down and the dace start to rise everywhere, you can increase the hook size with good effect. With dace there is no need for exact imitation, for they will take almost any fly. As a guide the following short list will be useful: Coachman, Peter Ross, Greenwell's Glory, Black Gnat, Wickham's Fancy, Alder, Red Tag, Dark Olive Quill, and Coch-y-bondhu.

General

The dace is quite common in England and Wales but is not found in Scotland or Ireland (except in the river Blackwater). The rivers which I know are likely to produce large fish are the Kennet, Windrush, Suffolk Stour, Dorset Stour, Lower Thames, and Hampshire Avon. A tributary of the Hampshire Avon yielded a 1 lb. 8 oz. 5 drm specimen to R. Wm. Humphrey in 1932, and the River Derwent produced a 1 lb. 8 oz. 12 drm specimen for S. Horsfield. The British Record (rod-caught) Fish Committee recognizes the Hampshire fish as the record.

Though of no great size the dace is a sporting fish that can be caught at any time of the season. It can be a useful quarry for match anglers, especially if the competition is held on a river not controlled by size limit. A great number of angling competitions have been won by the angler with a good bag of dace. Such a winner deserves his congratulations, for a match angler has to be skilful to end the day with a netful.

W. H.

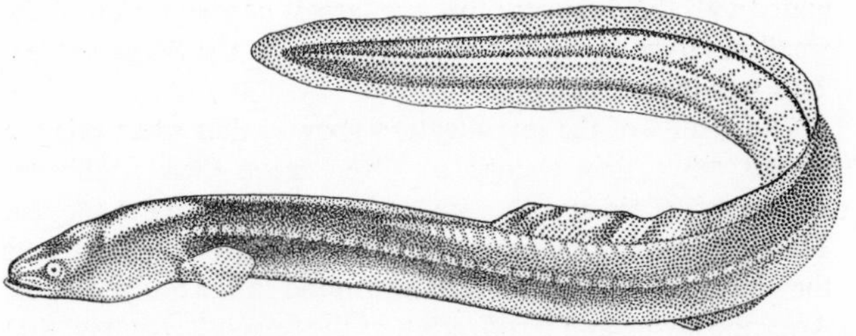

Eel

AAL
PALING

The eel (*Anguilla anguilla*) is a true fish, having gills and scales. Its scales are not readily apparent, being small, oblong in shape, and embedded in the skin. They are arranged in little groups placed obliquely and at right angles to each other. The scales show rates of growth clearly; they suggest that male silver eels ranging from 12 to 20 ins. in length have spent 4½–8½ years, and female eels of 14–26 ins. 6½–8½ years in fresh or brackish waters.

There is only one kind of eel in British waters; variations in colour simply indicate different stages in the eel's remarkable life-history.

The eel is a wonderfully mysterious fish. Only in comparatively recent years have we found out much about it. The final evidence of the eel's extraordinary migrations came to us only after the First World War.

Many years ago, a tiny fish was discovered on the surface waters of the Atlantic. It was shaped like a willow leaf, transparent, tiny-headed, and with a flattened body. In the first instance it was not connected with the eel, but in 1893 two marine biologists, Calandruccio and Grassi, finally proved that it developed into the young eel or elver.

The final solving of the mystery was left to Dr Johannes Schmidt, of the research ship *Dana*. He found one specimen of the young eel off the Faeroe Isles, a second specimen off the west coast of Ireland, and then more in the north-east Atlantic. His discovery induced him to make a systematic search for very young eels. Eventually he found them in large numbers, above the 500 fathom line to the west of the British Isles, and then all along this line from the Faeroes to the north of Spain.

It was thus established that eels need deep water for spawning purposes. Investigating further he found that as he travelled west from where the 500 fathom line began, he caught the larvae in larger numbers, but smaller in size. Finally his search ended with the discovery that the largest concentration of the smallest larvae lay in the northern area of the Sargasso Sea. This was in the year 1922.

The results of the investigation showed that when eels are almost adult they change to silver, leave their freshwater haunts in Britain and Europe, and make their way to the sea. This happens in the autumn; by the spring of the next year they have reached their breeding ground in the Sargasso Sea. After the laying and fertilization of the eggs it is assumed that they die, as there is no proof that any adults come back.

It is reported that transparent eggs, thought to be those of the eel, have been found in the top six hundred feet of the Sargasso, floating up from the deep spawning waters. The tiny larvae grow slowly and as they do so are carried, not far below the surface, in the prevailing Atlantic currents towards the coast of Europe. The geographical distribution of the eel is due to these ocean currents, which flow eastwards and north-eastwards from the middle of the Atlantic. It takes the larvae until the second summer to reach a length of two inches and by the third they are full grown at three inches. By this time they have reached the European coast. By the following autumn and winter they have reached the elver stage and in the spring they commence their run up the rivers.

Some of the details of this migration are still uncertain. There is a body of opinion which believes that the male eel usually stays in the estuaries while it is the female that runs up the rivers and streams to inhabit the ponds, ditches, and lakes.

There is also considerable doubt whether British eels ever succeed in getting back to their South Atlantic spawning grounds. The currents are thought to be against them on the return trip. If this theory is correct, it is the North American eels that return to perpetuate the species.

Where to find eels? They exist in many waters, but some are favoured by them more than others. Generally speaking you will find them in quantity in those areas where the rivers have a good elver run. Somerset, for example, has a big eel population thanks to the fact that there is a large elver run up the Parrett during the spring. As most waters in the county are inter-connected, every water gets its quota of eels.

Eels are to be found in disused clay pits, ponds, drains, canals, and rivers. They are also found in reservoirs, where, from the trout point of view, they are a menace. Strange to say, although big eels do undoubtedly exist in many reservoirs, they are usually extremely difficult to catch. In the reservoir at Durleigh, Somerset, for example, quite a number of eels up to

Eel

4 lb. or so are found at intervals in the sump, yet a number of attempts by anglers to catch them in the reservoir itself has met with little success.

Canals, as a rule, hold quite a large eel population. The Bridgwater and Taunton Canal is an example. This canal supplies the Bridgwater Docks with water and elvers work their way into it in considerable numbers from the Parrett via the Docks. This canal, like most others, has a series of locks to overcome the difference in ground levels. Although eels are to be found in most sections, they seem to concentrate more in the region of the locks, especially on waters that no longer carry any boat traffic. Usually they are on the lower side when both gates are shut but if the lower gate is open they can be found in the lock itself.

The largest eels prefer waters which have a mud bottom. Where the bottom is of rock, stone, or gravel they tend to run smaller. They prefer static or slowly moving waters to fast-running streams or rivers.

Stone walls that have crevices such as those under bridges or tunnels are a great attraction to eels. A local angler fishing for roach hooked and successfully landed a 6 lb. specimen from such a location. Disused brick-yard ponds often hold some outsize specimens and if I were going to try for an eel to beat the existing rod-caught record I should give some of these a trial.

Baits

Undoubtedly the best bait for eels in general is the lobworm, but it should be remembered that such a bait will also attract the smaller eels (and small fish of all kinds). Naturally if you are after real specimens you do not want to be bothered with small fry. Therefore you should select a bait that is too much of a mouthful for the smaller eels to manage, for example part (or whole if it is very small) of a small dead fish, which would be a ROACH, RUDD, BLEAK, or GUDGEON. Some anglers employ sprats for this purpose but they are not always obtainable. In the Thames, whole dead BLEAK are real killers.

Whether you use the whole fish or half at a time, make sure that the hook is well buried. A baiting needle is a great help as it enables you to draw the hook length through the body and out at the other end, drawing the hook well in.

Particularly large lobworms, pieces of meat, or offal have also proved to be good eel bait.

Tackle

The tackle for normal eel fishing should be a stout rod of the leger or pike-spinning type and a line around 10 lb. breaking strain, of either monofil or braided nylon or Terylene. Hooks can be the usual black-japanned, eyed type, or a good forged pattern around No. 4 in size. A pierced bullet or barrel lead should be run up the line and a link-spring swivel attached to the end.

Mount your hooks to monofil of about 9 ins. in length and of slightly less breaking strain than your line. Make sure your knots are good (have as few knots as possible). Use a half-blood knot with at least six turns to attach the hook to the monofil and a figure-of-eight knot for the loop at the other end. For this class of fishing, most anglers like to watch a float; a cork float of the *Fishing Gazette* live-baiting pattern ranging from one to one and a half inches is popular.

The use of a swivel when fishing for eels is essential, not only to counteract any spin from the fish itself, but to assist in the easy removal of the hook, especially if you are after the big ones. If a plain swivel is used, attach this to the reel line with a half-blood knot, pass the loop of the hook length through the other end, and pull tight, as you would when putting a hook to nylon on your looped line.

Choice of a reel is important. You can use a fixed-spool type, but I think a good centre-pin not less than 4 ins. in diameter is preferable. This gives much better control over a hard-fighting eel. Fill it well with line in order to get as quick a recovery as possible.

If you want to catch outsize eels, then you must use tackle of ample strength. An ideal outfit is a good, stout pike rod or light sea rod of 9–10 ft. The line should be not less than 20 lb. monofil or braided nylon or Terylene. Avoid twisted or what is sometimes termed 'cable line' at all costs. Hooks should be of good-quality forged pattern, mounted to stout nylon or flax. Some anglers use wire, such as Alasticum, which is non-corrosive. A reminder: do not forget to use a swivel.

Fishing Method

The average-sized eel is mostly taken during daylight simply because this is when they are fished for. Few anglers fish for eel during the hours of darkness. But it is when dusk sets in that eels really begin to roam around and the bigger specimens come out of their hiding places. All-night fishing, in my experience at least, does not pay off. The best times are the hour or so after dusk and before dawn. Eels seem to go off during the period in between. Most other eel fishermen with whom I have discussed this are of the same opinion.

Weather conditions are another important factor. Bright moonlight nights, for instance, are to be avoided, for eels do not seem to move then. So also are nights when the temperature drops suddenly or a cold wind springs up. Your choice should be dark, warm nights – the darker the better.

Take only essentials with you. Apart from the actual fishing gear, you should be provided with the following: a good torch, a sharp knife, a pair of angler's scissors, a strong sack, and a piece of string.

Take a companion with you if you can. It is no joke hooking an outsize eel in the dark when on your own. Handling the eel is quite enough for one person. Your companion can hold the torch.

Mount your hooks at home before leaving, or at least get to the water in plenty of time to do the job before dusk sets in. A dozen hooks should be sufficient. Mount a link-spring swivel to each hook length and put your baited hooks in a good tin box. This is a wise precaution, for I have known anglers who have laid the baits down beside them without such protection only to find that rats have made away with some.

Use a good rod rest or even a pair of rests after casting out. There are a number of ways in which you can detect bites. You can do it by sticking a piece of white paper on the side of the reel, or by laying a piece of light-coloured wool between the handles, or you can hold the line between your finger and thumb and feel the bite. I prefer the last, as it gives you an earlier indication and saves all fuss and eye strain. Some anglers I know clip a rod bell, as used in sea fishing, to the end of the rod. In addition there are, of course, a number of quite efficient bite detectors on the market, including electric bite alarms.

When you get a bite, do not be in too great a hurry to strike, for many good eels have been lost that way. Usually you will find that a few turns are taken off the reel, then the eel stops. Then a few more turns and another stop. The eel then has the bait in its mouth and away it goes taking off line really fast. It is during this period that you must curb the tendency to strike. Wait until it stops. Strike when it makes another run.

If good fortune is with you and the eel is well and truly hooked, it is then that the fun begins. You do not play eels, giving them a sporting chance as you would with other fish. The aim is simply to get the fish out of the water as quickly as possible, and you will be surprised how hard a big eel can pull. Exert maximum pressure all the time, keeping a tight line, and keep winding so as not to allow the eel to go down on you. If it once manages to get down to the bottom, more often than not you can count the battle as lost.

Your rod may be stout enough to lift the eel safely. If so, then wind up as tightly as you can, and grasp the line tightly to the rod, or alternatively hold the reel drum firmly and lift the eel straight out. This you can do with eels of medium weight. If your rod has not enough lifting power or the eel is too strong then you have to employ other means.

If the bank is low or gently sloping it is possible to slide the eel up. If, however, your bank is on the steep side, a good landing-net is a great help. It needs to be fitted with a long, stout handle, a big ring, and a net of good quality and small mesh. Here, too, that companion can be of real service.

When big-eel fishing at night, you do not waste time by trying to take the hooks out in the dark. This is where the sack and the scissors come in. With those eels you can manage to lift out on the rod, you get your companion to hold the mouth of the sack open, raise the eel until it is suspended over the sack, snip the line just above the hook, and drop it in. Tie the mouth of the sack tightly and there you are. You can bang the eel on the head in the sack, or at least try to, for eels take a lot of killing. With eels too big to lift out on the rod, grasp the line about a foot above the fish, and again lift it up and into the mouth of the sack.

To attach your line to the swivel on another baited hook length, either make another loop or use a half-blood knot. But remember – not less than six turns before you thread back through and pull tight.

General To what size do eels grow in this country? It is a difficult question to answer. If old records can be believed, there have been some real monsters – eels, for instance, of well over 20 lb. The heaviest of recent years was one of 16½ lb. taken in a net from the Whitadder, near Berwick, in 1926.

It is difficult to understand how the record rod-caught eel, an 8½-pounder taken near Bristol in 1922, and on view in a tackle shop there, has held on to the top place so long. There are eels to be taken which could raise the record weight very considerably. I am sure of this from personal experience, having seen three eels in my part of the country quite capable of breaking the record by a considerable margin.

The first was one I hooked while fishing a clay pit for pike. It was possibly the largest of the three. It took the live-bait at one go and, after a long struggle, escaped just when it seemed on the point of defeat. I should say it was the equal of a number of conger I have taken around the 15 lb. mark.

The second I found dead on the surface of a good-sized

pond. It was not marked in any way, and had apparently died from natural causes. On a spring balance which had been tested and found not far out, it weighed 11 lb.

The third had brought about its own downfall. It had been hooked by an angler and broken away, taking with it a length of stout gut, which had become entangled around a snag. It must have freed itself later, but died afterwards, for next day I found it close in to the side. Rats had eaten at least a third of the body from the head downwards. As the remainder weighed over 8 lb. this eel must have been around the 12 lb. mark.

Many anglers fish for normal-sized eels for the table. When it comes to a matter of calories, even the salmon with 1,173 per lb. has to take second place to the eel, with 1,635. As for other freshwater fish, none of these has more than 500 per lb.

Eels are, of course, found not only in fresh water but in coastal shallows also. Good-sized silver eels are to be found in the sea itself, especially in the region of estuaries.

Raymond Perrett

Gudgeon

GRONDEL

The gudgeon (*Gobio gobio*) is rarely fished for deliberately by serious anglers, except when it is required for live-bait. When fully grown it reaches a length of about 5 or 6 ins. although some specimens of 8 ins. have been taken. It is in fact a smaller version of the BARBEL. You can distinguish a gudgeon from a small barbel by the number of barbels or feelers which hang from the corners of the mouth. The gudgeon has two of these, while the barbel has four. The LOACH, a similar small fish, has six. Gudgeon vary in colour, being grey or brown, irregularly speckled, and generally silver with dark spots on the flanks. The dorsal and caudal fins have a number of brown or grey speckles.

Gudgeon are fairly widely distributed throughout England though rare in Cornwall. They are rarely found in Scotland, and there is only a small, local distribution in Ireland. They spawn in May or June, when a female will lay as many as 3,000 eggs. These are transparent and sticky, and are shed over clean gravel, which they adhere to so that the flow does not wash them away. Although gudgeon much prefer the flowing water of rivers they are to be found in the sluggish water of canals, and even in lakes and ponds. Gudgeon like a river to have a bed of gravel, on which they gather in large shoals. They often come on to the shallows at the water's edge, and lay-bys are favourite places for a shoal to get together.

Gudgeon feed on most forms of aquatic insect life, worms, and small crustaceans, which they find by searching around the gravel or silt on the bed of the river.

Baits and Tackle

No tackle can be too light for gudgeon fishing, since the gudgeon is such a small fish. Use a light rod matched with a fine nylon line. Almost any kind of reel will do – a hooked gudgeon is not likely to pull off yards of line or have to be played out before being brought to the net.

Hook sizes 14 and 16 are generally recommended for gudgeon, but I have found a No. 12 not at all too large for sizeable fish. Bait it with a morsel of crust, a maggot, or, best of all, a small piece of redworm.

The best kind of float is a small crow quill, weighted with one medium split-shot.

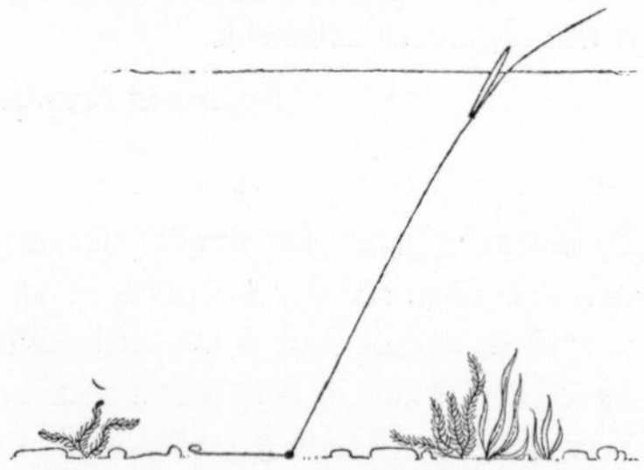

Gudgeon tackle for slack water. Crow-quill float weighted with one shot and with six inches of line between weight and bait.

Fishing Methods

The gudgeon is surprisingly strong for its size, and will put up a lively struggle on suitable tackle.

If you can stir the bottom with a rake, and then put some ground-bait into the swim, the gudgeon will start feeding almost at once – if they are there. If bites are not forthcoming, move a few yards downstream and resume fishing because the gudgeon there will start feeding as the water coloured by the raking drifts down. Insects and other items disturbed by the rake will also drift down to the fish.

Where there is a steady flow to the water, adjust the float so that the bait just trips along the bottom. If it is set too high off the bottom you will not catch many gudgeon; nor will you lure the fish if the bait is dragging along the bottom. Use the plummet, because it is essential to know the depth, and set the float accordingly.

Gudgeon usually pull a float right under, or, if hooked on leger tackle, give the rod tip a strong thump as they take the bait. This often raises false hopes in the angler fishing deeper water for larger species.

Gudgeon

General

The gudgeon record is shared by three fish at 4¼ oz. The first was caught on the Thames at Datchet by G. Cedric in 1933. Then in 1935, W. R. Bostock caught one from Hoggs Pond, Shipley. The third was taken from the River Soar by J. D. Lewtin in 1950. Several other fish have been taken at this record weight, but not officially recorded.

Furthermore, it is on record that a 4¾ oz. specimen was caught from a lake at Woolwich in 1955 – but the fish was returned to the water and therefore not accepted as a new record. However, every coarse-fish angler stands a chance of catching a new record fish because gudgeon are known to reach a weight of 8 oz.

W. H.

Loach

MODDERKRUIPER

There are two species of loach, the stone loach (*Nemecheilus barbatula*), which is by far the commoner, and the spined loach (*Cobitis taenia*), which is not found in Scotland, Ireland, or Wales, and in England seems to be limited to the Midlands and Wiltshire. The spined loach takes its name from the two spines situated one on each side of its head.

Both species of loach are of a brown, mottled colour and average about three inches in length. Around the mouth they have a cluster of six barbels, or feelers, which vary in size between the species, the stone loach having two long and four short, and the spined loach six of equal length. Loach may be confused by the inexperienced with GUDGEON or with very young BARBEL, but the number of barbels will readily identify them. The loach has six, the barbel four, and the gudgeon only two. An unusual feature of the loach is its scales, which lie flat and do not overlap.

Both species make excellent spinning and live-bait for PERCH, PIKE, TROUT, and SALMON. Loach fished alive on leger tackle have also accounted for BARBEL.

The stone loach may be found in fast-flowing streams and brooks in most parts of the British Isles; it is also found quite frequently in canals and in still water. Its favourite hiding place is among the stones on the bottom. Being almost entirely carnivorous, it is always ready to make a meal of any aquatic creature small enough for it to tackle that the current brings near. Spined loach have similar habits.

Fishing Methods Loach are rarely fished for deliberately except as bait. The best way of catching them is therefore the simplest and quickest, namely, with a net. A triangular landing-net frame which has been fitted with a fine meshed net (minnow mesh) and attached to a four-foot handle is ideal. It is best to wade in the stream with the net moving ahead along the bottom. Swift movements of the net around the larger stones should catch plenty of fish.

General If you have loach bait left over at the end of the day's fishing, you can take them home, sort them into size groups, and preserve them in formalin solution for use later as spinning baits. Incidentally, loach caught in sufficient numbers and cooked soon after catching are reckoned to be a delicacy.

W. H.

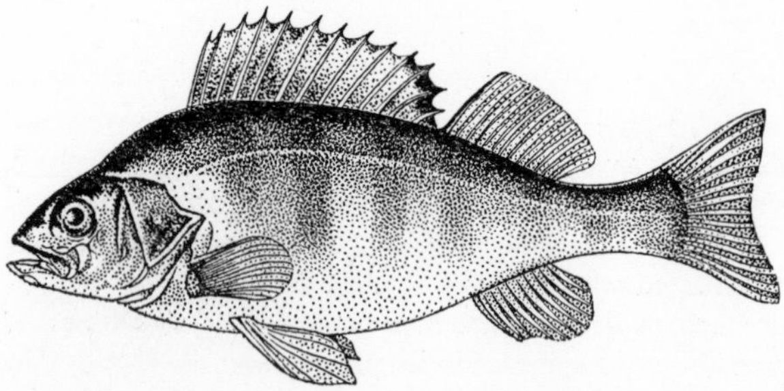

Perch

BAARS

The perch (*Perca fluviatilis*) is not likely to be confused with any other fish, thanks to its striped pattern and its double dorsal fin.

The back is grey-green, blue-green, dark blue, or grey-brown, and the flanks are pale green with a silver lustre and several darker transverse bars extending from the back down to the middle flanks. The bars narrow off towards the centre flank, and the belly is silvery-white or silvery-green. The transverse barring varies in intensity from one fish to another, and from one water to another, and the number of bars varies between five and nine.

The first dorsal fin is greyish in colour, with a tint of violet, and bears a large dark spot at its rear. The second dorsal is yellowish with green or pink tints or streaks at the edges. The fins on the underside are pink, orange, or red, and the pectorals are brownish or buff. There is considerable variation in body and fin colour according to the water, the time of year, and the age of the fish.

The body shape is narrow and laterally compressed with a distinct hump at the back, leading up to the fore-edge of the first dorsal fin. The first fin is supported by spines which are very sharp, the second by one or two spines at the leading edge and branched rays along the remainder. The scales are comparatively small and extremely firmly attached to the body, so that they are difficult to remove. When handled, the fish has a rough raspy texture on account of the tough scales. The gill-covers are triangular towards the rear, with a spine at the apex of the triangle. Carelessly handled this will prick the angler's hands, as also will the spines of the first dorsal fin.

Perch

The tail is small and clearly forked, being rather small for the size of the body.

Lake perch often grow to larger proportions than river perch but, unless conditions are fairly good, they are very prone to over-population, in which case the average size falls off, and growth rates become poor.

The normal fish is capable of fairly good growth and can attain 2–3 ins. during the first year, reaching 6–7 ins. by the end of the third year. This rate was far exceeded by the fabulous perch of Arlesey Lake, Bedfordshire, where the fish were at one time said to reach about 8 oz. during their first year. This is hardly surprising considering the number of large perch which have been caught in this lake. (Arlesey is an old clay pit. Recently, alas, the big perch seem to have disappeared.) In other waters where food is short and populations are vast, the very opposite often occurs. Three-year-old fish represent a near maximum for size, adding little to their stature over the following years.

Generally perch shoal in large numbers, especially when very young, the fish of a particular shoal being of the same size. As they grow older the shoals become smaller, until among the very large fish of specimen size there is a tendency towards solitary behaviour as the appetite becomes more rapacious.

The species is highly predatory, even when small. Its diet is very mixed, including minnows, loaches, gudgeon, and small fry of every kind, as well as freshwater shrimps, molluscs, caddis grubs, insects generally, and worms. Normally, perch do not eat vegetable food, but when feeding amongst silkweed they sometimes take the weed in their efforts to obtain the creatures living among it. They will also take the angler's bread or cheese baits when these are kept moving, mistaking them for some small water creature.

Perch hunt by hiding and surprising their prey rather than by chasing it, although they may sometimes be seen in marginal waters swerving after some small fish. A surprise attack by perch often results in the small fry scattering or leaping at the surface, as the angler sometimes observes when he has baited his swim for roach, and attracted large numbers of small fish at the same time.

Spawning occurs among the weed or reed stems in shallow water near the margins. When the first few inches of gelatinous ribbon have been extruded from the fish, they swim among the weeds entangling the ribbons of eggs among them as if to draw the ribbons out of them. A great many of the eggs are eaten by creatures hunting amongst the foliage during spring. Spawning is usually during March or April, but is occasionally later, after a late spring or a severe winter.

Once hatched, the young fish, complete with yolk-sacs beneath their bodies, lie among the weeds until the sac is completely absorbed and they have proper control of their bodies. They keep to the shallows in large shoals, making for slightly deeper water each year as they grow older. The mature fish tend to feed in mid-water, moving at intervals into deeper layers in search of prey and in order to see prey at the surface more easily. Once the fish get older and become solitary they tend to take up residence in some suitable hole, amongst tree roots, or by undercut banks, somewhat similar to the holes chosen by large CHUB, the difference being that perch prefer to be off the main stream and in the quiet water.

When winter approaches and the weeds die down, the fish move, with their quarry, into deeper water and become more active in patrolling large areas of water in the search after food. Shoals can sometimes be seen roving along the marginal waters between forages into the deeps.

In ponds and lakes the behaviour is similar, the larger fish taking up deep holes during the colder weather and conducting their search for food from this through a limited area of territory.

Baits Perch will take worms, maggots, grubs, and insects of all kinds. Minnows, GUDGEON, and other small fry are also acceptable, and a hungry perch won't turn up its nose at a recently dead small fish either. They will also take bread and cheese baits either because they are temporarily on short commons, or, as explained above, because they mistake them for some small creature. Molluscs and freshwater shrimps are also welcomed. Perhaps the best way to sum up the appetite of the species is to suggest that it will take anything that moves – provided it can catch it, and provided the size is within the limits imposed by the mouth. This gives fair scope. I have heard of a $1\frac{1}{4}$ lb. perch being caught on a 4 oz. perch live-bait!

Brandlings, marsh worms, redworms, and lobworms all make exceptionally good perch baits, but the lobworm is probably the best of all. A large lobworm can be hooked on a No. 6 hook, or on multi-hook tackle made up with size 8 or 10 hooks. Triangle hooks are not suitable for perch fishing except on spinners or dead baits, where some anglers prefer them.

Many anglers take their first perch on a maggot bait and never forget it, using the bait in later life as confidently and successfully as any other. The objection to the use of maggots for perch is that the bait so readily takes small fish of other species and is therefore likely to be grabbed before the big perch manage to find it.

Much the same objection applies to caddis and other grubs. All the same, these do take perch. Often good specimens are caught by the confident and delicate presentation of such baits. For the specialist seeking large perch, however, they tend to be too small to give much hope of consistent results.

Minnows, gudgeon, and small fry are probably the best all-round perch baits and tend to catch good-quality fish. Almost any small fish between 2 and 5 ins. in length is suitable, and, used on a hook suited to its size (4–6), may be presented dead or alive. Float, leger, and paternoster tackles all permit the use of live-baits, which can be successfully presented at any depth according to water conditions.

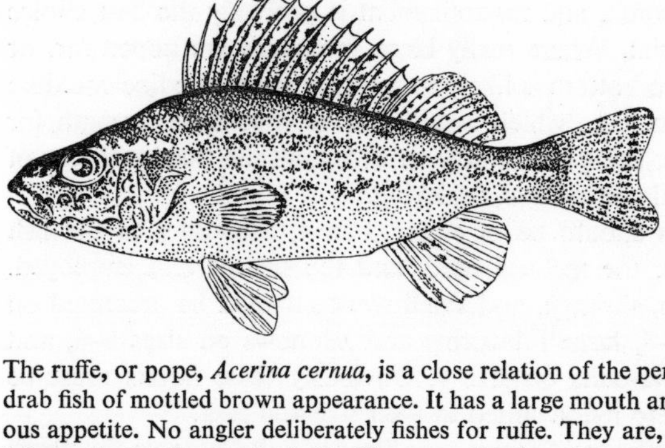

The ruffe, or pope, *Acerina cernua*, is a close relation of the perch. It is a drab fish of mottled brown appearance. It has a large mouth and voracious appetite. No angler deliberately fishes for ruffe. They are, however, taken only too frequently in the Thames and other rivers when fishing worm and maggots for other species.

Dead-baits are also valuable when mounted on suitable mounts or flights, or presented sink-and-draw.

Frogs, slugs, elvers, lampreys, and crayfish are baits which must be included in the perch angler's armoury. They are not often used, but on some waters and in the right conditions they can be very killing – especially when other baits fail.

Tackle For casual perch fishing the sort of rod generally used for ROACH will frequently suffice, but if good specimens are sought it is far wiser to use a rod with a little more power, both to help in casting large baits, and to give the angler a good chance of coping with the fish taken. An Avon-type rod is fine for river fishing, and a built-cane three-piece of similar dimensions, but with a slightly stiffer action, is suitable for still waters. For spinning, a two-piece rod of the kind used for light TROUT spinning is first-class, but the use of a PIKE rod is to be deprecated.

Choice of reel depends largely on personal inclinations, centre-pin and fixed-spool reels being equally useful, except perhaps for spinning, where the fixed spool is better for casting light baits. The chief requirement of the reel is that it should be capable of carrying the necessary amount of line (a hundred yards is ample for most kinds of perch fishing); also that it should be free-running and simple to operate. Many anglers use light multiplier reels with great success, but these do have the serious disadvantage that they tend to make line lie in coils on the surface. Multipliers are reels with a geared recovery mechanism. They are free-running for easy casting and are fitted with an adjustable drag for playing a powerful fish. They are fished on top of the reel. See p. 33.

Lines of 3–4 lb. breaking strain are suitable for all but the largest perch, and monofilament is probably the best choice of material. Where really large specimens are hoped for, or where the bottom is likely to produce snags, the line could be of 5–6 lb. b.s., which would also be a suitable strength for spinning, being better able to withstand the wear and tear of continual casting and retrieving.

Hooks should be of sizes 10 to 4, according to the fish expected, the method used, and the size of bait employed. Maggots, shrimps, and small worms should be presented on sizes 10–8, large lobworms and minnows on sizes 8–6, and larger live-baits on size 4. Obviously these hooks must be fastened to nylon suited to their size and task.

The ordinary Thames-type float is quite suitable for perch fishing, but it is not necessary to shot the float too low in the water since perch often fiddle with the bait before making a definite run. The most favoured type of float is a 4–6 in. quill with a tubby cork centre, but anything larger is ridiculous.

Fishing Methods

Strictly speaking, ground-baiting is not much practised for perch, but it is always useful to toss in a few small worms at intervals about the swim, and small pieces of whatever hook-bait is in use will frequently bring the bait itself to the attention of marauding fish. Many anglers like to cast a spinning lure through the swim to draw fish from other parts of the water into the vicinity of the bait, others like to throw a piece of bank-side turf into the swim to arouse interest among passing perch. Probably the best method of ground-baiting is simply to use a little cloud bait (made up of small particles of bread and bran for instance) at intervals to attract the small fry. Once a good shoal of small feeding fish is established in the vicinity, the local perch dash in to make a surprise attack, and the small fry can be seen darting and leaping in all directions.

In deep water float-fishing tackle should be used to search the swim at all depths at intervals, but in shallow waters the bait is best presented within a foot or so of the bottom. If the water is fast, the bait should be shotted to get it down quickly, and in any case the float should be balanced so that it does not disappear at the slightest touch, especially if it is used to support a live-bait. On paternoster tackles used with a float, provided the weight is on the line, the float can be left lying on one side on the surface.

For ordinary float-fishing the tackle is adjusted to the required depth and cast into the swim, where it is allowed to slip along with the stream, or wherever it is taken by the efforts of the live-bait. Usually this means that the bait fish will sooner or later bring the tackle into weed beds, where the angler must decide whether to move it clear lest it tangle, or leave it alone in the hope that it may locate a hiding fish. Sometimes good perch are taken right in the middle of weed beds, and the problem of extricating them then has to be faced.

If you want to anchor the bait in a position where it has a restricted radius of movement, you can do this by using paternoster tackle fitted with a float at the top, a weight at the bottom, and the hook link fixed to the side eye of a three-way swivel attached to the line at the desired depth. When the tackle is cast into position, the weight and float between them control the line. The angler leaves some slack line at the rod tip to allow the run to develop freely. Sometimes it is preferable to fish such tackles without the use of a float at all, in which case the line should be fished tight from the rod top, and the reel delicately set to run freely when a bite occurs. Tackle of this kind enables the fisherman to place his bait fairly accurately close to the weed with a reasonable certainty that the live-bait will not be able to take refuge there. It is also useful for placing the bait out in midstream among the sluggish runs where roach or small fry congregate, or among the holes in the weed. In still waters the paternoster is particularly effective in getting the bait out beyond marginal bottom weed, and holding it in position. When this method is adopted the distance from the weight to the swivel must be adjusted to allow for the fact that the line runs in a slantwise direction from the weight at the bottom, otherwise the bait will tend to be far too low down on the line.

Paternoster tackle can be varied by using a running line with the weight attached to a separate leg of nylon with a swivel at the top end. The main line is then passed through the swivel and the hook attached. A stopper shot on the main line is set at the desired distance from the hook and can be adjusted up or down with ease to set the bait at the depth required. The advantage of this is that it permits a taking fish to draw line through the swivel eye without feeling the resistance of the bottom weight (which may be a pear lead between a quarter and three-quarters of an ounce).

This method is, of course, closely allied to, indeed almost inseparable from, *legering*, and is in fact so called in many circles. Leger tackles are very effective in still waters. You can make up the tackle just described, or simply use a running line passing through the eye of a swivelled weight such as the Arlesey Bomb, or a pear lead and swivel. Again the weight is stopped on the main line with a shot just below it to prevent it falling down to the hook. The length of trail is largely a matter of personal opinion. For most purposes, a trail of about 18 ins. is right, but occasions will arise when this must be lengthened to 3 ft or shortened to 6 ins.

For effective legering the rod is placed in two rests, arranged so that the rod points in the same direction as the line. This means that a running fish is unlikely to feel any lateral vibration from the rod top when it takes line from the reel, which must, of course, be free-running if a centre-pin is employed. Fixed-spool reels are useful for this kind of fishing and permit the angler to fish with the pick-up open and the line quite free to run off the edge of the spool. An electric bite alarm can be used, or the angler can fit a small dough bobbin to his line to give an indication of bites. The bobbin is always more efficient if it is spindle-shaped and small enough to run easily through the first two or three rod rings when a take occurs.

Deciding just when to strike is sometimes a problem. Usually it is unwise to 'hit' the fish too soon. On the other hand if the strike is too long delayed the fish may swallow the bait and be hooked in the stomach, which means that it has to be killed. A brief pause of two or three seconds is recommended to allow the run to develop, particularly with a large bait. If this causes fish to be missed altogether the time should be lengthened; if they are hooked too far down the gullet the angler must adapt his methods accordingly.

Sink-and-draw is in effect a form of spinning with a dead-bait and its purpose is to simulate a sick or wounded fish moving through the water. The bait is worked by casting it out, allowing it to sink, then drawing it up towards the surface by raising the rod tip; then the operation is repeated until the bait is back under the bank again. The swim is methodically searched in this manner on subsequent casts. This is a very effective way of taking good perch.

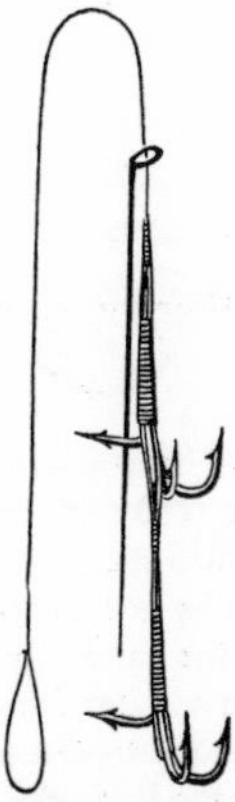

Dead-bait flight without spinning vanes. The needle is pushed inside the bait and the straight points of the hooks stuck into its flanks. Such a lure will wobble rather than spin.

The bait can be a minnow or gudgeon, elver or lamprey; often a worm fished in this way is very telling. Small dead-bait flights are sometimes used to mount the bait, but for perch many anglers prefer simply to use a baiting needle and thread the bait on the main line. Occasionally such a bait is taken by a marauding PIKE. Then the angler is in for a fight. He will lose the pike if his line is cut by the teeth of the fish. It is hardly worth while to use wire tackles for perch fishing on the off-chance of a pike, but soft flax line, which is less easily cut through by a pike's teeth, can be used on the last foot or so. This sort of line tends to become chewed and flattened instead.

The baiting needle should be passed through the body of the bait fish from mouth to vent, and the hook should be attached to the tail end so that when the fish is drawn towards the angler it will appear to swim head first. To sink the bait a small spiral lead is clipped on about a foot or eighteen inches up the line. This causes the bait to sink naturally head first, so that both

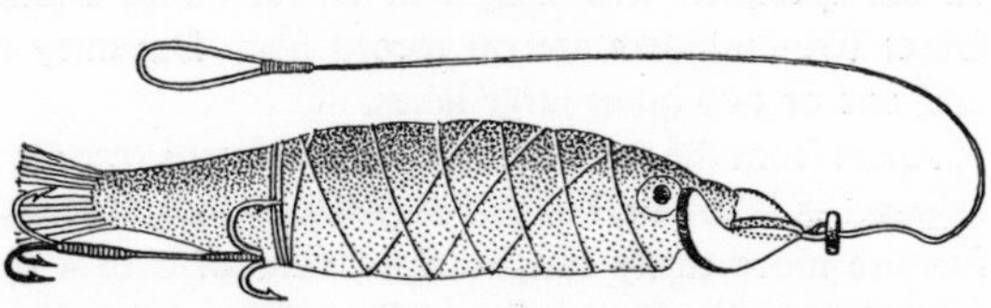

Small dead-bait mounted on spinning flight and suitable for perch. Vanes at head of bait give spin. The bait is bound on to the flight with fine wire or cotton.

the 'sink' and the 'draw' movements imparted by the angler simulate the movement of a living fish. If a spinning flight is used, the bait must be mounted on the needle provided, and then bound on with a few turns of fine copper wire or cotton to prevent it from flying off during the cast.

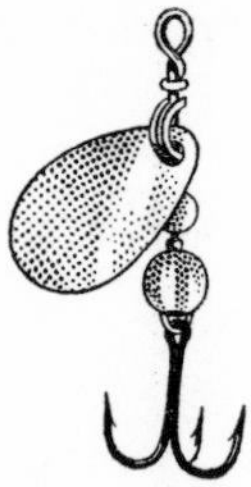

Mepps spoon, deadly in sizes 0–2 for perch, pike, trout, and even salmon.

The tremendous variety of spoon, plug, and spinner baits makes the art of spinning a fascinating business, and one which often accounts for good perch. So many kinds of lure can be used that a description is not possible here. Generally lures such as a Kidney or Colorado spoon, or a Vibro spinner of about half an inch to one inch are very effective. So are Mepps sizes 1 and 2. Home-made spoons are also popular, and small plugs, quill minnows, or small silver and golden devons are equally suitable.

Spinning is essentially a roving occupation and is at its best during the colder months when the fish are on the move. The method is to investigate thoroughly likely-looking holes or eddies, and to search the open water by fanwise casting from a selected spot at intervals.

Celluloid anti-kink vane. The reel line is tied to the swivel eye. The keel shape of the vane stops the spinner from passing on twist to the line. Plain swivels will not stop twist on their own. Ball-bearing swivels need no anti-kink devices.

Usually, slow spinning is the most efficient. 'Slow and deep' is a good rule where perch are concerned, especially in winter. The angler should allow the bait to get well down before commencing the retrieve, and should vary the rate, pausing momentarily at intervals to give the bait a realistic movement.

It is perfectly possible to spin with a centre-pin reel, although casting is perhaps limited. Many anglers find that hand-lining the line back through the rod rings imparts a very natural movement to the bait and takes good fish.

When using a revolving bait an anti-kink device must be used between bait and reel line. For light baits, anti-kink vanes are suitable. For heavier baits an anti-kink weight may serve better.

General

The British record perch is a fish of 5 lb. 15 oz. It was caught by P. Clarke in the Suffolk Stour, in 1949. A 5 lb. 14½ oz. fish is recorded from Farlow's Lake near Iver, and in 1957 a 5 lb. 12 oz. specimen was caught in Diana Pond, Bushey Park. Other five-pounders are on record from Daventry reservoir and one or two other large lakes.

Apart from the record fish, river specimens recorded are not as good as lake fish, but this may simply indicate that the lake fish are more easily caught. Specimens of over 4 lb. are recorded from the Dorset Stour, Bure, Thames, Avon, Kennet, Severn, and Great Ouse, and these great rivers are obvious places for the specimen-hunter to try. Nevertheless, the indication is that the biggest fish are taken from still waters, canals, or reservoirs.

Perch

Perch are common in most parts of the British Isles, except in the extreme north. If anything, the species is less common in southern Scotland than elsewhere in the British Isles.

H. T.

Pike

SNOEK

The Pike (*Esox lucius*) cannot possibly be confused with any other British freshwater fish. Long and slender, built for sudden spurts of acceleration from ambush rather than for staying power, they are predominantly green on the flank, dark on the dorsal surface, and camouflaged to match the reed beds in which they often lurk. In the young fish this camouflage takes the form of light, often yellowish, bars. The adult fish are marked with primrose spots. Fins and tail often have brownish, or even red, edges. Dorsal and ventral fins are set to the rear. The head is long and the jaws are powerful, with sharp grabbing and gripping teeth in the lower jaw. The roof of the mouth is covered with hundreds of rearward facing 'ratchet' teeth which prevent the prey, once gripped, from slipping out again. The eyes are sited on top of the head for upward vision in attack and set to give binocular vision, which enables the fish to 'sight' on its prey and judge distance when darting at it. Prey fishes such as the roach have monocular vision, which gives all-round warning of approach. The pike is not so concerned with self-defence (though quite large fish of 8 lb. or more are sometimes gobbled, cannibal fashion, by bigger relatives); it needs to look forward and upward. It is the only British freshwater fish that can look you squarely in the face with both eyes at once. Many anglers find this disconcerting.

The small pike, of 6 ins. or less, that one sees from time to time poised like little arrows over weed growing close to the surface are probably fish in their first year. The growth rate of pike thereafter is geared to the food supply available in the water, which may vary a great deal. In an extensive, shallow, weedy lake where rudd are plentiful, for example, there may be a very speedy growth rate in the first few years, perhaps as much as 3 or 4 lb. per year, declining gradually thereafter. A fifteen-year-old pike may be very large indeed, possibly a 40-pounder. On the other hand, in poorer waters where the roach are stunted, the pike may grow much more slowly and may reach a maximum of only five or six pounds.

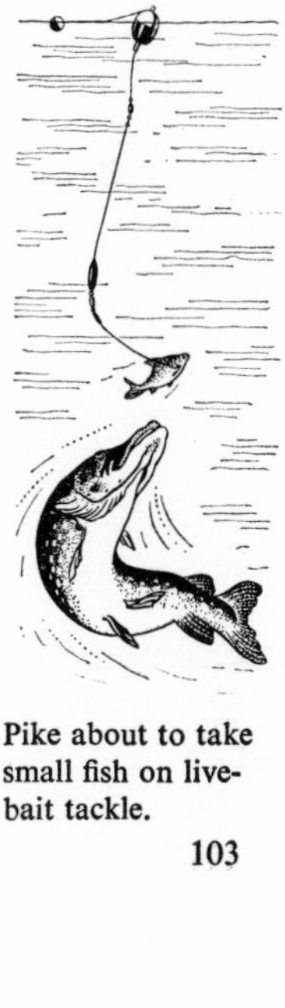

Pike about to take small fish on live-bait tackle.

Male pike are considered to be much smaller than the females; a suggested maximum size for the former is 10 lb., but the matter is still open to doubt.

There are all sorts of estimates of the life span of pike, from the famous and quite spurious Mannheim pike which was said to be 267 years old (A.D. 1230–1497) to as little as fifteen years. So far as I know, no serious scientific investigation of this question has been undertaken; it is notoriously difficult to gauge a pike's age by scale reading.

Pike are, *par excellence*, solitary fish, only pairing briefly in the spawning season. Sometimes it is possible to catch a number of pike from the same spot, one after another, but I think it is likely that their massing together is not the shoal instinct in operation but is merely fortuitous; for some reason the small fish are huddled in one corner of the lake and the pike have got to know of it independently.

Spawning takes place in the spring. The fish begin to pair in February and shift their quarters to the shallows. In lakes where the winter rains flood the grasslands pike will often move on to these. Reeds too seem to attract pike at this time. If you walk the banks of a pike lake on a sunny day in early spring you will sometimes see great swirls in the marginal reeds as you disturb the fish, or you may see the reeds knock together and a procession of pike swim out from them. A few years ago I saw what could only be described as a flotilla of very large fish move out from the bank in this way. Some of them were more than 30 lb.

In spawning, the female pike deposits a very great number of eggs, the majority of which are swallowed by waterfowl or eels before they hatch out. The famous nineteenth-century natural historian Frank Buckland estimated that a 30 lb. female pike might contain more than half a million eggs. There seems to be no particular correlation in size between the female pike and her spawning partner. I remember once hooking a twenty-pounder in the shallows in late February on a floating plug. During the fight she was followed all the while by a small jack of a couple of pounds, which, indeed waited patiently while the hen fish was on the bank being unhooked, was still there when she was returned to the water, and finally swam off in her company. Clearly at any other time of the year the small jack would have made a couple of quick mouthfuls for the big female.

Pike feed almost entirely upon fish. Their basic diet will consist of whatever species is commonest in the water. Large pike, certainly, have a great relish for small fish of their own species, so that one of the best baits for a very big pike of which the whereabouts are known is a small pike fished dead or alive. The old fallacy that pike are not inclined to take TENCH is little heard of now; on a summer's morning I have seen 3 lb. tench skip like roach out of the water when chivvied by large pike.

Other creatures living in or on the water are not immune. Waterfowl are taken regularly in some waters (though I have noticed that coots have a peculiar immunity). Frogs and small mammals that venture into the water also fall frequent victims. All this is well authenticated, but there are other, darker stories as well, of gold watches being found in the bellies of pike (the owner having met a watery death not long previously) and of large animals and bathers being bitten. Only by the greatest freak of chance, I suppose, could anything like this happen.

We have seen how in the spring pike move into the shallows for the purpose of spawning. Where do they spend the rest of the year? The answer to this, of course, is: where the bait fish are. The usual picture given is of the pike's taking up permanent ambush quarters, in a reed bed, for example, or under the stump of an overhanging tree, having, so to speak, its own area of domination which it will defend to the death from other pike. There is a certain amount of truth in this. In winter, fish such as ROACH tend not to move about a water so much as they do in the summer, so the pike takes up winter quarters near the roach concentrations. This is especially true of large lakes, where quite extensive areas of water which look inviting enough will be found to yield very few pike, while several fish in succession may be taken from a single swim. In the summer, however, pike tend to range about much more extensively, just as the small fish do.

Orthodox practice is to fish for pike wherever there is cover for them; a favourite place, for instance, is around the margins of a lily-pond bed. Bays of reeds and rock projections are also held to be good places for pike. This is undoubtedly true, but chiefly of the small and medium-sized fish. All the big (15 lb. plus) pike I have ever taken have accepted a bait, spinning or live, in the open water. I do not think that really big pike skulk around in ambush very much. When they decide to feed, they make a field day of it, moving out into the open water and harrying the shoals all day. No doubt they have what might be called a retiring place somewhere, and if you happen to drop a bait on their noses, it may be taken there. But when they really feed they are in no way circumscribed.

In rivers, the position is rather different; clearly the pike still go where the small fish are, but their choice of lie is more limited. The haunts of pike in rivers are weir pools, eddies, and lay-bys, bays out of the main stream. By and large, pike do not like fast, heavy water or shallow riffles.

Baits For pike live-baits on still water most fishermen use the species found most commonly in the area. ROACH, RUDD, PERCH, and small CARP will all take fish. The great Alfred Jardine found that using a species unfamiliar to the pike of a given water was particularly killing – GUDGEON, for instance, not often found in lakes, or even goldfish.

On rivers, much the same kinds of live-bait are used, but RUDD are less common and DACE and small CHUB come more into the picture.

For dead-baiting, any of the small fish mentioned above is suitable. (It is important, of course, to pierce the fish's swim-bladder to make certain that it will sink.) Considerable success, however, has been had with herrings and sprats bought at the fishmonger's. Big fish have a well-known predilection for big baits, and a herring of a pound or so is substantial enough to interest a good pike. The fish does not necessarily have to be used whole.

Fred Taylor emphasizes that the bait does not have to be fresh; he records successful dead-baiting with really stinking fish. (I myself have caught pike with a dace-bait that I could hardly bear to put on the hook.) If you cannot get hold of fresh herring, bloaters are acceptable.

For normal autumn and winter spinning artificial lures are legion, and the novice angler will be hard put to make a choice. Action, colour, and size are the vital points which have to be considered in the purchase of an artificial, and it might be convenient at this stage to look at some of the standard baits with these considerations in mind. As far as action goes, some lures revolve (spinners and most spoons) while others merely wobble (plugs and some spoons). A bait with the most violent

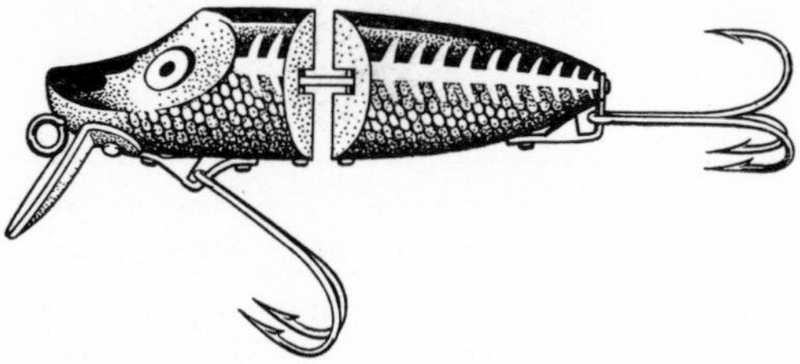

Jointed pike plug. Note nose plate which makes plug wriggle and dive when wound in.

action is not necessarily the best; I once owned a rubber plug bait which went through the water with a really demented wiggle, but I never caught a pike on it. Action seems to be more important in rivers than in lakes; presumably still-water pike rely more on eyesight and less on the sensitive lateral line which picks up the vibratory movements of small fish than do river pike. Plugs with a wild action are more effective in still water; bar spoons with a marked vibratory effect work well in rivers. What matters as much as anything is whether the angler himself is happy with the way his lure is working. If he fishes with confidence he fishes well.

The same thing applies to colour and brightness. As far as plug baits are concerned, where bright metal is not involved, reds, greens, whites, and yellows in various combinations seem to do best with pike. Very bright metal spinners and spoons are not to be recommended. I have always done far better with a tarnished metal spoon than with one that shines brightly on both sides. Very often, spoons are painted with a matt finish on one side for this reason. How bright a lure you use will depend a great deal on water conditions. Use a dull lure in clear water and a brighter one when the water is clouded.

One thing the novice angler will be up against is that the lures available in the tackle shops are usually on the small side. Most spoons seem to average no more than 2 ins. in length. If you are lucky they may be available in sizes up to 3 ins., but generally that is all. A 3 in. fish is not particularly exciting to a 20 lb. pike, and if possible a bigger offering should be arranged. One big spoon on the market is the Hardy's Jim Vincent, which is $5\frac{1}{4}$ ins. in length. Certain big plugs are available also, but they have to be sought out. For serious pike fishing, therefore, the lure should be not less tha $2\frac{1}{2}$ ins. long, and bigger if possible. Big pike have been taken on small lures, but such captures are exceptions that prove the rule, no more.

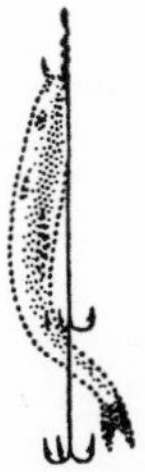

Largish dead-bait mounted on wob bler tackle. The bend given to the tail of the fish will ensure that the bait swerves about realistically when retrieved.

It might be useful for the beginner to have a short list of lures that are well tried. Among spoons, the Colorado, Mepps, bar spoons of various designs, kidney spoons, and elongated Norfolk spoons are all tested fish killers in their big sizes. Among plug baits, the plastic ones seem to be more effective than the jointed wooden variety. So far as I know, no British manufacturer has anything to offer as good as the plug baits imported from the United States. Phantoms and devons are not used much by pike fishermen (though some very good fish have been taken on a five-inch silver devon), but the Wagtail, in a large size, will kill pike.

Tackle One of the difficulties in choosing tackle for live-baiting is that a much greater weight has to be cast in this game than in any other branch of coarse fishing. Many expert live-baiters swear by a large bait, of $\frac{3}{4}$ lb. or even more. Even a 4 oz. bait is a problem to cast, especially when it is remembered that there is the additional weight of the lead and the float to be considered.

With a really big bait, casting is virtually out of the question. The bait has to be thrown out by hand, the reel line being spread out on the ground, or, in the case of a fixed-spool reel, the pick-up being left open and free from obstruction. To throw the smaller, standard bait, a reasonably hefty rod is necessary. Sometimes also, particularly in lake fishing, a long throw is desirable.

This means that a certain amount of sport has to be sacrificed as far as the smaller pike are concerned, but the specialist angler who is out for really big fish will not mind this. For him, specialist rods have been developed, notably the Stepped-Up Mark IV, designed by Richard Walker, and another to the specifications of Dennis Pye, the Norwich expert on the Norfolk Broads. Both of these rods are of split-cane. So far, except in the field of spinning rods, there has been a marked reluctance on the part of coarse fishermen to take advantage of fibre-glass. This material, it seems to me, would prove as useful to pike fishermen as it has been in the last few years to sea fishermen. I find a long, light, surf-casting rod admirably suited to live- or dead-baiting for pike.

Whatever rod you choose, do not let it be too short. A long rod can occasionally be a nuisance in fishing heavily overhung waters or from a boat, but the extra casting power it gives, and the control one is able to exercise over a hooked fish by means of it, amply make up for this. Ten feet, I think, should be regarded as a minimum length. To facilitate casting, the reel fittings should be well up the butt, and should be designed to hold the reel firmly. I prefer a screw fitting.

A centre-pin reel of good line capacity seems to be best suited to live-baiting, though there is something to be said for using a multiplier (see p. 33) or a sea-type fixed-spool reel, the last-named particularly if much casting has to be done from a bank constricted by trees and bushes. I prefer a centre-pin as a rule because the cast is an easier swing, not so likely to throw off a bait.

The line can be of monofilament nylon, but I prefer one of the braided synthetics such as Terylene, since these give no stretch to speak of, an important point when striking a fish. I do not think 15 lb. b.s. too heavy to recommend, since with the comparatively heavy weight involved, the line is liable to shock-loading during the cast. The biggest pike, too, seem to live near horrible obstructions, sunken trees being a favourite haunt. A really big pike diving for safety takes a lot of stopping! The trace, of course, must be of wire. Alasticum is still the best bet, although it has to be carefully checked for kinks developing during fishing. The twisted wire covered with nylon which is now on the market looks good but is untrustworthy. It suffers from the same defect as the old gimp did: the wire rusts inside, and the weakness is not apparent until it is too late.

Traditionally, a tandem of special treble (a hook with three points on one shaft) hooks known as a snap-tackle is used for attaching the live-bait. This, perhaps justifiably, has been stigmatized as involving undue suffering for the bait, and, used wrongly, can in fact kill the bait in a short time. Many pike fishermen these days, myself included, use a single treble hook mounted amidships or lip-hooked. With the single-hook tackle it is noticeable that while small pike are quite often missed on the strike, it is rare not to hook a good one successfully.

There remain to be discussed the float and the lead. Traditionally again, a tubby, *Fishing Gazette* pattern float is recommended, the bait being kept down in the water by a spiral lead of appropriate size. Both these items of tackle come in for some trenchant criticism by Richard Walker in his *Still Water Angling*, and it seems to me that there is much in what he says. In the first place, there is no point at all in using a very big float unless a really big bait is being used. Even in this case, a more streamlined float is much less likely to arouse suspicion in the pike, since it will offer less water resistance when it is drawn under. Walker suggested a bomb-shaped rather than a pear-shaped float for this reason. For small baits, a good-sized cork-bodied Avon float is perfectly adequate.

As far as the lead is concerned, the spiral type is more satisfactory when fished on a wire trace than it is on a nylon one, but even in the former case it has a distressing tendency to come off during the cast or in the water. A drilled leger lead, stopped with a swivel, is much more useful.

The tackle for dead-baiting is just the same as that described for live-baiting, until the trace is reached. Clearly there is no need for a float or a lead. Two treble hooks are used in tandem, mounted on a wire trace as before. The hooks are set into the bait, one behind the gill-cover, the other about midships, and the wire is then threaded by means of a baiting needle through to the tail root and out.

Tackle [Spinning] For the most part, a light SALMON spinning rod is well suited for pike. These rods are usually of split-cane, but there is an increasing tendency to use fibre-glass in their manufacture. If you do decide on glass, choose hollow glass, not the solid kind. You will find this has a better casting action. The length usually recommended is between seven and eight feet, but I prefer a longer rod for the reasons mentioned above. A screw reel fitting is recommended; continual casting tends to work the reel loose on simple sliding fittings. If you intend to use a fixed-spool reel, make sure that the butt ring is a big one, one of those designed for the purpose. The rod I have described will cast conventional artificial lures and small dead fish.

A standard-sized fixed-spool reel is preferable to any other type, especially if much of your spinning from the bank is done in constricted surroundings, since with a fixed-spool reel it is easier to flick out a bait under a canopy of trees and bushes. Load the spool with 8 lb. monofilament; I think it rather foolish to go below this breaking strain if there is a possibility of hooking a heavy fish.

This is the tackle to use in most pike spinning contexts, but in certain circumstances it is not ideal. In the summer, for instance, good sport may often be had by 'stalking' pike. In shallow lakes, the fish may often be seen near the surface in sunny weather, lying over the weed which may come to within a foot of the surface. For this game it is best to use a lighter rod than in standard spinning. The pike are usually smallish fish up to 5 lb. or so, and great sport may be had with a trout-spinning rod, a fixed-spool reel loaded with 5 lb. b.s. line and a floating plug which is fished very slowly on the surface.

When the weeds are down, and the water reaches its winter level, a very large natural bait wobbled through the water is an excellent lure for a big pike. Heavier tackle is necessary, however; I myself employ the gear described earlier for live-baiting.

Fishing Methods [Live-Bait and Dead-Bait] The least successful way of live-baiting in a lake is to choose a spot, cast in and wait, all day if necessary, for a pike to come along. Live-baiting should never be too static, unless the angler knows that a particular specimen has taken up residence in the place he is fishing, and decides that a siege is necessary. If you know of numerous spots on a given water which in the past have proved productive, a useful plan is to visit each of these in turn, never spending more than ten minutes on each, unless it proves that pike have 'packed' into one particular small area, as they sometimes do.

If your lake is spanned by a long bridge, then you are lucky for it should be possible from this vantage point to command a good acreage of water, and if there is a breeze you can work over many pike lies without recasting.

It is impossible to give written directions on where to fish. Every water varies, and experience is the only guide. On a calm day, it is possible to learn a good deal about the movements of pike. In a shallow lake particularly they will be seen 'striking', swirling in the water and scattering the shoals of small fish. If you can drop your live-bait near a pike feeding in this manner, it is virtually certain that he will take it.

Live-baiting in rivers can produce excellent results. The slacker waters of a river are usually fished – weir pools and backwaters especially. Slow-moving stretches, and eddies where the float may be worked round again and again may also prove fruitful. Very often, pike are not so evenly distributed in rivers as they are in lakes; there may be especially 'pikey' stretches with which the angler will become acquainted as his experience of the water develops.

The old idea that very cold weather and successful pike fishing go well together seems to be pretty well exploded now. How the notion grew up remains a mystery. More important than the temperature is the matter of how settled the weather has been. A sudden drop in the temperature will kill pike fishing stone dead for a day or two, though the same does not seem to be true of a rise. The kind of day I prefer is one often experienced in autumn, a misty, soft day with plenty of cloud but no heavy rain. In my experience, a real downpour is fatal to pike fishing while it lasts, though sport may pick up immediately the rain stops. A thaw after a short spell of hard weather often produces excellent pike fishing. When a lake is ice-bound, there are certain to be patches of water which are clear of ice earlier than the rest of the lake. When the thaw starts it is very much worth while to try these spots even though there may be only a limited area in which it is possible to fish. In these circumstances you may often see big pike cruising round the edge of the ice, and if you keep out of sight there is every chance that they will take a bait dropped where they can notice it.

Only when there is a downpour of rain or when the water is completely frozen over should you give up all hope of a good day's pike fishing. Some of my best pike have been taken on days which, conventionally, were not worth fishing – one twenty-pound-plus fish came on a day of brilliant sunshine in early March, another from a hole in the ice at the bitterly cold fag-end of a January day.

A few years ago, Fred Taylor of Aylesbury and some others reported in the angling press that they had had a good deal of success with dead-bait *legered* on the bottom of a lake. This was received rather sceptically by anglers who had been nurtured in the belief that any bait for a pike had to have life or simulate it. However, the method worked in many parts of the country, and it became plain that a new method of pike fishing had been born.

Ground-baiting is sometimes useful when dead-bait is to be used, herrings being chopped or minced before being introduced into the water. I have an idea that fish oil, cod-liver oil in large quantities, or pilchard oil in small quantities, might be as effective in this context as it is in sea fishing. This, however, is a theory I have not tried out in practice.

When a pike grabs a dead-bait there are usually two distinct parts to the run. The fish picks up the bait in its jaws, moves a little way with it, pauses to turn and swallow the bait, then moves off again. The strike should come at the beginning of the second run. If it is delayed too long there is a possibility that the pike will gorge the bait and you will have to kill it.

Although dead-baiting will take pike in most conditions, it comes into its own as possibly superior to other methods in hard weather when the pike become lethargic and loath to move far after a bait. Thus, while they cannot be bothered to chase a spinner or move up in the water to take a live-bait, they will pick up a dead-bait that lies in their path on the bottom. The deepest water of the lake is the best bet for this kind of fishing.

In light summer fishing, a floating plug is the best bait to use. No other artificial will really do, since there is a good chance that the lure will sink into the weed.

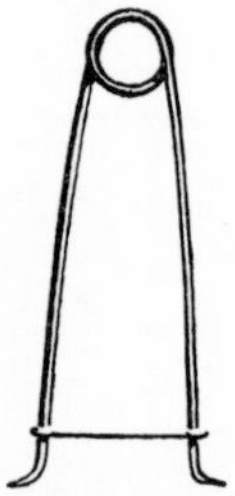

Pike gag. When the catch at open end is released, the jaws spring apart to hold pike's mouth open so that hooks can be removed.

Having spotted your fish, the most important thing is to keep out of sight. Do not underestimate the wariness of pike, especially in these circumstances. Cast well over the fish and fish the lure very slowly towards him, aiming to bring it a few feet from his nose. If all that happens is that he follows it for a short distance and then turns back, do not keep casting, but put on a different lure and give the fish a few minutes before trying him again. Pike taken this way often fight spectacularly, even the small ones. When removing hooks from a landed fish a gag is often useful. It enables the angler to prise out the hooks without getting bitten in the process.

Fishing Methods [Spinning]

The usual advice to beginners is to spin slowly and deep. This is rarely possible with an artificial lure on most pike waters, and the best thing to do is to find out by trial and error what

Perch

Perca fluviatilis (page 94)
Specimens 3 lb and over
Record 5 lb 15 oz 6 drams*

Pike

Esox lucius (page 103)
Specimens 20 lb and over
Record 53 lb*

Pike-Perch

Lucioperca lucioperca (page 116)
Not native to Britain
Record 11 lb 12 oz

Pope

Acerina cernua (page 97)
Record 3 oz 13 drams

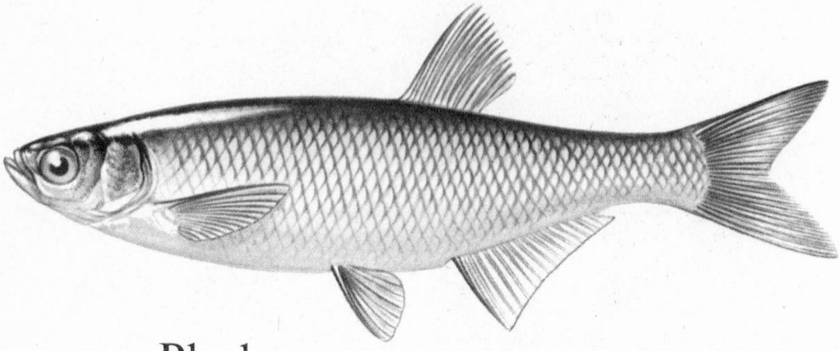

Bleak

Alburnus alburnus (page 46)
Record 3 oz 8 drams

speed of retrieve the fish like on your water at a given time. There are occasions, for instance, when a really fast retrieve seems to persuade them to take when they will not look at a lure worked at conventional speed.

As far as the fishing itself is concerned, a useful method of spinning a particular spot is something like this: one cast down the bank along which you will shortly be walking, then a few short casts close in around any features which look as if they may harbour pike – tree stumps, lily pads, or reeds, then a few casts out as far as possible into the open water. It is wise not to race down the water trying to cover as much as possible in a short time, but on the other hand there is no point in spending too long in a particular spot if there is no response.

Spinning a dead-bait is the method favoured most by the late Jim Vincent, the great Hickling Broad pike fisherman of the period between the wars. The tackle is simple: a treble hook on a short length of Alasticum wire. A baiting needle is used to thread the wire through the vent of the fish and out through its mouth, and a swivel is twisted on. The retrieve should be very slow; experience will teach you how to impart a sink-and-draw motion to the bait and how to make it flutter enticingly or fall away in a most attractive manner.

Dead-bait flight for small bait, suitable for light summer fishing over weeds. In smaller sizes, ideal for perch and trout baits too.

There are tackles available, known as flights, which are designed to make a small natural bait spin and wobble. These are not seen so much as formerly. In practice it will be found that a simple home-made mount like the one just described will be just as effective. A small bait, of course, can be fished on the lighter gear described for standard spinning, and very small baits indeed can be used for light-tackle summer fishing, for they are light enough on leadless tackle to be worked over the weeds.

General

Pike seem to bring out the most extreme feelings in anglers. Either they abominate the species or they are fascinated by it; there seems to be no middle way. I should say here and now that I have always been a pro-pike man, or rather a pro-big-pike man, for there is no greater anticlimax than to go out equipped for 40-pounders and catch a succession of 2- and 3-pounders. Some fishermen hate the thought of pike and can't look at one without thinking of how much delectable roach flesh has been sacrificed to build up its poundage. The anti-pike mania can take extreme forms. I shall never forget, years ago, attending the annual general meeting of a fishing club, in the course of which a stout, red-faced man got to his feet and made an impassioned appeal for volunteers to go to the water we rented and wipe out the pike. Fortunately for those of us who like pike fishing, pike aren't wiped out so easily.

Less vehement anglers prefer to dress up their prejudices with a show of reason. Pike fishermen usually argue about the balance of nature and declare that, if it weren't for pike keeping their numbers down, the lesser fish would multiply and become stunted. The answer to this is that in many waters where there are pike the roach and so on are stunted in any case; and that there are plenty of examples to be found of specimen roach (or rudd, or whatever) coming from waters where there are no pike. The truth seems to be that the presence of pike is not an important factor in extensive waters; there are other, much more significant factors at work. In small, enclosed waters, there is a strong case to be made out against pike.

What the question boils down to in the end is whether or not one likes pike fishing. Speaking for myself, I think that all the roach that went into the making of a 20-pounder gave their lives in a good cause. If small carp-family fish interest you more than pike you will disagree. There seems little hope that the two points of view will ever come together in a compromise.

What is certain is that pike give most coarse-fish anglers in this country their best chance of a big fish. Pike do grow large. Even in a farm pond, where the average size may be only 2 lb., there is always the possibility of a 10-pounder turning up. If one is fishing one of the great lakes of Ireland or Scotland, or the Norfolk Broads, or some delectable private lake, perhaps, in the heart of England, there is always, at the back of one's mind, the feeling that this might be the day, that the next time the float bobs under the resistance will not be that of an ordinary pike, but of some great monster that will immortalize the angler who catches it in angling history. In some ways I would rather catch a record pike than break the record for any other species.

There are many, many enormous pike of legend. Some of them, like the one that chased the parish clerk across the pool in Staffordshire, may be discounted at once. Other monsters may be given more credence. The Loch Ken pike, said to weigh 72 lb., is the most important of these, since evidence, in the shape of the creature's mighty skull, still exists, and from its dimensions it is clear that the fish could have attained the weight claimed for it. The Whittlesea pike, a 50-odd-pounder taken when Whittlesea Mere was drained in the seventeenth century is also well authenticated. The Irish record fish is established beyond doubt – a 53-pounder taken by J. Garvin in 1920 in Lough Conn, County Mayo. The English record, a $37\frac{1}{2}$ lb. fish, was taken from the Hampshire Avon at Fordingbridge in 1944 by C. Warwick. There is a Scottish fish of 47 lb. 11 oz. taken from Loch Lomond in 1945. Pike a little over the 30 lb. mark seem fairly plentiful, in the sense that a number are generally reported each season in the angling press, but the English record has proved very difficult to beat. A 40 lb. English pike seems a distinct possibility, however.

It is possible, I suppose, for a big pike to turn up almost anywhere from some protected and keepered water where the fish are left to grow large and lusty. Small waters that are regularly fished are unlikely to produce very big fish, since in such places it is very easy to over-fish pike. There remain the great still waters of Britain and Ireland where the fishing pressure can never exhaust the pike population in the ordinary way. In England, the Norfolk Broads are a vast repository of specimen pike, as has been proved in recent years by the exploits of Dennis Pye, who has caught more than two hundred pike over 20 lb. since the war, and a number over 30 lb. The Lake District, curiously enough, does not seem to produce the big pike one would expect from such waters. Possibly there is not a great deal of piking done there, possibly catches are not reported (and there may still be a good deal of the activity known as 'trimmering' going on; with this illegal method a large float, such as a bottle, is allowed to drift freely with a large live-bait attached to it). English rivers vary in the quality of pike fishing they yield. The Thames and the Great Ouse, two of the major southern rivers, rarely produce a really good specimen. The Hampshire Avon is a good deal better, as is its neighbour stream, the Dorsetshire Stour. The Wye, where permission to catch coarse fish may be gained, has some tremendous pike in it; it once produced a record fish and may do so again. The north of England seems to provide little quality pike fishing, though the Yorkshire water of Hornsea Mere is an exception to this. The river Lune is possibly an exception, too.

Pike are not indigenous in Welsh waters, and are not widespread, though there are a few lakes where excellent pike fishing may be had – Llangorse in Breconshire is one and Bosherston in Pembrokeshire another. Lake Bala used to be, and may still be, a good pike water. There are certainly some enormous pike in the lower Towy, a salmon river, but so far it has been difficult to get to grips with them; no live-baits are allowed and artificial lures must be of a very large size to lessen the chance of their being taken by salmon kelts.

The lowland lochs of Scotland are said to contain some very big pike, but so far little specialist fishing has been done, the local anglers not regarding the fish as of any consequence.

In Ireland, the very large lakes no longer provide the pike fishing they once did, since the Inland Fisheries Trust began schemes to reduce the number of pike considerably, chiefly by means of trapping. In the Irish midlands, however, there remain countless small lakes which probably provide the angler with his best chance of a 20-pounder and where a 30-pounder is an ever-present possibility. If you want a record fish, though, the best plan is to scan Ordnance Survey maps and seek out the estate lakes where permission to fish has not been granted for a hundred years. Then win the football pools and buy the owner out. Engage extra keepers with watch dogs, then one mild October morning stroll down to the lakeside with a bucket of live-bait . . .

At the time of writing, it is clear that sooner or later a really big controversy is going to shake up the angling world over the question of live-baiting. Certain anglers now regard the practice as cruel and feel that with the advent of dead-bait legering it has also become superfluous. These feelings do their owners credit, but, personally, I cannot go the whole way with them. This is not the place to go into the ethics of fishing, or to examine the motives, conscious and unconscious, that make anglers of us, but I do feel that it is possible to be over-squeamish about a sport which, let us be frank, does involve catching fish. As far as the second claim is concerned, I am not at all convinced that dead-bait legering is suitable for all occasions and waters, and I am sure that live-baiting gives the best chance of a good pike in most waters, although most of my pike fishing has been done in shallow, weedy lakes where, admittedly, dead-baiting seems not to be as effective as in some other types of water. It is worth noting, by the way, that the legal position is quite clear. A decision of the courts before the war established that live-baiting is not regarded legally as cruelty.

Clive Gammon

Pike-Perch

SNOEK-BAARS

The Duke of Bedford, a very keen fisherman and naturalist, first introduced the voracious pike-perch (*Lucioperca lucioperca*) into the lakes at Woburn Abbey, near Bedford, in about 1910. This fish is definitely not a hybrid, although a great many anglers seem to believe that it is a cross between the two well-known fish from which it gets its name. It is an entirely separate species, Continental in origin, which, although virtually unknown to may British anglers, is a member of the perch family, Percidae. It is very much like the PERCH in many ways. It has, for example, the perch's two handsome dorsal fins, the first and spiny one being erected when the fish is about to make an attack on an intended victim. The fins on the lower part of the body are broad and very well formed, yet look quite delicate. The fish's predatory nature is indicated by the large and heavily-toothed mouth. Pike-perch grow much larger than the British record perch and nearly as large as the heaviest PIKE. In common with both pike and perch, they are true predators, always ready to attack any fish small enough to be swallowed.

Pike-Perch

The pike-perch is fairly common throughout Central Europe, where it is known as *Zander*, *Sander*, *Sandel*, *Gos*, and *Snockbaar*. There are, however, several varieties, two of the more prevalent Continental types being the *L. lucioperca volgensis* and *L. lucioperca sandra*. The variety *volgensis* is confined mainly to Austria and South Russia, particularly in the Volga, while the *sandra* type is found in the Danube, North Russia, Scandinavia, Hungary, and North Germany. America also has pike-perch, which are common in certain waters; there they are known as wall-eyed pike.

Some of the Woburn Abbey lakes were netted in 1948, and a number of pike-perch were transferred to a pit at Leighton Buzzard, but they do not appear to have bred. Later, in 1951, about thirty young specimens of some 5 ins. in length were obtained and introduced to Claydon Lake, near Winslow, Bucks, where a few fairly large specimens have since been caught, including an 8-pounder which is the largest recorded in this country so far. This fish was caught in 1956, which suggests that pike-perch have a growth rate of some 7 or 8 lb. in five years! In 1960 the Great Ouse River Board imported a consignment of about five hundred 'fingerling' pike-perch from Sweden and released them in an enclosed water in the River Board area as an experiment to establish their growth-rate.

Baits and Tackle

Pike-perch are notorious predators and may be taken on live-bait, spinning lures, and plugs. The tackle you would normally employ for big PERCH will also suit pike-perch, but where the fish may run large a change to PIKE tackle is advised.

Choice of spinning lures will present few problems, since the pike-perch will take plugs, devon minnows, and any small 'flashy' spoon, e.g. the Abu Sonette, Colorado, Kilko, Kidney, and Vibro. A hook flight fitted with a spinning vane, of the well-known Archer type, will make an ideal lure when mounted with a dead natural. Any small fish, such as LOACH minnow, GUDGEON, BLEAK, etc., can be used to bait the flight.

The bait, or lure, should be joined to the reel line by a wire trace of some 18 ins. to 2 ft long, with an ordinary barrel swivel at the line end and a spring link swivel at the other end for connecting the lure. These swivels are essential to prevent the line from twisting and kinking.

Fishing Methods

Pike-perch are credited with an indomitable fighting spirit and, fished for on reasonably light tackle, they are reputed to give really exciting sport.

When spinning, give the lure a lively movement as it travels through the water by frequently moving the rod from one side to the other. Such movements create the impression that the lure is a small fish moving with a zigzag motion, altering course continually. At the same time, give the rod tip a few jerks in order to transmit a swift darting movement to the line. But, while handling the rod, don't forget to manipulate the reel. The reel handle should only be wound between each movement of the rod, and three or four turns should be all that is necessary.

As you come to the end of each spin make sure that the rod tip is pointing down at the water so that the bait or spinner stays in the water as it moves to the bank edge. Some predators will follow the lure right in close, and take it a few feet from the rod tip. If the lure breaks water too soon, the fish sheer off, and lie low for a considerable time.

Pike-perch can also be taken on feathered mackerel lures (see p. 302) or even streamer flies.

Use live-bait tactics as for large PERCH.

General

There's little doubt that the time will come when pike-perch will be caught from many different angling waters in Britain. Once they have become firmly established in this country, specimens weighing up to around 30 lb. may be caught.

W. H.

Roach

BLANKVOORN

The roach (*Rutilus rutilus*) is subject to considerable variety in colour and shape. The back is blue-black, blue-green, grey-green, grey-brown, or green, and the flanks are either predominantly silvery or bronzed. The silver-flanked fish is the more common, probably because all young fish are of this colour, the brassy colours developing in certain fish in maturity. The underside is cream, white, or buff. Within the limits described colour varies according to age, type, and locality.

The dorsal fin is darker to conform with the colours of the back. It is generally a red-brown colour, and sometimes red-streaked. The fins of the lower body are pink-tinted but may

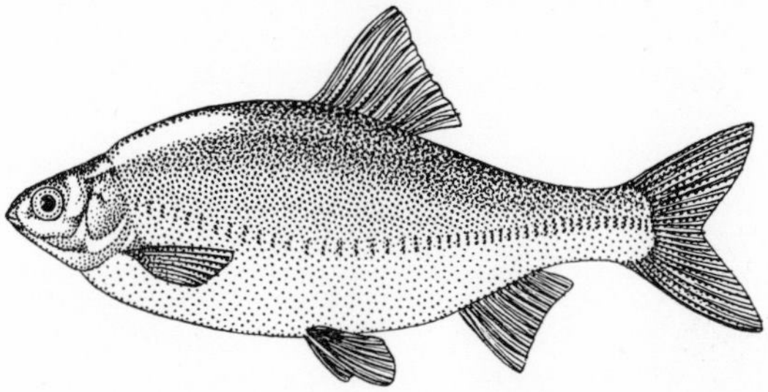

Roach

be grey, crimson, or yellow with red streaks. The tail fin is similar to the dorsal fin.

Body shape varies considerably in maturity, but young fish tend to be slim and spindle-shaped. Some fish retain this characteristic throughout their lives while others become decidedly hump-backed and deep-bellied. Yet others tend to become broad-backed and reminiscent of the CHUB. Three varieties of roach, resembling DACE, RUDD, and CHUB, were described by Schmidt in his *Scandinavian Fishes* (1892) and these conform roughly to the descriptions given here. Schmidt considered the differences to be largely due to heredity rather than to environment and gave each type a sub-title: *Rutilus rutilus var. crassa*, the chub-like roach; *var. elata*, the rudd-like roach; and *var. elongata* the dace-like roach. These distinctions are not today accepted by most zoologists, but most anglers will have found roach roughly corresponding to one or another of the types.

It is tempting to suggest that the slimmer varieties are found in fast waters while their plumper cousins belong in lakes and ponds, but this theory is far from being borne out by the facts. Deep-bellied, bronze-flanked fish are typical of the Hampshire Avon for instance, and are also frequently found in gravel pits and reservoirs. The slimmer fish so often found in lakes are also commonly to be found in the Fenland drain waters as well as in the Thames, Medway, Trent, and Great Ouse. In many waters, such as the Kennet, roach of two distinct types are to be found, the golden-flanked deep-bellied fish inhabiting the same reaches as the slim, silvery ones. Bronze-flanked fish are less often found in the Thames, where there are nevertheless plenty of deep-bodied fish. This suggests that Schmidt was quite correct in ascribing these differences to heredity and genetical structure rather than to environment.

With so much variety in food supplies from one water to another it is hardly surprising that researches into growth rates show apparently conflicting results. In optimum conditions, for example, such as those found in the Hampshire Avon and one or two other waters such as reservoirs, which occasionally produce large fish up to 3 lb. or so, the growth rate is high. A two-year old fish might attain a size of 4½–5 ins., putting on a further inch each year and reaching the Thames angler's size limit (8 ins.) in five years. Such fish could reach the 3 lb. mark at an age of about fourteen or fifteen, having achieved what is for a roach a fairly good old age. After this, growth falls off and the fish 'go back'. At the other extreme, in waters where food supplies are limited by overpopulation or poor conditions, the fish may fail to attain 8 ins. by the time it is nine or ten years old.

The great majority of roach waters lie somewhere between these extremes and average conditions can produce fish capable of 3–3½ ins. length by the end of the second year. These may become sizeable in six or seven years, which leaves them plenty of time to put on further weight before reaching advanced age and 'going back'.

Average waters will contain a fairly good head of fish of about a pound in weight. Two-pounders or near two-pounders will probably also be present, but this weight will generally represent the peak of growth. Two-pound fish are, of course, few and far between in comparison with the millions of 6 in. naïve youngsters which the angler so often grumbles about. Losses due to predators and other natural causes naturally increase as age increases.

Roach occasionally interbreed with other allied species which happen to be spawning in close proximity to the roach shoals. Hybridism is accidental, and arises from fishes on the fringes of the shoals intermingling, eggs from one species being fertilized by milt from the other. Hybridism of this kind arises rarely between roach and BLEAK, commonly between roach and RUDD and between roach and BREAM.

The roach/bleak and roach/rudd hybrids are unlikely to give rise to problems, though they are difficult to identify. In the case of the bream/roach hybrid, the resultant mixture often reaches specimen proportions. This can inspire false claims for record or specimen fish.

The bream/roach cross is often referred to as a pomeranian bream, and was once thought to be a separate species. It is now recognized for the hybrid it actually is. It is intermediate in appearance between roach and bream and may resemble either parent predominantly, having a stongly forked tail and a slimy body, and combining depth of body as found in bream with the roach's thickness of body. This means that it may weigh upwards of 2 lb.

Such fish can be recognized instantly and quite definitely by counting the number of branched rays in the anal fin. The true roach bears only nine to twelve such rays, the bream between twenty-three and twenty-nine. The hybrid bears between fifteen and nineteen and is, therefore, clearly neither roach nor bream, and cannot easily be mistaken for another species.

It is impossible to define typical haunts of the roach with any accuracy because they inhabit waters of widely different kinds, their haunts being as variable as their structures and, in any event, changing according to the time of the year. Certain generalizations are possible, however. Other things being equal, roach tend to seek out hard bottoms, preferring gravelly, sandy, rocky, concrete, and sometimes even hard clay bottoms, to soft surfaces such as silt and mud.

Against this must be considered the fact that roach are very fond of weed, which provides cover from predators, and offers good feeding. Where there is plenty of weed on the bottom or reedy margins, the roach will seldom be found very far away – especially during the summer.

Very little is known with any certainty about the roach's seasonal movements because little research has been undertaken. Most available evidence is the result of direct observation by generations of anglers who usually know where they catch their fish at various times of the year. The reasons for those movements which do occur are not hard to find.

During the months of April to June, earlier or later according to the severity or mildness of the year, the fish move into the weeds and reed margins, often in very shallow waters, and well up in the minor tributaries. In lakes and ponds the choice is restricted, but even here the fish tend to move out of the deeper waters, and make the best of available weed and shallows.

Spawning is communal, and no obvious selection of mates is observable except occasionally among older and larger fish where the shoals are themselves smaller and fewer. In this event the spawning groups are smaller and, if space permits, big fish tend to separate from the smaller ones. The eggs are deposited on the weed stems and left to fend for themselves. By June the roach are seeking out the faster reaches to recover from the rigours of spawning. Now they occupy mill-tails, weir pools, and the swift streamy stickles, but they still prefer shallow waters.

About July the shoals tend to move out into the deeper runs, taking up residence in the typical gravelly scours and runs between the weed. They seem to prefer to remain in or by the 'stream', where their search for food is assisted by the hatching of myriads of eggs provided by various insects and crustaceans, so that they have a virtual conveyor belt continually bringing food along. With the onset of colder weather, however, the fish tend to spread more, moving away from weed and into deeper waters scattered about the whole river. By the time the weeds have rotted, the roach are fairly firmly established in the deeps, returning to the shallows only during warmer spells.

As the winter floods approach, the shoals are continually on the move, patrolling many miles in the course of the day in the never-ending search for food. When the floods arrive, the lay-bys, eddies, and ox-bows provide temporary refuge from the worst of the fast water, and the shoals are not slow to follow the river up and over the banks on to the meadows and grassy fringes where some welcome extra rations are provided.

During periods of drought the fish instinctively avoid being left high and dry, receding with the water into the centre channels where it remains comparatively deep. They are now continually moving, hunting or being hunted until, when spring comes, the fresh weed growth and the breeding season bring welcome cover and a whole glut of extra food in the form of the many creatures which live and breed amongst the weed. Here the fish remain until they themselves have spawned.

Throughout the year the general diet of the fish is subject to some modification. During the early season silkweed and the profusion of insects provide the basic food, but later in the year it is to the adult insects as well as to molluscs and crustaceans that the fish must look for food, though they still show a marked liking for silkweed. By autumn, food is scarcer and the fish must move about in search of freshwater shrimps, snails, leeches, bloodworms, and other food forms still available. Sometimes they are forced to exist on fat reserves remaining from the summer, and as they become leaner they become also beautifully conditioned. In still waters some fish fall into a state of semi-hibernation from which they only arouse themselves when the temperature rises considerably. During winter, still-water roach fishing is less attractive than river fishing for this reason.

Baits

Provided the fish are in a feeding mood they will eat or sample practically anything which looks or smells edible, as long as it appears also to be natural. This means that the roach angler has a very wide range of baits, including the tiniest insects at one extreme, and large lobworms at the other.

The *maggot* or gentle is the larval form of the common blowfly and is in fact a very fair imitation or representation of innumerable grubs and larvae which roach are accustomed to finding in their natural haunts. This is probably the chief reason for its great efficacy as a traditional roach angler's bait.

The size of the maggot is not itself important, although many anglers prefer to sort out the smaller maggots or 'squats' and retain these for ground-baiting, using only the largest and best for hook-bait. What is important is that the maggot should be lightly hooked in such a way that it retains its liveliness and wriggles provocatively on the hook. To ensure this the hook must be sharp, and the point is simply nicked through the tough skin at the head (which is the blunt end of the maggot).

Maggots are used on a No. 16–12 hook, singly or in pairs, when the fish seem to mistake the two maggots for one extra large one. Sometimes they are effective in bunches of three to five on a 10–8 hook, and on odd occasions roach will even feed madly on bunches of eight or more and refuse all else.

Coloured maggots are favoured by many anglers and 'rainbow' maggots of every possible colour can be purchased for the purpose, or the angler can stain or dye his own. In cold weather maggots should be kept in a warm place to prevent their becoming comatose, and in hot weather they should be kept cool to prevent them from turning into the chrysalis stage. Maggot dispensers which may be kept in the coat pocket during cold spells can be obtained; in hot weather the fisherman has to improvise, keeping his baits in a shady place during the day.

If maggots are kept for any length of time they produce a small, oval-shaped, brown chrysalis which is itself an excellent roach bait, especially when the fish are feeding on or near the surface. This is best presented singly on a 14 or 12 hook, and requires to be carefully hooked lest it splits apart. Roach often take the chrysalis bait very daintily and the slightest tremble of the float should be struck. Chrysalids can also be useful as mid-water or bottom-fishing baits.

There are dozens of different kinds of *caddis grub*, and all make good roach baits. Some anglers like to hook them within the case, others prefer to remove the case first by pinching one end, at which the grub usually emerges smartly at the other. Caddis grubs look rather like maggots with legs, and are usually daintily taken. Sometimes, however, the roach take very confidently indeed and the float sails away unmistakably. Caddis grubs are difficult to keep for any time, and should be immersed in water and kept in a cool, shady place.

Practically any *worm* will make a good roach bait, but much depends on the mood of the fish, which will often take one kind and reject another without any apparent reason. Lobworms, redworms, and brandlings are the established favourites and can be presented whole, or in pieces. The smaller worms are best whole, unless experience indicates that fastidious roach are taking only small pieces. The tail of a lobworm is a traditional roach bait and is often highly successful. Worms can be presented on Pennel double-hook tackles, but are usually more effective for roach on single hooks, the size of the hook depending on circumstances. Small hooks are not good bait-holders and a size 8 or 10 is usually suitable for all but the very biggest worms. The angler should not be afraid to employ these occasionally on number 6 or even 4 hooks when legering.

Considering how very versatile *wheat* baits are it is surprising that they are always considered in second place to worm or maggot baits. When properly presented they take roach just as well, often bringing better-quality fish, and they are far less trouble to hook than worms or maggots, as well as being more wholesome to use. They are slowly receiving the recognition they deserve on waters where maggot and worm baits have recently been subject to a ban.

Wheat grains are used whole, but require stewing first so that the husk splits. Hook sizes 14–10 are suitable, according to conditions. In meadows where the wheat fields run down to the water's edge wheat is particularly effective, especially when also used sparingly for ground-bait.

Wholemeal or bleached white *flour* can be made into a dough which makes an excellent roach bait. Self-raising flours are best avoided, as these spoil during the day, once they are made up. Wholemeal flours produce a brownish dough which is especially attractive during the early season but needs to be presented in small pieces on a 12 or 10 hook because it tends to fall easily from the hook.

Bread paste is similar to dough but can be made up rather stiffer to suit individual preferences. It should be made from the white inside of a day-old loaf, new bread being unsuitable for paste making. The bread is well broken up in a piece of strong, clean cloth and the corners of the cloth are drawn together to make a sort of bag. The bread is kneaded well, then the cloth is dipped in the water for a few moments, and the bundle is again thoroughly kneaded to make it homogeneously wet. When removed, the cloth is screwed up and excess water ls wrung out, the resulting paste being kneaded again to give it an even consistency. Opinions differ about the consistency required. Some anglers prefer a paste which falls from the hook as it is withdrawn at the end of the cast. Others like to stiffen it with flour, custard powder, or even cotton wool. Others flavour or colour the paste with honey, sugar, aniseed, or pilchard oil, using blancmange powders or custard for colouring. For general roach fishing the paste is used in pea-sized pieces moulded on a hook of about size 10, but specimen seekers like to use a walnut-sized piece on a No. 6 hook. On the frequent occasions when fish are very fussy, a tiny piece the size of a dust shot will work wonders, on the very point of a very small hook.

For bread flakes only new bread is suitable, the flaky white inner bread being used. A small piece is pressed on the bend of the hook and remains in place by its own plasticity. The outer irregular flaky edges should be left as they are, as these swell up in the water and pieces break off and drift down ahead of the bait to present an appetizer which brings the fish in search of the hook bait. Care must be taken that the harder nucleus of pressed bread is not masking the hook point, as this would seriously impair quick penetration.

The outer crust from old or new bread is a tempting bait for roach, especially during winter, and when presented as a slowly sinking bait. Irregular pieces about a quarter of an inch long can be used, or the crust may be cut off in little squares. The hook should pass right through the crust to the other side. Then the point is brought back through so that the crust sits on the bend of the hook but leaves the point clear.

'Bread crumb' is the inner layer of bread immediately under the crust. The bait is used as flake or crust and often makes a very tempting bait.

Crust. Stick point through crust into crumb.

Stale bread cut in quarter-inch cubes is a very effective bait during the winter and also during the early season. The hook is worked into the cube so that the point is not showing, but is nevertheless close to the surface. The cube falls from the hook easily, but is worth trying just the same.

Cheese makes an excellent legering bait. Fresh slab cheese, softened between the fingers and moulded on the hook like paste, will frequently tempt the fish when no other bait succeeds. The cheese may alternatively be used in cubes or mixed with bread paste to give a cheese flavour which is very useful when cheese is in short supply and bread paste plentiful. Many anglers use softer cheeses such as Danish Blue or Gorgonzola with great success.

Silkweed is the green thread-like weed found on masonry, piles, and lock gates and it is an excellent roach bait during the early season, before the fish work into deeper water. The hook is simply drawn through the weed so that strands cling to it. These are wrapped about the shank or bend several times to prevent the weed coming too easily off the hook. Silkweed can be collected and used with considerable success in streams which are not in the immediate vicinity of weirs or locks. It must, however, be kept in water in a shady place or it will deteriorate very quickly.

Hempseed and bird seed is boiled gently until the husk splits and the white plumule appears through the split. Soft-cased seeds can be hooked through the case, but hemp is placed on the bend of the hook, which is inserted into the split in the case. The case is springy enough to clip on the hook bend and hold the seed in position. Use a small hook; sizes 14–10 are best. The angler requires very good reflexes to strike hemp bites successfully.

Other baits include elderberry, which is fished like hemp, and often used in conjuction with it; freshwater shrimps, which, hooked in the bend of the back, are effective in many waters; and freshwater molluscs such as mussels and snails. Woodlice, beetles, moths, caterpillars, slugs, and pond skaters all have their uses when the angler's supply of baits is low, and cereals such as pearl barley can also be valuable. Wasp grubs, baked to improve their toughness, are also excellent baits, and bloodworms and boiled potato and macaroni are all useful at times. Presentation is half the battle when seeking roach. Most edible substances will take fish under the right conditions when properly fished.

Ground-bait may be made up from old bread crusts soaked in water and then kneaded to remove surplus water until a pasty consistency is achieved and the mixtures can be thickened with porridge, rusk, and bran. It may be obtained in prepared packets from the tackle dealer. The secret of successful ground-baiting is 'little and often', with a small piece of the ground-bait wrapped about the hook-bait at every other cast.

The substance used as hook-bait can itself be used as ground-bait, simply by feeding a little into the swim at intervals.

Maggot anglers often use swim-feeders to do this. Those using paste or cheese like to throw in a small pellet near the hook at intervals. Care must be taken not to provide so much ground-bait that the fish have no desire to search for the hook-bait. With experience you will learn how to cast an eye over the swim first so as to discover where the ground-bait should be thrown in order to reach the bottom in the vicinity of the hook-bait. In still waters, ground-baiting should be very sparing indeed as there is no current to disperse the ground-bait once it reaches bottom, and it may go sour in a day or so if too much is used, temporarily spoiling an otherwise fruitful swim.

Tackle

The only generalization possible about roach rods is that they should be as light as prevailing conditions will permit, which in itself allows for tremendous variety. The rod and line must match. (Test-curve figures for the rod will give maximum breaking strains.) In most waters the rod must be suited to the strength and type of water fished rather than to the roach it is designed to catch; indeed recent developments in tackle show an ever-increasing number of rods designed for named waters.

The great exception is perhaps the match-type rod, which is designed for taking large numbers of fairly small roach quickly. This usually has a marked tip action and is used whenever possible with very light terminal tackle. The length may vary between 12 and 16 ft, and the rod is often of Spanish reed, with a spliced built-cane, whale-bone, or fibre-glass tip. Tubular fibre-glass or steel rods are nowadays slowly superseding these Spanish-reed match rods, owing to the greater versatility and power, commensurate with length, which they provide. These rods still bear a marked tip action, however, and are excellent for competition work in many kinds of water. Used in conjunction with a fixed-spool reel and light or even medium tackle, they make up in length whatever they lack in casting power. They enable the match fisherman to control his light tackles well out in the stream and at considerable distances. Nevertheless, they are at their best in fairly sluggish or still waters.

For medium waters, where a brisker flow is experienced and competitive results are not essential, a tip-and-middle action is preferable and the rod can with advantage be somewhat shorter (between 10 and 12 ft). A whole-cane butt with a spliced-cane middle graduating to a built-cane tip will provide this action, but the middle and tip could instead be entirely of built-cane or tubular fibre-glass. Again, tubular fibre-glass and steel are becoming increasingly popular in this type of rod and can provide the somewhat heavier casting power and tackle capabilities that are needed. If there is such a thing as a general roach rod it would be of this kind. Matched with a fixed-spool reel and low breaking-strain line, this provides a very versatile kit suitable for a wide range of water conditions and capable of handling big roach.

In exceptionally fast waters such as the Avon, Kennet, or Dorset Stour, a far sturdier rod is preferred, in order to cope with the tremendous strains imposed on the tackle by the force of water, especially when it is considered that the strike may frequently occur with the tackle twenty or thirty yards away. Avon-type rods (see p. 32) are made up in built-cane throughout; for this kind of rod this material has easily withstood growing competition from tubular fibre-glass and steel. Avon-type rods should give an all-through action which continues under the corks of the butt in the angler's hand, and are highly suitable for all kinds of roach fishing in very fast waters. They can also cope with tight-line legering.

Between the three standard patterns described will be found many modifications suited to particular local conditions and fishing methods, all of them usually known as 'roach rods', but each as different from the other as it is possible to imagine.

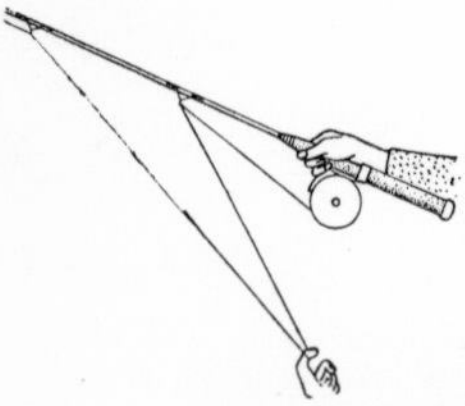

The Nottingham cast. For this, loops of line are pulled from between the first and second rod rings and released as the cast is made. One loop is shown here. The method gives extra distance.

Reels offer less of a problem for the fisherman because they are far more versatile and can easily be adapted to conditions simply by changing the line strength. The fixed-spool reel is highly popular, but the older centre-pin, when built in modern alloys with precision bearings, holds firmly in the affections of many anglers. For leger work, and for methods which do not require continual line manipulation, the fixed-spool is easily the best tool, but for long-trotting and precision work, such as tripping the bottom, nothing gives quite the same sweetness of control in the hands of an expert as a first-class four-inch-drum centre-pin. In the last resort, choice of reel is an extremely personal matter.

Fishing Methods

The majority of roach caught during the season undoubtedly fall to the float-fisherman, who has innumerable modifications of the style at his disposal. The various forms of float-fishing are usually adopted not simply from preference, but according to the water conditions prevailing, or the depth at which the fish are feeding at a given time.

On arrival at the waterside the angler does his best to sum up conditions and adopts the method which appears to be most suitable, changing it as conditions and the behaviour of the fish indicate. It is not at all unusual for an angler to make use of almost every possible variation of float-fishing in his search for the taking method, or indeed simply to take better-quality fish than those caught hitherto.

The slowly sinking bait is a method without equal in still or very sluggish waters and when conditions are right it enables the angler to present his bait at any desired depth simply by adjusting the position of the float. It is also a method suited to very light tackles. The float may be a four- to six-inch porcupine quill or a light 'bobber', with only one or two dust shots to cock it. The shots are always used fairly near the float to ensure that they have little or no effect on the sinking of the bait, which must settle slowly in the water under its own weight. If the tackle has to be cast any distance it is usual to attach the float by its base only, or to arrange the lower shot just over halfway down the cast to prevent the bait from fouling the float in its passage through the air. More often the style is used within fairly easy casting distance of the bank. When used with maggots, bread crust or cube, it can be most effective.

This method of course can be used in conjunction with swimming the stream tactics as discussed below. In many waters the angler learns to strike at the merest tremble of the float, which to him at least signifies a bite. Frequently, for example, the bait is taken before it has reached the bottom of the cast and before the float has properly cocked.

Swimming the stream requires a current which carries the bait downstream of the angler for several yards before it is withdrawn and cast again. The float can be set to any suitable depth, which is varied to discover the 'taking' depth. The terminal tackle is adapted to suit conditions, which might be light enough for the use of tackle like that described for the

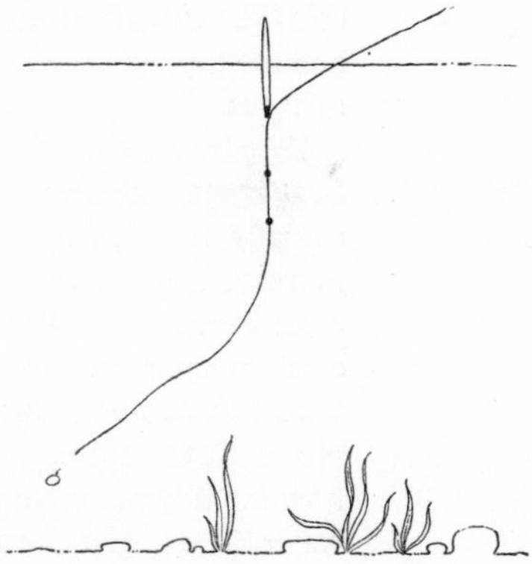

Slow-sinking rig with weights close to float.

slowly sinking bait, but with the shots arranged to get the bait down quickly.

In slightly heavier waters a larger quill or cork-bodied quill is used, with the shotting arranged so that about an eighth of an inch of the float is above the surface. Heavier tackles can be employed to give extra casting distance when it is necessary to fish farther out in the stream, or when the length of the swim requires that the float should be visible at a distance.

Normally the tackle is cast into position and allowed to drift fifteen yards or so downstream before recovery. It is important, however, that the float should not precede the bait, and this is achieved by exerting a light check on the float with the rod tip. As line is paid off the reel the check is maintained, or the rod is moved downstream to follow the float. This normally allows the bait to swing just in front of the float at the prescribed depth. In swimming the stream in this way it is sometimes advisable to stop the float momentarily so as to give an upward swing to the bait; this movement is often effective in attracting a curious fish. Many anglers always strike at the end of each swim as a matter of course. Bites are usually signified by a definite plunge of the float, but in over-fished waters where the fish are extremely suspicious the angler must be equally suspicious and strike at any undue movement of the float. The method requires some skill and familiarity with the water being fished. It is probably used by most anglers at some time in their everyday fishing.

Where the strength of the stream permits it, and the bank is suitable, the method can be used to search many yards of water by trotting downstream as much as fifty yards. In this event the style is usually called *long-trotting* and requires the use of somewhat heavier terminal tackle to give the angler good visibility and better control when it is a long way off. In this event, the float must usually be attached at both the base and the top, and the line is greased to ensure fast striking at a distance.

Tripping the bottom involves the same basic method, but the float is set higher on the cast, with the result that the bait is actually tripping along the uneven bottom throughout its journey. The operative word here is 'tripping', because unless great care and skill are exercised the bait will undoubtedly catch in some obstacle and give rise to a very promising false bite. The depth throughout the swim must first be carefully plumbed, therefore, and the float set slightly above this, just how far depending very much on the speed and depth of the water. The angler must make minute by minute adjustments to his tackle, as experience indicates, to get the float at the right depth.

Once cast, the float is checked throughout the swim. Again, the amount of checking must be just enough to trip the bait over obstacles and along the bottom, and yet not so much as to cause it to behave unnaturally in the water. The style calls for considerable skill and experience on the angler's part, but is highly effective in catching good-quality fish.

When these swimming-the-stream or long-trotting styles are in use, it is obvious that the amount of line between the angler's float and rod tip will vary considerably from time to time. This line must be kept as straight as possible to give effective striking at a distance. When the wind or current causes bights or curves in the line lying on the surface, these must be straightened out by lifting the rod tip, switching the line straight, and placing it back on the water again. All this must be done without unduly disturbing the float and bait. 'Mending the line', as this is called, requires some experience.

Laying-on is suited to still and sluggish waters, but cannot be satisfactory in very fast waters. The depth is first plumbed, and the float set so that the cast is a foot or so longer than the depth. When the tackle is cast into position, the float fails to cock because the weights are all in a heap on the bottom with slack line between them and the float. The float is withdrawn a few inches by taking in some reel line, and this straightens out the cast and cocks the float slantwise. The chief advantage now immediately apparent is that the shots lie hidden on the bottom with the bait a foot or two away, and the float and line are well away from the bait, presenting no silhouette on the sky-line to frighten suspicious fish. Properly presented, the bait is usually taken fairly confidently and bites are signified by a leisurely and dignified plunge of the float which should be met with an immediate strike. Many anglers find that this method brings fewer but better fish to net. It is particularly suitable when the fish appear to have gone off feed somewhat during the middle of the day.

In brisker waters the method can be even more versatile, although setting it up properly requires continual attention and adjustment, and more concentration is necessary on the angler's part. When the tackle is cast into position, it rests only for a short time, as the current, acting on the float and line, tends to swing the bait downstream and towards the bank at intervals. Between each swing there is a brief period of equilibrium during which the bait can be taken. When the bait is under the near bank it is recovered and cast again.

Laying-on tackle is sometimes used with a drilled bullet in place of several shots. The bullet is stopped in position with a single shot about eighteen inches from the hook. This leaves the line free to run when a fish takes. However, if the fish begins to submerge the float, the full buoyancy of the float will offer considerably more resistance than the few shots which have been removed, so this must first be countered by adding shots immediately under the float, or by bending a piece of lead wire about its base.

Stret-pegging is similar to the method described above and is used to fish out holes and uneven bottoms in fairly brisk water. The float is set as for laying-on with a small drilled bullet, but an extra shot is attached a foot or so above the bullet to restrict its movement somewhat. The tackle is cast down and across and held in position with the rod tip from which it is fished. The bait is fished through the 'hole' by moving the rod tip downstream a little, or by paying out a few inches of line at intervals. Bites are felt on the rod tip or detected by the float.

With a few exceptions *legering* requires the use of a drilled or perforated weight through which the line is free to run in the direction of a taking fish. The weight is usually stopped in position with a single shot anywhere between 18 ins. and 3 ft from the hook, the length of trail depending on conditions. Since floats are not used, bite detection is usually more difficult and some means of bite registration must be devised.

The shot leger is perhaps the simplest form, requiring only a single small shot as weight, and is suitable for sluggish or still waters. The bait is allowed to lie on the bottom and in shallow waters the angler can watch the fish take, and strike accordingly. When fishing in clear, but deeper waters or at

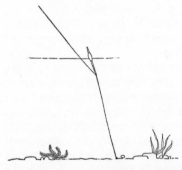

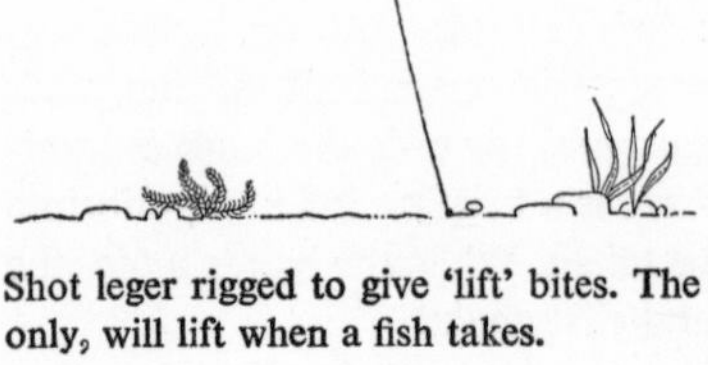

Shot leger rigged to give 'lift' bites. The float, attached by the bottom only, will lift when a fish takes.

longer range, he must depend on movements of the slightly slack line between the rod tip and the surface to detect bites. The method is useful for fishing a worm or maggot bait but is difficult to fish in waters where the flow is at all marked, or where the bottom is particularly snaggy.

In slack-line legering for roach, the leger is made up with a pear lead and swivel, the swivel being attached to the pear, and the line running freely through the eye of the swivel. Alternatively, an Arlesey Bomb or Capta-type leger weight can be used. The bait can be fished at almost any distance provided the water is sluggish or still, or moving at a slow uniform rate. It is cast down and across the stream, and as soon as all slack line has been retrieved, a foot or so of line is eased forward through the rings to allow the line to hang in a curve. Bites are indicated by a movement of the line, which straightens out quickly; an answering strike usually secures the fish. The method is especially useful when the angler is fishing from a very high bank which doesn't allow him to get down to the water's edge, as the rather large curve of line so caused is frequently very sensitive as an indicator. As soon as the current begins to run fast, however, the method is not definite enough and a dough bobbin must be employed to give bite detection.

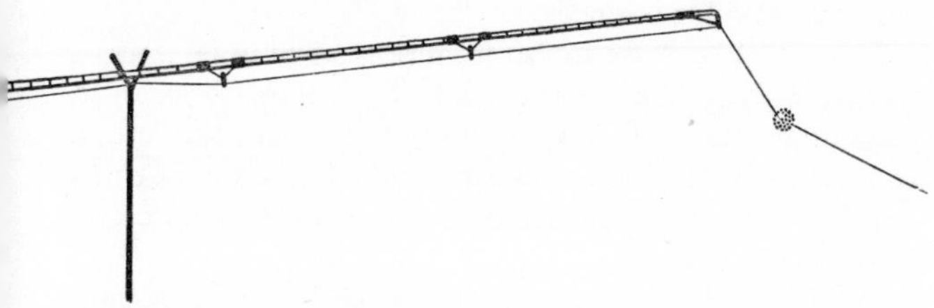

Dough-bobbin bite-indicator

The dough is attached to the line itself, either at the rod tip, or between the butt ring and the reel, and left to hang down a foot or so. This gives a definite indication of bites. Some anglers prefer instead to use an additional rod tip called a 'swing-tip' which is attached to the end of the rod with the line passing through its rings. This attachment has a flexible portion at its base so that it hangs limply below the rod top. Weighted with dough to suit prevailing conditions it will swing quite definitely when a bite comes.

Tight-line legering: in faster waters where slack-line methods are not suitable, the angler legering for roach has no alternative but to fish a tight line, relying upon movements at his rod tip or the pluck of the line in his hand to register bites. Normally the rod is fished with part of its weight on a rest and the butt across the angler's knees, his fingers being closed over the line to feel for the sensitive touch of a fish.

Weights used for tight-line work vary according to conditions, the pear and swivel or Arlesey Bomb being suitable for still waters or medium-fast waters. In very fast waters, however, a flat-based Capta lead, coin lead, or coffin lead must be used to prevent the tackle being moved by the force of the current.

Sometimes, however, it is preferable to have the bait moving, in which case the weight is selected so that it is moved downstream at intervals. To prevent line-twist as the weight rolls, an Arlesey Bomb or pear-and-swivel lead should be employed. The bait is fished until it is under the bank, when it must be cast again. If the current fails to move the weight of its own force, a light lift of the rod tip should dislodge it.

The methods described here are all suitable for taking roach under varying conditions, and are all normally used downstream. Recently some anglers have had good results by legering upstream, but considerable care is required to distinguish bites from movements of the tackle in the stream. Upstream legering requires considerable practice and is not recommended for beginners.

Many anglers prefer to fish from rests when using legering tactics, while others insist on holding the rod throughout, without any support. If a rest is used in conjunction with a comfortable seat it does enable the angler to exert more easily that high degree of sustained concentration which most leger methods demand.

Fly-fishing: this is not much used for roach, but can be most effective at times when the sun is high and the weather very hot, and the fish are only casually taking odd tit-bits from the surface and ignoring bottom or mid-water baits. A light TROUT outfit is very suitable and almost any fly will do provided it isn't too big. For fast waters buzzy, hackled flies are preferable, but in slow or still waters the winged patterns are better. Suggested patterns are as follows. Dry flies: Alder, Black Gnat, Coachman, Coch-y-bondhu, Blue Dun, Greenwell's Glory, Wickham's Fancy, Red Tag, Willow-fly, Zulu, Medium Sedge, Medium Olive, Stone-flies, and Mayflies during their season. Wet flies: Peter Ross, Blue Dun, Hare's Ear, Zulu, Butcher, Alexandra, Black Gnat, Red Spinners, Greenwell's Glory, Black Spider, Palmer, Red Quill, etc. (See pp. 155–80).

Roach

A fairly fine tapered cast is to be preferred and the flies should be small (on 12–14 hooks). Often roach will rise to the dry fly without actually taking it, and sometimes they will roll upon it before taking it. The wet fly is then to be preferred. If it is presented just below the surface it is often effective, a slowly sinking wet fly being the best of all.

General

The British record roach of 3 lb. 14 oz. was taken by Bill Penney from Lambeth Reservoir, Molesey, in 1938, a 3 lb. 10 oz. fish was taken by Wilfred Cutting in Hornsey Mere in 1917, and fish of over 3 lb. have been recorded from the Thames, Dorset Stour, Hampshire Avon, Kent Stour, Norfolk Bure, Test, Colne, Bain, Trent, Loddon, Medway, and Brue as well as several others. Similar fish occur in reservoirs and gravel pits, including Kilpin Pond, Howden; Bickling Lake, Norfolk; Staines South Reservoir; Hornsey Mere, Yorkshire; Ellen Hall Park, Staffordshire; and others.

No doubt an exhaustive list of 3 lb. roach caught would fill pages. Two-pound fish have been very much more common in recent years than previously, and the chances of the ordinary angler's attaining this target are probably better than they have ever been.

Experience gathered by River Board officials during clearing and netting expeditions suggests that bigger fish are available in many more waters than anglers ever suspect.

Roach are found in still and running waters of every kind all over the British Isles as far north as Loch Lomond, but are less common in the extreme west of England and Wales. Until recently, roach were unknown in Ireland and the name roach is used to describe the true RUDD, which is common there. Recent introductions have undoubtedly occurred and roach are now found in the Foyle river system, Fairey Water, and the Mourne. No doubt the species will in time spread farther.

H. T.

Rudd

RUISVOORN

The rudd (*Scardinius erythrophthalmus*) is also called red eye, azurine, blue roach (and, in Ireland, roach).

The back is green-brown, grey-brown, green-blue, or intermediate. The flanks are pale yellow in the young fish, becoming brassy as it gets older, and finally a golden metallic colour tinged with red. The belly is cream, yellow, or off-white and the dorsal and anal fins are blood-red or pink, or in some fish yellow, or yellow streaked with red. The tail is orange or pink, and streaked with brown or grey. In some waters younger fish are silvery like ROACH and their colour in maturity is less golden, and some fish, when seen in the water and when first removed from it, have a bluish appearance in the back and flank, which has no doubt given rise to the notion that they were 'blue roach'. All so-called 'blue roach' have upon examination proved to be rudd.

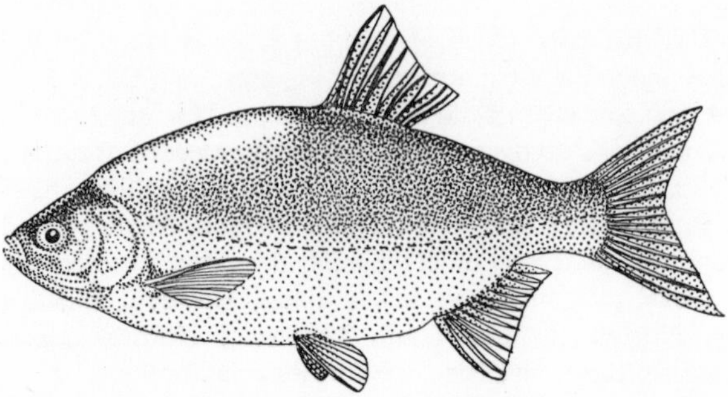

Rudd

The body in mature fish is strongly compressed laterally, the back being humped, and the abdomen full and rounded. The abdomen is also keeled between the pelvic and anal fins. The mouth is strongly oblique and the lower jaw projects boldly beyond the upper, indicating that the rudd is a surface feeder. The fore-edge of the dorsal fin is set well to the rear of the pelvic fin, and in mature fish its top edge points rearwards.

Rudd are subject to some variation, particularly in colour; an albinotic form, the golden rudd, is a favourite with aquarists. The yellow-finned forms are found alongside the red-finned in the same waters, which suggests that differences in fin colour are due to genetic rather than to environmental causes.

The growth of rudd is probably more variable than that of any other fish species except possibly PERCH, chiefly because of their tendency to overpopulate the water. In suitable conditions, however, they grow more quickly than ROACH, reaching 2 ins. during the first year, and 4 in the second. During their third year they are capable of breeding and may attain a length of 6 or 7 ins., and by the time they are five they may reach the ½ lb. mark. In poor conditions a ten-year-old fish might still be undersized.

Rudd interbreed occasionally with ROACH or BREAM, and the resulting hybrids are fairly common in waters where the species are mixed.

The rudd/roach hybrid is difficult to recognize, falling as it does intermediately between two species which are already closely allied and similar in appearance. If the position of the dorsal fin suggests roach, while the strongly upturned mouth suggests rudd, the angler should suspect hybridism. Only a dissection by a specialist would satisfactorily prove the case. Since these hybrids do not often reach specimen proportions this is neither necessary nor desirable.

The rudd/bream hybrid is different in that it does frequently reach proportions which would be sought in a specimen rudd. It is, fortunately, easy to identify by counting the number of branched rays in the anal fin. The true rudd bears between ten and thirteen such rays, the BREAM between nineteen and twenty-three. The hybrid bears between fifteen and eighteen branched rays and can thus be positively identified as such by any angler who makes the count.

Any fish which is big enough to warrant a claim as a record or specimen fish should first be subjected to this check. Immediate identification in this way will avoid much disappointment later if the fish does happen to be a hybrid. Most enlightened specimen groups, newspaper columnists, or club officials will be certain to apply this test if the fish is presented to them for prize or record claim purposes.

Rudd are generally thought of as lake and pond fish, but they also occur, though less often, in rivers, where they inhabit the slower reaches and sluggish pools. The river fish are usually as large as lake fish although the best specimens are invariably recorded from lakes and still waters. The fish do especially well in lakes, provided that food supplies are good and the water is suitably alkaline, with good weed growth. Unfortunately the species breeds profusely and in many waters there is a tendency to over-population. The fish then become stunted over a period of many years, and growth rates are extremely poor. When waters of this kind are ruthlessly netted, the fish transferred elsewhere often show a sudden improvement in growth and those which remain also improve temporarily until population gets out of hand again. Such waters can be improved with lime and fertilizer and other agents to increase food supplies for the fish. Where rudd are of good quality there are often good PIKE also, and the suggestion that pike stocking might assist in over-populated waters deserves consideration. Possibly the introduction of PIKE-PERCH would considerably help in balancing the population, since these fish are just as predatory as pike, and rather more active.

Rudd are confirmed surface feeders and live in mid-water most of the time, although older specimens become less attached to the surface, tending to feed nearer the bottom to obtain a more varied and satisfying diet. The shoals consist of fish of all sizes, the older and larger fish often lying in the centre of the shoal, or deeper in the water. They are fond of the shallows, especially among thick bottom weed which extends upwards to the surface, and often shoal among reeds, their thin-sectioned bodies being well suited to swimming between the stems.

Rudd patrol the lake during the day, working from the margins to the deeps or vice versa, according to the prevailing winds and the water temperatures. They seem to prefer the sheltered part of the lake or pond where wind neither ruffles the surface nor lowers the temperature. They spawn in the weeds between May and June, and are often found still unspawned in mid-June, when the slightest touch of the hands on the flanks is sufficient to cause spawn to be shed. Towards autumn they feed less often, particularly in exposed waters. By December they become quite comatose and cease to feed except on exceptionally warm, sunny days, when they may feed for a brief spell at about midday. This semi-hibernation lasts until February or March according to the severity of the season.

Rudd are widely scattered in all parts of England, being chiefly confined to still waters, but are found notably in the Great Ouse, Nene, Fenland waters, and the waters of eastern England, becoming less common towards the west and rare in the extreme north and in Scotland. The species is common in Ireland, where it is known as 'roach'.

Baits

Almost any ROACH bait will also succeed for rudd and improvisation with grubs, pond skaters, and insects from marginal weed will often prove successful. Among the best baits are bread derivatives, worms, maggots, chrysalids, and natural and artificial flies presented on fly tackle.

For *bread* flake, the soft inside crumb from a fresh, new loaf is squeezed on the hook with the edges left irregular, or it may instead be first squeezed in the middle to make a compact nucleus through which the hook is inserted. Fished as a slowly sinking bait this is excellent.

Bread crust can be pressed overnight by damping it in the steam from a boiling kettle and then placing it in a tie-press. In the morning the rubbery crust which results is cut into squares or triangles for the hook, or may simply be bitten in irregular pieces. For most fish a piece about a quarter of an inch square is quite large enough.

Stale bread cut into quarter-inch cubes and fished on a No. 10 or 12 hook makes a good mid-water bait.

Flour pastes from white or wholemeal flour are very telling baits, but the self-raising flours tend to spoil during the day and plain flour should be used for preference. Bread paste, made as described for ROACH, is also successful, and cheese-flavoured baits are extremely good on many waters.

A single *maggot*, lightly hooked on a No. 10 or 12, will often take good fish, but a pair or a bunch can be used when the presence of larger fish is suspected. The slowly sinking maggot is a useful technique. Hook sizes will vary according to the water.

Bloodworms are an extremely good bait, but must be presented on small hooks (say an 18 or 20). Fished on the bottom, or among the weed margins they will take good-quality fish. Redworms and brandlings are also tempting to rudd, especially when presented on slowly sinking tackle. Worms fished on the bottom often take better fish.

Maggot chrysalids (and indeed the chrysalids of any small insect) are very valuable when fished with a bubble float on the surface.

Small *slugs* take good fish, but require to be carefully cast lest they fly from the hook. Young snails, of about a quarter-inch shell size, are splendid baits. They should be hooked through the soft edge of the shell. Rudd often take these as they sink.

Freshwater *shrimps* are sometimes very good baits when lightly hooked through the back so as to leave the shrimp free to wriggle.

During the period when *ants* are mating over the pond the fish will frequently look at nothing else.

Powdered ground-baits which provide a floating cloud, with a small amount of slowly sinking, finely ground biscuit or bread, are by far the best. A moored crust attached by cotton to a stone is valuable in bringing feeding fish into the vicinity.

One of the best rudd ground-baits is made of a mixture of dry, floating crust covered with biscuit. The biscuit flakes off

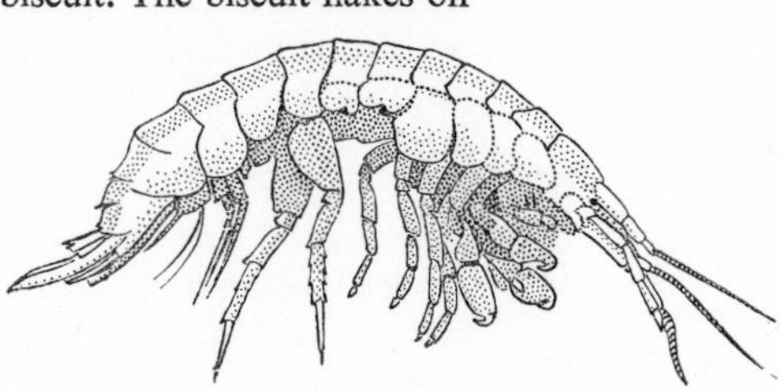

Freshwater shrimp, *Gammarus pulex*, about four times life size.

the floating crust in a fine sinking cloud, and the bait is presented in the midst of the cloud. This often takes the bigger fish.

Ground-baiting should always be sparingly applied, particularly in still waters, where a little goes a very long way. When rudd fishing it is always useful to throw in a few small pieces of the hook-bait at intervals.

Tackle The ROACH rod is very suitable for rudd fishing, but in most waters fairly long casts are often needed and for these a rod with all-through action is better. In rivers and canals the match-type rod can be used with considerable success.

Choice of reel depends on the angler. Some prefer centre-pins for canal and sluggish river fishing, but in lakes or ponds a fixed-spool reel is more suitable. Line of about 3 lb. breaking strain should be right with this, weed permitting. Where ultra-fine tackle is needed, the terminal tackle and hook link could with advantage be reduced to 2 lb. b.s., or even 1 lb. b.s. Care must be taken to inspect the cast at intervals if frequent long casting is employed.

Floats: porcupine quills are much favoured in many waters, but bubble floats and perch bobs are often used when longer distances must be covered. Almost any float can be used provided it gives suitable visibility at the distance and is properly shotted.

When shots are used on the cast they are usually distributed over the top half or just beneath the float to allow the bait to sink slowly. Where longer casting is needed, at least one shot must be arranged more than half-way down the cast to prevent the hook from flying back around the float in mid-air. Bubble floats can be free on the line, with a single dust shot just below the bubble to prevent it from sliding down on the hook link. The line is then free to run through the float when a fish takes. The line above the float must be well greased to ensure that it floats.

Fishing Methods By far the best form of presentation for rudd is at, or close to, the surface. In deep lakes, the bottom weeds often grow up to within a few feet from the surface. In marginal waters these weeds usually break surface and fish feeding in the margins can often be seen. Those feeding farther out, however, are often to be found at a depth of up to 10 or 12 ft, just above the upper fringes of the deeper-rooted weed. In a river this might be considered deep water, but in such a lake it is fairly close to the surface. Baits presented at such depths, and over deep weed, are frequently very effective in taking good-quality fish. Often the better specimens feed here during the daytime, and cruise into marginal waters only at night, or at about dusk.

Fish feeding at some distance from the banks usually do so very confidently. They can sometimes be detected by their occasional rises at the surface. Failing this, especially in waters where the fisherman is not familiar with the bottom contours and the location of weed beds, it is necessary to search the water methodically by making long casts, covering a different sector each time. Fanwise casting like this, with the process repeated at different range, is often the only way to discover confidently feeding groups of fish.

For this long casting, fairly heavy tackle must be employed, so it is fortunate that rudd are not particularly tackle-shy provided they have not first been alarmed by the angler. At distances of 20 to 40 ft from the bank, this is quite unlikely. The fish tend to be short-sighted and when they are lying in deep water their effective 'window' is limited, even if it is not already impaired by the colour of the water.

When feeding fish are found, it is sometimes useful to overcast, drawing the float back to the right spot. This avoids unnecessary splashing over the heads of the fish, as the heavy tackle hits the water at some distance from the angler. The rudd are far less likely to be scared by a gently moving float passing over them – indeed they will often take the bait while the tackle is still moving.

When the fish are feeding deep, the float submerges in no uncertain manner, but if they are within 4 or 5 ft of the surface they often run sideways with the bait, causing the float to skate across the surface without actually disappearing. A little experimenting with the timing of the strike soon establishes whether or not to hit the float immediately it moves. Usually, there's a lot of line to pick up when the angler strikes at such distances, and this makes some delay inevitable. It is tempting to use a spinning rod for such fishing, in view of the long casting and the stiffer rod action it gives, but this is unwise unless the rod is long enough to take up a good deal of line on the strike.

Inshore rudd are fairly shy of the angler, and the very fish which feed so confidently thirty yards out can become extremely wary when cruising within a few yards of the bank. For this reason, good weed cover is very valuable to the angler.

In very large lakes, *boat fishing* is popular, especially in the shallow but extensive waters of the Norfolk Broads, which are noted for their rudd. In this region it is usual to moor the boat by driving the oars into the bottom some distance away from the tall Norfolk reed fringes which so often harbour shoals of feeding fish. The method is then to cast towards the weed, fishing a few feet from the stems. If fish are not quickly located it is wise to move in, tether a floating crust or two within a couple of feet of the reeds, and then move back to the original moorings again. Usually this brings fish into the area in sufficient concentration to make the fishing worth while. It is, however, vital that movement and fuss in the boat are kept down to a minimum to avoid scaring the fish away.

A further problem in shallow waters is that of ground-baiting. If any amount of solid ground-bait is used to concentrate fish in a particular area, it is quite certain that the local aquatic birds will spot this before the fish do. These arrive on the scene incredibly quickly and proceed to dive and feast on the ground-bait. Nothing is better calculated to ruin the morning's fishing and the angler has no alternative but to move elsewhere until the coots and moorhens have disposed of his ground-bait. If ground-bait is used it should be sparingly offered, or be of a cloud-like consistency which has not sufficient bulk to attract the birds.

Rudd are very partial to a fly, wet or dry (see pp. 156–8), although the wet fly is probably better. Any light TROUT outfit will suffice, provided it will cast a reasonably long line without fuss, and a tapered line is not essential. If dry flies are used the line must float, however. If the wet fly is preferred it is often considerably improved by adding a maggot to the hook, or alternatively by using a piece of white cloth or kid leather as an imitation. Almost any small fly on a 8–10 hook is suitable, but anglers with a fancy for tying flies would be wise to include the snippet of white kid on the dressing.

Flies can be presented with a fixed-spool reel on ordinary bottom tackle by means of a float, controller, or bubble float on the line above the fly. A single shot a couple of feet from the fly will help to make the cast clean, or, better still, a lightly leaded fly will keep well clear of the bubble float during casting. The bubble or float can be loose on the line, with a single split-shot just below it to prevent it sliding down the cast. This gives the fish a very free take, since they can pull the line through the float. The angler needs sharp eyes to strike on the movement of the line. Some experience is needed to enable him to recognize bites.

If a controller (see p. 28) is required, a small piece of balsa wood can be used, with a hole at one end through which the line is passed. A piece of Norfolk reed, with a little wire loop whipped on one end, or a 5 or 6 in. porcupine quill will serve just as well. *Rudd*

General

The British rudd record was a fish of 4 lb. 8 oz., taken by the Rev. E. Alston from a mere in Norfolk which has since dried up. Probably the best-known rudd waters are Slapton Lea, and the Norfolk Broads. Most suitable ponds will contain fish of 2–3 lb., but these, being older and wiser, are very difficult to catch. Probably the best rudd to be found anywhere live in the remoter loughs of southern Ireland.

H. T.

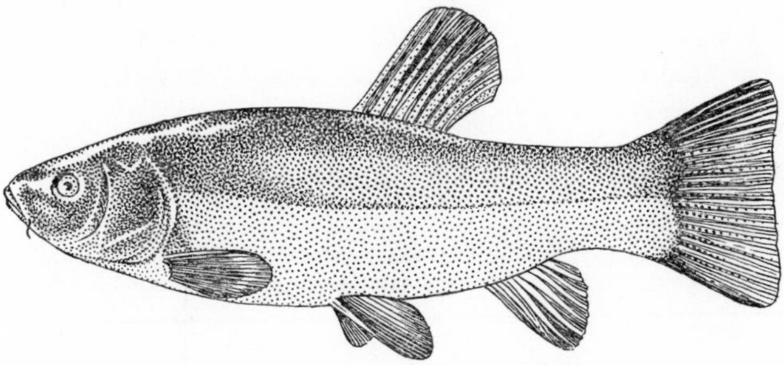

Tench

ZEELT

The tench (*Tinca tinca*) is one of the most easily identified of the coarse fishes. The depth of its colouring may vary a little according to environment, but it is usually a dark green on the back, blending into a greenish-bronze on the sides with a lighter belly or underside. All the fins, including the tail, are neatly rounded, the eyes are noticeably small and tiny scales well embedded in the skin give it what can best be described as a 'leathery' appearance.

The skin has a copious coating of protective mucous or slime, a feature which gave rise to an old fallacy which endowed the tench with the title of 'doctor fish'. In bygone days this slime was held to possess curative properties for certain human ailments and there was also an old belief that other fishes cured themselves of disease or injury by rubbing themselves against the slimy flanks of the tench. At one time it was believed that the hungriest pike would never devour a tench because of its usefulness as a 'doctor'. This quaint notion has long since been disproved, however, for tench have been found, though not very often, in the stomachs of opened pike. The tench's coloration, an excellent camouflage in its normal environment, is the probable reason for its comparative immunity from the predatory pike.

Rate of growth is governed by various factors, such as size of waters, locality, and availability of natural food. Another factor, nowadays, is the strain or ancestry of the parent fish, for many of the tench now used for stocking are descended from imported artificially reared fish which are of a faster-growing strain than our native tench.

Generally speaking, large well-weeded waters produce the biggest tench. Small ponds do not usually yield large ones, but even in these smaller waters tench will usually grow large enough to offer the angler worth-while sport. Scale readings and checks on tagged fish suggest that naturally bred pond tench are not fast growers. They appear to take about five years to attain a weight of 2 lb., seven or eight years to grow to 3 lb., and about ten years to reach the 4–5 lb. class. In large well-weeded waters, rich in natural food, growth will be appreciably faster, and even in lesser waters growth may be faster in the case of introduced fish of good stock.

Tench are primarily still-water dwellers, their natural habitat being static waters such as lakes and all kinds of pools and ponds. They thrive well enough in canals and they get along quite well in sluggish rivers and broads, but in the faster-flowing rivers you can only expect to find them, if at all, in quiet backwaters away from the main current.

Even in their natural habitat tench have their favourite haunts. Only in very small ponds and weed-free waters can they be found generally distributed. They have a pronounced liking for the cover afforded by weed-growth and rarely roam very far from such cover if it is available. In and around lily-pads, among banks of weed, and among rushy fringes; these are the favourite haunts of tench. They are not, as a rule, frequenters of the deeper water, preferring the shallower areas where the weed-growth is more abundant.

Though not as widely distributed as some species, tench are to be found over a fairly wide area of the British Isles. They inhabit suitable waters throughout England and Wales, in parts of Ireland, and in the southern counties of Scotland. They are most prolific in southern England, but are fairly common in waters as far north as Lancashire and Yorkshire. Farther north than this they become far scarcer. In recent years tench have become an increasingly popular quarry with coarse-fish anglers, and more and more angling organizations are stocking suitable waters with these hardy and easily trans-

Tench

Tinca tinca (page 143)
Specimens 4 lb and over
Record 9 lb 1 oz

Burbot

Very rare these days. No record recognised

Grayling

Thymallus thymallus (page 181)
Specimens 2 lb and over
Record 7 lb 2 oz*

Salmon

Salmo salar (page 188)
Any salmon is a worthwhile fish
Record 64 lb

Sea Trout

Salmo trutta (page 237)
Good fish start at 4 lb
Record 22 lb 8 oz*

Salmon Smolt

Salmo salar (page 189)
Immature fish weighing a few ounces

Salmon Parr

Salmo salar (page 189)
Immature fish weighing a few ounces

ported fish which will settle down and grow to a worth-while size even in waters containing only stunted populations of other species.

With tench, spawning seems to take place over a rather longer period than is usual with most other species of coarse fish; they have been found ripe with spawn as early as May and as late, even, as September. The spawning time is probably governed by water temperature, varying according to locality, but May to early June seems to be the usual breeding period.

The female tench shed their eggs on to the weed-growth in the warmer shallows to be fertilized by the more numerous males of the shoal. Much of this haphazardly deposited spawn is consumed by other fish, but the fertilized eggs which survive hatch out in about seven days.

Although the tench will sometimes seek food at mid-water and, occasionally, even at the surface, it is for the most part a bottom-feeder. The bulk of its food is picked or rooted up from the mud of the bottom and it is there that a bait intended for tench will normally prove most effective.

The natural food of the tench consists largely of vegetable matter, aquatic worms and molluscs, and the larval form of all kinds of aquatic insects. Chironomid larvae, more familiarly known as 'bloodworms', are a favourite food. Very often, streams of tiny bubbles rising to the surface will betray the presence of tench rooting in the mud in search of these small worm-like larvae. At such times, however, they are often uninterested in any bait the angler may offer. Water-snails, too, are another favourite item of the tench's diet. It is often possible to observe violent movement of marginal weed-growth as tench forage among the submerged stems, probably in search of these molluscs.

Tench are notoriously unpredictable in the matter of feeding. At times they will fast for quite long periods, yet on occasion they feed ravenously and can be caught fairly easily. They seem to be particularly susceptible to changes in water temperature and feed only within fairly narrow limits, showing little interest in baits when the water is below about 55°F. or above 70°F.

This reluctance to feed at low temperatures makes the season for successful tench fishing a short one, lasting only from the opening of the coarse-fishing season in June until about the end of September. With the onset of the winter months the tench go into semi-hibernation, settling themselves in the mud of the bottom in a torpid condition. Hibernation does not seem to be so complete in rivers, where tench are occasionally caught during the winter months, but even in these waters tench fishing is likely to be an unrewarding occupation after the end of September.

Although they are, from the angler's point of view, summer fish, tench have a strong dislike of bright sunlight, and in very sunny conditions they seek shade and show little interest in the angler's offerings. The first few hours after dawn and the last few hours before dark are usually the most promising for tench fishing at any season, but especially during a spell of bright sunny weather. There are times when tench will feed at intervals throughout the day and, if it is not too cold, throughout the night, but more often than not the hours from dawn to sun-up and from sunset until dark offer the best prospects for the angler seeking tench.

Baits There are three hook-baits which are consistently successful lures for tench; these are worms, maggots, and bread. Tench can be taken with other baits at times, but when they cannot be tempted with one or other of these three, prospects of sport are very poor indeed.

Tench have a liking for *worms* of all kinds but, when circumstances permit its use, the most effective worm bait of all is a large, active lobworm. This is a bait big enough to appeal to the largest tench, and too big to interest unwanted small fish. It has the disadvantage, though, of being also attractive to eels and where these prove troublesome a bread hook-bait is the only solution.

On some waters where *bread* is used extensively as groundbait, tench develop a taste for it and take it in preference to any other bait. For fishing over a clean bottom, bread can be used in the form of paste, kneaded from the crumb of the loaf, but if the bed is muddy or weed-covered a cube of bread crust is preferable, being more buoyant and less likely to become obscured in the mud or bottom weed.

Maggots are a hook-bait well worth trying when tench cannot be tempted with either worm or bread. When tench are rooting in the bottom mud, feeding in earnest on bloodworms and other small larvae, they seem to become preoccupied with this natural food. At such times large baits are often ignored, but a small bait such as a maggot or the tiniest of redworms may prove effective.

Tackle To fish for tench with fine tackle is to risk the frequent loss of hooked fish. The tench is a powerful fish and its favourite escape manoeuvre when hooked is to head for the nearest weed-bed. Even if it is only of average size, fine tackle will not stop it and once it reaches its goal it is as good as lost. With reasonably substantial tackle it is still not too easy to coax a weeded tench into open water again.

In any case, there is little to be gained from using very fine tackle for, unlike most species, tench do not seem to be unduly deterred by a line that is plainly visible. Its small eyes suggest that it is not very keen-sighted, and in its natural weedy habitat a line is not likely to be too conspicuous. A practical line for tench fishing is one having a breaking strain of between 4 lb. and 6 lb., depending on the extent of the weed hazard and the size of fish expected.

Lines of 4 lb. to 6 lb. b.s. call for a rod with a test curve of about 1 lb. A 10 or 11 foot Avon-type rod will serve in most cases, but a longer rod is often an advantage when fishing over rush fringes or marginal weed beds. Lightness is not of great importance as tench fishing does not call for frequent casting, and for most of the time the rod is supported in rests.

In most cases any good centre-pin reel will suffice, for most tench fishing is done at fairly short range, but a fixed-spool reel can be an asset when fishing at longer range from a boat, or around islands of weed some way out from the bank. The fixed-spool reel usually has the advantage, too, of an extra spool, which enables one to use alternative line-strengths.

Hooks need not be large. The tench's mouth is fairly tough and a small hook will hold quite well once it has penetrated. A selection ranging from No. 8 down to No. 14 will meet most tench-fishing requirements. Eyed or spade-ended hooks can be used, tied directly to the reel-line, but hooks whipped or tied on to separate hook-lengths are often more convenient. In the poor light which so often prevails at the most favourable tench-fishing times, attaching a looped hook-length is much easier than knotting a small hook to the reel-line.

Tench fishing is essentially still-water fishing and there is no need for a float that will support a heavy string of lead shot. The sole purpose of the float is to act as a bite-indicator, and the smallest float that can be comfortably seen will suffice. All that is needed for short-range fishing is a small porcupine quill or, if it is more visible in the circumstances, a 4 in. length of white peacock quill. A slightly larger quill may be necessary when fishing in poor light or at longer range.

Fishing Methods

If large catches of tench are expected, some preliminary preparation is usually necessary. Gaps and open patches in marginal weed-growth are always favourable tench-fishing pitches and it usually pays to clear such a patch if none exists rather than fish the open water. A makeshift weed-drag can be made by festooning barbed wire around a piece of old iron bar or tube, but a couple of rake-heads bound back to back make a handier and more portable device. Tied to a strong rope, the drag is thrown out and drawn ashore repeatedly until a sufficiently large patch is reasonably free from weed.

Some anglers are convinced that this weed clearance actually attracts tench by disturbing the bottom mud in which they find much of their natural food. This may appear so at times, but when possible it is better to do the dragging well in advance of the actual fishing time. It is a big advantage, too, if quantities of ground-bait can be thrown in at regular intervals, to encourage the tench to venture out and feed in the cleared area.

If the hook-bait is bread, the ground-bait can be waste bread, dried in the oven and ground up in a coarse mincer. If worms or maggots are on the hook a quantity of chopped worms or small maggots should be included in the basic bread ground-bait. A proportion of mud or wet sand mixed with the ground-bait will ensure that it sinks quickly to the bottom in the desired area.

For tench a sensitive float-fishing method should be used whenever possible, so that any slight interference with the bait can be detected. Sometimes tench will take a bait boldly and make off with it in no uncertain manner, but very often they are cautious in the extreme, sucking in and blowing out the bait repeatedly, without moving away with it. A sensitive float is needed to indicate bites such as these.

In still water, *laying-on* is an effective way of presenting a bait on the bottom. The float should be a porcupine quill or piece of peacock quill just large enough to be comfortably visible. A single lead shot, just heavy enough to cock the float, should be fixed about 18 ins. from the hook. The distance between shot and float is set at slightly less than the depth of the water, so that the shot is supported by the float and only the baited hook lies on the bottom. The advantage with this method is that a taking fish can pick up the bait without feeling the weight of the lead shot; the snag is that the float gives no positive indication of a bite until the fish moves away with the bait.

A more sensitive arrangement when tench are feeding cautiously is the *shot-leger*, often referred to nowadays as the 'lift' method. The terminal tackle used is the same; a small quill float and a single shot just heavy enough to cock it. With the 'lift' method, however, the shot is placed quite close to the hook, about 2 ins. away, sometimes only 1 in., and it is usual to attach the float by its bottom end only. The tackle is fished with both the baited hook *and* the shot lying on the bottom. The distance from float to shot must be carefully adjusted so that the float is *just* cocked when the shot is on the bottom. Because of the need for precise adjustment of the float for depth, the method can be used only when the water is reasonably calm.

With this arrangement the float registers the slightest interference with the bait. When a tench picks up the bait it also picks up the shot, and the float, relieved of its weight, rises and falls flat on the surface. A swift strike when the float is rising will often hook a tench before it has a chance to eject the bait. Often this 'lift' technique is the only method likely to succeed.

Float-fishing methods are not practicable, of course, in the dark; nor is a float very convenient when there is a strong wind which blows it about and drags the bait along the bottom in an unnatural way. In conditions such as these, however, tench seem to bite more decisively and the float is not so important. Instead, a running leger can be used; that is, a running leger weight loose on the hook-length, with a small split-shot squeezed on about 12 ins. from the hook to act as a stop for the leger weight. The running-weight should not be too heavy; just heavy enough to anchor the bait in the desired spot.

In the absence of the float some other form of bite-indicating device should be used for tench, for they are usually quick to discard a bait if they feel the pull of the rod top. The old

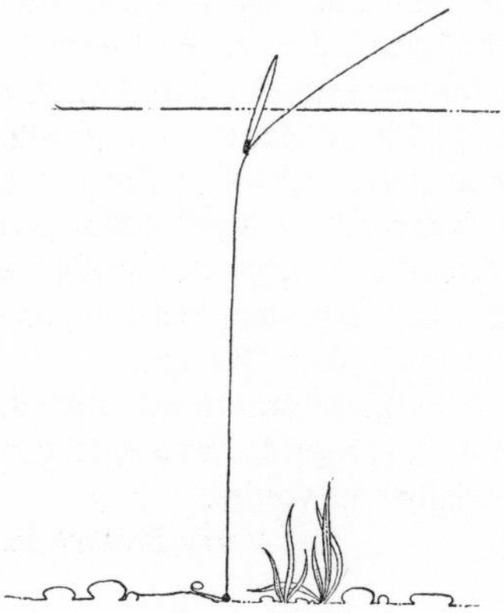

Lift rig for tench

dough-bobbin bite indicator is quite effective when the tench are biting boldly. After the bait has been put out, a loop of line is drawn from between the reel and the first rod ring. A knob of bread paste or a ball of silver paper is squeezed on to this loop to act as an indicator, which will move in response to any slight pull on the line. Much handier, however, are the electric bite indicator and the swing tip, two useful devices which are superseding the old dough bobbin.

Although tench are almost wholly bottom-feeders there are times when they can be caught at the surface. In lakes and ponds where bread is used extensively as bait a certain amount of discarded bread drifts into the marginal shallows. At dusk, when most anglers have departed and all is quiet, carp and tench will often move right inshore, scavenging around the fringes of the pool in search of these pieces of floating bread. These margin feeders can sometimes be taken with a floating bread bait fished under the rod top.

The rod is set up in rests and the bread-baited hook is lowered so that the bread floats on the surface beneath the rod top. A foot or so of line must be drawn from between the reel and the first rod ring, so that a taking fish will not feel immediate resistance when it sucks down the bait.

This margin fishing will sometimes take a few tench when all other methods fail, but conditions must be right. The water must be still, or the floating bread will drag unnaturally on the surface. Also, the angler must be inconspicuous. There must be no disturbance of any kind to drive the tench away from the shallows.

General The probable maximum weight to which tench grow is a matter for conjecture. On the Continent tench of up to 17 lb. are said to have been bred in fish-ponds, but as these were artificially bred this cannot be regarded as natural growth. The British rod-caught record for tench stood at 8 lb. 8 oz., for thirteen years but in 1963 John Salisbury beat this with a 9 lb. 1 oz. tench from a private lake at Kemmingford Grey. It is almost certain, though, that even under natural conditions tench grow larger than this. Occasional bigger fish, ineligible for the rod-caught record, have been reported, including one of 12 lb. 8 oz. taken in 1951 from the River Kennet.

Rod-caught tench of over 6 lb., however, are exceptional. From most waters a tench of 4 lb. is regarded as a specimen and fish of over 5 lb. are especially noteworthy.

Harry Brotherton.

Game Fishing

Glossary

Bulge The hump a trout makes at the surface without actually breaking it, usually when feeding on an insect just below the surface.

Devon minnow A small torpedo-shaped spinning bait with vanes towards the front end and a treble hook attached at the rear.

Drag The V-shaped ripple made on the surface when a dry fly is moving unnaturally across the current. Trout will not look at a fly presented in this way.

Dropper When two or more wet flies are fished on a single cast, the droppers are the flies fixed to the cast by short links and spaced between the end (point) fly and the fly-line itself.

Dry fly A fly tied to sit on the surface and to imitate an insect on the surface film.

Dun A fly of the mayfly family (the Ephemeridae) just after hatching but before shedding its final skin and becoming the perfect fly, or spinner, which is then ready for mating.

False-cast To get out line by casting above the water without dropping the line on the surface, lengthening the amount of line in the air at each forward cast until there is enough out to cover the fish.

Floatant Silicone or paraffin preparation to make line or fly float well.

Fly-line Heavy line of silk or synthetic fibre to which gut or nylon cast and flies are attached. It is the line which the angler casts; cast with fly attached has to follow. Dry-fly lines are tapered so that they can be put down on the water gently and accurately. Wet-fly lines are level. A fly-line is usually about thirty yards long. Some dry-fly lines are made to float without greasing.

Fly reel Usually a simple reel in which the drum is caged or enclosed. There is a permanent check or ratchet on most fly reels.

Greased-line A method of salmon fishing for low-water, summer conditions. Small, sparsely dressed flies are used. The line is greased to make it float.

Grilse A salmon returning to the river from the sea after one year.

Gut Silkworm gut, still the best material for dry-fly casts though nowadays often replaced by tapered nylon.

Feather tied round the shank of a fly to imitate the legs and thorax of an insect. For a dry fly, the hackle comes from a cock, the stiff points helping the fly to float. Wet-fly hackles are softer and come from hens. The movement of the soft fibres under the water adds to the life-like appearance of the fly. *Hackle*

A salmon spent by spawning. *Kelt*

An aquatic insect in the larval stage. Flies are tied to imitate these and are fished below the surface. *Nymph*

Salmon in the first stage of its river life. *Parr*

An artificial spinning bait; the body is made of two flat pieces of plastic or rubber, overlaid. There is a spinning vane at the head. *Phantom*

The last foot or eighteen inches of a nylon or gut fly cast. Since the point inevitably becomes shortened when fresh flies are tied on and old ones cut off, spare points are carried and tied on with a blood-knot. *Point*

Releasing extra line from the hand as the line falls to the surface, in order to make the line and fly fall softly, also to gain extra distance in casting. *Shooting line*

A young salmon that has turned silver and is ready to leave the river for the sea. At the previous stage, when it is marked rather like a small trout, it is known as a parr. *Smolt*

Ephemerid fly in its final stage, ready to mate. A spent spinner is the same fly after mating and when it has fallen dead, or dying, on to the water. *Spinner*

Flies with a long 'wing' made of hair or feather. They imitate prawns, shrimps, or young fish fry, and are used in salmon, sea-trout, and lake trout fishing. *Streamer fly*

A hook with three points on one shaft. *Treble*

A fly designed to fish below the surface. *Wet fly*

Tackle for Game Fishing

There are many possible rods with which to fish for salmon, trout, sea-trout, and grayling in different waters and different conditions. Choice is largely governed by the type of water you are most likely to fish.

Rod	*Fish*	*Reel and line*
1. 6–7 foot brook-trout dry-fly rod	Smallish brown trout (4–14 oz.)	3 inch fly reel and No. 1 (IFI)* tapered line

* Fly-lines are both numbered and code lettered thus: No. 1 or IFI. Increasing numbers denote increasing weight of line.

Rod	*Fish*	*Reel and line*
2. 9–10 foot river-trout dry-fly rod	Larger brown trout (½–4 lb.) on larger rivers	3¼ inch fly reel and No. 2 or 3 (HEH or HDH) tapered line
3. 9–10 foot wet-fly rod	Small (4 oz.), large (2 lb.) brown trout	3¼ inch fly reel and level line
4. 11 foot wet-fly boat rod	Large lake brown trout (½ lb.–6 lb.)	3¾ inch reel and No. 3 or 4 (HDH or HCH) tapered line
5. 11 foot dry-fly rod for reservoir trout	Large lake trout (1 lb.–6 lb.)	3¾ inch reel and No. 4 (HCBG) forward tapered line
6. 9–11 foot sea-trout rod (wet- or dry-, but usually wet-fly)	Sea-trout of 1 lb.–12 lb.	4 inch reel and No. 3 or 4 (HDH or HCH) tapered (dry-) or level (wet-fly) line
7. 12–14 foot, double-handed salmon fly rod	Salmon of 5 lb.–30 lb.	4 inch reel and 40 yard tapered line
8. 9–11 foot salmon spinning rod	Salmon of 5 lb.–30lb.	Multiplier or fixed-spool reel
9. 7 foot split-cane trout spinning rod	Brown or sea-trout	Fixed-spool reel and light nylon monofil line
10. 8 foot steel boat trailing rod	Brown or sea-trout, salmon	Drum reel with heavy check and monofil line

Here again the range of alternatives looks somewhat confusing at first sight. However, in game fishing more than in most forms of the sport choice of rod is practically decided for you by the water in which you expect to do most of your trout or salmon angling.

The point is that any rod will be unmanageable or inadequate if it is inappropriate to the water fished. Just the same, some sort of compromise is possible.

If you expect to fish in the West Country and Wales, most of your rivers will be fairly small. A fair choice if you intend to go in for dry-fly fishing would be something between the first two rods on the list, say an eight-foot split-cane dry-fly rod. You may be a trifle undergunned on the Usk but you will be glad of the short rod when creeping and crawling among the bushes of the Little Exe. An eight-foot rod will throw a line far enough to catch most trout, for it is a fact that most fish are hooked within 15 yds. of the angler.

Wet-fly fishing (see pp. 217–21) is widely practised in the West also. This requires a longer, softer-actioned rod to pick the submerged line off the water. Wet-fly rods for river work are usually between 9 and 10 ft in length.

Still keeping to the same part of Britain (though the pattern could be repeated in Ireland, Scotland, and many other places) you may decide that your first choice is reservoir fishing for big trout. In this instance you have magnificent opportunities at Blagdon Reservoir or at Chew Magna. To punch out a dry fly in a stiff breeze to where the fish are feeding on these waters, you will want a split-cane rod that has a great deal of backbone and will throw a heavy line without strain to itself.

To change the scene entirely: if you intend to fish the limestone lakes of Ireland or the Scottish lochs from a boat, you will want a longish wet-fly rod. So I stress that you must decide (*a*) your area of maximum fishing opportunity, and (*b*) the technique (i.e. wet-fly or dry-fly) which you most want to employ.

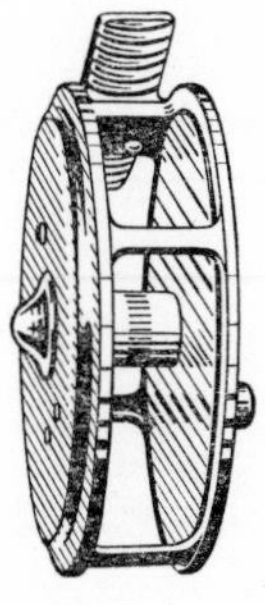

Fly reel

Fly rods and lines are expensive. Perfectly good split-cane rods can be bought for £8 but they can cost as much as £30. You get the craftsmanship you pay for. Fly-lines cost from £3 to £5 but, properly used, have a long life, especially as most of them are reversible and can be used at the opposite end when wear develops. A good fly-line should give at least four seasons' use.

The remaining fly-fishing equipment is relatively cheap. A reel can be bought for from £3 to £5. Flies (see pp. 159–80) work out at about 8*d*.–1*s*. each, nylon leaders at about 5*s*. each. Apart from these you will need a folding landing-net and waders.

Artificial Flies

Some definitions – How to describe an artificial fly? Broadly speaking, there are three sorts: specific imitations of known insects, generalized impressions of small aquatic life, and 'fancy' flies which resemble nothing known to man or fish.

Flies fall into two main categories of use: wet and dry. A wet fly is designed to fish below the surface. A dry fly floats on the water.

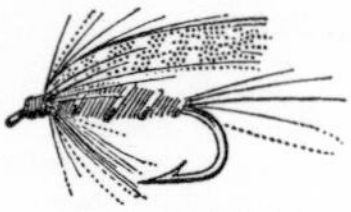
Wet fly

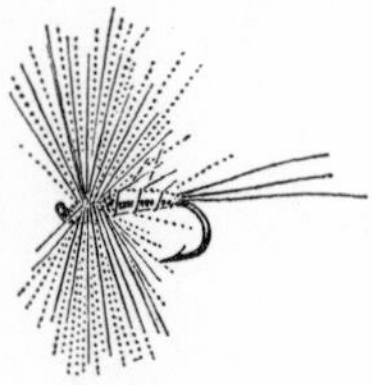
Hackled dry fly

Artificial nymph

In practice, however, there is some overlapping of function. The wet-fly fisher often finds it useful to fish his fly in the surface-film. Dry flies are sometimes fished awash and to describe them as 'dry' in these conditions is a fine quibble. The wise angler fishes his fly the way that catches fish.

Of recent years anglers have elaborated methods of fishing which employ artificials made to resemble the natural fly in its immature state. These particular creations are fished near the bottom, and are called nymphs. In fact they are wet flies in all but name – perhaps they are called otherwise out of deference to chalk-stream pundits whose traditions are against wet-fly fishing. Certainly fish could detect little difference between many wet flies (which are not allowed on most chalk streams) and nymphs (which are); the distinction is purely artificial. When fishing such waters, however, it is wise to conform with tradition and local opinion.

The parts of a simple winged trout fly are as follows: wing, hackle, body, and tail. A simple hackled trout fly is merely: hackle, body, and tail. Most artificial impressions of insects are modelled from these basic constructions.

Oddly enough, the most complex flies resemble nothing in nature. They are compositions in colour, texture, and form intended to exploit the skill of the fly-dresser creating them. Most traditional salmon flies and many of the 'fancier' sea-trout flies come into this group. These beautiful creations have caught fish for generations, but simpler flies catch just as many if given the chance.

The Wet Fly

Wet flies have a long and rich tradition of usage, and some of them have remained almost unchanged since the time of

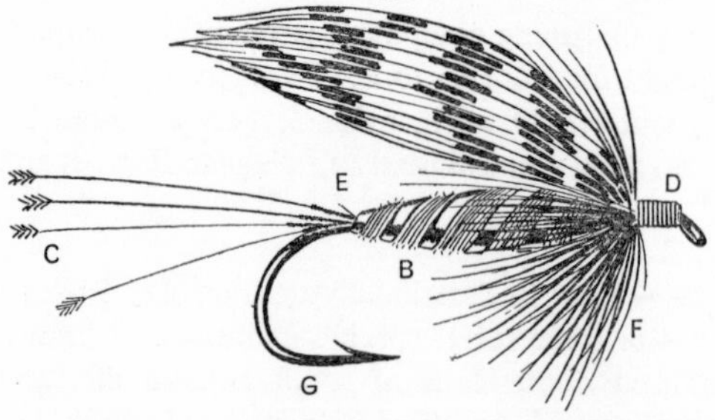

Wet fly: (A) wing tied swept back for easy entry into water; (B) body, made of silk or fur and ribbed with tinsel; (C) tail from feather fibres; (D) head whipped silk secured with varnish; (E) tail tied in at rear of body; (F) soft hen hackle; (G) bend of hook.

Walton and Cotton. Most wet flies are designed to suggest the underwater development of various river flies, or, in other words, to resemble the natural nymph.

They can be constructed to the winged or to the hackled pattern, the former being slightly more difficult to assemble. For practical fishing, in good water, there is little to choose between winged and hackled flies as regards killing.

Winged wet flies are dressed with the wing raked aft to facilitate entry and passage through the water. A well-constructed wet fly often has a wing dressed almost flat along the body. Flies with wings cocked up at a steep angle should be avoided. Hackles on winged flies should be soft and sparse and the fibres should be long enough to reach the point of the hook.

Wingless flies usually have a good deal more hackle. Generally, the soft hen hackles are employed, but the steelier cock hackles are sometimes used for special purposes. A thickly hackled fly is often used as a top-dropper when the angler wishes the fish to see a substantial outline against the sky.

Some general rules: select sparsely dressed flies with hackles of good colour; if they are winged, see that the angle of the wing is right and that it extends to the bend of the hook; the fly should have its parts in proportion to each other.

The Dry Fly

Dry flies too may be hackled or winged, but most modern anglers tend to favour the hackled pattern. Hackled dry flies are constructed to the simple hackle, body, tail formula.

The hackles of dry flies should be stiff and shining – selected from the necks of elderly cockerels. This enables the fly to 'sit' on its hackle points, so to speak, without penetrating the surface film.

Winged dry flies can be tied in several ways, of which the chief are up-winged, forward-winged, and spent. These are intended to imitate the insect at various stages of its life-cycle.

Dry flies vary greatly in quality according to the materials used. A good dry fly, if dropped on to a hard flat surface, should bounce appreciably.

Nymphs

Nymphs are still a matter for much experiment by anglers. Two main forms have evolved; namely, those with body and thorax and a sparse hackle, and those with merely a body. The latter is the simplest sort of artificial possible, and often the most effective.

Nymphs are fished deep, since the natural nymphs live under and between the stones. Weight is given to them as a rule by wrapping the hook-shank with wire or lead foil, but some experts prefer small double hooks, unleaded.

Plastic and other 'manufactured' nymphs should be regarded with distrust. If shape, colour, and weight are correct they should catch fish, but many are too light and they have an inferior texture for the purpose required.

Intermediate Forms There are some artificials which are intermediate between wet and dry, and which, although technically 'wet', are designed to fish on the surface. Typical of these is the chironomid, an impression of one of the many sorts of midge larvae which are found in still water. These creatures cling to the surface-film and breathe through small tubes like a submarine's snorkel.

Lures Among 'flies' which resemble nothing on earth must certainly be included salmon flies, many sea-trout flies, many lake-trout flies, and a wide and startling assortment of Terrors, Demons, Matukas, and other colourful offerings.

Some lures, however, may suggest such specific creatures as, for example, the elvers. Lures often do well in rivers which have a summer elver run. More often, however, lures are used in estuaries where they may suggest the migrating elver, the sand-eel, and the young of colourful marine fishes such as the WRASSE.

Lures must be adequately hooked. Two or even three single hooks in tandem are not too many if the lure extends to 2 or 3 ins., as is common. Lures dressed on a single hook are almost useless in the writer's experience, since fish pluck at the trailing feathers and go away wiser.

They are dressed from soft plumage from fowl and duck, with brighter items added for more positive effect. Peacock, jay, and dyed swan fibres are typical lure materials.

What We Think a Fish Sees Before we can even begin to study artificial flies objectively we should ask ourselves what it is that the fish sees. (See pp. 20–22.) This subject is fraught with difficulty. A fish has the brain of a fish, not of a man, and the images presented by its eyes are interpreted in ways that are obscure. Game fish are known to see certain shades of colour in certain conditions, but which colours and in which conditions is still a matter for speculation by the ordinary angler. Scientists have given us no cut-and-dried statements on this point. Furthermore, in spite of all that has been written about the fish's window (see p. 21) some experienced observers feel that there is room for doubt, in that trout, for example, do not always react the way fish-window diagrams say they should. It is probably wise to work on the assumption that fish see a good deal more than we imagine.

It is untenable that the artificial fly must be matched exactly with the natural in order to obtain good results. Experience is against this belief and so is common sense. If such a criterion were in force, we should never catch fish, simply because the exact imitation of a natural fly is quite beyond man's ingenuity. Even the most skilled of professional fly-dressers admit that their work is crude when compared with the living insect. Simply to imitate colour is difficult enough. Few anglers possess the equipment or technical knowledge needed for pinpointing the exact tint transmitted by a certain fly in certain conditions of light. Translating this tint – when known – into the raw material of the fly-dresser calls for skill far above average. We can only hope to approximate.

Fish see flies flying above or resting on the water-film. They will leap at airborne flies. Flies resting on the surface expose their undersides to the fish. This suggests that elaborate winging on the upper side of the fly is largely wasted effort.

Wet flies come in for quite a different form of scrutiny. Fish look at them from below, from the side, or even from above. Wet flies depend on size, approximate colour, and action for their success. Dry flies rely on size and colour only.

With artificial flies, then, the best we can manage is a compromise based on size, colour, texture, form, and action. The last of these will be discussed later. Fortunately for fishing, our approximations work quite well in practice. When they fail, it is not necessarily the angler's fault but rather because the artificial fly has touched one of the many physical limitations intrinsic in its nature.

Trout Flies – General

Probably no branch of angling has had so much time, expertise, and sheer ingenuity squandered on it as this – the creation and design of the trout fly. The intention at root is simple – to persuade trout that scraps of fur and feather wrapped together in certain ways are in fact an insect of the water. The fascination of the trout fly lies in trying to make it perform this illusion. No matter how often the angler gets away with it, the trick never loses its interest.

There is no exact parallel elsewhere in fishing. Salmon flies are lures and are taken for the same greedy reason that pike snap at a spinner – because they glitter and because they move. There is no real illusion there. There is even less illusion in coarse fishing, where anglers use as bait tasty food which fish eat readily.

A mere catalogue of trout flies would make dull reading. In any case, each expert angler has his own preferences. Some fishermen use fewer than half a dozen patterns throughout the season.

Size of fly is at least as important as pattern, perhaps even more so. Trout can be very particular about fly size. Essentially, this can be traced to the factors of relative visibility and (in wet flies) to the depth at which they are fished. Other things being equal, the larger the wet fly the quicker and deeper it will sink. Conversely, the larger the dry fly the greater the depth at which a fish may be lying and still see it.

In Britain we are still afflicted with a quite nonsensical system of ambiguous hook numbers. Despite protests from anglers over the years, the British Tackle Federation has not standardized its hook sizes. Currently, anglers and angling writers refer to either the Redditch Scale or the New Scale. Sometimes anglers mention hook sizes without indicating to which scale they are related!

The New Scale was introduced by Pennell, who later expressed regret at the confusion he caused. The Redditch or 'Old' Scale is to be preferred and this is the scale referred to in this and subsequent chapters. The Redditch Scale of trout hooks runs from size 20 to size 7. A size 20 hook measures $\frac{5}{32}$ in. overall, not counting the eye. A size 7 hook measures $\frac{3}{4}$ in.

Quality and type of hook become increasingly important as the angler gains in experience and learns to discriminate. Bad hooks are not common, but they do appear. Trout-hook making is a highly skilled operation because of the fineness of the wire used. Tempering is all-important. Under-tempered hooks tend to be soft and will straighten in the fish. Over-tempered hooks are brittle and will snap. The correct mean is a tough, springy hook carefully balanced between these two extremes.

Hook shape is very much a matter of individual opinion and preference. The trade rely mainly on what they describe as 'Wide Gape Trout', 'Limerick', and 'Round Bend' – most makers list their own specialties, but these are essentially more or less ingenious variations on the above.

Sneck – the amount the point is off-set to the shank – is again a matter for preference. On the whole I prefer hooks with little or no sneck. A sneck-less hook with a widish gape and a round bend meets all reasonable requirements.

Eyes are traditionally upturned on dry-fly hooks and downturned on wet-fly hooks. This is largely a fad. Down-eyed hooks suit either dry or wet flies.

Most anglers buy their trout flies, but an increasing number find that simple fly-tying is a relaxing and interesting winter hobby. Information on how to tie simple trout flies is given later in this chapter.

The traditional home of the dry fly is the English chalk streams. Yet floating and semi-floating flies were used in other parts of the country long before the day of Halford and other notables. The chalk-stream anglers rediscovered the dry fly, exploited its possibilities on their particular waters, and turned the whole thing into a high cult.

Chalk-stream dry flies are mostly small in size and are modelled on specific natural flies. Dry flies as used in rain-fed rivers and lakes are often larger and less specific in design. They aim to suggest floating insects, but no insect in particular. C. F. Walker and other recent writers have laboured to persuade anglers to particularize their lake-fly dressings. R. C. Bridgett argued the same more than forty years ago but seemed to make few converts. There are good arguments for both sides.

The 'basic' trout fly, so to speak, is the simple wet fly. It has a rich history. There have been many schools of fly-dressing and we can only admire the artistry and observation of those long-dead anglers, often anonymous, who contributed details to fly-design which have since become universal.

Essentially, one must begin the story of the wet fly in Ireland, where it was first elaborated in all its fullness. Each district had its dresser of note, and as the work of these dressers became tested and approved they often turned professional. The work of the great Irish fly-dressers of the eighteenth century such as Cummess and Gorman is a pleasure to study.

The Irish were impressionists and manipulated their home-produced materials into fluid shapes around the hook. Colour and texture were considered of prime importance; form and size less so. Even today, it is by no means certain what the old-style Irish flies were intended to suggest. But years of painstaking trial and error ensured that they caught fish.

Scotland, too, had its impressionists. A famous school of dressers sprang up on the Clyde. Clyde flies are often winged; and they are long in the wing. The wings too are often mounted at a steep angle, thus breaking the fundamental wet-fly rule. Out of the water Clyde flies look almost ungainly. But in the water, fished according to Clyde methods, they catch fish.

And this must always be our final criterion of a good fly; it is our only sure indication of what a fish sees.

The Yorkshire and North Midland schools had different ideas. The streams they fished were often stony and fast and their flies were sparsely and softly hackled, with slim bodies. Some of our best impressions of nymphal water-flies come from this area, patterns which have been in constant use for 150 years. Silk bodies with hackles of water-hen, coot, or partridge were developed into the so-called 'spiders' which have earned a place in the box of every trout fisher.

Wales too has made her specific and general contributions to the art of fly design. Vaughan senior is a famous name among trout fly-dressers and that splendid all-purpose fly the Coch-y-bondhu is unlikely ever to lose its appeal. There are a great many excellent and effective traditional Welsh patterns.

Modern developments in trout fly-dressing stress the value of synthetic materials. Nylons, Perlons, polymides, and plastics of every shade and type are now in common use to augment the traditional fur and feather of the older schools. Although professional fly-dressers skilfully weave their way through the welter of materials there is a real danger of the amateur getting lost. A good rule is: when in doubt, use the simplest material for the job.

The basic intention is the same today as it was in Walton's time – to deceive the trout. Whether you do it with a piece of polyvinal material or with a scrap of common sheep's wool salvaged from a fence makes no matter.

Sea-Trout Flies

By quaint reasoning there is still a tendency to equate lake flies and sea-trout flies. They are not synonymous and never have been. Big tinsel-bodied lake wet flies will catch sea-trout sometimes just as sedge-suggesting river flies will catch lake fish. But, as groups, flies for lakes and flies for rivers are apart. Sea-trout in lakes often respond best to flies you would never use in a river.

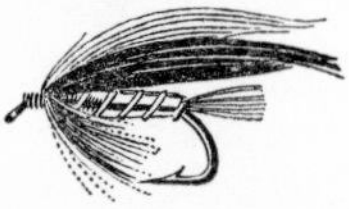

Typical sea-trout lure

On the whole, sea-trout flies are mostly 'fancy' flies of traditional design, the most important innovation since the war being the introduction of fluorescent wool, chenille, and monofil. Used correctly, fluorescent materials catch more sea-trout. Used incorrectly, they catch no better than any other dressing.

With sea-trout flies self-weighted tubes were another useful development. These tubes, of aluminium lined with plastic, carry a sparse dressing, frequently of hair. A fine wire treble is mounted at the tail. A small brass head can be used as a sinker.

Salmon Flies

The modern trend is quite definitely towards hairwing flies dressed on self-weighted tubes with a treble at the tail. Salmon anglers find that these inexpensive flies catch quite as many fish as the glorious traditionals with their kaleidoscopic colouring. Moreover, hairwings fish better.

Yet there is still a place for the Jock Scotts, Black Doctors, Silver Wilkinsons, and so forth if for no better reason than sentiment. After all, salmon fishing is largely a ritual, and the ritual killing of our greatest game fish does seem to argue the poetic rightness of using something more aesthetically satisfying than a bunch of brown dog-hairs mixed with a bit of bottle-top foil. It is a great pleasure to select, mount, and fish the traditional fully dressed salmon fly. But if the reader is interested in results at a low cost he is advised to stick to tubes.

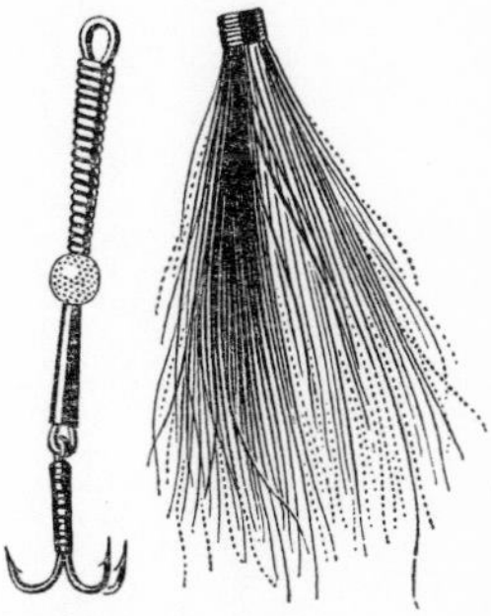

Hairwing, streamer, or tube-fly

Amateur Fly-Dressing

The dressing of simple dry and wet trout flies, flies for sea-trout and tubes for sea-trout and salmon, presents no real difficulties. Time and a little patience are more important here than great manual dexterity. It is easy enough to buy shop flies, but there are two arguments in favour of tying one's own: (i) it leads the angler's interest into a new and absorbing field; (ii) it enables flies of the desired sort for any particular water to be produced cheaply and at will.

The beginner will soon be confronted with the mystique of fly-dressing. In the end he may decide to join the coterie, learn its language, and produce mysteries of his own. The cult of the hackle is typical of fly-dressing mysticism, a hackle of course being a small feather usually from the ruff or neck of a domestic fowl. The hackle cult centres on the Andalusian and other breeds of show fowls. A high-grade Blue Dun neck is regarded as very choice material and the highest-quality Blue Dun necks may fetch as much as £5 or even £10 in private sale. Such feathers, in fact, are almost literally worth their weight in gold. A friend of the writer has a Blue Dun neck some 110 years old – possibly the oldest specimen in Britain. Produced originally as a utility item, this neck has now become a priceless collector's piece.

Equipment and Materials: A small amount of mechanical equipment is needed. The following will be found adequate: a fly-tying vice with a pointed nose, and fitted with a table clamp; a silk-bobbin holder; hackle pliers; fine scissors; an adjustable lamp of the Anglepoise type; a few hundred hooks of various sizes; Durofix adhesive; some cobbler's wax; silk in various shades; and a selection of tubing for tube-flies. That leaves us with the material to collect.

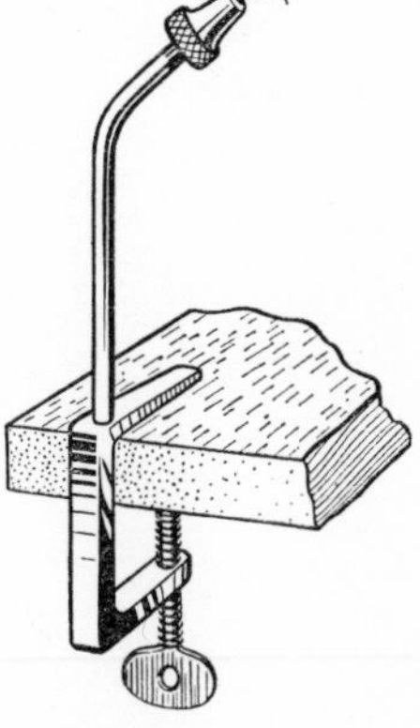

Fly-tying vice

In amateur fly-dressing, a little goes a long way. A moleskin lasts for ages. A single heron primary will continue to supply blue-grey fibres long after the angler has forgotten where he picked it up. Variety rather than quantity should be the key-note of a collection of materials. The importance of quality – as regards the colour, texture, and soundness of the material – goes without saying.

Once the fly-tying beginner gets behind the magic and mystery he finds that simple materials often make the best flies, and many materials can be picked up by walking through the countryside with one's eyes open.

Here are some typical items which will start a useful collection:

Red, black, brown, and honey cock and hen hackles
Pheasant feathers (from neck, rump, and tail), cock and hen
Mallard duck and drake feathers (flank and neck)
Jackdaw throat hackles
Partridge (back and breast)
Teal feathers (flank, breast, and neck)
Snipe and moorhen wings
Peacock eye-feathers
Heron primary feathers
Blackbird, swallow, and thrush feathers (various)
Martin, sandpiper, corncrake, and rook feathers
Furs: rabbit, mole, squirrel tail, water-rat
Tinsels: silver oval and flat; gold oval and flat
Wool: various colours
Silks: red, purple, yellow, brown, and olive shades
Fine gold and silver wire

Many of these materials can be collected during walks in the country. Some – such as peacock – may be purchased from the suppliers of tying materials. Feathers from protected small birds such as swallows and martins can be obtained around nesting-sites, sometimes from discarded nests. £1 spent with a coastal wild-fowler or a poulterer will supply more assorted plumage than the fly-dresser will use for the rest of his life.

Tying Trout Flies: A simple trout fly that will catch fish consists of only two parts – body and hackle. Let us suppose that we want to tie half a dozen flies suitable for use in a moorland stream and likely to take fish at more or less any time throughout the season. No attempt is made at imitating any particular insect; we aim here at a general impression which could be any of a dozen species of hatching nymphs.

A March Brown Pheasant Tail is a splendid general pattern. Tie it to hooks of size 10, 12, and 14 Redditch scale.

The materials needed are a cock-pheasant long centre-tail feather and a few brown partridge hackles, plus a piece of fine gold wire and a spool of brown silk.

Fit the hook into the vice, eye pointing to the right of the operator. Wrap the silk around the shank opposite the hook-barb and overlap to trap it. Smear a little Durofix, or similar quick-drying cement, on the silk and along the shank. Trim away any waste silk hanging.

Place four cock-pheasant tail fibres against the hook and trap the tips with two turns of silk. Repeat with the end of the fine gold wire. Holding wire and fibres to one side, wind the silk evenly along the shank to within a quarter of an inch of the eye of the fly.

Now wind the fibres as evenly as possible forward over the silk. Tie off near the eye with two turns of silk. Follow up with the gold wire. Tie off.

Now take a partridge hackle. Tie it in at the shoulder of the fly by the tip, stroking the remaining fibres to the rear. Wind the silk forward to the eye. Using the hackle pliers, give the hackle two or three turns around the shank and trap it in position with the silk while holding it taut.

Trim the hackle flush. Secure all material by giving the fly a neat silk head. Make the final tie with a half-hitch and solidify the silk with a little Durofix. Trim.

Very many amateurs could tie such a simple fly in less than a minute.

Fly-dressers seldom agree over details and there is no reason why they should. Laying aside the dogmas of fly-dressing – the 'principles' – tying flies really boils down to neatness and security. Neatness pleases the workman in us and makes for more efficient assembly. Security is achieved by correct assembly and the use of cellulose cement. Flies that come apart during fishing are a source of wasted time and annoyance.

To catch a trout a fly needs only a body and a hackle. Indeed, one can dispense with the hackle. The fly is then a fair representation of a nymph and, if fished in the manner suitable for such an impression, will catch fish admirably.

Winging: Most of us, however, love to pretend that we can imitate living insects in all their details. We add tails to our flies; sometimes we give them wings. Wings, however, have a rather special use, for by making a more bulky silhouette they enable fish to see the fly in darker water.

Winging a fly such as a March Brown Pheasant Tail takes a certain amount of dexterity. This particular fly is best winged with a brownish feather to suit its dull hue. A hen-pheasant feather does the job very well.

After tying in the hackle but before forming the head of the fly, tie in the wings. Cut two slips of fibres from opposite sides of the feather. Place the slips together and pinch them firmly with the finger and thumb of the left hand.

Place the wings in position and secure by winding the silk very firmly over the butts. The grip must not be relaxed. After about four turns of the silk the wings should be checked for alignment. Complete the head and varnish. Special winging pliers help with this operation but are not essential.

Flies for lake trout, rainbow trout, grayling, and other fish can all be constructed in this way. For fur bodies, the fur is spun around the silk before winding. Tags and tails may be needed according to the pattern used. Other materials such as quill and herl are wound on in the same manner as the pheasant tail fibres.

Salmon Flies: The tying of built-wing salmon flies is a highly skilled job and one beyond the ability of all but advanced amateurs. It is purely a labour of love – and an expensive one at that. The materials for traditional salmon flies become dearer and harder to obtain each season.

The practical angler who ties his own salmon flies, as I do, has no need to purchase exotic plumages. Hairwing flies and flies made from simple materials such as turkey, swan, and duck will catch fish quite well. In fact, many experts prefer these simple flies.

Although the big salmon 'irons' are no longer as popular as they were it is useful to have a few with one for early spring fishing. They sink well and are not hard to release from the jaws of kelts; and there are days when one catches nothing but kelts. Bodies of flat silver tinsel with a low broad wing and a black or brownish hackle do well if sunk deep. There is nothing hard about constructing such flies.

For late spring and summer fishing, tube-flies have quite swept the field, the nylon tube itself being simply a piece of discarded ball-point pen tubing. Self-weighted tubing can be bought. A brass head prevents skating on the surface.

To dress a tube one presses it on to a darning needle of suitable size. The needle is gripped in the vice, so that the tube is firm and has no tendency to turn. The dressing is then assembled around the tube. To mount for fishing, one runs the brass head up the leader followed by the tube and both are retained by a treble hook tied to the leader end. When a fish is hooked the tube washes up the leader and the dressing is preserved. An important advantage, this, on days when one hooks nothing but toothy kelts.

Another advantage of tube-flies is that one can increase or decrease the size of the fly according to conditions. If a 1 in. tube is in use and conditions suggest that this is too small, one has only to remove the treble and add another tube, and at once one has a 2 in. tube-fly.

Furthermore, by varying the dressings on the tubes one can build up composite flies. Two $\frac{3}{4}$ in. tubes plus a $\frac{1}{2}$ in. tube, each variously dressed, will give a 2 in. fly to suit whatever the conditions demand.

Almost no useful suggestions can be made about dressings since salmon flies vary from dingy March Browns to concoctions that would shock a rainbow. Dull hues will catch fish when brilliant ones fail. I like silver tinsel for spring work, gold for summer. Hair has a better action than feather.

Many sorts of hair can be used to dress tubes. Squirrel – fine and silky – is good; so is polar-bear, if you can get some. Polar-bear dyes well and has a brilliance all of its own. Moreover, it is proofed by nature against damp.

Artificial flies still offer a huge field for practical research and development. The last answer is never the final answer. Fish react to subtle environmental changes about which we know little, and this tempers their reaction to flies, real and simulated.

Years of experience lie behind traditional patterns so they should not be lightly discarded. Personally, I use traditional patterns and materials with a leavening of moderns and experimentals.

F. W. Holiday

Natural Flies

Entomology Related to Angling. For hundreds of years fly-fishing in Britain was an elementary sport, in that anglers were aware of only two or three of the commoner water-flies. By about 1850 observation, experiment, and the development of the fly-dressing art had extended the original few flies to well over a dozen.

The early fly-dressers, having the acuteness to realize that they couldn't imitate the natural exactly, used their wits and dexterity in order to simulate or suggest. Towards the end of the last century, however, new influences spread from the southern chalk-streams. Pocket-lenses, manuals of entomology, and tools for removing the contents of a fish's stomach became part of the angler's kit. Every known water-fly was catalogued and artificials were produced aiming at exact duplication.

Today, the tide has long turned. Although entomology for its own sake is an interesting hobby it is rather pointless to mix it up too much with fishing. Minute knowledge of every stage of each insect's life-cycle is not an indispensable requirement for the catching of fish. Some of us feel that the schools of exact imitation of the last century were really cults of bluff and magic designed to impress the uninitiated. To that extent they did real harm by frightening many people away from fly-fishing.

Some good, however, did come out of this excursion into the study of water-flies. Anglers gained a clearer image of how insects live and develop. The fanatical collection of specimens showed that many flies vary widely, even among individuals of the same species, which of course made exact imitation even more fatuous. In reaction, most common-sense anglers took to using artificials which suggested an average fly of any given species. Thus was the bubble of exact imitation pricked.

Since the Second World War one or two first-class textbooks of entomology have been produced, chief of which is J. R. Harris's *An Angler's Entomology* (Collins' New Naturalist Series). A great many fly-fishers lean heavily on this standard textbook, for although exact imitation is an absurdity, there is a short list of flies on which it pays to be knowledgeable. By studying these in relation to our fishing it is possible to increase one's bags of fish.

Flies of River and Stream

It is a traditional, and sound, practice for anglers to fish differing flies according to the month. In the past, Welsh anglers used to differ their patterns according to which wild flowers were in bloom. This was good reasoning because the flowering of plants is a much surer guide to the weather than a date on the almanac, as we know to our cost in Britain's climate. Like plants, flies need moisture and warmth.

Some anglers and writers use the Latin names of natural flies for more exact identification. Although essential for scientific purposes, this practice can easily become pedantic, and a pedantic fly-fisher is well on the way to becoming a bore. The names used in this chapter refer to flies as defined by J. R. Harris, who is now the standard authority.

The flies of chief interest to river anglers divide into four groups: Day-flies (Ephemeroptera), Sedge-flies, Stone-flies, and miscellaneous insects.

Natural Flies

Day-flies. This is the most important – although not the largest – group of anglers' flies. It includes the Olives, Iron Blues, March Browns, Pale Wateries, Mayflies, and Blue-winged Olives.

Specimens of these flies are found in most clean running water in Britain. Some species, however, tend to be localized, conditions sometimes favouring one at the expense of another.

All day-flies have a similar life-cycle. The nymphs emerge from eggs deposited, usually in shallow water, by the parent fly. A stone turned over at the edge of a stream nearly always uncovers one or two day-fly nymphs, which may be seen scuttling for shelter. Nymphs hatch into flies by first swimming or drifting to the surface. The fly must then free itself from the nymphal skin, or 'shuck', during which operation it is quite defenceless and falls an easy prey to fish. Once free of its shuck, it flies off the water as a dun. The drier and warmer the weather the quicker the fly can leave the water and thus escape the trout.

The dun stage of the fly's life is of varying duration according to the weather and may be minutes or even days. Sooner or later, however, the dun – which has now taken refuge amongst bank-side vegetation – is ready to shed its skin once more. In its final form it creeps forth as a spinner or perfect fly.

With day-flies, then, we have three distinct forms: nymph, dun, and spinner. To these may be added a fourth phase, that of the spent gnat; this is simply a spinner which has laid its eggs and sunk, dying, on the water.

Trout can be caught on artificials suggesting any of these stages. Broadly speaking, however, most fly-fishers are interested in dun and spinner impressions unless the fish are very obviously feeding on the other forms.

Natural flies must be considered in relation to the two main types of river system we have in Britain. These systems are: rain-fed streams and chalk-streams. Rain-fed streams usually rise in moorland; their flooding after rain and subsequent fall are often rapid. Frequently they are swift and stony. Chalk-streams rise from springs in the deep chalk strata. They are clear and slow-flowing and flooding is rare. They afford ample cover for huge numbers of day-fly nymphs. Rain-fed rivers on the other hand often offer little cover, since their weed-beds are sparse. Their fly hatches therefore are often meagre and patchy.

The rain-fed or rough-stream angler – and this includes something like ninety-eight per cent of British fly-fishermen – has a different approach from that of the chalk-stream angler. The former usually mounts a fly-pattern suitable for the day and the season. The latter often prefers to wait until flies hatch in the sheltered reaches he fishes and offer him a chance to identify them.

We will now consider the day-flies common to both types of river along with the fly-dressings which suggest them. This short list of day-flies starts off with the commonest of the Olives – the Large Dark or Large Spring Olive. Some Welsh and West Country anglers call this fly the Blue Dun.

The L.D.O. is found throughout Britain. It hatches in the coldest weather and is very welcome to winter-starved trout. The L.D.O. dun is a fly about half an inch long with bluish-grey wings and a brownish-olive body.

A good dressing for the L.D.O. is the Blue Upright, a traditional Devonshire pattern. A Welsh friend with over fifty years of fly-fishing to his credit converted me to its use. There may be some difficulty in obtaining the correct hackle for this fly, which should be a dark blue game-cock hackle with stiff shining fibres – just one of the occasions when a cock's hackle is used in a wet fly:

Hackle: Dark blue game-cock
Tail: A few game-cock fibres
Body: Peacock stripped quill to give well-marked light and dark bands
Hook: 10 and 12 (Redditch Scale)

The spinner stage of the L.D.O.'s cycle is suggested by a simple Red Spinner pattern. When using a 'team' of three wet flies it is good practice to mount the Red Spinner as a bob-fly. Or a cock hackle can be used in place of hen and the fly fished dry:

Body: Red silk ribbed with finest gold wire
Hackle: Pale honey hen
Tail: Fibres of honey hen
Hook: 10s and 12s

The only other Olive the angler need worry about is the Medium Olive. True, the Small Dark Olive sometimes appears but a separate pattern is not warranted.

The Medium Olive is the Yellow Dun of our grandfathers. It is a smaller fly than the L.D.O., with blue-grey wings and a bright yellowish-olive body. One of the best patterns is the Rough Olive, another old West Country dressing:

Body: Olive seal's fur, well mixed with a pinch of orange
Hackle: Dark blue hen
Tail: Fibres of blue hen
Hook: 12s and 14s.

The March Brown is localized in distribution. There are heavy hatches of the fly on some Welsh rivers; in some other places it is seldom observed. It is a largish rather coarse-looking fly of drab, mottled appearance.

March Brown patterns are legion and catch fish even in water which never harbours the natural. This is almost certainly because the dingy brownish dressing suggests the hatching nymphs of several fly species. A useful pattern is the Hackled March Brown:

Body: Brown rabbit's fur ribbed with finest gold wire
Hackle: Dark partridge
Tail: Pale mallard fibres
Hook: 10s and 12s

The Iron Blue is a small fly which enjoys cold blustery weather. Some anglers reap their best baskets of spring trout with an Iron Blue pattern, especially in April and May. Hatches are variable; sometimes heavy. Fish feed greedily on the nymph.

There are many dressing variations of the Iron Blue, but a simple and very effective tie is as follows:

Body: Tag of scarlet silk. Blue-grey mole's fur ribbed with scarlet silk.
Hackle: Light blue dun hen
Tail: Fibres from Rhode Island Red cock
Hook: 12s and 14s

The name Pale Watery is a convenient label for several similar species of flies, including the Sky-blue Dun, the Blue-winged Pale Watery, and the Pale Evening Dun. These creatures are as lovely as their names.

The Pale Wateries appear from mid-May onwards. They are medium-sized flies and always look most conspicuous when the light glistens on their wings as they rise from the water. The writer has enjoyed excellent catches using Pale Watery patterns.

Two dressings will be adequate for most anglers – a wet:

Body: Bright yellow silk ribbed with finest gold wire
Hackle: Pale blue dun hen
Tail: Fibres of a honey or white cock spade-feather
Hook: 12s and 14s

and a dry:

Body: Amber or pale orange silk ribbed with finest gold wire
Hackle: Stiff, shining honey cock
Tail: Fibres of honey or white cock
Hook: 12s and 14s

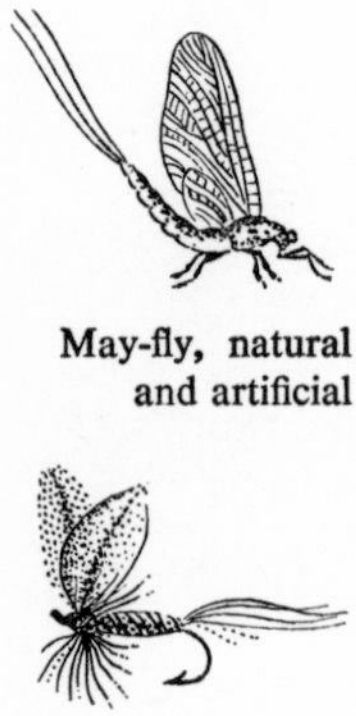

May-fly, natural and artificial

Mayfly: The Mayfly is the largest and best known of the day-flies. It seems, however, to be becoming less common and one frequently hears the complaint that hatches are not what they were. This may be due in part to the fact that, with deeper drainage and regular dredging, rivers are getting rid of their water much faster nowadays. Mayfly nymphs thrive in a habitat of mud and sand.

On chalk-streams the Mayfly hatch is an event of some importance. This is less true of rough streams, many of which – for example, the Usk – hardly know the May. I have, however seen the Usk covered with duns of the Yellow May, a fly not much smaller than the May and probably just as succulent to the fish.

One Welsh river ends its course in flat country where suitable beds of muddy sand are retained. For two or three days each year there is an enormous hatch of Mays and the fish will look at nothing else. A few miles upstream, however, not a fly will be found.

The dun stage of the Mayfly's cycle is known as the Green-drake. The spinner stage is known as Grey Drake (female) and Black Drake (male).

Of all the very many Mayfly patterns that have been devised probably none is better than Goulden's Favourite and its variations. This dressing makes use of the fact that the glittering wings of a hovering Mayfly appear to be orange when viewed in a certain light. Richard Walker once gave me some of his Mayflies, which are constructed on the above principle. On the few occasions when I have fished during our brief Mayfly hatch I found these to be very effective.

Here is a useful variation of Goulden's Favourite:

Body: Olive 'Raffene' (artificial raffia) ribbed with scarlet floss silk (doubled)
Hackles: First hackle: Dark Rhode Island Red cock
Second: Hot orange hen
Third: Grey mallard, left natural or dyed green
Tail: A few cock-pheasant centre-tail fibres
Hook: 8s and 10s (Mayfly hooks)

This pattern can be fished either dry or wet. Wet fishing is often useful at the tail-end of a spate, when Mays are hatching and getting washed down-river.

The Blue-winged Olive (B.W.O.) is common to a great many rivers. On the Teifi it is almost the only day-fly to hatch in quantity during the summer. It is a largish fly with four conspicuous bluish wings and can be observed rising languidly from the water on thundery, airless days in July and August.

The B.W.O. has the reputation of being a difficult fly to match successfully with an artificial. The truth is that trout can be mighty fickle in the heat of summer and unless there is a really heavy hatch of B.W.O. they just don't bother to feed.

In some conditions trout seem to prefer the B.W.O. spinner to the dun, perhaps because they can see it better.

Here is a simple pattern for the B.W.O. dun:

Body: Olive tying silk ribbed with finest gold wire
Hackle: Grey-blue game-hen
Tail: Brownish fibres from a cock's spade-feather
Hook: 10s and 12s

The B.W.O. spinner has long been dubbed the 'Sherry' spinner owing to its tawny colour. An excellent dressing is as follows:

Body: Ruddy fibres from a cock-pheasant centre-tail feather ribbed with finest gold wire
Hackle: Dark R.I.R. cock
Tail: R.I.R. cock fibres
Hook: 10s and 12s

Sedge-flies. The sedge-flies, or caddis-flies, offer the angler exciting and interesting fishing. Even the biggest trout, fish which have long fallen into the reprehensible habit of eating nothing but small trout and minnows, will rise to a sedge.

The sedge begins life as a larva living on the river-bed in a tube made of silk, to which is attached a variety of materials such as sand, tiny twigs, and gravel. On rivers fished by the writer, trout stuff themselves with sedge-larvae, especially in the spring. Fortunately, the immense number of larvae prevents their extinction from this cause. I calculate that a typical pool on the Teifi may be supporting anything up to 10,000 sedge in their cases.

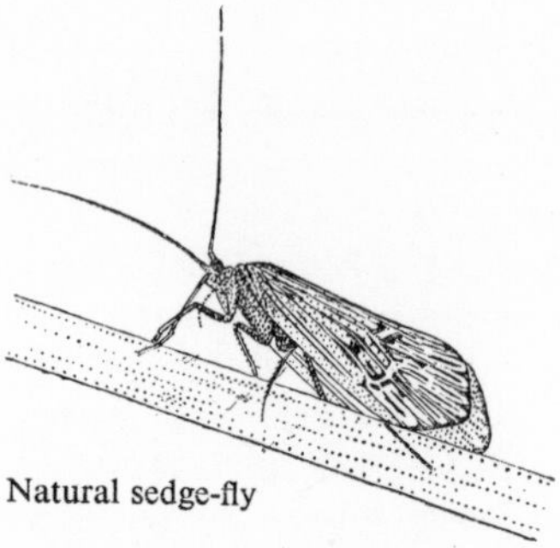

Natural sedge-fly

Although there are 185 sedge-fly species in Britain only a very few are of particular interest to the angler. Fish are usually caught on what might be called 'generalized sedge-suggesting patterns'. A few species, however, are worth suggesting by more specific dressings.

Broadly speaking, sedges are flies of the summer; the ones most useful to the angler are those which hatch in the evenings. Sedges love humidity; damp warm air is their delight. Dry air – whether warm or cold – they dislike. Evenings of very fine misty rain or humid nights with a hint of thunder in the offing are the ones on which to expect heavy sedge hatches.

The angler experienced at fishing the sedge knows what to look for. The swirl of a good fish at dusk on a damp evening as described is a sure sign that sedges are hatching. And that means that one of the best opportunities in fishing is on offer.

The sedges most familiar to the angler are: Grannom, Great Red Sedge, Cinnamon Sedge, Grey Sedge, Brown Silver-horn, and Silver Sedge.

There are many brownish and greyish sedges which can be suggested by a single pattern. A good pattern is that given by R. C. Bridgett, in his book *Sea-Trout Fishing* published in 1926, under the name Silver March Brown.

Here is the variation used by the writer:

Body: White rabbit's fur ribbed with flat silver tinsel
Hackle: Brown speckled partridge

Wing: Mottled hen pheasant
Tail: Pale mallard fibres
Hook: 10s and 12s

This is an excellent all-purpose sedge pattern. The hen-pheasant wing may be dressed narrow or full, the former for dusk, the latter for night use. In the dark this fly will also pass muster for a moth.

Specific sedge patterns will now be considered. Many of these are of day-flying sedges, for a trout's power of discrimination of course wanes at the onset of darkness.

Grannom: Grannom are the earliest of the sedges to appear, usually hatching towards the end of April on a mild wet day. The angler will suddenly observe hundreds of small ash-coloured flies weaving and circling low over the water and banks. Nearly every trout in the river will be busy feeding.

Observation persuades me that fish take the Grannom at the instant of eclosion, i.e. as it frees itself from its nymphal shuck and flies off the water.

Here is a traditional pattern for the hatching Grannom:
Body: Mole's fur dyed a dark green in picric acid.
Hackle: Two light brown partridge neck feathers
Hook: 14s

In practice a simple hackled March Brown often does nearly as well. Fished deep, trout probably mistake it for the ascending pupa. Thus:

Body: Dark rabbit fur ribbed with finest gold wire
Hackle: Brown partridge
Hook: 14s

Grannom are also known as 'Greentails', since the females develop a bluish-green cluster of eggs. Some anglers like a small amount of bluish floss silk to suggest this feature.

Silverhorns: There are several sedges of this name, all of them very common in summer and widely distributed. The most useful of the group for the angler is perhaps the brown variety, for which almost any sort of small brown-hackled fly can be used.

Grey Sedge: Some species of Grey Sedge are not unlike the Grannom although they appear much later, being flies of June and July. On warm fine evenings trout and sometimes sea-trout can be seen feeding greedily on Grey Sedge, at the margins of the pools, and especially beneath bushes. Various patterns have been suggested, none of which I have found entirely satisfactory. Harris suggests a grey fur body, grizzled dun hackle, and woodcock wing. Thomas Clegg once tied me some with a woodcock wing and a mixed seal's fur body which did quite well.

Cinnamon and Great Red Sedges: These are the classic sedges of the chalk-waters. They are also the largest. The Silver March Brown generalized pattern gives fair results as a wet fly, but for the dry-fly fisher there is little to beat a well-hackled Red Palmer.

Silver Sedge: The Silver Sedge, as the name suggests, is a silvery fly with ginger legs. In the summer, on lakes, it can save the angler's day. Watch for it hatching in the quiet sunlit water around weed-beds.

Here is a useful wet pattern:

Body: Two strands of wool, one plain and one lemon. Lay together and wind down the hook
Wing: Silver-grey mallard
Hackle: Reddish-brown partridge or red cock
Hook: 10s

Grouse-wing: On some lakes there is a sedge, related to the Silverhorns, whose mottled wings suggest the mottled plumage of a grouse. A rare example, this, of a fly being named after the fly-dressing material used to simulate it.

Here is a typical dressing:

Body: Maroon silk ribbed with finest gold wire
Wing: A slip of grouse tail fibres, rolled
Hackle: Red cock wound in front of wing
Hook: 10s

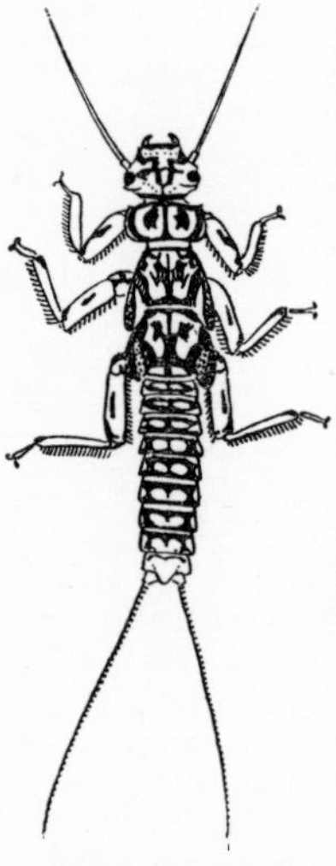

Natural stone-fly larva

Stone-flies. Stone-fly nymphs are crawling creatures, hence the North Country name 'creepers'. They are fearless and may be picked up for inspection.

The nymphs are very active, and most species crawl ashore before emerging as adult flies from the nymphal shuck. This limits their value in trout fishing, since there is no moment of eclosion when the nymph lies on the water completely at the mercy of fish.

Brown Trout

Salmo trutta (page 210)
Specimens 3 lb and over
Record 18 lb 2 oz

Rainbow Trout

Salmo irideus (page 231)
Specimens 3 lb and over
Record 8 lb 8 oz

Char

Salvelinus alpinus (page 252)
Seldom over a pound

Pollan

Coregonus pollan (page 251)
Not a sporting quarry

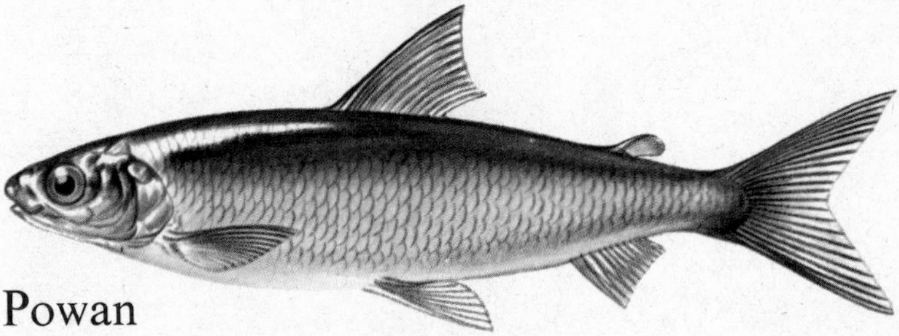

Powan

Coregonus clupeoides (page 250)
Not a sporting quarry

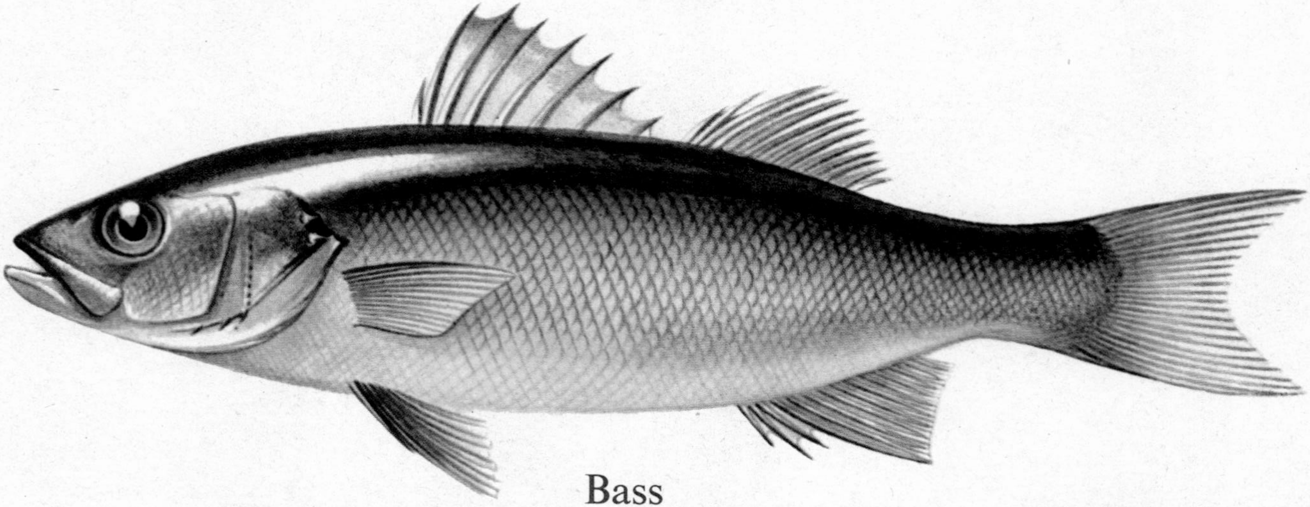

Bass

Morone labrax (page 260)
Specimens 8 lb and over
Record 18 lb 2 oz

Large stone-flies and their nymphs are traditionally difficult to simulate successfully and no very successful pattern has been evolved.

February Red and Early Brown: These are the earliest of the stone-flies. The first of them is one I have never encountered, although it is said to occur in Wales. The Early Brown is common and widely distributed. Like all stone-flies it has a long narrow body and strong legs.

A traditional general pattern which suggests both these species and can hardly be improved upon is tied thus:

Body: Orange tying silk ribbed with finest gold wire
Hackle: Brown partridge
Tail: Partridge fibres

Needles: Needle-flies are locally common, especially towards the end of summer. As the name suggests they are slender flies. The artificial is said to kill well in September. Dark Spanish Needle is a traditional Yorkshire tie for this fly; a partridge-and-orange, very sparsely hackled, is a fair simulation.

Large Stone-fly: This insect makes an appearance in late April, when the angler may observe them crawling clumsily about in wet grasses fringing the water. They are commonly as long as 1½ ins.

If big stone-flies are hatching it is a sure sign that their nymphs must be crawling ashore prior to that event. The natural nymph of the stone-fly is large enough to be used as bait.

Artificial patterns of the Large Stone-fly are notoriously mediocre in effect. I have occasionally taken the odd fish by using the following simple pattern.

Body: Dark rabbit fur and olive seal's fur mixed and dubbed sparsely on the hook
Wing: Hen pheasant dressed full
Hackle: Brown partridge
Hook: 6s

Willow-fly: Heavy hatches of this fly are sometimes noticed. The angler brushing through bank-side vegetation sometimes finds his jacket strewn with them. Again, this means that the fish will be active against the nymph as it crawls ashore. Fished slowly near the bottom any small, dark, weighted nymph is likely to catch fish in these circumstances. A simple but effective tie is a P.T. nymph of the sort commonly used on the Avon.

Body: Two even layers of fine copper armature wire. Overlay with cock-pheasant tail fibres ribbed with fine gold wire
Hackle: None, or two turns of black hen
Hook: 10s

Miscellaneous Insects. *Hawthorn:* The artificial Hawthorn is a mystery fly. The natural has a short season. It is easily mistaken, however, for such species as Black Gnat and Heather Fly, which may explain why the artificial Hawthorn kills fish throughout the summer.

There are several tyings for the Hawthorn. The following is probably as good as any:

Body: Black floss silk dressed slim
Hackle: Black hen
Hook: 10s

As a dry fly the above pattern can be usefully modified by adding a few turns of white cock hackle at the throat, thus making the fly a 'bi-visible'.

Alder: The Alder (or Orl Fly) is another mystery fly. It makes its appearance in early summer and looks rather like a medium-sized sedge. It hatches on land but crawls about on vegetation near the water.

Do fish feed on the natural Alder? There seems to be real doubt, for there have been frequent reports of Alders falling into the water and failing to stir the interest of fish. The artificial, however, does catch fish – perhaps due to its sedge-like appearance.

A simple pattern is:

Body: Peacock herl dyed claret
Hackle: Black hen – two turns
Hook: 12s

Coch-y-bondhu: The Coch-y-bondhu is said to be the red and black beetle familiar on Welsh mountainsides in early summer. Breezes often carry the flying beetles over the water in great numbers. The traditional artificial is deservedly famous, for it is probably the best beetle-impression ever devised, and trout are very fond of beetles.

Body: Peacock herl dressed oval in a plane parallel to the hook-bend
Hackle: Hen coch-y-bondhu (black centre, red tip)

Tail: Bend of hook wound with flat gold tinsel
Hook: 10s, 12s, and 14s

A Coch-y-bondhu with a body ribbed with flat gold makes a good fly for sea-trout and a splendid top-dropper for summer lake fishing.

One Welsh expert prefers long-fibred cock coch-y-bondhu hackles instead of the above.

A variation of Coch-y-bondhu, known as Cochyn, is popular on the Usk. Mr A. S. Pleace gave me the following dressing:

Body: Green peacock herl
Hackle: Dark R.I.R. hen, long in the fibre
Hook: 6s and 8s

Black Gnat: This fly has been given a lot of attention over the years, probably too much. It is a small blackish fly with pale wings, rather like a diminutive house-fly. A small Hawthorn makes a satisfactory artificial.

Lake Flies

There are at least as many species of lake flies as there are flies of the river. While some flies frequent both still and running water this is certainly not always the case, as C. F. Walker has shown. Opinions are still divided on whether to simulate actual lake species or to use traditional patterns which were adopted, presumably, merely because they caught fish. The choice is open. Nevertheless it is useful to have a working knowledge of lake insects, since at times fish most certainly do feed on one specific species.

Pond Olive: Pond Olives are day-flies. They are found throughout the season in nearly all clean, still water. The fly is about $\frac{5}{16}$ in. long, and has a dark olive body and bluish wings, although some specimens have reddish or orange bodies. The spinner stage has an orange body and colourless wings.

A good pattern on warm dull days is the Orange Partridge.

In the late evening a spinner pattern may be fished dry. The following tie is useful:

Body: Hot orange floss silk ribbed with fine gold wire
Hackle: Honey cock
Hook: 12s

Lake Olive: This has a shorter season than the Pond Olive, with which it is often confused. The best dry imitation is a Red

Spinner dressed to rather a large hook. There are several wet dressings to simulate the dun, but I find that a Rough Olive pattern does as well as anything.

There are many other species of lake day-flies but the above two are the most generally useful to the angler.

Chironomoids: On many sheets of still water, especially lowland reservoirs, a familiar feature of the fly-life are the long-legged midges of the genus *Chironomus*. These bizarre-looking creatures – like flies on stilts – sit around the margins of Blagdon, Chew Valley, and other reservoirs in vast numbers. They have no dun stage. At Blagdon they are known as 'Buzzers' or 'Racehorses'.

Fish feed freely on the pupal stage. The chironomid pupae hang from the water-surface before hatching and the big trout cruise around sucking them in. I have seen Chew Lake boil with big trout feeding in this way.

A lot of ingenuity has gone into devising patterns to simulate Buzzer pupae, but there are so many different species and they have such different coloration that it is almost anyone's guess what the fish are taking. The angler who carries red- and green-bodied pupae will probably do as well as those who try to simulate each variety.

Here is an effective simple pattern:

Body: Red (or green) floss silk wound from round the bend of the hook to the shoulder
Thorax: Two turns of peacock herl
Legs: A single turn of soft black hen
Hook: 12s

Corixid: These insects – the Lesser Water Boatmen – are oval, bug-like creatures with a pair of legs like paddles, which swim below the surface. They should not be confused with Water-skaters, which live on the surface.

Some anglers report success with yellow seal's fur bodies ribbed with broad silver to simulate the air-bubbles that cling to this insect's body.

These are the main groups of natural lake flies of interest to anglers. There is of course some overlapping between lake and river fauna. The Coch-y-bondhu for example is as likely to fall into a stream as into a lake; so too with the Alder.

Although the study of lake flies is very interesting it should be made clear that most anglers catch most of their fish on artificials and lures which bear little relationship to real insects.

However, more will be said about this in the section on TROUT fishing.

F. W. H.

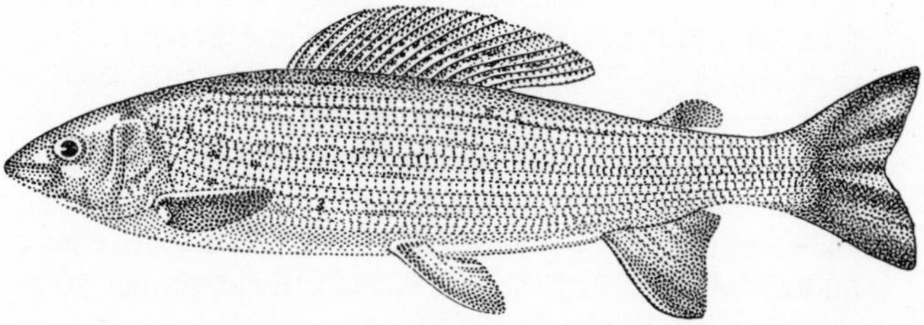

Grayling

The grayling (*Thymallus thymallus*) is a beautiful fish. Its skin is shot with colours like a piece of oiled silk and its streamlining is flawless, even though the big dorsal does appear a bit ungainly when one is used to the trim lines of trout. The grayling is of course a member of the salmon family and has the adipose fin of that fish as proof. Just to be contrary, however, it spawns at the same time as coarse fish.

Grayling tend to run small when compared with trout, and in some waters they are very small indeed. Fish of 5 lb. and over are uncommon in most rivers; a 2 lb. grayling is a good fish.

The variable distribution of grayling has been a matter for discussion over the years. There is some evidence that grayling may have been introduced into Scotland and northern England by monks, and certainly the spread of this fish south and west is patchy and localized. In Wales, the main pockets of grayling would seem to be importations.

The grayling is not usually classed among the bottom-feeders, but the river bottom is clearly where most of its food is obtained. The shape of its mouth certainly argues a predilection for river-bed foraging.

It does, however, feed on insect fare and in suitable conditions will rise to surface fly with alacrity. On the whole, grayling may be considered for fishing purposes as wet-fly fish or, in other words, mid-water feeders, but on chalk-streams, where floating duns can be exhibited under ideal conditions, the dry fly too will take its quota. All of which suggests that the grayling should be studied in relation to the water in which it is found.

Grayling, unlike salmon and trout, spawn in early summer and are at their best in autumn and early winter. Grayling fishing, in trout waters, thus permits a useful and pleasant extension of the fishing season. Many trout anglers fish grayling until Christmas.

Flies

In Britain, grayling don'ι seem to be very discriminating about flies. Most of the grayling I have caught and those I have seen captured by other anglers took flies which are best described as 'generalized impressions' (see pp. 161).

The fancy patterns are popular, especially those with a yellow or red wool body. Even more effective – because more conspicuous in dull light – would be flies dressed with a tag of fluorescent floss. Red is a good colour for dusk, but yellow shows up best in discoloured water.

Flies in sizes 10, 12, and 14 (Redditch Scale) should be adequate for most conditions that permit of fly-fishing. In heavy water or falling water after spates more grayling will be caught by trotted baits.

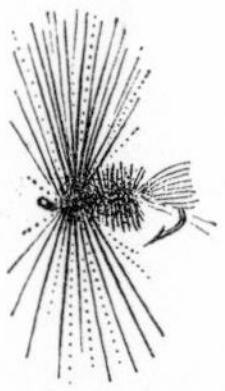

Grayling fly, a Red Tag

Again, I don't think one need lose a night's sleep over patterns. If grayling are rising to particular flies they should be offered the appropriate dry trout fly. Red Tag has earned some fame as a grayling fly, but almost any wet fly with a trace of tinsel and colour will catch grayling feeding in mid-water.

Tackle

The best general rod is probably the familiar 9 ft trout rod. With this goes a line of suitable weight and a 3 in. reel. The line can be either dressed silk or self-floating. For fly-feeding fish weighing probably no more than $\frac{3}{4}$ lb. there is a good case for fishing as light as possible.

Fishing Methods

Fly: Time and again we find angling experts expressing opinions which seem quite opposed. Beginners are often confused about this, and even experienced anglers are provoked into writing cynical letters to the editors of magazines. There is often, however, a very ordinary explanation. In nearly every case of this sort the expert is quite right for the water he fishes and for the conditions he describes. It is not the writers who are at variance but the fish, who may react quite differently even in adjacent portions of the same stream.

Several differing views have been expressed on fly-fishing for grayling. The grayling is said to be particular about which artificial fly it will take; it has also been described as an indiscriminate feeder. Charles Ritz calls the grayling: 'a Germanic type: consistent. Only accepts small flies . . . and certain shapes and colours.' E. Horsfall-Turner says: 'For inconsistency I have yet to meet the equal of the grayling.' It should be noted that while Ritz fishes mostly on the Continental chalk-streams, Horsfall-Turner is most at home on the chalk-streams of Yorkshire. I am sure that the observations of these two anglers are correct for the locations where they usually fish.

So it seems that grayling vary widely with locations (as indeed do sea-trout). The first thing in grayling fishing, therefore, is to study the fish in its particular setting.

In rivers where grayling do appear to feed erratically I believe the reason is simple. For most of the time they are bottom-feeders, but when conditions of light and temperature change they are able to switch rapidly to surface feeding. On very clear chalk-streams where heavy hatches of fly are commonplace they tend more to surface feeding and in the process no doubt learn to discriminate between one size and colour of fly and another.

The grayling's rapid change-over from surface rising to mid-water and bottom feeding often baffles anglers. If more fishermen went to the river with both fly tackle and bait-trotting tackle and used either as seemed appropriate to the conditions I believe that heavier bags of grayling would be recorded.

Certainly it is useless to flog the water with fly when grayling are browsing on the bottom muds. The method that seems to capture the best of both worlds, so to speak, is the wet fly. This can be fished just under the surface or deep, at will.

Dry Fly: Grayling, as mentioned earlier, are largely bottom-feeders, and hug the mud. Normally a shoal lies deep, occasionally rising to mid-water. For a grayling to take a floating fly, therefore, it needs to do something in the nature of a slick manoeuvre. When the fly floats within the grayling's cone of vision the fish must move quickly in order to catch it before it moves out of view. As a preliminary the fish may have to rise through several feet of water, by which time the fly has drifted a few feet below the lie. The grayling therefore will have to swim a few feet downstream before it can get opposite the fly to take it into its mouth.

This delayed-action type of rise must be expected with grayling. This is especially so when the angler knows where the shoal are lying and, rather naturally, hopes for a rise immediately above the spot. Instead the rise may come several feet below.

From the above it is easy to reason that a good deal of slack line needs to be cast in order to prevent drag on the fly while it moves on its comparatively long travel. Slack line coupled with precision in casting has always been hard to achieve. One method is to throw a hard straight line with the fly aimed a few feet beyond the fish. At the limit of the 'shoot' the tip of the rod is brought back rather sharply. If all goes well, the fly drops on the desired spot and the line falls slackly on the water. Clumsy presentation, however, will plop the fly on to the water like a stone. Luckily grayling like to forage in the tails of the runs, where the streamy water does, to a certain extent, camouflage imperfections in the angler's casting.

Wet Fly: The chief secret of successful wet-fly fishing is knowing where the fish are and what they are feeding on. This is a good deal more difficult than catching a fly floating on the surface and identifying it with the aid of a textbook. Grayling may be nosing through weed on the look-out for freshwater shrimps and snails, or they may be busy nymphing in the tails of the runs. Equally, they may be lying on the bottom and rising periodically to floating duns. The wet-fly fisher needs to have a pretty good working knowledge of the stream he is fishing. It is important to acquire this even if it means sacrificing an hour or two of fishing time. Time spent thus is not wasted.

Grayling like brisk-flowing streams with muddy bottoms. Now these requirements are not very common. Most brisk-flowing streams have stony or gravel bottoms; most muddy bottomed rivers are usually sluggish and canal-like. All of this gives certain clues. Since grayling like the type of water described we will probably be able to eliminate at least fifty per cent of a typical river as being unsuitable. A brief examination, by means of wading and sampling the bottom with a stick, will soon establish its nature.

Unlike trout, grayling are shoal fish, and where you catch one you may well catch more, if care is taken to get the hooked fish out of the shoal area as soon as possible. On the other hand they are not quite so sensitive to disturbance as trout. If the water is rested for a few minutes after a fish has been caught it will often be found that the shoal has resumed its position and is still feeding.

The casting routine as described for TROUT is used for presenting a fly or a team of flies. Personally, I usually start at the surface of the water and work downwards if fish are not showing. If the air is very cold and dry, however, a sunk fly or lightly leaded nymph would be first choice.

In winter it is often necessary to dredge the bottom. Some

anglers dislike this way of fishing, but it is often the only one that will give results.

Nymph patterns dressed on small double hooks are used on the Clyde and elsewhere. Some anglers prefer singles weighted with lead or copper wire. Unweighted wet flies can be sunk deep by using a self-sinking fly-line.

Striking and Playing: Striking presents no special problems. The grayling has rather a small mouth, which is one reason why some anglers insist on small flies. I have never found these fish particularly hard to hook.

Angling hares are started all too easily and are often pursued down the years until we regard their phantom existence as fact. It seems to have been Izaac Walton who first 'discoursed' on the grayling's tender mouth. Walton was a poet rather than a scientist and all poets are allowed a little licence. But the wretched hare had been started and anglers are still chasing it three centuries later.

Half the trouble, I think, is caused by faulty playing. On being hooked, a grayling likes to lie sideways to the current, its big dorsal erected, so that it can exert maximum resistance against the rod. It is quite useless to try and pull a grayling against a stream that is running at all strongly. If you try to do so you will simply lose your fly. Some anglers who make this mistake go away complaining that grayling have tender mouths but it would be truer to say that some anglers are ham-fisted.

The correct way to net a grayling – indeed any river fish – is to get below it in the stream and drift it over the net. If this is impossible owing to the nature of the banks the fish should be drifted into slack water and 'walked' up-river.

The smaller the fly in use, the less pressure you dare exert. With a small trout fly it is unwise to pull a fish against even a weak current, because you may well lose it in so doing. If you look for it there is always a safer way.

Bait-fishing – Trotting: Since grayling are bottom-feeders for most of their lives and are in season during winter it follows that bait-fishing is quite appropriate to their capture.

The maggot is the usual bait for grayling, although some anglers prefer small redworms. The best rod to use is one of 10 or 12 ft. A roach rod of Spanish reed with a fibre-glass tip has been recommended for grayling trotting but I know anglers who use 10 ft split-cane fly-rods and count these none too powerful when pitted against winter currents. So-called 'trotting reels' – which were, in fact, free-running centre-pin reels – have now been largely superseded by the fixed-spool reel. This seems to me a pity, for a well-made centre-pin is not only pleasanter to use, but is, I fancy, a better tool for the job. I have trotted baits for hundreds of hours with both fixed-spool and centre-pin reels and, personally, I prefer the latter every time. It is smoother in operation and gives one more intimate contact with the bait and, after hooking, with the fish. Centre-pins, too, are kinder on the line, which fixed-spool reels tend alternately to twist and unwind. Also, soft-plaited Terylene lines can be used; on fixed-spool reels, with their tiny drums, these tend to coil-cling.

Grayling float

Whatever reel is used it should be loaded with 100 yards of 4 lb. line. The cast should be tied direct to the line. Some anglers use a yard cast as fine as 2 lb. b.s., but in the high waters of winter this may spell breakages.

A bob-float is needed. A pike pilot-float can be easily adapted for grayling trotting. Some anglers like to shot the line; other prefer to shot the float itself. Some again like several biggish shots immediately below the float and one or two dust shots near the bait. I prefer my shots to be spaced down the line with the lowest not nearer than a foot to the hook. An unshotted line is not easily controlled in a fast stream and the bait is often carried towards the surface. If I want to fish shallow I prefer to do so by lowering the float. The bob-float, by the way, should have a lick of orange fluorescent paint to make it easily visible.

If the water is not too cold, wading is in order. This enables you to command all the best swims, which otherwise would have to be attacked from the bank. In any case, a 12 ft rod permits a reasonable command of the water, especially on smaller rivers.

The whole point and purpose of trotting is to present the bait to the fish in advance of the float. That is to say, the float should be periodically retarded in its drift so that the current, acting on the line, will swing the bait forward and upwards. The amount of swing of course will depend on the strength of the current and the amount of shot on the line.

All this sounds simple, but in practice it takes some concentration and delicacy of touch to manage a bait neatly in currents of varying speed. Too much retarding will cause the bait to eddy around uselessly; too little will permit the float to overrun the bait and haul it through the water.

Natural Grasshopper: One of the most curious pieces of grayling lore is the trend towards fishing natural grasshoppers.

Why grayling in particular should be associated with grasshoppers I don't know, for you can catch many sorts of fish on these lively insects, especially trout.

Grasshoppers begin to appear in quantity around midsummer. They can be captured in the early morning, when they may be observed sheltering around grass-roots waiting for the sun to come out. Although they are strong insects, their limbs are brittle and are easily destroyed by rough handling. They are best kept in a bottle, the mouth covered with gauze or perforated plastic. A wine-bottle with a long neck makes a good container.

Live grasshoppers are quite deadly if fished on the surface, where the vigorous kicking of their hind-legs quickly attracts fish from a distance. Unfortunately they soon drown, and the energetic display is brought to an untimely end. This means that one needs a good supply of the insects for an evening's fishing.

Grasshoppers are a fairly big bait and I find that a tiny Stewart tackle is the best mount for fishing them. A hook fixed in the fibre on the shoulders and another near the tail is the most humane way of securing them. Careless hooking will soon kill them.

There are several possible ways of fishing the live insect. No sort of real force can be used when casting, so the trotting outfit already described may be pressed into service, but without the shots and with the length running down to the hook greased. One can use McMillan's self-floating monofil for this job.

The floating, kicking 'hopper is then trotted down the slack water at the edges of pools, the float being retarded only enough to keep float and bait well separated. A fish that comes at a live grasshopper is not easily discouraged, and if it fails to seize it the first time it will try again and again.

Some anglers use an artificial grasshopper, a sort of hybrid between a wet fly and a lure. These creations are fished subsurface and are said to do well on occasion.

Weather: Grayling seem to be much more tolerant of weather changes than most game fish. On cold days their feeding periods seem to extend over a longer time than do those ot trout. Grayling fishing seems to be best on chill days when the sky is not too bright and the stream is full but not flooded. In these conditions, in late autumn, a dry fly often does surprisingly well. Like most fish, however, grayling do like a measure of stability in the weather and it is not suggested they will take no matter how stormy the conditions. A glass that rises and falls at short intervals – owing to the arrival of succeeding depression fronts – is likely to put every fish in the stream off its feed. The only exception to this that I have ever discovered is the common eel.

Autumn is the best time for grayling, especially during a spell of Indian summer, with its warm days and tangy nights. Unfortunately on tree-lined streams one usually gets a fall of leaf and this can make fly-fishing quite hopeless. Oak leaves seem to be exceptionally bad for fishing.

General Grayling are a betwixt-and-between fish. Although classed among the coarse fishes for purposes of River Board legislation they are tolerated – if that is the word – as a member of the Salmonidae. Few anglers fish for grayling specifically except as a sort of stop-gap during the trout closed season. This is clearly a natural reaction. One generally takes the best that is available, and when we fish for grayling during the winter the feeling that we are slumming in the piscatorial sense is inescapable, although rather tough on the grayling.

Probably many trout fishers underrate the grayling's fighting qualities. They hook grayling during the spring and summer, while trout fishing, when the fish has hardly recovered from spawning, and a spent fish can scarcely be expected to put up a lively struggle. On rivers where grayling are quite overshadowed by other game-fish, there is often no provision at all for catching them when they are in condition – that is to say, during late autumn and winter. On these rivers – the Teifi for example – it is impossible for an angler to catch a grayling when it is fit simply because, at that time, no angler has the legal right to be fishing.

Charles Ritz, in his book *A Fly-fisher's Life*, rates the grayling highly. However, he also says: 'In my view the sporting qualities of a fish are dependent neither on its size nor its weight, but on the effort of concentration, the skill, and the mastery it demands from the fisherman.'

The record grayling, incidentally, is a 7 lb. 2 oz. fish, taken from the River Melgum in 1949.

F. W. H.

Salmon

ZALM

There are several species of salmon, but *Salmo salar*, the Atlantic salmon, is the only one found in British rivers, unless one counts a few errant Pacific Spring salmon from Russian stocking of north European rivers. The salmon can be confused only with large SEA-TROUT, both fish having the same silver sheen and, of course, the adipose fin of the salmon family. However, they are easily told apart. The sea-trout has the characteristic long upper jaw-bone of the trout, extending beyond the centre of the eye; in the salmon this bone ends about level with the middle of the pupil. Again, the salmon has about ten scales diagonally between dorsal fin and lateral line, and the sea-trout has sixteen.

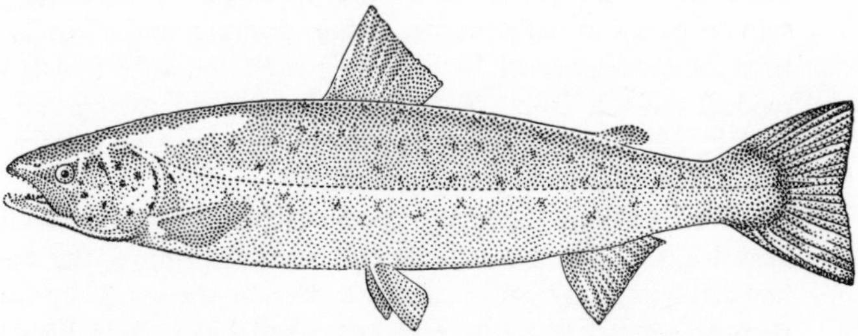

Salmon

The Atlantic salmon has been described as the greatest freshwater fish in the world. This is only half true, for the salmon spends the larger part of its lifetime in the sea and only returns to freshwater to spawn. In so doing it becomes the angler's most prized quarry. The life-cycle of the salmon is a fascinating one. It is hatched on the redds, or shallow gravel spawning beds, often in the tiniest hill streams. It spends the first two weeks of its life fighting its way up through that gravel and living between the stones, which it uses as a shelter from its many enemies. During this period it lives on a yolk-sac, containing nourishment, which is fixed beneath its throat like a small balloon. After this, it lives in the river for about two years as a parr, during which time it would look remarkably like a small brown TROUT were it not for the characteristic parr markings (rather like bluish finger prints) along its flanks. Next, it changes its coat to silver and moves down to the sea, when it is known as a smolt. In the sea it puts on weight at a great rate, owing to the rich feeding there, but the mystery is that no one knows precisely where in the ocean the salmon go for this feeding, for they are seldom caught in trawls.

The salmon may return to the river to spawn at one, two, or three years. If it returns within one year, it is known as a grilse on this maiden spawning run. A percentage of salmon find their way back to their own rivers, the ones in which they were born, but by no means all.

The salmon return to the rivers in spring and fight their way upstream with every fresh surge of rain-water that comes down from the hills until they reach the spawning shallows, or redds. There the female excavates a deep hole. She uses her tail to do this, but the tail itself does not do the digging; it is the vortex created by its movements that shifts gravel and quite large stones from the river bed. After courtship – in which the male fish lies alongside and moves against her – she deposits hundreds of eggs at a time in the redd. As she does so the male instantly becomes excited and sheds his milt. Recently it has been discovered that, possibly as an insurance against infertility, a salmon parr is usually present at the spawning and sheds his tiny cloud of sperm too. Because he is right under the female's oviduct this results in a high fertility level. The amazing thing is that this little fish, who has not yet even put on his sea-going coat, is already sexually mature.

After spawning, the female covers each clutch of eggs with gravel again. Finally, after several such spawnings, the exhausted salmon try to fight their way back to the sea. They are then emaciated like eels and are called kelts. It is illegal to catch kelts. A high percentage of them die before they reach the sea and few of the survivors return to the river after several more years of sea life to spawn again.

As far as the angler is concerned, the salmon's whereabouts in the river are highly predictable. The homing salmon is a travelling fish with a sense of purpose and a goal ahead of it. When conditions are right, i.e. when fresh water is coming down to urge it on, it moves on upstream and is usually uncatchable. However, it must rest, and the resting places or holding pools are where the angler finds it. In these pools the salmon lies are usually well known and do not vary except when flood conditions alter the contours of the river bed. Salmon often pack into a pool in numbers when water conditions become low. They are then usually torpid and uninterested in any fly or bait. The strange thing is that salmon do not eat when in the river but live off their sea fat. However, they will still snap at the angler's artificial offering.

Three-quarters of the success attained in salmon fishing results from knowing where fish lie. This is especially true in spring, when the uniformly high level of water tends to make most parts of the river look alike.

Salmon are fond of stones and rock, since sands and muds irritate their gills. The rock salmon-lodges in most rivers have names because they have been noted for generations. A walk along the river with an experienced rod is the best way of learning its more obvious taking places. Failing such helpful advice the angler will have to make up his own mind on where fish lie. Naked bed-rock on the bank-side is usually a good indicator, for quite probably it extends underwater, where it will be hollowed into caves and pockets. Fish will tenant these desirable places. Almost any 'ease' or quiet spot out of the main current around such bed-rock is likely to harbour a salmon.

Some rivers are peppered with boulders, but most of these can be ignored unless they fringe deep holes or pots where fish can take cover. Long featureless pools, especially those with mud or clay bottoms, can also be ignored. But close attention should be given to 'necks' where gravel banks abut the stream. Rocks may well be embedded in the gravel underwater, affording fish a harbourage.

Croys or piers are constructed on many rivers and I never cease to bless the men who constructed them, often a century ago. A successful croy usually has a deep hole at its foot where the fish lie. Quite often, however, the salmon will creep many yards up or downstream into the slack water at the sides of the adjoining runs. Some croy-pools no longer hold fish, usually because the current is too fast, the stream having changed over the years.

The lies or taking-places mentioned here assume that the river is at average spring level – full but not flooded. In flood conditions, before fish have taken up their lies, they can be expected almost anywhere, but especially in the broad shallow tails of the big pools.

Tackle

Fly Tackle (*Spring*)*:* The long, heavy salmon rods of Victorian Britain have now given way to smaller, lighter rods. Few anglers today use a rod longer than 14 ft and many prefer one of 12 ft. This latter is a trifle light for spring fishing with a sunk line, although of course much depends on the size of the river and the amount of wading possible. A well-made 12 ft rod has the advantage of being light enough to use single-handed, once one's wrist becomes conditioned, while the 14-footer needs both hands.

Choice of rod material is a personal matter which depends on the size of one's purse, the amount the rod is going to be used, and other factors. Tubular steel makes a powerful and efficient rod; split-cane is most commonly used; glass competes heavily with both on the score of price and toughness.

A self-sinking line of suitable weight for the rod in use is essential for spring fishing. Ungreased silk – the classic line material – is now being ousted by Terylene. A 4 in. or 5 in. reel with a strong adjustable check will be adequate for the casting-line and the 150 yds of 15 lb. Terylene backing. Stout nylon leaders tapering down to about 8 lb. b.s. should be adequate for all medium ranges of flies. Some anglers use 10 or 12 lb. material and this is certainly advisable in heavy water. Spring is no time to experiment with very fine tackle.

It is useful to carry a supply of single-hook salmon flies from size 2/0 downwards, supplemented with a few big hairwings dressed to the Waddington system; personally, I prefer Waddington flies to tubes. For most spring fishing a black-and-silver fly dressed on a 1/0 single is as good as anything. The ritual salmon-killing flies of the tackle-dealer's shop window are for the angler who wants to enjoy his fishing in the aesthetic sense. Complicated salmon flies give a great deal of pleasure and interest to many anglers, but in the strictly practical sense they are unnecessary. If you can afford it by all means order a good stock of Durham Rangers, Jock Scotts, and Dunkelds from a professional craftsman. You may be tempted to spoil a few by fishing with them but you will wisely keep the rest in moth-proof cases to show to friends. A whole century of salmon fly skill and tradition are enshrined in these flies so they are well worth studying if only as *objets d'art*.

Most salmon on our water are caught on home-made flies dressed from teal, mallard, and turkey together with assorted wools, hairs, and furs. These concoctions look shaggy and dingy as they drip wetly in the palm; their effectiveness is their only virtue.

Spinning Tackle (*Spring*): Artificials such as devon minnows of some 3 to 4 ins. long are standard items for spring fishing. A strong spinning rod, 8 or 9 ft long, and a large fixed-spool reel or a multiplying reel are the usual supporting tackle. A ball-bearing swivel is tied into the line, three feet above the minnow to minimize line-twist. One or two small drilled lead bullets are suspended on a bit of line from the topmost eye of the swivel. These help to prevent kink, but they also serve another purpose. The idea in salmon spinning is to fish so that the leads knock on the bottom. When a light minnow is used it will be found that this fishes several inches higher than the leads. It is certainly easier to free a rounded piece of lead from a snag than it is to shake free the multiple points of a treble hook. Moreover, with practice, it is possible to feel the leads tapping on the gravel and thus be sure that the minnow is fishing at maximum depth.

Some anglers use bottled sprats and others preserved baits,

but I find that a small herring, with head and tail removed, fished on the usual dead-bait spinning mount is quite as effective. Eel-tails are said to be good although they are leathery, lifeless objects. The smell of a fresh herring is better than either eels or sprats. Colour seems to me to be immaterial, although some anglers insist on dying their baits.

Prawn is almost a dirty word on many waters, being regarded as hempseed used to be regarded in coarse fishing. In spring, fresh prawns are expensive and hard to procure. Bottled or artificial prawn is the usual compromise, but it has always seemed to me a weak compromise since the peculiar properties of this bait lie in its strong odour.

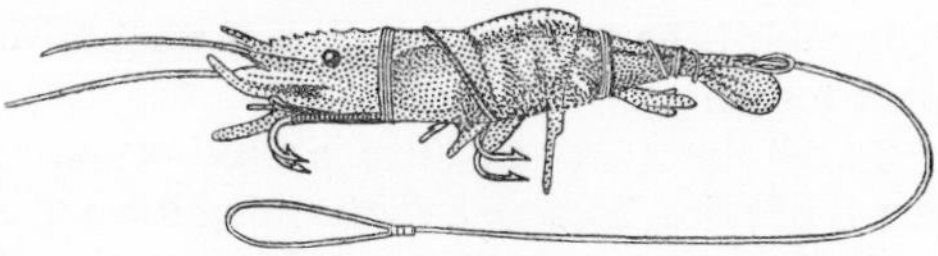

Prawn tackle

Natural prawns, of course, are almost colourless. Therefore perhaps it is no wonder that salmon are often alarmed when a brilliant scarlet artificial prawn is hauled through their lies. They seem either to attack in desperation or to flee to the farthest ends of the pool. It is this that has given prawn-fishing a bad name. But if the angler can obtain natural fresh prawns, or big shrimps, there seems to be no valid reason why these killing baits should not be used in moderation.

Tackle for Greased-line Fishing: The rod depends on the size and general character of the river being fished; a big Scottish river, for example, requires a 12 ft rod. Personally, I use a 9½ ft rod for the much more modest English streams, although it is sometimes necessary to supplement this with a rod measuring 11 ft.

Self-floating lines have already been described. Alternatively, one can use dressed silk line which has been given a rub-down with silicone line-grease.

The leader should be tapered down to 6 lb. There will be occasions when this looks too thick for the crystal water and strong sunlight. If the water is open and snag-free and you can, if necessary, chase your fish, then a 4 lb. point may be a worth-while risk. This is especially true when nymphing.

Since greased-line fishing was first evolved, a good deal of attention has been paid to light, sparsely dressed flies for this work. Greased-line flies should be short in the body and light in the wing. None of the materials should extend much beyond the bend of the hook. A series of light greased-line salmon irons are available for these flies. Teal, mallard, and hen pheasant are the commonest dressing-materials, although many anglers now prefer hair.

Fishing Methods The Atlantic salmon is a species with many local variations. In some rivers fresh fish run every month of the year but most rivers have a bias towards either a spring run or an autumn run. Quite often there is a run of summer fish. Heavy estuary netting over the last 120 years, however, has progressively culled the spring and summer fish-runs; many salmon now run and spawn in winter and the survivors are back in the sea before the season opens. In any case, if caught, they are returnable kelts or spent fish. This is what private netting has done for us.

'Early' rivers – where there is a run of spring salmon – are pearls of price, because a fresh spring fish is the salmon at its peak of perfection. Summer salmon, although desirable, soon become 'potted' or stale, especially when low water follows spate. Autumn salmon – often the biggest fish of the season – are already starting to exhibit the dark hues associated with the spawning process.

Spring salmon are usually caught by deep spinning, preserved sprats, devon minnows, and prawn being the usual bait. Flies – when the water is fly only – are commonly of the tube type, often lightly leaded, with a treble in the tail. Many rivers are seldom heavy enough, even in the spring, to warrant anything much bigger than a 2/0 'meat-hook' – the largest standard single salmon hook. But in big rivers a really big tube-fly is probably the best bet.

Summer fish nowadays are caught on greased-line fly or by light spinning. They can be caught on sea-trout flies, but some anglers prefer the worm-bunch or a small prawn. Autumn fish fall between spring and summer as regards methods used. The water can be quite low in a dry autumn, in which case small greased-line flies catch fish, but heavy water calls for a return to the big flies and baits of spring.

In very low water, when the fish are a trifle stale, the best method for sport and interest is probably nymph-fishing. L. R. N. Gray showed in Ireland that 'impossible' fish can be caught by this method. The nymphs used were the ones designed and dressed by Thomas Clegg of West Calder.

Spring Fly: Spring salmon fishing can be summed up in the sentence: 'Fish down and across, fish deep, fish slow.' The fish will be lying sluggishly at the bottom of the deep holding pools with no particular interest in moving objects. The fly needs to be at the same level as the fish, and no great distance from it, before a take is likely.

All this is, of course, a broad generalization. On the warmer days which one gets even in March the fish sometimes move up into the slack water at the sides of the runs. It is then a standard routine to fish this water before covering the pool proper.

Most anglers seem to agree that a small treble hook, as used behind tube-flies, obtains a better hold than the standard single salmon irons, particularly those in the bigger sizes.

The actual casting of the fly consists in laying line, leader, and fly at an oblique angle downstream according to the speed of the current and the position of the lie. Adequate time must be allowed for the fly to sink to a position where the fish can see it.

Some anglers don't work their fly. Again, it depends on the speed of the water and the lie of the fish. To pull the fly for a couple of feet just as it is passing the fish encourages a take, but this can easily be overdone. Salmon will not chase about after a fly in cold water; they want it brought to them.

The angler should never hesitate about changing the size or type of his fly if he thinks it is fishing too shallow. The fly must be down near the bottom – but of course not be so heavy that it catches in every stone.

Fly in Summer: Fly-fishing for salmon in summer is almost entirely confined to the technique known as 'greased-line' although, in fact, most anglers no longer bother with grease but use a self-floating line. The only occasion when spring fishing technique with sunken line is used in summer is when fishing the falling waters of a big, cold flood. Greased-line fishing is based on the fundamental principle of fly-fishing – that the combination of cold water and warm air means fish will rise to take surface fly. But cold air and warmer water mean the fly must be taken down to the fish (i.e. sunk). From May onwards, on average, the former conditions apply in most British rivers.

Greased-line Fundamentals: No one seems to be very sure why a salmon takes a greased-line fly – or indeed any fly. It seems certain that salmon do eat small items while in fresh water, despite the belief to the contrary. While it is one thing for a vigorous fish to snap at a large glinting lure being drawn past its nose, it is quite another when a slightly stale salmon rises like a trout and takes a small fly off the surface. The motivation in the two cases must be different. All this is still an open field for speculation and experiment.

Greased-line fishing is probably the most finely controlled method of wet-fly fishing possible. This is why so many anglers find it interesting and attractive. The following typical advantages may be noted:

(i) The depth at which the fly fishes can be controlled by fishing flies of the appropriate size and type.

(ii) The speed at which the fly fishes can be controlled by rod and line manipulation.

(iii) Control is possible over the track or path of the fly.

(iv) The angler can see the fish as it takes his fly.

L. R. N. Gray has been at some pains to try to teach me his theory of greased-line fly sizes. He writes: 'There is no doubt at all on most fly rivers that salmon are unbelievably fussy about the exact size of the fly when conditions indicate the greased-line. I have, however, long firmly believed that what they are actually fussy about is not so much the size of the fly as its distance below the surface according to the temperature of the water and the pace at which it is fished.' This puts the case in a nutshell.

Standard greased-line flies are normally dressed on the light salmon hooks mentioned in the tackle section. Some experts – including Mr Gray – supplement these greased-line flies with small tube-flies and flies in the sea-trout range of sizes. All of them, however, are fished according to the greased-line method.

Salmon and sea-trout that have been a little time up the river are often very circumspect about taking a fly. Mr Gray considers that they want the fly and its reflection in the surface-mirror to be a certain distance apart. There may be optical reasons why this should be so. The weight of a fly, the pace of the current, and the manner it is fished all bear on the distance a fly sinks beneath the surface. And on this rate of sinking – or lack of it – it would seem that the success or failure of greased-line fishing depends.

The most important point of all in greased-line fishing is for the angler to keep out of contact with his fly. It is interesting to note that the same applies to CARP fishing. The salmon must be free to take the fly and turn away without feeling any resistance from the rod just as a carp must be at liberty to take a bait and move away without feeling the attached apparatus. In greased-line fishing the angler must make no attempt to strike or hook a fish which breaks surface as it reaches for the fly. If it is given a moment or two's grace the fish will hook itself; hasty striking will almost certainly pull the fly out of its mouth.

Salmon are conservative creatures while in the river. They cherish their favourite lies with a zeal matched only by the most home-loving town-dwellers. They will leave home for a short time but soon hurry back. When a fish rises to take a greased-line fly its next move is to return whence it came. If the angler tightens after the fish has turned down it will be hooked firmly. In practice most anglers school themselves to wait – after seeing the boil to the fly – until the downward-moving fish has taken up the slack line lying on the water. If the fisherman finds this too nerve-racking he should close his eyes and wait until he can feel the fish.

A high proportion of salmon hooked in this manner will have the hook embedded in the 'scissors' at the corner of the mouth. Such a hold is very secure.

Most casting in this form of fishing is across and up or across and slightly down, depending on the pace of the current. The aim of the exercise is to make the small fly swim across the river at a speed in keeping with its size and on a slack line.

Expert greased-liners know when fish are likely to take a fly and when conditions are unfavourable. Only experience can tell you when the glint of the sun on the leader is so acute that it will scare the fish. Likewise, the shadow of line and leader, moving over the bottom, will often repel more fish than the fly attracts. Conditions on a river are changing constantly. On some days for example air temperature falls rapidly towards evening owing to the lack of moisture, and although greased-line may be appropriate during the middle part of the day, the evening conditions may indicate a return to sunk fly, perhaps of quite large size.

The angler will need to do a good deal of study of the low-water salmon lies on the river he is fishing in order to get the best out of them. Salmon like cover and deep water into which to retreat. Unlike sea-trout, they are rarely caught after dark. This is probably because sea-trout actively feed in fresh water while salmon merely pick at trifles.

Manipulation of Greased-line Fly: Manipulating a g.l. fly calls for concentration and dexterity. Common sense is a good guide. Fast dragging and inert drifting are the two extremes to be avoided; the mean to aim at is the smooth even travel of the fly. Why salmon should prefer a fly near the surface to be fished round smoothly when they often take a sunk fly fished quite fast is problematical, but the reason has probably something to do with turbulence in the wake of the fly, which, at depth, perhaps goes unnoticed.

The speed the fly fishes is controlled by the line bag (or 'mend'), which is simply a loop of line thrown either upstream or downstream as the case requires. An upstream bag relieves pressure on the fly and causes it to fish more slowly; a downstream bag draws the fly onwards, ever faster.

Mending a fly-line is a manual skill like shuffling a pack of cards. It is performed by flicking the rod point in a small half-circle. With practice this can be done without jerking the fly and without slapping the line on to the water. Mending should be used no more than is necessary, for even the neatest mend causes a slight disturbance, and a clumsy mend executed on a glassy pool will send every fish rushing for cover.

The angler will soon learn when mending is needed and when it is unnecessary. For a part of the drift the current itself, acting on the line, will move the fly at a suitable speed. When the fly starts to drag too fast the angler will mend upstream. When the fly fishes into slack water the angler mends downstream and thus encourages the fly to keep moving. There are endless variations and combinations of this pattern.

Nymph Fishing: In very low water when the fish are tending towards staleness (a common feature of our abstracted rivers) often the only method of catching salmon is with a trout-size nymph. Pheasant-tail nymphs, famous on the Avon, and the dainty patterns devised by Thomas Clegg are both equally suitable.

The main points to study when nymph-fishing are these:

(i) The shadow of the leader and the line should not travel in advance of the nymph.
(ii) The nymph should drift inert or draw only very slowly.
(iii) The nymph should fish near the level of the fish.

In the conditions described, salmon will spot a nymph dressed on a H 14 hook from several yards away and will often move in order to intercept it. They open their mouths and suck the nymph in – which means that the line really must be slack or the fish will feel the resistance.

The difficulties of playing a salmon on a trout hook are obvious. Pressure from the rod must be avoided at all costs. If the fish is constantly persuaded to run, and thus exhaust itself, the trout hook will do its job.

Salmon on Dry Fly: Comparatively few anglers use dry fly for salmon, but it is a perfectly effective method of fishing. Unlike trout, salmon do not position themselves in order to rise steadily to summer hatches of fly. Very occasionally they can be seen rising to Olives but more usually they go for insects of bulk and size.

Dry flies for salmon are of the bushy Palmer type, which presumably resemble moths, sedges, and similar fare.

In a recent friendly encounter on the Dee at Aberboyne between Lee Wulff, U.S.A., and Jock Scott, Great Britain, Mr Wulff demonstrated the effectiveness of his dry salmon flies by catching fish under test conditions. It is interesting to note that, on this occasion at least, dry fly beat greased-line fly by one fish to nil.

In salmon fishing, perhaps more than in any other branch of angling, traditional methods tend to congeal and ossify into dogmas which sundry authorities insist should not be tampered with. Although the wet fly, both sunk and greased-line, still remains the chief method of attack on Atlantic salmon, it would seem that the dry fly is due for a renaissance unsuspected even as recently as five years ago.

Summer Spinning: It must be agreed that many anglers do all their salmon fishing with a minnow. Although spinning in spring is widely regarded as a fair method of getting fish out of high, cold rivers there is possibly less to be said in favour of the minnow when the water is low and warm.

The late Alexander Wanless – arch-champion of the threadline – wrote devotedly of the pleasures and problems of spinning for salmon. The methods he advocated – natural minnow, fine monofil lines, and light spinning rods – are still widely used. His other brain-child – the fly controller – has been thrown out of court.

Some experts insist on a distinction between threadline spinning and light spinning. By definition, the words 'thread-lining' imply the use of lines of 6 lb. breaking strain and below; the words 'light spinning' imply the use of lines of from 8 to 12 lb. As a further mark of distinction some anglers in the latter group use multiplying reels instead of fixed-spool reels.

A rather important principle is at stake here, the point being that if salmon can be caught on 6 lb. lines then there is no point or purpose in using heavier tackle. Where salmon run small, a 6 lb. line, given luck, is adequate. The trouble is that a 6 lb. line today may be no more than 4 lb. tomorrow through wear-and-tear and the twisting action inherent in all threadline reels, and a 4 lb. line is dangerously weak for even a small salmon. A tapered fly-leader with a 4 lb. point rapidly increasing to a substantial thickness is of course quite a different thing.

Much depends on whether one can follow one's fish. It is easy to do so on some rivers, impossible on others. Places where the angler must hook, play, and land his fish all at the same spot call for a strong line if any sort of success is to be achieved. There are 8 lb. lines available today that are no greater in diameter than the 6 lb. lines advocated by Wanless. So, in theory, perhaps the light spinner is still 'threadlining'.

Natural minnow, shrimps, and small prawns are readily taken by summer salmon. These can be spun upstream, across-and-up, across-and-down, or downstream.

In low-water conditions fish can be taken by casting a very small devon minnow upstream and recovering it fairly fast. Quill minnows are very good for this type of work, but the hook flights should be bound against the body of the quill instead of being left 'flying', to ensure that the minnow spins true and fast. Minnows that spin lop-sidedly or fail to revolve easily are useless for fishing purposes until suitably repaired.

Some anglers like to use a spun shrimp. There is a good supply of these in summer and they make a good bait by reason of their strong odour. Shrimps should be spun slowly, down and across, so that fish have a chance to smell them. Fresh shrimps can be netted, or bought from the shop, and will keep for several days if pickled in strong brine.

Elvers can also be used. Failing these, or as an alternative, a glass-jar minnow trap will soon catch a quantity of minnows big enough for salmon spinning. Hen minnows in spawn are best, if procurable.

From July onwards, fresh mackerel is often available locally. A 'lask' of mackerel, cut from the side and back of the fish, is very attractive to salmon.

Some fishermen dose their baits with pilchard oil. Salmon have an acute sense of smell, so anything that appeals to this sense is well worth trying. Baits pickled in formalin should be avoided. Salt is best for short-term pickling.

Good artificials to use are the spoons in which the blade hangs freely on a pivot. The smallest sizes – say ¾ in. – are big enough for low-water spinning. Big spoons with a 1½ in. blade are excellent in high water.

Dull-coloured quills and devons seem to do best in low

water. A dark brown back with a gold belly is a useful choice for summer fishing. In spring, all silver is preferable.

There is room for experiment with fresh natural baits. The sand-eel for example, is easy to collect and is abundant at many coastal resorts. Fish feed freely on the eels both along the coast and in the estuaries. Sand-eels can be spun or fished on the sink-and-draw principle. In brackish water the live sand-eel will catch fish if lip-hooked after the manner of a live minnow. In estuaries, however, these baits are likely to receive the attention of bass.

Rolling the Worm-bunch: The worm-bunch is a deadly method of baiting for salmon. It can be used throughout the season but kills best when fish are moderately fresh-run. The worms to use are the big blue-headed dew-worms which slink out of the lawn after a summer shower; a torch used after dark will reveal them. Keep them in a well-aired box in moss mixed with a little wet pond-weed. If a close-fitting box can be obtained this may be sunk in a shady part of the garden. Give the worms a feed of diluted fresh milk mixed with a little boiled oatmeal twice a week and they will wax sleek, tough, and fat.

The tackle consists of two large single worm-hooks tied about 4 ins. apart in tandem. Good-quality round-bend hooks with the bend measuring about ½ in. across are the ones to use.

The size of the lead is important. The best plan is to obtain a stock of ¼ oz. drilled bullets, thread a couple of these on to the line, and fix them two feet above the hook by means of a split-shot stop. Some anglers also like to incorporate a swivel.

The number of bullets to use must be found by experiment. When the bait is cast square across the pool it should be weighted so that it rolls round slowly in an arc. Too much weight will anchor it to the bottom and too little will cause it to move too fast. Depth of water, speed of current, and the nature of the bottom are variables which make more or less weight desirable. For this reason some anglers use quickly detachable leads.

A clean gravel, shingle, or pebbly bottom is best for this method of fishing. On strange water, occasional snagging is to be expected and then the main thing is to avoid force. If the bait fails to come in on gentle recovery of line then the angler should walk twenty yards up or downstream and pull from a new position; the hook can then nearly always be shaken free. Getting annoyed and jerking the line savagely only serves of course to fix the hook into whatever is holding it.

It is well worth while carrying a small home-made otter for freeing tackle. One about 6 ins. long, keeled with lead, with a wooden pin which retains the line in a slot will do the trick.

The hooks are baited with three or four worms hooked by head and tail, and held together in a compact bundle with an elastic band.

The fishing itself is systematic. The angler casts and allows the bait to trundle round in a slow arc. After taking a pace he re-casts, and so on. The water is therefore covered foot by foot and no fish is missed. On smelling the bait salmon will come upstream to meet them.

After some experience in the method the angler will learn to distinguish between a small trout tugging at the tail of a worm and the vibration made when a salmon takes the bunch into his mouth and starts to chew them. Expert anglers quickly shake small trout off and re-cast.

A strong rod, eight or nine feet long, of cane or fibre-glass, suits this type of fishing. An efficient fixed-spool reel holding 100 yds. of 12 or 14 lb. nylon is satisfactory. Since fish may have to be held in heavy water there is no sense in fishing too light.

Whatever may be said against worming for salmon it must be agreed that the method takes fish from waters which are too small and too overgrown to be fished in almost any other way. Fished with skill and understanding the worm-bunch will kill fish that are otherwise impossible.

Playing and Landing: Never, at any time, should the fishing-rod be pointed at a hooked salmon. During casting, a rod is a special sort of lever, but after hooking a fish it becomes a highly sensitive spring or buffer which protects the comparatively fine tackle from the strength of the fish. But it can only do its job if it is held correctly; that is with the line forming a 90° angle – or thereabouts – with the rod tip.

The angler soon develops the power of automatic observation. Bank-side bushes and trees are danger-points when playing a fish, partly because their roots usually extend into the water and partly because they prevent the angler moving freely along the bank. Other danger-points are where fences and hedges bisect the bank.

Most fish are reluctant to leave the pool where they are hooked, especially in low water. When the water is above average height the fish are of course more mobile and they show much less hesitation in leaving the pool. In conditions of high water, therefore, the angler needs to pay much more attention to his own mobility along the banks than when the water is low.

Salmon

There are no hard and fast rules because rivers vary so much in size and character. On some rivers one can follow a salmon for a mile without once having to climb the bank. On other waters the angler may have to play his fish from the top of high banks fringing deep water.

Some salmon adopt a curious and dangerous trick of moving upstream at a very slight angle to the current, usually when below the fisherman, and thus 'ottering' themselves across the river. The angler thinks he is dealing with a quiet fish until, suddenly, he finds that it is a hundred yards away and nosing roots under the opposite bank.

Where possible, one should always play a salmon from below, so that it must fight both the rod and the current. Some fish of course refuse to stay above and shoot downstream, so that they have to be chased on foot. When a fish is downstream and there is no chance of getting below it, it can usually be 'walked up'. The angler puts a good bend into his rod and keeps it well up; then he walks slowly and deliberately upstream. Three fish out of four will follow for many yards before starting to object.

The behaviour known as 'sulking' is usually caused by the angler being afraid of the fish. The salmon stands on its nose in the deepest part of the water and nothing will shift it. If the angler out-thinks the fish, however, by shifting the angle of pressure and keeping it constantly on the move then it will have no time to sulk. The angler must make the salmon work; otherwise he has lost control of the situation.

Gaffing, as we all know, is a bloody and ugly affair, more often bungled than performed neatly, and thoroughly hateful to many anglers. Gaffs should in fact be left to poachers and their ilk. The best way (and the safest way) of landing a salmon is to beach it. When beaching fish always keep as far back as possible, for if the angler is well out of the way the salmon will kick and wriggle its own way on to the dry stones. The tailer (a wire slip-loop which can be tightened over the fish) is best when the water is too deep for beaching. There is a modern tailer on the market with a trigger-operated noose which works unfailingly. I look foward to the day when gaffs are regarded as obsolete.

General

There was a time, half a century ago, when salmon were fished to a rather stringent set of rules; in low and medium water, fly only was used; in high water a certain amount of spinning was condoned, even if not encouraged. In those distant days no angler who considered himself a gentleman would ever have dreamed of selling his catch. Fish were given to friends or distributed discreetly via the gillie to the poor of the parish. Decorum was expected from the salmon fisher and guests who hoped to be invited to fish again had to show good manners. The economic state of the country at that time permitted the ownership of salmon fishings together with the requisite staffs of keepers, gillies, and retainers. Fishing for salmon expressed a way of life as much as did the hunting of foxes. The petty details of tackle were left to the servants and the angler was concerned merely with the actual fishing. At least one of the old-time salmon anglers was in the habit of handing his rod to the gillie whenever a fish was hooked, on the tacit assumption that the hooking was everything, the playing nothing.

Times change and although there are still some grandiose backwaters of salmon fishing left, especially in Scotland, the main picture has altered completely. The chief trouble is that the salmon is a valuable fish and soaring prices have introduced problems undreamed of by our forebears. In 1777, on the Teifi, spring salmon sold at 6*d*.–8*d*. per lb. and later in the season its price dropped as low as 1*d*. or ¾*d*. By 1867 the price had risen to 1*s*. 6*d*. per lb. The retail price at the time of writing is no less than 19*s*. 6*d*. per lb. Any fish that is worth nearly £1 per 1 lb. of its body-weight is clearly going to present problems of a sort unknown almost anywhere in the world. The fact that a salmon today is worth between £7 and £14 on the market has introduced a mercenary flavour that many salmon anglers abhor.

On the best salmon rivers the fishing is let in beats for the month or for the season. The owners of these fishings are usually interested in them as a commercial enterprise. Therefore the more fish killed by the lessee the better, for a beat with a substantial bag entered in the record-book commands a better price in subsequent seasons than a beat where few fish have been caught.

This pernicious system tends to turn the salmon angler into a fish-killing machine. If he sticks to the old-time code of ethics and uses 'fly-only' when the water is not in good fly condition then his bag tends to fall. And this could mean that when he inquires about that beat in later seasons the agents will tell him that there are no vacancies. The agent wants a client who will kill plenty of fish.

Anglers of moderate means are faced with the problem in a different way. They may rent or lease a beat for a short period, perhaps in conjunction with a friend, but even on a second-rate river the transaction will cost them a useful sum of money. Such anglers would be inhuman if they failed to explore the possibility of recouping their outgoings by selling the fish they caught. Economic pressure therefore persuades them to fish hard with every legal method allowed by local rules. Catching salmon on fly has become a luxury which only rich men can afford. The anglers must be constantly haunted by the thought that every fish lost to the bag adds £10 to the bill.

So it goes on down the scale. On most Association water 'everything goes' and the salmon are hammered with spoons, devons, plugs, worms, and prawns from the moment they enter the river. Stretches of fly-only salmon water are becoming ever more rare because they are a contradiction in economic terms. I count myself lucky to have a rod on what is one of the few surviving pieces of fly-only water in South Wales.

If the honest angler is subjected to these distasteful pressures, the dishonest poacher is tempted even more. We have all heard about the dynamite, fixed nets, and gaffs that are in nightly use and such devices are now supplemented by novelties like Aqualungs and underwater harpoons.

Who is to blame for salmon-fishing having become an avaricious rat-race? Is it the modern economic set-up, and the insatiable demand for fresh salmon, or the lazy and mechanical fishing equipment so readily available to all? The reader must judge.

Possible solutions are studded with difficulties. In the end, some sort of national control seems inevitable. Salmon fisheries are too valuable to be left to take pot-luck. The salmon is hounded by all and sundry; its only crime is that it is eatable.

Cost: Salmon fishing costs work on a sort of sliding scale. The more you pay, the more you get, other things being equal. Unfortunately other things are seldom equal and the lessee of an expensive beat often has to swallow the disappointing pill of spring and summer drought. Or it may turn out to be one of those unpredictable years when the runs of fish are below average.

Fishing on a good-class river is unlikely to be had for under £100 a month, to which must be added running costs. Luck coupled with hard fishing is unlikely to recoup the angler by much more than fifty per cent of his outgoings in an average year. Most anglers of course expect to sell the bulk of their fish.

A great many anglers rely on hotels for their salmon-fishing.

About £10 per week is average for fishing in a fairly decent river, but to this must be added the River Board licence fee and, of course, hotel board charges. With some hotels the fishing is included in the overall tariff. Personally, I favour this arrangement. For one thing it argues that the majority of the guests will be anglers, since few people care to pay for services they don't intend to use. To be an angler in an hotel catering mainly for non-anglers can be a frustrating experience, for one then has to make arrangements for late meals, drying clothes, etc. – facilities which the true fishing hotel provides without being asked. A typical hotel of this sort usually charges from £12 to £20 per week, depending on the quality of the fishing and the time of the season.

Ownership of the fish is a question that should be investigated at the outset. Some hotels claim all the catch; others claim first fish. The majority let the anglers dispose of the fish how he will. Most hotels have deep-freeze facilities or can arrange access to them. Since I don't care much for frozen food, I usually pack my fish in dry grass after cleaning and send them off individually by parcel post clearly marked 'Perishable'. Ecstatic letters from friends witness the success of this system.

Association and club waters vary from good to indifferent. Many Associations issue visitors tickets *ad lib.* and this fact alone ensures that the water is overfished. A better system is the issue of multi-colour tickets which restrict the holders to fishing only on certain days.

Association fishing for salmon usually costs from about £2 to around £7 or perhaps £10 per week. Many Associations charge the visitor a higher fee than the locals. Day tickets on fairly decent water will cost from 10–15*s*. and upwards. On many rivers, however, day-tickets are not available.

Free fishing for salmon does exist and I know of such waters where fish are killed regularly in the right conditions. There is, of course, intense competition, and bait fishing and spinning are the usual forms. There is some good free salmon fishing on some of the Irish loughs and Scottish lochs, but the stranger nearly always needs the advice of a local angler – amateur or professional – if he is to do at all well.

Estuary and salt-water fishing is highly variable. Some estuaries fish fairly well; others are practically hopeless. A great many factors are involved – geological as well as biological. The angler must find an estuary where salmon are caught and make a detailed study of it at all states of tide throughout the season. Most estuaries have pools at the head of the tideway and these are well worth visiting at low water.

Most estuary fishing in England and Wales is free; in Scotland it is usually owned. In any case, anglers may not use private land to reach the fishing without permission.

The Future: Some experienced salmon fishers are inclined to wonder cynically whether salmon fishing has a future. Drift-netting has reached the proportions of a national scandal. Trawlers – many of them foreign – creep round the mouths of all our salmon rivers; in effect there is no such thing as a territorial limit. For the first time in history our great fish-markets are becoming glutted with salmon, and the end is not hard to visualize. Just as they made the hake and the plaice rare fish, so the trawlers will prove ruin to salmon-runs.

Seine-netting for salmon has been traditional for many generations in our river-mouths and prior to the invention of the railway it did little harm. But once the netsmen found that they could sell every fish they caught to the lucrative city markets, the situation changed and netting became big business. The main trouble with private seine-netting has always been its haphazard and unscientific mode of operation. It can be said that high water means that a good proportion of salmon run up-river, while low water restricts them to the off-shore water and the estuary. The seines therefore reap their richest harvest during low water and have lean times during wet years. On most rivers there is a weekend 'slap' when netting is not allowed. In theory, this is to allow fish to get up-river, but tides and low water may be against salmon running and the slap therefore is ineffective. On Monday, the nets catch the fish that should, in theory, have run on Sunday.

This is all so unsatisfactory as to be almost unbelievable. Here we have given over the well-being of our salmon fisheries to the flukes and fortunes of the British climate. Could anything be more muddled and short-sighted?

Scientific management is quite unknown on British salmon rivers. These valuable and useful national assets are producing perhaps fifteen or twenty per cent instead of the possible hundred per cent of yield. No government has ever expressed a progressive policy for rivers, and fishery research is stifled through lack of funds.

The Bledisloe Report: Salmon fishing is likely to be governed for many years by such findings of the Bledisloe Committee as the government decides to implement. This committee was appointed to review the Salmon and Freshwater Fisheries Act and to report thereon. Here are some of the more important suggestions:

(i) The installation of counting-meters in rivers frequented by migratory fish.
(ii) By-laws to control inshore netting of salmon and sea-trout.
(iii) When commercial fishing has lapsed, Boards should be empowered to abolish the public right to net and undertake netting on their own account.
(iv) Sale of salmon and trout should be conducted under licence only by accredited persons.
(v) Revised scale of penalties for poaching.

This is the essence of the Bledisloe Report as it may affect our fisheries in the future. How much, if any, of the above will be implemented is not yet known at the time of going to press, but even if each clause were implemented it would still fail to put our fisheries on a scientific and rational footing. It is simply a token gesture in the right direction.

Common Sense and the Salmon: The Fisheries Sections of River Boards are financed almost wholly by anglers, riparian owners, and other ratepayers. Out of the £750,000 paid by anglers in Wales over the last ten years in licences, the seine-nets contribution was about £450. The nets are admitted as catching 61 per cent of the fish and on many rivers the proportion is thought to be as high as 80 per cent.

It is clear that fisheries can never improve while this quite astonishing anomaly exists. The bulk of the revenue from the fisheries goes into private pockets. Meantime, Boards are under-staffed and under-financed. A bailiff, for example, may be expected to watch effectively anything up to a hundred miles of stream, which is clearly impossible.

Commercial catching of salmon is desirable, but it should be managed by the Boards by means of modern fish-traps operated by staff under the control of the Fishery Officer. Revenue from these would finance the operating of the Boards, pay for more bailiffs, and vastly extend the present meagre research plans. Scientific farming of the rivers would mean more fish available to the consumer market, more fish for the angler, and a great increase in the tourist trade on which so many rural communities depend.

Given adequate legislation, modern salmon fisheries could be created. A Chief Fishery Officer needs certain basic data before he can draft plans. Specimens of the sort of data that no

Grey Mullet

Mugil chelo (thick-lipped)
or *Mugil capito* (thin-lipped) (page 308)
Record 10 lb 1 oz

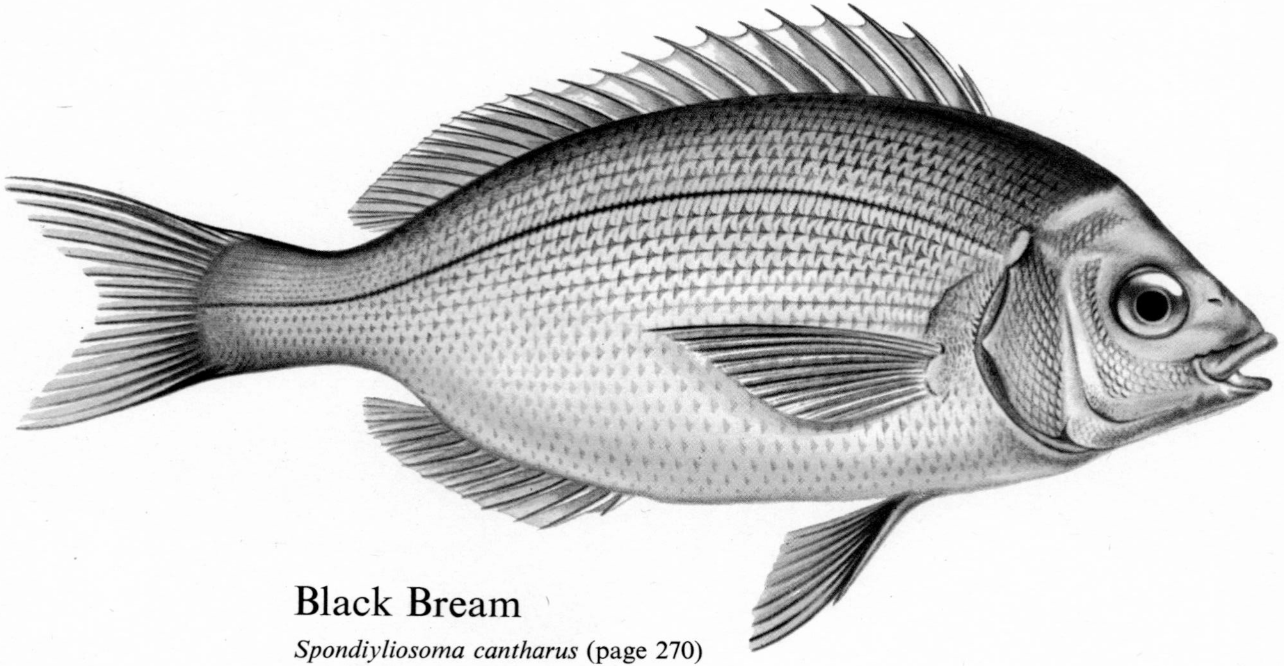

Black Bream

Spondiyliosoma cantharus (page 270)
Record 6 lb 5 oz*

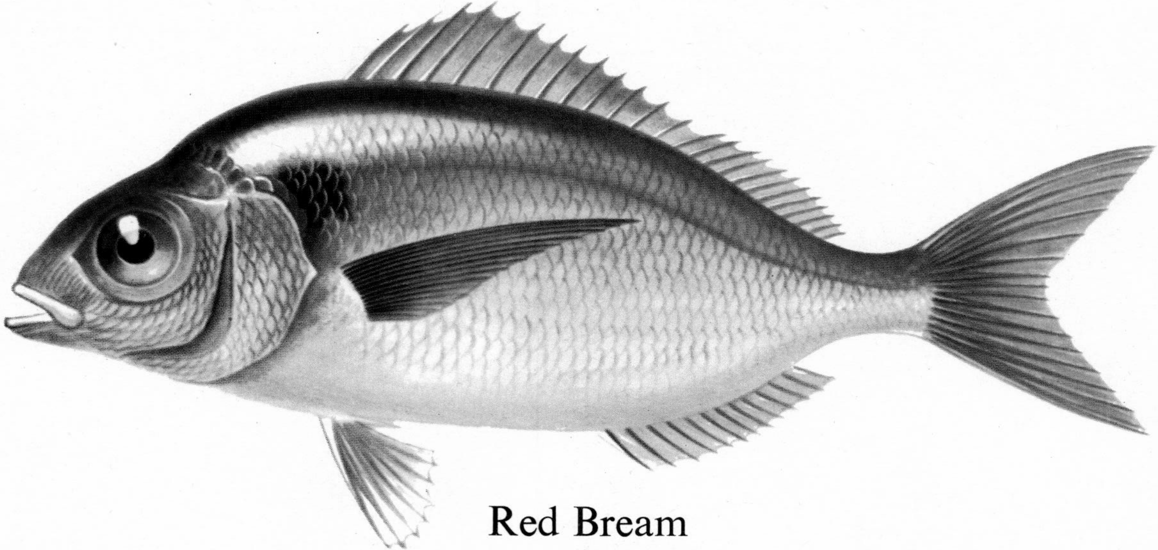

Red Bream

Pagellus centrodontas (page 271)
Record 7 lb 8 oz

Cod

Gadus callarias (page 274)
Record 44 lb 8 oz

Haddock

Gadus algilfinius
Record 8 lb 12 oz

River Board, at present, possesses about its fisheries are:

(i) Number of fish migrating per season.
(ii) Number of fish migrating per month.
(iii) Type of fish (i.e. grilse, spring fish, small summer fish, etc.).
(iv) Average annual yield of sea-going smolts.
(v) Average smolt survival rate.
(vi) Number of salmon killed in relation to number running.

No River Board can answer these questions with any degree of accuracy. Yet without this information planning is futile.

Nature is nothing if not highly adaptable. If, in a large breeding flock of poultry, you kill every bird that shows a white feather, it will be found, in the course of time, that white-feathered birds have become rare. This well-known phenomenon is known as culling. The same applies to salmon. On many rivers concern is felt at the declining spring runs and the growing shortage of summer fish. Instead of these desirable strains, nature now supplies the 'Blueback' or 'Greenback' salmon, which runs late – in December or January – spawns, and at once returns to the sea. The Blueback could be nature's answer to ruthless spring and summer netting which has culled the desirable strains from our rivers.

In many Welsh rivers the vacuum caused by the disappearance of the spring and summer fish has been filled by sea-trout. But sea-trout, too, are netted and only a small proportion of fish over 3 lb. find their way upstream.

It can be said in conclusion that the art and delight of salmon fishing depend on the abolition of both drift and seine-netting – and at no distant date. On the Scottish east coast more than 10,000 grilse are said to have been taken by drift-nets this season alone. Foreign trawlers can be seen fishing boldly well within the three-mile limit. The fish that dodge these devices have still to evade the estuary seines. The few that are left can be taken by the angler, who pays heavily for the privilege.

It would be unfair to the reader not to state the facts in this not entirely cheering chapter. By joining the Salmon and Trout Association he can help save the sport from untimely extinction. But in the end I feel certain that scientific management will be given a free hand in our fisheries and once more they will become highly productive of both good food and good sport.

F. W. H.

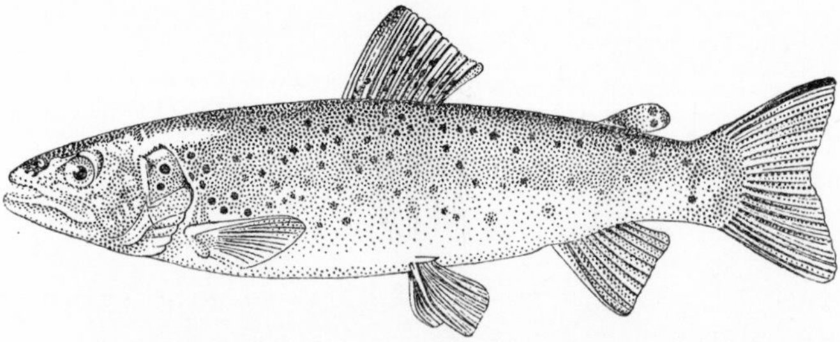

Trout

FoRREL

Salmo trutta is the native British brown trout. Almost everyone knows what a trout looks like but almost no one could give you a definition that was worth much. Trout are one of the most plastic races of fish known. They can adapt themselves to all sorts of streams and lakes; they will live in fresh water or in the sea; they adapt readily to a great many countries, and are a favourite species for stocking wherever fish are needed to provide both sport and food.

Like all fish, trout reflect the quantity and quality of the food they eat. A quick-growing trout fed on large amounts of small nutritious organisms has a small head, beautiful proportions, and delicate coloration. A slow-growing trout, half-starved, which has augmented its diet by cannibalism, is a lanky ugly creature.

Like all living things, trout react quickly to environment, and become conditioned to the water in which they live. There are strains of trout living in water with a plentiful food supply which are adapted to assimilate nourishment quickly and in quantity. On the other hand, trout from poor waters are usually slow-growing even when introduced to richer pastures. Yet both are the same species.

Although scientists consider that there is only one British trout, *Salmo trutta*, there are a great many local forms and varieties, some of them uncatalogued even today. Many waters have their own distinctive forms of trout, spotting, coloration, and even shape varying with the locality. In one part of a remote Welsh river there is a race of red-eyed trout which have not, so far, found their way into the textbooks.

Trout coloration tends to be darker when the water is acid, lighter when the water is alkaline. More will be said about this later. Spotting, its frequency and pattern, seems to be due to variable biological factors. Trout are seldom, if ever, spotted exactly alike.

Among quick-growing trout may be cited the famous Loch Leven strain which feed on very rich pastures. Other quick-growing trout are cultivated by various midland reservoir authorities, and by those in Somerset.

Quick-growing trout are also found in rivers with rich feed such as the Usk. These fish, when contained in the new Usk reservoir, made good use of the feed and numbers grew to 2–3 lb. with rapidity.

The chemical composition of water and its biological effect on living things is not our present concern, but the relative acidity of water is so fundamental to trout fishing that it may not be ignored. Rain-water, when it falls through unpolluted atmosphere is, for all practical purposes, neutral. Once it touches the earth this is no longer the case. Most water percolates through the top-soil and absorbs various chemicals and gases in its passage. It flows through and over rocks. By the time it reaches river or lake it has quite changed its character.

The best trout water is alkaline and is usually found in regions where limestone is a common rock-formation. Poor trout water is acid. Trout, of themselves, are largely indifferent to the acidity factor except when water changes rapidly as during a thunderstorm, but the small organisms which make trout fat are very dependent on the chemical state of the water. Snail, for example, is an important item of trout diet, and without lime in the water snails will not flourish.

Moorland streams are usually acid or, at best, neutral, but not always. Sometimes they flow over limestone bars, and these vastly improve the trouting. Lakes and streams fed from springs rising in chalk strata provide some of our best trout fishing.

Natural nymphs of Late March Brown (above) and Large Dark Olive.

Trout would soon starve if they relied on floating duns for a living, and even in the most prolific waters they feed on a wide variety of fare. In limestone lakes the snail is a substantial and fattening item, which the trout swallow shell and all. In moorland streams the natural equivalent of the snail is the caddis or sedge larva in its case. Trout stuff themselves with the cases until their stomachs are distended.

The freshwater shrimp, water-fleas, and nymphs are other sources of nourishment. Bigger trout, however, need larger items of nourishment; sticklebacks in lakes, and minnows in rough streams are a common prey.

Flies are really a sort of dessert after the main dish, for only rarely can a trout gorge itself on flies and consider that it has had a square meal. For this reason, trout rise freely only during a substantial fly hatch. Otherwise, they are busy foraging elsewhere.

Before we can practise wet-fly fishing successfully it is important to have a clear idea of how trout typically react to their environment at different seasons. The temperature and condition of the water is of fundamental importance to such behaviour.

Let us consider a well-grown trout through twelve months, starting with winter. The water is cold – probably never more that 35–40°F. if spring-fed. Our fish has spawned and it is weak and ill-favoured. In these conditions the trout is in a state of semi-hibernation. Trout do feed in winter but the feeding is irregular and not part of a pattern. In any case, aquatic food-forms are at a minimum.

Early spring sees little increase in water-temperature; indeed, it may fall. But the lengthening day has its effect on weed-growth and the small animals that are nourished thereby. Some early flies will hatch, especially the hardy Large Dark Olive. Therefore the nymphs of this fly will have been active for some days past and trout will feed on them especially during the middle part of the day, as well as on the hatched dun.

Much of our fish's early feeding therefore will be done deep down in the deepest and quietest pools. Bright sunshine may tempt the trout into the tails of the deeper runs for short periods, especially if the winter has been mild. But this will be only during the warmest part of the day.

Late spring sees the water a few degrees warmer, unless there are days of bitter north-east wind, which are only too common. More flies hatch and nymphal activity increases sharply. Our trout will now be feeding freely whenever a hatch occurs, but especially during the hours of about 11 a.m. to 3 p.m.

Early summer sees this trend even more strongly marked. Feeding will now be almost continuous during daylight hours. Intense sunshine, however, coupled with low water, will drive the trout to cover because it dislikes concentrations of ultra-violet on its skin. Although a trout enjoys the warmth it seems to sunburn easily.

Full summer sees an end to the day-fly hatches. Some, such as the B.W.O., seem to hatch all summer through, but these are not enough to sustain our lusty trout, which is now in prime condition. He quickly switches his attention to the minnow and to elvers if elvers run his river in quantity. Sedges and moths provide substantial fare during the short summer nights. Indeed, during the hottest weather he will do most of his feeding at night.

The approach of autumn sees a shortening of the day although the weather is often the best of the year for both trout and angler. Late-season hatches of day-flies begin and the trout takes a renewed interest in duns and spinners. He is now a fat fish and can be very choosey over the items of fare that float, crawl, or swim across his field of vision. Despite the nearness of the spawning season he can still give a good account of himself should he be silly enough to rise to a cleverly cast dun or to a sedge drawn over his lie at dusk.

In October he passes out of the angler's ken – a protected fish once more. His function during the coming weeks will be to find a mate, take part in the reproductive process, and then sink into a state of dreamless lethargy until the boisterous winds of March herald another spring.

This thumb-nail sketch of a trout's year is necessary so that we don't waste time over fishing methods that are unlikely to be productive. If fish are absorbed in feeding on nymphs at the bottom of six-foot pools it is clearly a waste of time to draw wet flies through the surface film. Conversely, if they are feeding on minnow, they are not likely to bother with the angler's nymph, solitary and tiny, fishing across the bottom.

Three-quarters of the problem of catching fish of any species is to diagnose correctly what they are feeding on at a given time. In trout fishing the other quarter of the problem is to show them similar fare in fly-form in an appropriate way.

In all game fishing we must remember the critical water-temperature of 50°F. Loosely speaking, water below 50°F. is 'cold' and water above this temperature is 'warm'. Trout tend to feed down in cold water and up in warm water. Cold water slows up a fish's metabolic processes so that it needs less food; warm water speeds them up and makes the fish hungry. There is of course an upper limit – about 75°F. – above which trout suffer discomfort and refuse to feed at all.

The temperature of the air in relation to that of the water is also important. A cool air-stream rapidly draws heat from water and fish dislike entering this cooling strata. An air-stream warmer than the water, however, quickly warms the upper strata and fish will rise into it freely. Although fish do hug the bottom when the water is cold they will nevertheless rise to surface fly if the air-stream is relatively warm.

It is always useful to check the air and water temperature. Some anglers use a thermometer; others – I confess I am in this slack group – use the backs of their hands.

Fly-fishing Tackle

The core of the fly-fisher's outfit is the rod, and the rod must be chosen with its purpose in view – that is to say, the sort of water to be fished and the weight and size of line to be lifted. Broadly speaking, a 9 ft trout rod will do everything an angler wants.

Rod and line *must* be selected together. If you already possess a rod then take it to the shop when you buy your line. A new system of identification marks, now adopted by the Association of Fishing Tackle Makers, no longer makes this precaution as necessary as was hitherto the case, but it is still worth doing.

The new method of standardizing fly-lines and 'fitting' them to rods rests on the sound fundamental principle that the only thing that matters, as regards casting, is the weight of the line. Today, fly-lines are made of silk, Terylene, nylon, or plastic; they may be level, forward-taper, or double-taper, and they may be devised to sink, to float, or to be 'neutral'. Each of these factors influences the weight of the working part of the line beyond the rod tip, a length of between 8 and 10 yds. Should this piece of line be of incorrect weight to suit the rod then poor casting is the inevitable result.

In future new fly-rods should carry the symbol ‡ followed by a number between 1 and 12. For example ‡ 4 means that the rod will handle a line which weighs between 114 and 126 grains per 10 yds of working portion. The ideal weight of line for such a rod would be 120 grains.

The angler therefore can select a rod, check the symbol on the butt, and buy a line bearing the corresponding symbol. The line may be of any type of material so long as the symbol and number indicates that it is of suitable weight.

Fly rods are now made of either split-cane, glass, or steel. Tubular glass is the least expensive and makes a good trout-rod, steel is powerful and long-lasting, but most fly-rods are made of split-cane. Greenheart, once common, is both heavy and uncertain in use.

Essentially, the weight and length of a rod depend on where and how the angler intends to fish. Small- to moderate-sized rivers argue light work for the rod and comparatively short casting distances, but bigger rivers and many reservoirs demand a rod stout enough to punch a longish line across high winds.

Some anglers seem to prefer a stout rod no matter where they fish. A 9½ ft rod weighing a little over 6 oz. is heavy enough for most reservoirs and big rivers. A light rod of this type can be wielded all day without fatigue.

The common belief that long rods increase the distance one can cast is a misconception. A tubular glass rod 8½ ft long makes a good long-casting tool.

Personally, I find that a 9 ft, 5 oz. rod made of split-cane is suited for most trout fishing and for sea-trout in smaller rivers. On reservoirs and larger rivers a 9½ ft rod gives a better command of the water and has enough backbone to play big fish.

A great deal of research, both by firms and by anglers, has been done since the war to discover the best type of cane for splitting and rod-making. Split Tonkin is the best and it is worth seeking, but there are plenty of inferior canes on the market.

Fly-Lines: Many trout anglers have turned with real relief to self-floating fly-lines, which require no greasing and have a tough, smooth dressing. These lines cast well and shoot beautifully. For reservoirs and medium-sized rivers the self-floating line is hard to beat, especially when there is a trace of summer scum on the water. It is useful for wet fly as well as for dry, provided one isn't scraping the bottom.

Smoothly dressed sinking lines are equally useful for fishing slow and deep in early spring. These take the place of the heavy ungreased silk lines which used to be the usual choice of wet-fly fishers.

Silk lines of the Kingfisher type are lovely to handle and to fish with, although they do suffer from clinging in the rod rings after greasing. Silk, however, being almost neutral in specific gravity can be fished more easily at varying depths than can lines which are either positive sinkers or positive floaters.

For trouting I like a double-tapered No. 2 dressed silk line on one reel and a No. 3 self-floating (Air Cel Supreme) line on another. These two, on the rods mentioned, have proved adequate on rivers as diverse as the Towy and Usk as well as Blagdon and Chew Lakes.

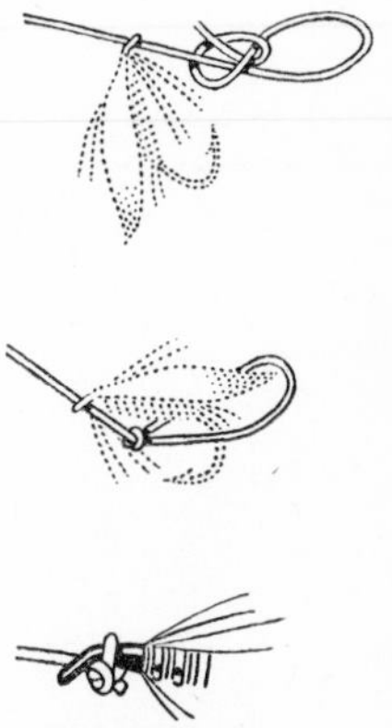

Turle knot for attaching fly to cast. Stage one, tie a slip-knot in end of cast. Stage two, pull fly through slip. Below, tighten slip-knot against metal eye.

Leaders or 'Casts': Gut is now obsolete and has been superseded by synthetics. Ordinary nylon monofil is not of much use for fly-leaders, since it is too limp, tangles easily, and quickly ties itself into wind-knots, but hard nylon is now being directly imported from the U.S.A. and makes a first-class leader. It is a tough, stiff nylon with small elasticity.

Many anglers still prefer continuous taper leaders of the type sold by Messrs Dunlop under the trade-name of 'Square Law'. I use these excellent leaders frequently and it is hard to suggest further improvement.

Dunlop have also produced a new material called 'Polygut'.

Tests showed that it lost little strength by soaking, sank easily, and was as stiff as silkworm gut. It did however glitter badly and took dye poorly; also it tended to 'neck'. Of the two materials I still prefer the familiar 'Square Law'.

Some anglers are finicky about the colour of leaders. Colour in itself matters little but any form of staining that helps prevent glitter is useful. A dull brown or dark grey is as good as anything.

Reels: A 3 in. reel for a 9 ft rod and a 3½ in. reel for a 9½ ft rod is about right. A narrow drum, adjustable check, and closely machined parts are desirable. A black or matt finish is much better than highly polished aluminium. Some reels seem designed to catch the eye on show-stands and would certainly throw off flashes at every cast when fishing.

Backing Line: Terylene or plaited nylon is the modern backing line, these materials having superseded the old-time flax and silk, both of which rotted. The backing line, of course, goes on the reel before the fly-line. Use as much backing line as the reel will carry in comfort. Terylene of 11 lb. breaking strain is about right. In reservoirs, a hundred yards of backing plus the reel line allow a safe margin where fish run big.

Combined 'priest', for killing fish wanted for the pot, and disgorger.

Accessories: A list of accessories useful to the trout fisher includes:

Landing net
Bag or creel
Book or wallet for leaders
Fly-box (a tobacco-tin will serve)
Large plastic bags for fish
Line grease
Bottle of detergent for de-greasing leaders
Dry-fly oil
Scissors
Bodkin for unpicking knots
Anti midge-cream
Artery forceps for removing hooks
'Priest' for killing fish quickly
A hank of string

Sooner or later the angler will need each of these and they take up little space.

Clothing: Most trout fishers use studded thigh-waders which are easy to slip on and off. Clothing should include a thick sweater for use under the fishing-jacket in cold weather.

Fishing-jackets should have a high collar, well-flapped pockets, and windproof sleeves. I like a type made by Barbours which has a removable hood zipped into an inner pocket for use in heavy rain. Fishing-jackets should be capacious enough to fit over one's ordinary tweed jacket and must be long enough to hang well down over the wader tops. This sort of outfit will resist heavy rain for hours on end.

Some sort of neck-cloth is desirable and there is nothing better than a silk square folded narrow and wound tight.

A pair of fishing-gloves is far from being a luxury. Fingerless gloves with nylon string palms and water-resisting wool backs are well worth acquiring. There is nothing worse than cold hands – unless it be cold feet.

Many anglers use polarized glasses, and some form of eye-protection is certainly needed when fishing sheets of open water in bright weather. Ordinary dark-glasses fitted with side-shields are my choice.

Fishing Methods

Upstream Wet Fly: Wet-fly fishing in rivers can be a semi-mechanical operation with very little real skill involved, or it can be as precise and delicate as the angler pleases. Certainly it takes little ability to drop a 'team' of wet flies into water and 'fish' them round. But this is very far from being the most effective way of wet-fly fishing.

Some anglers fish a single fly, or a leaded nymph, upstream. This is an exacting method, demanding delicacy of touch, quick reflexes, and good eyesight. The fly is cast precisely to selected lies where trout are known to be hovering, sometimes to a particular fish which the angler has spotted, using polarizing glasses.

Some experts at this form of fishing recommend that the angler tighten on the trout as soon as it turns with the fly; others try to spot the white of the opening mouth; most anglers study their lines. After some practice it is possible to detect when a fish has stopped the fly. One should then instantly tighten. All this takes a good deal of practice because one's timing must be gauged to a fraction of a second.

This form of fishing is good fun in low summer water, especially when a breeze ripples the surface, hiding the fall of the line from the fish and blurring the image of the leader. It is more effective to fish up and across than directly upstream, otherwise the point of the leader may reach the fish before the fly.

It is most important to de-grease the leader thoroughly for upstream wet fly. The fly *must* sink as soon as it touches the water. For this reason some experts use a weighted nymph fished on a fine point.

Those with the patience and reflex-control to master upstream wet fly have a deadly method of angling at their disposal. Trout of course lie facing the current. It is obvious therefore that the angler who wades quietly below the fish and casts his fly beyond them will hook his trout firmly in the side of the mouth. A wet fly fished down and across is all too easily plucked from the fish's mouth.

Better-quality fish are caught by upstream wet fly, probably because the fly acts more naturally. Big trout are less easy to fool than small trout. The upstream method is the most natural way of all of showing a wet fly to trout.

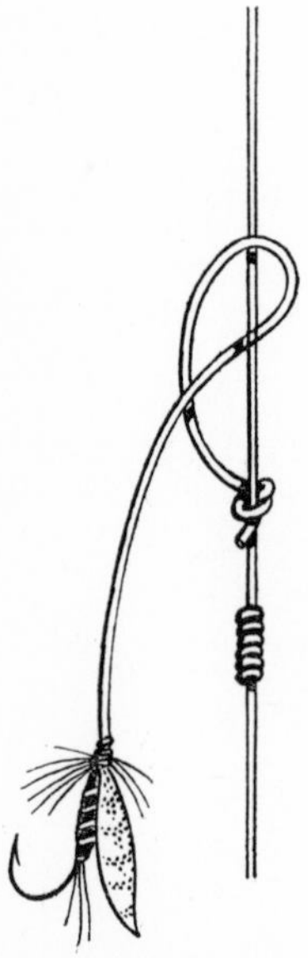

Dropper knot for tying wet-fly dropper to cast. Attach when possible above a blood-knot in cast, shown here as six small coils.

Standard Wet Fly: Upstream wet-fly fishing is best executed by wading, but depth of water and the nature of the banks may prevent this, the stream may be overgrown and the best trout may be lying under bushes on the far bank. Again, many anglers, especially when fish are not moving too freely, like to cover a bigger area of water. This is especially true when they are fishing in competition with threadline spinners.

In these conditions one uses standard wet-fly technique. This usually takes the form of casting across-stream or obliquely across and slightly up, or across and down. Instead of fishing only a few yards, as in upstream wet fly, one's flies now fish in a wide arc and cover a great deal more water.

The passive game of casting and allowing the flies to drift round on a more or less tight line has little place in good wet-fly fishing. The angler should submerge his flies in shallow water and study their appearance when immersed. Notice how a slight pull on the leader causes the hackle-fibres to work. Yet too much pulling will easily plaster the fibres flat against the hook.

Patterns which suggest nymphs should drift and be drawn across the current, but slowly. A nymph that flashes across the water at speed will never be mouthed by a big trout for although trout are unable to think, instinct warns them that nymphs in nature do not move at high speeds.

Tinsel-bodied fancy flies, of which the Butcher is a good example, can be fished in little spurts and pauses. Fish probably imagine them to be big water-beetles or small fish, which can move quite smartly on occasion. Even Butchers, however, should not be dragged against a strong current, for small fish and beetles travel by swimming down and across. Only in the slowest of backwaters can you work your wet fly upstream with the likelihood of catching trout.

Wet-fly angling has borrowed a good deal of technique from the developing art of greased-line salmon fishing. Wet flies are now fished more effectively than was the case thirty years ago. Both tackle and technique have improved, and we are a good deal wiser about what fish want in given conditions.

Wet-fly Technique: Assume the angler is fishing a North Country trout-stream in early April – an intermediate date for weather, for at that time of year the day may be bitterly cold or hot enough to make the fisherman sweat.

The angler looks at the water. It is full, bright, and promising. A warmish sun shines behind hazy clouds. Occasional specimens of various flies can be seen hatching and lifting off the water. Clearly the temperature is rising. Checking the water the angler finds it quite chilly, a mere 42°F. The air is much warmer, 54°F. Conditions here are favourable for surface fishing. A dry fly would do well. In any case, surface-fished wet flies are much to be preferred to deeply sunk nymphs.

The angler therefore will use his greased line, or a self-floater. If a particular sort of fly starts to come off in quantity he will of course use patterns to suggest that species.

But conditions may be quite different from the above. The day is dull with a hint of bitter rain hidden in the grey clouds. The water is cold; so is the air. Flies are few. The stream looks lifeless. The fish are down among the stones. Ungreased silk or one of the self-sinking lines is now indicated. It is a less pretty way of fishing than dry fly or surface wet fly; but it is the only way.

Some anglers work their wet flies vigorously; others do so hardly at all. It depends on the intensity of the light, the relative clarity or darkness of the water, and the speed of the flow.

Trout will not take a fly unless they can see it, and a small fly in darkish water may go unnoticed. One can of course use a larger fly but this is not always the best answer. Fish need to see the fly moving in relation to the current. This is the trout's only real assurance that the small insect-like object coming down on the water is in fact alive. Streams carry down a variety of tiny debris and trout sometimes make mistakes. And they are naturally doubtful about non-swimming items which may be simply twigs.

Normally a trout relies on vision to distinguish the animate from the inanimate, and the best way of doing this is to detect

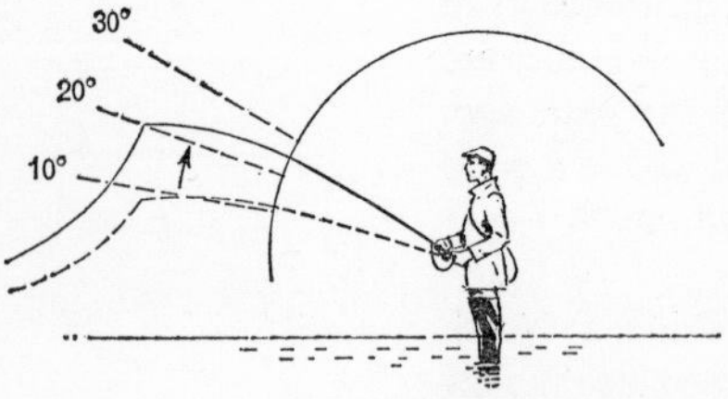
30°
20°
10°

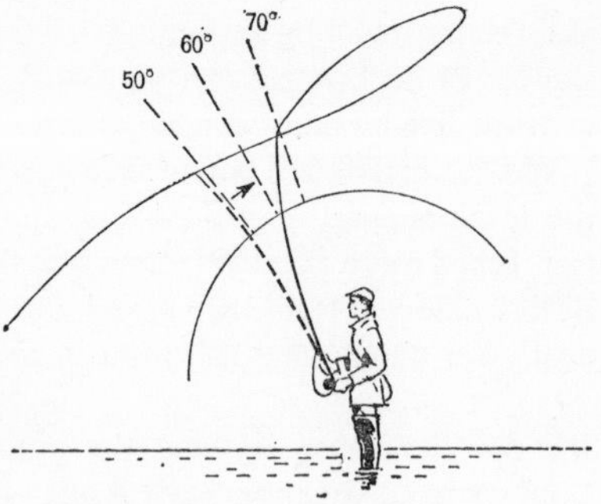
70°
60°
50°

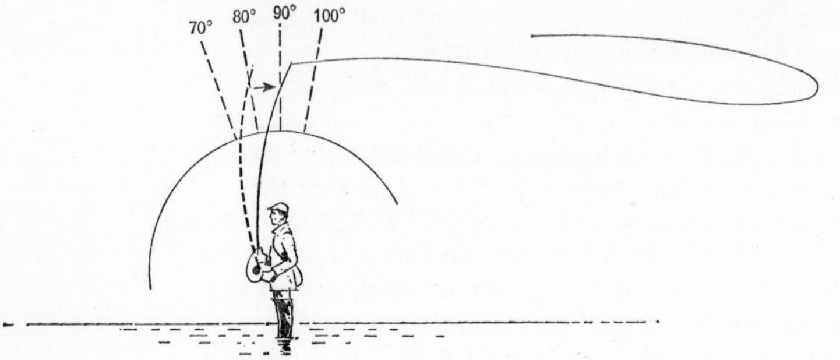
70°
80°
90°
100°

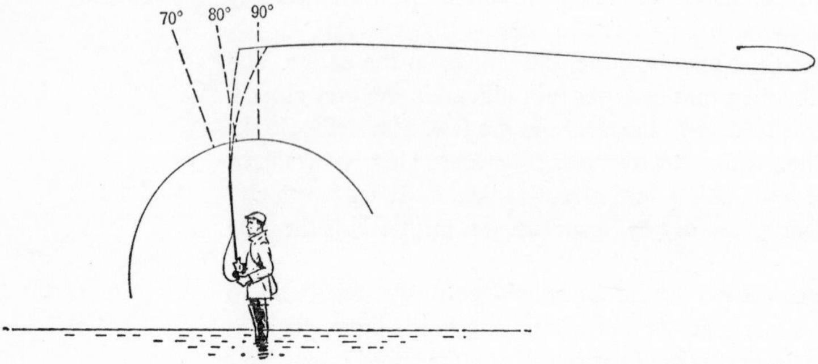
70°
80°
90°

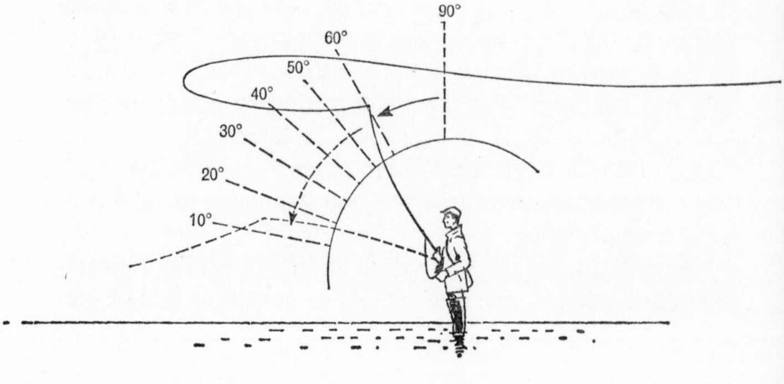
90°
60°
50°
40°
30°
20°
10°

movement relative to the current. An object that moves in a different direction from that in which the current would carry it is fairly obviously alive. Fish know this by instinct.

Working the fly gives it this necessary touch of vitality. Broadly speaking it may be said: quick working for fast streams and slower working for slower streams. Quick working will hook fish on dull days when slow working fails to get an offer. At the other extreme – in clear sunlit water – flies can be drifted without working, the slight drag from the line being quite enough to give life to the hackles.

Working the fly can be done in several ways. Some anglers draw line in slow pulls; others collect line in the palm of the hand. Still others tremble their rod tips. Personally, I try all these methods in rotation to find out which the fish fancy.

Most wet-fly fishers use a leader of three flies, but some North Country fishers put up more than half a dozen. It depends on what local rules allow and what you think fair. I use only a point-fly and a dropper high up the cast. If you can't make a basket with two flies then three or four are unlikely to help.

Dry-fly Fishing: The floating artificial fly offers advantages not always clearly appreciated. Fish see very much less of a dry fly than they do of a wet one. Many fish are caught on dry fly that would refuse a wet, simply because they can give the latter closer inspection. Most trout, taking waters as a whole, are hooked the instant the dry fly touches the water. They rise, so to speak, spontaneously.

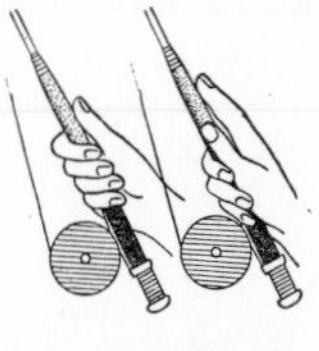

Two possible grips of the right hand for fly-casting.

Dry fly is often best in sunny conditions, because the leader point is less conspicuous when floating in the surface-film. This is especially true when there is a bit of dust and summer scum on the water.

Many studies have been made of what a trout sees when it looks up at a floating fly. E. Horsfall-Turner, for example, has photographed some extraordinary patterns of light and shade made by a dry fly's hackle-points penetrating the surface-film. The effect was certainly nothing like what we imagine.

(Opposite) Basic overhead fly-cast. Begin by drawing in line with left hand and then pick line smoothly off the surface, accelerating rod top. Between fifty and seventy degrees, the rod top is reaching maximum speed in order to throw line behind angler. At the vertical, the rod is checked and the line allowed to stream out behind. It is vital to pause while the line straightens. Maximum effort in the forward throw is made between the vertical and fifty degrees. The rest is follow-through. Spare, loose line held in the left hand is 'shot' (released) at about twenty degrees to help the fly to fall softly.

A trout probably sees a blurry image, faintly coloured, with a few insect legs penetrating the water. The 'educated' trout is no doubt influenced by the size and colour of the image more than by its mechanical details. All trout see the steel bend and barb of the hook, but since this is outside of their experience it is not taken into account.

Dry-fly Technique: The easiest way of fishing a dry fly is to wade and cast the fly up and across a slow current, line being gathered with the left hand until the fly is ready to be picked off and re-cast.

Often wading is impossible and the fly must be cast from the bank. It may be necessary to cast the fly in any direction – even downstream – in order to cover the fish. Casting across a current raises the hoary problem of drag. This is caused when the current moves the line or the leader in a different direction from that in which the fly is drifting. This motion is soon transmitted to the fly, which is then, in the worst cases, dragged bodily across the current.

There are several standard ways of preventing drag, all of them based on the principle of keeping the rod out of direct contact with the fly. Some anglers deliberately cast a wavy line, as opposed to a straight one. This is managed by driving forward fairly hard on the forward cast and giving the rod a slight lift and shake before the line straightens. To do this and achieve a measure of accuracy is not easy.

The line can also be 'mended' to counteract the dragging effect of the current. Placing the line upstream with the rod point has a similar but more positive effect.

The best way of preventing drag, however, is to remove the fly from the water before drag develops. It should be stressed again that the most killing part of a dry fly's 'travel' is the first few moments after it touches water. Some fish – notably grayling and sea-trout – do tend to follow a fly and take it some distance downstream, but trout don't do this to any marked extent. In brisk currents, therefore, where drag is very difficult to combat, the best technique is to use a short line, cast often, and allow the fly only a short travel. More water will be covered and more fish risen this way than by any other.

Dry fly on the quiet chalk-streams, casting to rising fish, permits of a more precise approach. The fly is presented a couple of feet above the position of the last observed rise and enough slack line is laid on the water to allow it to drift without dragging for at least a yard beyond the position of the trout.

In rough streams the angler can pick the fly off when he chooses. In clear chalk-water a pick-off too near the fish will certainly put it down, and the fly should first be allowed to drift beyond the fish until it starts to drag.

Hooking fish on the dry fly calls for restraint. It takes time for the trout to rise, take the fly, and turn down; and the bigger the trout the longer the time. The angler usually sees a swirl or bulge as the trout reaches for the fly. Unless it is allowed a second in which to take it and turn down there is a danger of pulling the fly out of the fish's mouth.

Various sorts of preparation are offered for making dry flies buoyant. Personally, I keep a little petrol in an air-tight jar in which a bit of petroleum jelly has been dissolved. Modern silicone preparations are clean and easy to use.

Lake and Reservoir Fishing: Lake and reservoir fishing for trout is worth careful study because, for very many anglers, this is the only sort of trout fishing they are ever likely to enjoy. In terms of weight and quality of fish, reservoir angling can be very rewarding. Indeed, few British rivers provide the feed to equal the best of our still waters, and feed is the key to good trouting.

Still-water trout fishing calls for patience, persistence, and intelligence. Many good river-anglers are hopeless on lakes and soothe their feelings by declaring that lake fishing is 'dull and featureless'. So it may be – if your bag is empty. Still-water fishing, unless tackled correctly, does breed tedium and

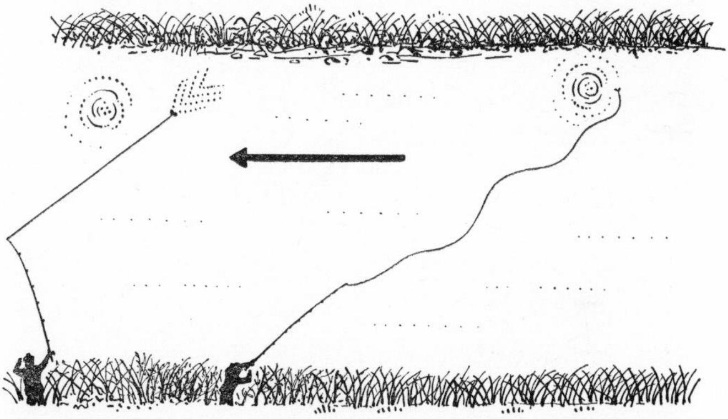

Drag The fly at left is dragging sideways before it reaches the fish because the angler has cast too straight a line. At right, the line is long and wavy so that the fly will have reached the rising fish long before any currents between angler and fly have started to put drag on the line.

disgust. It is pleasant to spend an hour by a lake. But to work all day and never see a fish sends many anglers back to their rivers wondering what others ever see in lake fishing.

The successful still-water fisher must know when to fish and when to desist. He must learn to detect when water is 'dour' and when it is productive.

First, he should know something about the climate in relation to his chosen lake. The altitude of the water is important too. Lowland reservoirs, such as Chew Lake, fish earlier in the season than waters which are 1,500 feet above sea-level. As a general rule: the higher the reservoir the later it fishes.

With lake fishing two factors are important: the colour of the sky and the amount of wave. Humidity – in so far as it encourages hatches of fly – also has an effect. Misty-grey is the best colour of sky for lake fishing. A low overcast or a drizzly mist are both good. A sunny, blue sky is mediocre. Fluffy white 'thunderheads' are bad, since they act as huge reflectors and pour light down into the water.

In conditions of strong light the trout see too much. Fish which have no trouble in finding and eating organisms as small as 0.100 in. in diameter can certainly spot a 3 lb. leader-point. Anything thicker must look like a rope.

A trout's vision depends on the reflection of light. Reduce the light (by dulling the sky) and they do not see so well. Break up the light-waves by introducing waves in the water and their vision is much reduced. Only then are we likely to catch them.

Can lakes be successfully fished in calm, bright conditions? Yes, but the angler must pick his times with care. Early morning and late evening are both favourable. As is well known, light is reflected off water at the same angle as its incidence, so that most of the light from a low sun is reflected off the surface instead of penetrating. The water becomes 'dark' and we can fish with some confidence.

Sometimes you will get dull skies and rippled water but have no luck. If the wind is north or north-east it is probably chilling the water and driving the fish into the deeps. Very dry air too is disliked by lake trout, probably because it is often at a lower temperature than the water.

Lake-fishing Technique: There is and always must be a certain amount of guess-work in lake fishing. If we could catch fish to a 'formula', angling would be a pretty dull sport. It is the gamble that attracts and keeps us flogging away when common sense cries quit!

What sort of tackle for lake fishing? For wading and bank-work I prefer a medium trout rod. Mr Ivens and others have told us with some authority that we should use a powerful rod of some 10 ft. There is good sense in this in that strong rods will cast long lines, but short rods will cast even longer lines. It is not necessarily wise, however, to use a rod designed for casting at the expense of its fishing qualities. I like to see my rod bend into a fish because this is the best guarantee that I am going to land it. It means that the hook is being pulled in firmly and that the fish has a spring against which to fight. To pull on a fish with a strong 10 ft rod or even a stiff tournament rod of shorter length means simply that the leader-point is being subjected to great strain. To counteract this some anglers use points of 7 and 10 lb. breaking strain. But stout points of course reduce the number of 'takes' in light-dark conditions. Others fall between two stools, using the prescribed stout rods but with fine points. As a result, numbers of fish smash their way to freedom.

One hears reports from time to time of anglers having their tackle broken by fish. This is something that can and should be avoided. At no time should a lake fisher point his rod tip at his flies while they are fishing. The rod is the angler's prime guarantee against breakage, but it works only so long as it is used as a buffer between the taking trout and the angler's fist. Point the rod at the flies and a heavy take will certainly break you. But hold the rod so that the line forms an angle of about 90° with the tip and it is impossible for even the biggest fish to break you on the take, always assuming that a light rod and a sound, although fine, point are in use.

I have watched scores of anglers breaking this common-sense rule and can only assume they have not bothered to think it out. The loss of a big trout is a high price to pay for carelessness. Yet it happens season after season.

Nothing takes harder than a lake trout. All the weight of their bodies goes into the first frightened plunge and it needs every bit of the spring in rod and tackle to resist breakage. A trout may take fifty yards of line and backing off the reel in under three seconds. A properly held rod helps the leader to survive this shock treatment.

Self-floating lines are very suitable for lake fishing. Alkyd-dressed lines and so-called 'bubble' lines shoot well and help give the angler distance, which is sometimes desirable. Also such lines float perfectly even in choppy water.

On some still waters the angler has the option of wading or boat-fishing. The question naturally arises: 'Is boat-fishing worth the extra cost?' As with most things in life, it depends.

Sometimes a boat means also the services of a professional gillie; sometimes one can fish alone or with a companion. Boats managed by professionals greatly reduce the amount of skill and water-craft needed by the angler. In many cases one finds that it is really the gillie who is doing the fishing and the angler is merely holding the rod. Placing the boat on a good drift, giving a pull on the oar to line the rodsman up with a rising fish – the gillie knows it all, or should do. Then if the angler keeps his fly in the water all will be well.

Managing one's own boat is of course quite different. The credit, if any, must certainly go to the angler himself if he catches fish. Will he do better in a boat than he would if he had waded? Obviously he will cover more fish, and the ripple-line, which always seems to be just out of reach on big lakes, is no problem. The lake angler who masters the problems peculiar to boat-fishing will probably – over many months – beat the average of the bank-angler. But, of course, individuals vary widely; many anglers simply prefer to wade.

Fishing upland lochans and hill-lakes provides plenty of inexpensive pleasure in lovely surroundings. No special problems are involved. Light trout tackle and small flies almost invariably work well. The factors of sky-colour and amount of wave mentioned above apply equally here.

Dapping: Dapping is not as easy as it is sometimes made out to be. There are two sorts: dapping from a boat using a 'blow-line' and dapping from the bank, usually of an overgrown stream.

Dapping from a boat is an accepted method in Ireland and Scotland. In Ireland, natural flies are used, especially the may-fly and the daddy-long-legs. In Scotland on Loch Maree and similar waters holding big sea-trout it is usual to dap with huge artificial flies. It takes a big fly to draw fish up from deep water. A dapping rod should be 12–14 ft long. It must be light and the top section needs to be pliable enough to play heavy fish without shattering.

The technique consists of dancing the fly – whether natural or artificial – along the crests of the waves. A breeze acting on the fluffy blow-line makes this fairly easy. Striking is much the same as when fishing a dry fly. The fish must be allowed time to turn down after boiling at the fly. On seeing the rise some anglers school themselves to glance away and wait until they feel the fish taking line. This is not a bad plan.

Nearly every angler at one time or another has tried dapping from the bank, usually on a hot summer day when any other sort of fishing is hopeless. Provided you can lever your rod through the mass of greenery and lower the big bushy Palmer-type fly to the surface without showing too much of yourself there is a good chance of rising a big trout.

Bait-fishing – Spinning: In recent years spinning conducted against trout has come under a cloud, many people believing that it should be banned. Some River Boards do ban trout spinning; others permit it, but uneasily. One has got to look at the subject objectively. On most waters in Britain today trout have to be stocked. Where trout are not stocked there are few trout. It is as simple as that. Having stocked the trout you must then decide what methods of fishing are to be allowed. Should one allow the easy methods or only the most interesting methods, or simply allow people to get as many trout as they can out of the water any way they choose? Opinions are widely divided.

The hotel owner is always worth listening to on this topic, since he earns his bread-and-butter by the quality of his fishing, and at the same time must please his guests and help make their angling a pleasure. Quite a number of hotels do permit spinning, but at least as many are 'fly-only'. On one water they have what is called a 'Flag Day'. When the river is too spated for good fly-fishing, flags are run up masts to indicate that anglers may spin or worm, as they choose.

The Chief Fishery officer of a River Board once listed for me the objections he had to spinning for trout. These included too large a proportion of young fish hooked and killed while abstracting the trebles, and the wholesale disturbance of nearly every inch of water in the river.

Spinning is easy. After ten-minutes practice even a small boy can throw a minnow across a river. The lack of skill needed for spinning has led to the spinning or fixed-spool reel being manufactured in tens of thousands, and many of our rivers are now raked by minnows from morning till night. It is not my purpose here to condemn this activity as unsporting but simply to point out that good trout fishing demands restraint, and the best form of restraint is to require the angler to be proficient at an angling form that calls for some skill and experience before he becomes a danger to the fish-stocks. Fly-fishing does impose this limitation.

In neglected streams of no great size there seems no logical reason why anglers should not spin on occasion. The snag, of course, is that neglected streams become fewer every year. Some do exist, however, and in Wales there are plenty still.

Any badly overgrown water where it is clearly impossible to fly-fish may be considered a fair target for the spinning angler. A light 7 or 8 ft rod fitted with a trout-sized fixed-spool reel loaded with 4 lb. monofil Perlon is a suitable outfit.

Baits may be artificial or natural. Quill minnow or preserved (salted) minnow are both good. Fresh minnows can be used, too, but they are soft and don't survive casting so well as the tougher salty ones.

One spins up and across. The minnow is recovered at a brisk pace but not so fast that there is turbulence behind it. Sometimes trout go well for a tiny silver devon spun very fast, usually when the water is clearing after a spate.

Wobbler tackles are good, too, and I sometimes use them in preference to the ordinary 'Mountfast' type of minnow-mount. The wobbler-lead is inserted inside the minnow and the trebles are clipped into the shoulder and flank. Wobbling minnows are best fished across and downstream.

Late May and June are probably the best minnowing months, with a revival again towards the end of summer. Low warm water is ideal for minnow, especially when the sun is off it.

Dip or Drop Minnow: This is an effective and not inartistic method which is not as widely used as it could be. For once it can be said (almost with relief) that nearly any sort of tackle will serve. A light rod, 10 or 12 ft long, is ideal. An old ROACH rod could easily be adapted by fitting a fibre-glass tip.

Mount a reel (any sort) loaded with about fifty yards of 6 lb. b.s. monofil nylon. Push a small torpedo-shaped lead with a hole through it inside a fresh or salted minnow. Thread the line through the lead, using a needle, and out the minnow's tail, and knot on a size 12 treble hook.

The idea is to fish the minnow, dip and lift, wherever a big trout seems likely. Undercut banks, deep backwaters, and rocky pots amongst boulders are the likeliest places. The angler can wade; he can fish upstream or downstream as he chooses; or he can prowl the banks, dipping and drawing the minnow at a whim.

Patience, a light touch, and a good knowledge of trout-lies will be developed by this form of angling. The experts get some excellent baskets of fish.

Nymph and Creeper Fishing: Some fishermen use a delicate and skilful method of baiting by using a natural nymph. Hooks as small as 20s are used. The fairy-like baits are placed ('cast' is too coarse a term) upstream, where they are allowed to trickle over the stones, aided only by a microscopic dust shot.

The Large Stone-fly creeper is the largest of our river-nymphs and two-hook tackles are recommended for 'covering' this comparatively sturdy bait, which is cast upstream, using a long, light rod.

In late May and early June the natural creeper can be deadly. A good deal of practice is needed to detect the bite with certainty, but on the other hand, as with all natural baits, trout do tend to retain their hold much longer than they would with an artificial. Experience at upstream wet-fly fishing is very useful for the creeper angler.

Clear-water Worming: One rarely sees worms in the clear waters of trout-streams and they must be counted as a rare item of fishes' diet. On the other hand elvers are common in summer and a young eel and a worm look very much alike.

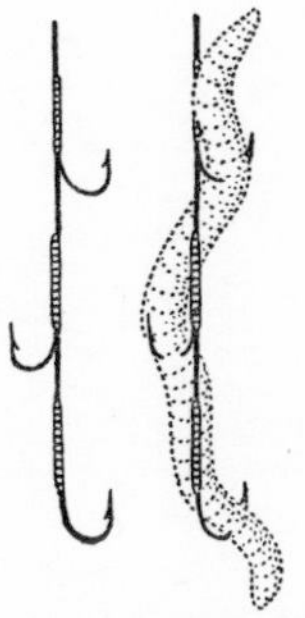

Three-hook Stewart tackle for securing worm. Two hooks will do.

If fly fails and worm is allowed then use it by all means. At dawn and again towards evening worm can have a fatal attraction for trout, even in near-drought conditions. Well-scoured redworms dug from an ancient dung-heap and subsequently re-packed in fresh water-weed or moss should do the trick. Those between 2 and 3 ins. long are the best.

Mount the worm on a two hook tackle so that head and tail hang attractively. One or even two small lead shots may be added to the line although some experts prefer none. A 4 lb. monofil line is about right if there is a chance of big fish. In a moorland stream it is safe to go as fine as 2 lb. A rod similar to that advocated for drop-minnow will serve for worming.

A worm is lobbed gently into the quiet gravel runs and the angler recovers line with one hand as it comes towards him downstream.

General

It is customary to assert that the only sporting way of catching trout is with a fly. Unlike some hoary statements which rest on doubtful premises the above remains as true today as when it was first stated. The most efficient way of catching trout is with a net or a fish-trap. Quite deliberately, anglers prefer to catch their trout by a method which calls for a high degree of skill, experience, and manual dexterity. This is not to say that fly-fishing is hard to learn, but it is hard to do really well.

Anglers have two chief motives for making trout-catching difficult. The first is to give the fish a sporting chance by allowing it to refuse to be caught. The second, stemming from the first, is to conserve trout-stocks.

Similar arguments of course could be advanced for other sorts of fishing. But these apply to trout in particular. Trout are a hard-sought species and large specimens – the breeding stock – are, unlike coarse fish, seldom returned to the water alive. Trout fishing needs to be difficult in order to protect the trout.

Apart from the severely practical consideration of maintaining stocks, fly-fishing is by far the richest, most diverse, and most interesting method of angling. It relies, as was mentioned in an earlier chapter, on illusion, and the successful illusionist needs to be part-artist.

Owners of fisheries and angling associations could do a lot more than they are doing to foster fly-fishing. For example more cheap day-tickets could be offered to young anglers who signed a promise to stick to fly only. Organizations such as the Welsh Fly-Fishing Association already run annual fly-only contests for juniors and generally do everything possible to urge youngsters to fish fly at all times.

The cult of the dry fly was driven too hard and died a natural death. Nowadays dry-fly fishing is simply one of several methods of fly-fishing, to be employed as and when the occasion warrants. Nymphs, fished near the bottom, are now widely used on many chalk-streams, and 'nymph' is simply a careful euphemism for a wet fly without wings. On waters other than chalk-streams the dry and wet fly have for long been regarded as equal partners, each contributing something to the sport. On most lakes anglers seldom use anything other than the wet fly, and count themselves no less sportsmen because of this fact.

For many years a number of books on dry-fly fishing led the public to think that this method was superior to any other. Many experts now consider that the upstream wet fly, working as it is in three dimensions, is the more difficult way of fishing. It is all a matter of opinion and each must decide for himself.

The huge upsurge of popularity for all sorts of fishing has almost driven trout fishing underground. The expensive clubs, offering rods at £400 per season, have always boasted a waiting-list of would-be members. But there used to be some less well-known waters where the trout fisherman could enjoy very good sport for under £10 a year, even around the bigger cities. These waters have now quite disappeared. Further afield, the rough-stream trouting of Yorkshire, the West Country, and Wales used often to be free for the asking, or at least quite cheap. But farmers who, even ten years ago, thought little of their fishing have now posted 'Private' notices or insist on substantial payment. With rates soaring on every river the fishing must now pay for itself.

The river-fishing picture is unlikely to improve. Even if all our rivers were pure the fishing could never stretch to meet the increasing demand, and I'm afraid we must like it or lump it. However, there is a reverse side to every coin. In trout-fishing this is spelled by the magic word: reservoirs. As we become more water-conservation minded there are likely to be more and still more sheets of fresh water, and local authorities are slowly becoming educated to the fact that, in these waters, trout are a lucrative and beneficial crop.

For the angler of modest means – which means most of us – reservoirs offer good value for money. In terms of sport, size and quality of fish, and the amount of fishable water available there are few rivers to compare with our best reservoirs.

A day-ticket on a reservoir enables the newcomer to get the flavour of the game without over-committing himself financially. The expert is assured of a season's sport for as little as £5, rising to £40 at our best reservoir, Chew Lake. Compared with the inflated cost of river-fishing this is good value.

Finally, to whet your appetite, the trout record at present stands at 39 lb.

F. W. H.

Rainbow Trout

The rainbow trout (*Salmo irideus*) is a handsome fish with a dark bluish-green back. Its sides are tinted with pinkish marks and it is profusely sprinkled with small spots. At Chew, where rainbows and browns are caught in roughly equal numbers, the rainbow has been caught up to 6 lb. According to H. E. Wallis, the average weight of the largest fish at Blagdon from 1905 to 1939 was 4 lb. 14 oz. for rainbows and 6 lb. 7 oz. for brown trout. The rainbow has been the subject of controversy ever since it was introduced into Britain more than seventy years ago. Even today, opinions are still divided on whether it is a desirable species to stock. There is a good deal of prejudice against rainbows on the grounds that they are inferior to native brown trout, and these arguments are strengthened when we notice that some Americans prefer brown trout to their own native rainbows.

How to define 'rainbow trout'? It is not particularly easy, since the blanket word 'rainbow' covers several related species, some of which are migratory and some non-migratory. When we reach the stage of sub-species and varieties the subject becomes confused and the best the average angler can do is to accept the definitions given out by some biological authority.

For convenience it may be assumed that there are three North American trouts which may be termed 'rainbow'. These are: the steelhead (migratory rainbow); *Salmo irideus* (non-migratory rainbow); and the Shasta rainbow. There are also numerous sub-species such as the cutthroat, Dolly Varden, Kamloops trout, and so forth. Professor John Snyder (U.S.A.) says: 'A steelhead is a sea-migrant of a particular species inhabiting the stream and it may be a cutthroat steelhead or a rainbow steelhead.' For practical angling purposes the steelhead and the rainbow trout proper may be likened to our own sea-trout and brown trout.

So far as is known, steelheads have never run British rivers. This is so even when rivers contain *Salmo irideus,* some of which might be suspected of having the migratory urge, just as some of our own brown trout stocks have it. An interesting, although inconclusive, case did however occur on the River Western Cleddau, where several anglers reported the capture of 'curious-looking salmon'. This river, at that time, had a commercial rainbow trout farm in its upper reaches from which fish sometimes escaped. Unfortunately the strange migrants were not sent for identification.

The value of the rainbow trout is said to lie in its speed of growth, its eagerness to rise to a fly, and the fight it puts up on being hooked. Objectors to the rainbow point out, however, that in many waters it fails to do well and the stocks have a tendency to disappear. Both faults could probably be traced to a strong migratory urge, for no migratory fish thrives if cooped in a lake.

The rainbow has other useful attributes. It enjoys warmer water than does the brown trout and will feed well even under a hot summer sun. It is also said to withstand mild pollution better.

Rainbows normally breed later than do brown trout. Some, indeed, are spring-spawners and are out of condition when the brown trout season opens, even if they are not actually gravid. For this reason it can be said that fishing for rainbows is at its best in late summer and early autumn.

Egg-binding seems to be a fault with rainbows and causes a good deal of mysterious mortality. Rainbows are rather particular about their spawning redds (or shallows) and should these not be quite suitable the female refuses to shed her eggs and dies. This trait may explain why some rainbows disappear without trace even from lakes.

However there are probably other factors at work and the problem of the vanishing rainbow is still of concern to managers of fisheries. In some waters the rainbow thrives and it is perhaps significant to note that these are usually alkaline. However, just to complicate the issue, at least one acid lake has been successfully colonized, so it may boil down to the fitness of the spawning redds, after all.

The belief that the introduction of a 'pure' strain of non-migratory rainbow would solve our stocking problems led to the importation of the Shasta rainbow, which was supposed to be a distinct non-migratory type. The Shasta, however, proved to be as variable as other sorts and in some waters it disappeared in the usual infuriating way. More research is needed before it can be said that this is due to spawning-bed troubles, migratory urge (fish can escape from lakes up feeder-streams, where many may perish), or food-supply. It may be a combination of all three factors.

Among the few British rivers 'adopted' by the rainbow are the Derbyshire Wye, the Chess, and the Derwent. Blagdon and Chew Valley are the chief lakes. Variable success has been scored on some other reservoirs and lakes. In one thirty-acre lake stocked with rainbows and brown trout rainbows were caught this season (1962) until May, after which only brown trout figured in the baskets. I was asked to comment on this phenomenon but could offer no useful solution.

T. C. Ivens tells how Shasta rainbows, introduced to a Midland reservoir, grew so fast that a fish only three summers old weighed 3 lb. 2 oz. Such growth however depends on a profuse food-supply. Where this is lacking one gets small rainbows tending to oust the browns.

There seems to be no cut-and-dried formula available for anglers who wonder whether their water is suitable for rainbow trout. The only effective method seems to be to have a trial stocking and check on the result. Waters with a pH factor indicating acidity are less likely to become successful rainbow fisheries than those with neutral or alkaline water. It would be interesting to know whether rainbows could flourish in acid lakes containing whitefish shoals. Experimental work is being carried on in Ireland, where between 3,000 and 4,000 rainbows have just been stocked in Lake Keeldra, Co. Leitrim, by the Inland Fisheries Trust.

Flies

Rainbow trout are usually caught on the same patterns and types as those used for brown TROUT. The rainbow, however, seems to be a more vigorous feeder than the brown. It tends to rise impulsively and this has earned it a reputation – and the mild scorn of some anglers – for being easier to catch.

This impulsive rising means that tinsel-dressed flies, drawn rather fast, often attract rainbows into rising in conditions where there is little natural fly on the water, and particularly in sunny weather. Moreover, some rainbows seem to rise more than once at the fly before taking it and being hooked.

It is useful to have a really bright fly in the box for rainbow trout in sunny weather. Here is a really sparkling pattern that often does well:

Body: Gold tinsel from the bend of the hook to the shoulder, dressed flat
Wing: Fibres from the eye of a peacock eye-feather
Hackle: Soft hen dyed pale blue, dressed very sparse
Tail: G. P. crest
Hook: 8s, 10s, and 12s

This fly should be drawn smoothly and steadily through the upper few inches of water. Fish probably take it for fry or a beetle.

Tackle Fly tackle as suggested for brown TROUT is quite suitable. For fishing the bigger lakes, such as Chew, a 9½ ft split-cane rod, a No. 3 self-floating line, and tapered leaders down to as fine as 4 lb. breaking strain are very satisfactory. The precaution of always pointing the rod *away* from the fly saves breakages by taking fish as explained earlier.

Fishing Methods It can be confidently asserted that the only rainbow trout the reader is likely to catch will be on a fly. Fishery management and stocking take a great deal of work and patience as well as money, and the people who do this work are naturally reluctant to see the fruits of their toil reaped in an inept or mechanical manner. Spinning, which used to be allowed at Blagdon, is now banned. Most reservoirs containing rainbow trout are 'fly only'.

It is a pity to catch rainbow trout by any other method than fly since they are free risers and often feed without restraint in conditions when brown trout are inactive.

Rainbow trout often take quite savagely. On hooking, they are almost as active as sea-trout, repeated leaps and swift dashes with rapid changes of direction being the rule. These tactics often culminate in a long fast run into deep water.

Beginners sometimes stand mesmerized on hooking a rainbow. The fish may dart rapidly shorewards leaving the angler with a lot of slack line. Reeling in is then too slow and one must haul the line down the rod with one's free hand until contact is established.

Tactics for Still Water: In lakes holding both rainbow and brown trout there seems to be no special way of ensuring the capture of any particular species. Certain areas on certain lakes, however, do seem to favour one fish or the other. The diet of the two species would seem to be closely similar.

On hot days when there is little activity among the brown trout it is likely that most of the fish in your basket will be rainbows. I get the impression that rainbows rise to a fly from a greater depth than do browns. Warm, windy days with a strong sun, diffused by cloud, are especially favourable.

Cogent-sounding arguments are often advanced in favour of fishing down-wind (from the lee shore) against equally cogent arguments for fishing on the weather shore. Anglers are often persuaded by thoughts of personal comfort rather than of the predilections of the fish they hope to catch. There was an occasion on Usk Reservoir when over a hundred fishermen were angling in the Welsh Fly-Fishing Championship. It was a day of strong south-west wind and rain, and despite the importance of the event and the kudos attaching to the winner, most anglers had congregated along the bays on the lee shore with their backs to the wind. Few fish were caught; only a dozen were weighed in all day. I asked the steward, who lived on the lake, where he thought the fish would be feeding in those conditions. He indicated a portion of the opposite weather shore where there were extensive weed-beds.

Lake fishing can be cold, hard work and it is only natural to seek the more sheltered positions on a bad day. But the lake angler often has to decide whether the object of the exercise is a basket of trout or a day in the open air. Feeding fish care nothing for the angler's comfort.

Occasions when the chop is so heavy that the water has been discoloured for some feet from the bank offer good conditions in which to catch big rainbow trout. Not only does the murk hide your leader but it dims the clearer water beyond, where the fish are feeding.

The routine here is to cast obliquely across-wind and allow the line to bag as it drifts rapidly inshore. The fly of course is first dropped into the clearer water off shore. Fish follow the fly and seize it before it can 'escape' into the gloom near the bank.

General

The rainbow trout is the most successful foreign game fish to have been introduced into Britain. Two other game fish have been tried: the American brook trout (a species of char) and the hutchen. The brook trout enjoyed a limited success, and according to Dr Winifred Frost, quoted by Fitter, is to be found in Wise Een and Wraymires in the Lake District and in Moss Eccles Tarn. The hutchen, or Danube salmon, seems to have failed completely.

In rainbow literature the work of Dr E. B. Worthington is extensively quoted in connexion with the investigation he carried out on the Derbyshire Wye into the complaint that rainbows were driving out the native brown trout. In fact it would seem that the rainbow was maligned. Pollution from upstream, especially from Buxton, was having a negative effect on the brown trout, despite extensive stocking. The rainbow was not inconvenienced to the same degree and it naturally filled the gap left by the diminished browns.

In the Bristol reservoirs, where the water is chemically pure, the rainbow and brown trout appear to thrive together amicably in the same environment.

Although it is the custom to stock rainbows artificially in most waters where they occur, the species does nevertheless breed naturally in several locations. Haddon Hall and Newstead Abbey, together with the rivers Gwash, Cam, Granta, and Rhee, are typical of such places. Rainbows are said to breed, too, in the Chiltern streams Chess, Gade, Misbourne, and Mimram.

Many rivers today are in a state of semi-pollution caused by the nation-wide use of detergents. Research is in progress to prevent detergents causing foam at the filter-beds and in the rivers, but from the angling viewpoint this may not be so good as it sounds. Foaming detergent can at least be seen, whereas foamless types may flourish unnoticed. Detergents rely on alkyl-aryl-sulphonates for their effectiveness and these chemicals are toxic to fish. Surface-active chemicals of the anionic type, from household and farm detergents, spread widely over the water-surface and their effect is to slow down the rate of oxygen-absorption. 9·4 parts per million of surface-active liquid has been found to kill brown trout. Rainbows would seem to be slightly more resistant.

From the Derbyshire Wye experience it looks as though mild pollution is diminishing the brown trout population in more rivers than is perhaps obvious. If the migration problem can be successfully tackled it may well be that in the future rainbow trout will provide good trout fishing in streams which have long been past their best as brown trout fisheries.

The risks attendant on introducing foreign species are now better appreciated than they once were. There have been several unwise importations, particularly the hideous Wels or Danubian catfish. Diversity of species has its attractions but it can be easily overdone, especially when the native forms suffer.

Rainbows have been introduced successfully into New Zealand. Lake Alexandrina in South Island contains excellent fish which are said to be descendants of the steelheads stocked in North Island's Lake Taupo.

The world record rainbow was a fish of 37 lb. taken in Pend d'Oreille Lake, Idaho, U.S.A. In this lake a land-locked salmon provides a supply of large food for big trout. It is difficult to see why whitefish should not occupy the same position in British waters. F. W. H.

Sea-Trout

Sea-trout, sewin, white trout, and migratory trout are synonyms for the form of trout (*Salmo trutta*) that travels between sea and river for the purposes of feeding and breeding. When we recall that the freshwater brown trout is considered a very sporting fish it will be appreciated that in the sea-going form the qualities of vigour, speed, and stamina are developed to a superlative degree.

All sorts of theories have been advanced to explain why a race of trout should find it beneficial to migrate, none of them wholly satisfactory. One explanation put forward is that since food is short in acid rivers the trout go to sea in order to feed. This theory, however, fails to explain why sea-trout are found in rivers of rich feeding such as the Hampshire Avon and the Dorset Frome. A bold theory, put forward by Mr Fred Page, suggests that sea-trout are in fact hybrids resulting from salmon and brown trout matings. But biological authorities assure us that such crosses have never been observed in nature and, in any case, would be sterile.

A great deal of interesting work is being done by the Salmon Research Trust of Ireland, which has produced numbers of salmon/sea-trout hybrids at its Inver hatchery. The growth of these fish was very good and exceeded that of salmon or sea-trout of similar age. It was hoped to tag and release these hybrids as large smolts just over two years old, but ill-luck dogged this experiment and the greater proportion of the stock died after routine treatment with fungicide. Research is fraught with difficulty and the real nature of the sea-trout is still a mystery. Dr D. J. Piggins, however, reports that it is possible to transform sedentary brown trout into sea-going smolts after appropriate endocrine treatment.

The name 'sea-trout' covers a multitude of sea-going, coastal, and estuarial trout forms, but the sea-trout of popular parlance may be described loosely as a trout with the proportions and wandering habits of a salmon, which indeed it closely resembles. The most scientific way of distinguishing salmon from sea-trout is by a scale count: the former have 10–12 scales from lateral line to dorsal fin, the latter 16.

Sea-trout are restricted almost entirely to our western seaboard, although they are caught in nets along the beaches of north Norfolk. They seldom enter rivers there, however. One netted at Blakeney recently carried a Scottish Dee tag. A few rivers as far east as Dorset contain them. Elsewhere they make occasional appearances but clearly find conditions not quite to their liking. Their presence in one or two Sussex rivers suggests that abstraction and pollution have driven the sea-trout from the east coast rather than the operation of any natural factor.

Broadly speaking, the sea-trout is a fish of the summer. Some rivers do have spring runs – in the Towy, for example, fresh sea-trout are caught as early as April – but a useful run of fish seldom occurs much before late May. These early summer fish are the best of the season, being clean, in perfect condition, and of substantial weight. The weights range from about 3 lb. to 7 lb. with a sprinkling of specimens as big as 12–17 lb.

Sea-trout smolts migrate during May and weigh, on average, about 3 oz. In July, August, and September they run up-river again, having quadrupled their body-weight in the sea. Indeed, many now weigh well over a pound. These young returning sea-trout are known as whitling.

From June onwards sea-trout run up the rivers freely. They are fond of hot, fine weather and anti-cyclones, and dislike muggy weather with depressive electrical clouds. I find that they run best when the weather is fine and the springs are in full flow. Much information can be derived from a study of the springs that feed the river. Springs are fed from underground reservoirs, and once these become exhausted the rivers rapidly fall to drought level and sea-trout stop running.

In the biggest rivers the ideal time for a sea-trouting holiday is probably the middle fortnight in June. Given hot sun, cool breezes, and a reasonable flow of water, the best sea-trout of the season will be found filling the lies. Fishing in July and August is often disappointing. September is often good, although the average size of the fish is reduced owing to the large numbers of whitling in the rivers.

As with salmon, there are early and late rivers, so it pays to make careful inquiry before booking advance accommodation on a strange stream. Small rivers may contain sea-trout from August onwards, and broadly speaking the smaller the river the later it is likely to be, but there is no hard-and-fast rule; some quite small waters have a June run.

The sea-trout first put in an appearance, of course, in the lower reaches and in bigger rivers it may be some weeks before they penetrate to the middle and upper water. This point is important to the angler who finds himself fishing water forty or fifty miles from the sea. He may find it pays him to drive twenty miles downstream.

Tackle and Flies

Ordinary TROUT tackle is satisfactory for sea-trout fishing. Generally speaking, a 9 ft trout-rod of split-cane or glass with a 3 in. reel, loaded with a suitable silk or Terylene tapered line, is all the angler needs. Specialists who fish for heavy sea-trout at night often prefer a slightly heavier outfit: a 9½ or 10 ft rod and line to suit. It is true that big fish can be more easily subdued on the heavier outfit and if a water is known to contain reasonable numbers of sea-trout over 8 lb. then the heavier tackle is recommended. But personally I use the trout-weight tackle at all times except when there is the likelihood of hooking a salmon. Having landed sea-trout up to 6½ lb. on a 4 oz. rod I am increasingly loath to use gear more suited to light salmon fishing, which is how one must describe heavy sea-trout tackle.

A 9 ft tapered leader of non-glint nylon is ideal for sea-trout, and the ones sold by Messrs F.O.G. Tackle, Ross-on-Wye, under the name of 'Square Law' have proved excellent in every way. Some anglers use a fly on point and a single dropper tied in high up the cast; some use one fly; others prefer three. I find that I hook two fish on the point-fly to every fish caught on the dropper.

Flies for sea-trout must be considered in relation to the habits and traits of the fish. Fresh-run sea-trout will take almost any sort of bright fly, but after a short time in fresh water this naïve phase expends itself and the fish rapidly become shy and discriminating. After a day or two in the river sea-trout adopt the habit of feeding mostly at dusk and at night. The angler's flies, therefore, must be selected with these generalizations in mind. When fish are clearly fresh-run – e.g. soon after a spate – almost any sort of tinsel-bodied fly stands a good chance of attracting them. When they have dropped into the dusk/night feeding routine it pays to treat them as if they were cautious brown trout.

Here are a few flies which the writer likes to use: Silver March Brown, Silver Invicta, Gold Mallard, Rusty Sedge, Magpie Scad, and Butcher. These should be dressed to hooks size 12, 10, and 8 (Redditch).

Fishing Methods

The chief methods of fishing for sea-trout may be briefly listed thus: fly-fishing, spinning, rolling or running worm, and drop-minnow. On certain big lakes a specialized form of dapping from a drifting boat is also used. Of these methods fly-fishing is widely considered to be the most sporting and the most interesting. It should be added also that it is the most killing method if performed correctly.

The mystique of gaudy flies and varying fly-patterns cannot be dismissed entirely as the product of man's fertile imagination. Personally, I feel that any sort of reasonable fly will catch sea-trout provided conditions are promising and the fish are not too stale. Yet I am also led to the curious belief that fly-patterns vary in value according to the angler who uses them. This sounds mysterious; and so it is. There is undoubtedly a quality in fishing described as 'confidence'. The angler who has confidence and faith in the luring qualities of a particular fly will certainly catch more fish with it than the angler who thinks that that pattern is no good.

Confidence stems partly from use and experience. The angler who catches fish on a particular fly naturally tends to develop confidence and faith in that pattern. In short, the angler needs to be intellectually convinced that the fly he is using is a good one.

Concentration plays an important part in fishing; the most successful anglers are all masters of the art of concentration. But no one so far has explained very clearly what concentration does for the fisherman in terms of cause and effect. An American research scientist recently recorded how certain laboratory experiments 'went to pieces' as soon as he handed them over to assistants after prolonged periods of concentrated personal attention. No obvious physical cause could be traced for the deterioration. It seems almost as though certain effects can be obtained by sheer will-power.

Every angler who desires better-than-average results should pay attention to the possibilities of this field. For success in sea-trout fishing I would say that the following points are desirable:

Conger Eel

Conger conger (page 280)
Record 84 lb

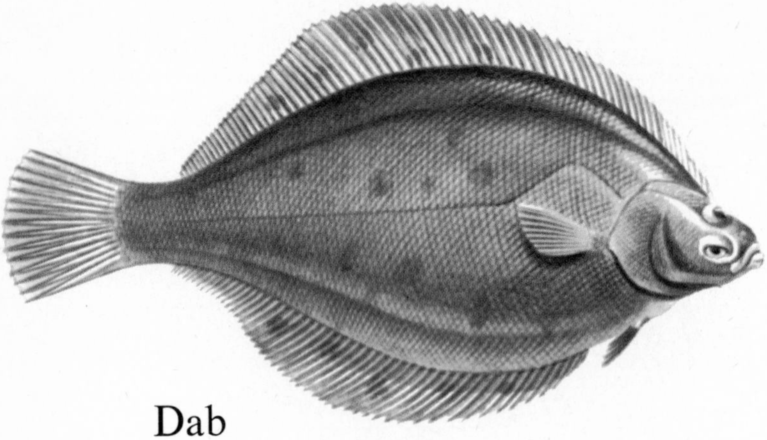

Dab

Limanda limanda (page 286)
Record 2 lb 10 oz 12 drams

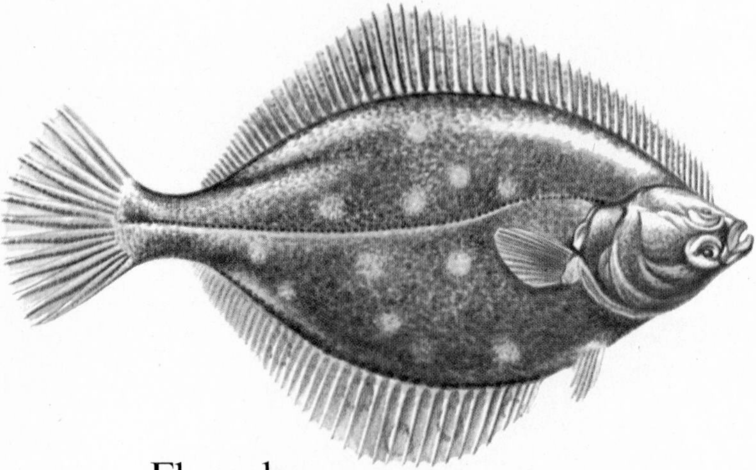

Flounder

Pleuronectes flesus (page 288)
Record 5 lb 11½ oz

Lesser Spotted Dogfish

Scyliorhinus caniculus (page 287)
Record 3 lb 12 oz 8 drams

Greater Spotted Dogfish

Scyliorhinus stellaris (page 287)
Record 21 lb 3 oz

Spur Dogfish

Squalus acanthias (page 287)
Record 16 lb 12 oz 8 drams

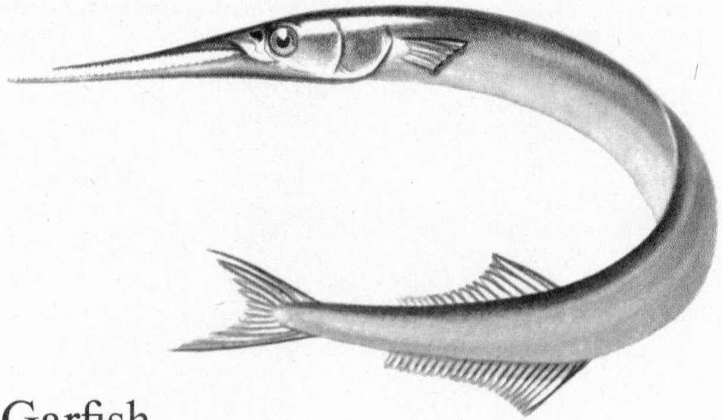

Garfish

Belone belone (page 290)
Record 2 lb 9 oz 2 drams

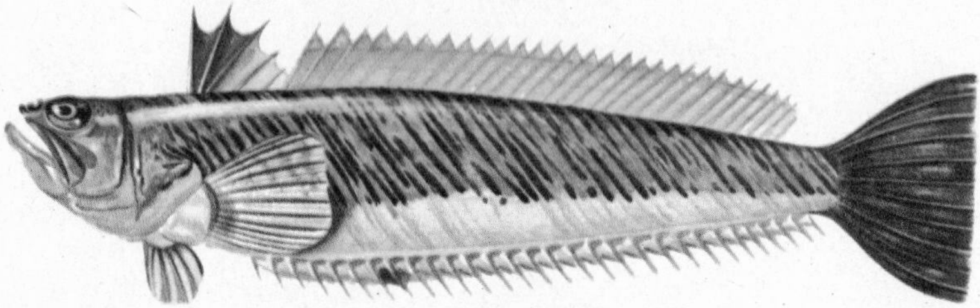

Great Weaver

Trachinus draco
Record 2 lb 4 oz

(i) The angler should feel relaxed in mind and body.

(ii) He should train himself to forget everything except catching fish.

(iii) He should fish buoyantly, never doubting his own ability to succeed.

The relationship between the angler's mental outlook and the process of catching fish on a hook is admittedly obscure, but I am quite convinced that there is such a relationship. Angling literature is full of references, and anglers frequently report that when they feel frustrated or depressed they seldom have any luck. Since the acts of casting and working a fly tend to become automatic it seems doubtful that such lack of success is due to ordinary physical reasons.

In fishing, success and failure breed like rabbits if given the chance; if you desire the one you need to discourage the other. But it is not always easy.

Day Fishing with Wet Fly: The best time for day fishing with fly is usually as the river falls after a spate, since the water is then dark enough to hide the grosser features of one's tackle and the fish are fresh-run and keen. In the right conditions some heavy baskets can be taken.

Greased-line or sunk line can be used for this fishing, the relative temperature of air and water being the deciding factor as explained earlier in the salmon chapter (see page 195). In these conditions, sea-trout are usually lightly poised in the water and will readily dart after a fly fished across their 'window'.

A partly greased silk line makes a good compromise. The silk is greased to within a couple of yards of the tip, but the last two yards and the whole of the leader are thoroughly cleaned with detergent. The angler can then fish his fly at varying depths and speeds according to the angle of his casting and the direction of his mends. By greasing the whole of the line one can fish the fly almost on the surface; liberal use of the degreasing pad enables a fully-sunk fly to be fished. This is a flexible method.

Low-water fishing by day is a different proposition, since clear water and a bright sun raise great difficulties. The best chance usually lies in the runs, especially if these are shaded by trees. The open sun-lit pools are usually impossible.

Trout-size flies are suitable for low-water fishing. Patterns can be matched with natural fly on the water or the angler can use small 'fancy' copies – flies with a floss or wool tag. Patterns dressed to simulate the nymphs of natural flies are also effective. Fishing tactics are exactly the same as for brown TROUT (see p. 219).

Night Fly-fishing: Most experienced sea-trout anglers concentrate their fishing into the hours at dusk, through the night, and at dawn. Night fishing is an acquired taste. Most anglers are not very enthusiastic about their first excursion, but the keen ones soon find that night fishing is not only more productive but has an appeal unknown to the daytime fishers.

Why do we fish at night for sea-trout, when salmon and brown trout are caught by day? The chief reason is that, while spring and autumn salmon run when the rivers are full and camouflage of one's tackle is unnecessary, sea-trout are summer fish and the angler needs the cover of darkness. In summer, brown trout fishing by day is notoriously dull, and in fact many anglers fish for brown trout at night also.

It should be remarked that all rivers are not equally suited for night fishing. Many Irish and Scottish waters take on a rich tawny colour, and in these the daytime fishing is as good as, if not a good deal better than, the fishing after dark. Fish are slow to take a fly in coloured water after dark.

Most West Country and Welsh rivers on the other hand are so clear that the cover of darkness is essential for sea-trout angling. Sea-trout are extremely shy fish, and if we were prevented from fishing at night in these rivers we should catch very few summer fish at all.

Too much tackle is a liability. After a good deal of experiment I find that the following items are essential:

A big landing-net
A rubber-covered torch
A spare leader, mounted with flies, wound round the hat
Adequate clothing
Thigh waders
Food and a hot drink

These, together with the fly-outfit and a commodious tackle-bag furnished with the usual small items, are sufficient.

Before going night fishing a preliminary daytime inspection of the water is necessary, especially on a strange river. Walk the bank slowly and make a mental note of the following points:

(i) Discover where the fish are lying and look for the areas where they are likely to feed after nightfall. Usually they lie in deep water under cover of rock or trees and at night they move into shallow water adjacent to this cover – often the tail or the sides of the pool, sometimes the neck.

(ii) Check the wading conditions. If necessary, conduct a trial wade where you propose fishing. Make sure there are no nasty snags such as lengths of barbed-wire washed down by floods.

(iii) Check nearby vegetation and measure it against casting-distances, making sure that there is at least one spot where you can cast unimpeded. Remember that it is hard to estimate the distance of trees at night.

(iv) Find a good place to land your fish. Notice whether they can be beached on a sand-bar or whether you will need to net them. Check your route down and upstream on the assumption that you may hook a really big sea-trout and have to follow it.

(v) Last, but most important, decide whether there are in fact sea-trout in the pool you intend fishing. Locals may advise, or by looking into the water with polarizing glasses you may be able to see the fish. Failing this, you must rely on the probability of the pool's holding fish because of recent catches by other anglers up and downstream from that point.

This sort of inspection only takes ten minutes but it does much to remove frustrations before they arise. It helps one to approach night fishing in a determined and workmanlike manner.

Night fishing starts at full dusk – usually about 10 to 10.30 on a June evening, although heavy surrounding vegetation and a cloudy sky may permit an earlier start. The best of the fishing is from 11 till about 1 a.m. My own routine is to be on the water from 10 till 1.30 a.m. and again from 3.30 till 6 a.m.

Making a good bag of sea-trout at night demands hard work and a good deal of patience. It is important to weigh these demands against the prize offered. Many anglers, in my experience, fancy that they can dabble at fishing and still show interesting results. They play around till dusk and then go to their hotels to sleep soundly. It depends what you want; if you want fish you have got to work. To fish all night is more exhausting, physically, than doing a day's hard work. Apart from the sport, however, the angler gains by sleeping like a log and eating like a horse.

Reaching the pool of his choice the angler puts up his rod, makes sure everything is neat and secure, then considers the prospects in relation to the conditions. Here are a few pointers that indicate the sort of sport that may be expected:

(i) Swirls and dull plops, indicating feeding fish. The sea-trout will most probably be feeding on one of the numerous sedge-species. The angler notes the general area of this activity so that he can fish down to it the moment it is dark enough.

(ii) Fish jumping clean out of the water. An unfavourable sign. It means that the fish are uncomfortable – either through falling water-temperature or through changing chemical conditions. (Thunder and flood-water both alter the chemical balance.)

(iii) 'Arrowheads' seen at the tails of pools. This means that sea-trout are moving up-river. If they are fresh fish they should take a fly keenly. If they are rather stale – coming from pools lower down river – they will be much less easy to lure.

(iv) Heavy 'boils' seen near the shallows. This means that sea-trout are taking minnows. Show them a silver-bodied fly without delay.

(v) White mist forming just above the surface. An unfavourable sign. If the angler is fishing while the mist is forming he may none the less get a few fish. Once the mist thickens all fish activity ceases, and deeply-sunk fly is then the only chance.

(vi) 'Scotch' mist or light drizzle. A favourable condition, especially when it brings on a hatch of sedges and other nocturnal flies.

(vii) Rising moon. Unfavourable if the sky is clear and it is a full moon. Fishing in the shade of trees offers the best chance. If moonlight alternates with cloudy periods the angler can fish under cover of cloud and use the moonlight to change pools, check tackle, and refresh himself.

Casting at Night: At night one's tackle is harder to manage. A tangled cast goes unnoticed until it has developed into a first-class bird's nest. Darkness is a liability as well as an asset.

The angler should always start on his pool by making a series of short casts. If the water is shallow on the near side he should continue to short-cast as he wades quietly to cover the farther water. It should never be forgotten that sea-trout seek the shallowest water at night, often only a few feet from the bank. Some anglers start operations by throwing a long line, but I feel sure that they disturb a great many fish that could be caught. When I have been forgetful enough to cast over shallow water at night (instead of first casting into it) I have often sent shoals of sea-trout scattering in all directions. On occasion, I have practically trodden on fish in no more than six inches of water. Given caution, these fish could have been caught.

Some casting instructors insist that the rod should work in a single plane when executing the overhead cast (see p. 220), the theory being that the velocity imparted to the line on the back-cast will cause it to turn over well clear of the rod tip. All this is quite true when you are fishing in still water and can get a clean pick-off and impart high velocity to your line. In night fishing, however, when the tip of the line may be several feet under water, things are not always so simple. More often than not the line is picked up from downstream at a rather low velocity. I find that it helps if the rod is shifted sufficiently to avoid the line, which often comes across rather low. If distance is desired, a single false-cast in the required direction instantly gives the line enough velocity for it to be cast and shot in the normal way.

A most useful cast for the night fisher is the so-called Spey cast, which is merely a roll cast incorporating a change of direction. In my own mind I call it the sling cast because that is the sort of action it imparts to the line. In a roll cast the line is never thrown behind the angler as in an overhead cast. It is rolled forward low over the water with a circular movement of the rod tip. These casts are useful in confined places where there is no air-space behind the angler. Readers who wish to plunge more deeply into the technicalities of casting should consult the standard work on the subject: *The Angler's Cast* by Captain T. L. Edwards and E. Horsfall-Turner.

Fishing a Pool at Night: Let us suppose that we are fishing a pool holding a fair head of sea-trout, some of them fresh-run, others not quite so fresh. The pool is a hundred yards long and lies over rock and gravel. On the near side it shallows gently to a few inches of water. On the far side a steep bank flanks water deepening from a few inches just above the neck to as much as six feet in the middle. A moderate current flows down the pool against the opposite bank.

We start off by greasing our line to within a yard of the tip and mount a rather mangled Invicta on point. This fly has caught several fish and will catch more, given luck. Top-dropper is a big silver-ribbed Coch-y-bondhu. The leader is degreased with a pad soaked in detergent and water.

Sometimes fish feed towards the neck of this pool on sedges brought down from the river above. Sometimes they are found only in the wide, shallow tail. If it is an inactive evening the sea-trout may remain doggedly in the deepest water, brooding or perhaps dreaming on the bottom. Each of these situations calls for a slight change in tactics.

It is now a quarter to eleven, so we start at the neck in water no more than six inches deep. The point-fly is dropped at the edge of the down-flowing current. It is necessary to cast systematically so as to cover every yard of likely water. Big sea-trout can be lazy takers and they like to have their supper served, so to speak, in bed.

Nothing results from twenty minutes of this work, so we wade out quietly and prowl along the meadow until we reach the pool-tail. A huge swirl in mid-stream indicates that a fish or two are moving. This water is no more than two feet deep, but luckily the night is dark, so our nylon leader must be quite invisible. We wade for two yards with snail-like slowness and start to cast.

A fish takes the fly at first offer. The line held in our left hand trembles; we tighten instantly by the twin motions of pulling the line and lifting the rod point. The rod curves and there is the solid feel of good fish. The sea-trout chases for cover like an alarmed hare and it is a few minutes before we have him lying on his side in thin water, spent. After resting the pool-tail for a few minutes we try again but receive no further offers.

Since it is now 11.30 we decide to fish the deeps under the far bank. A certain amount of summer algae has got on to the line, tending to sink it, so this saves us the trouble of using the degreasing-pad. The Invicta is taken off the point and a size 8 Magpie Scad is substituted. The fat green wing and harl body give a big silhouette, which is what is needed for deep-water fishing.

We walk back to the neck of the pool, wade down thirty yards, then start to fish as slowly and deeply as possible. By mending line upstream twice every cast we are making the fly come round almost on the stones at the bottom. After a few minutes a curious nibbling sensation is transmitted down the rod. We strike by pulling line and by moving the rod a trifle. There is a sudden lurch as a fish turns away and kicks the leader with its tail. The rod doubles and we are fast into him.

For a few minutes this fish is the boss. We feed slack line through the rings until the fish is on the reel. The rod point dips until the reel trills in alarm and gives line to relieve the strain. The sea-trout churns in a half-circle fifty yards away and leaps thrice.

In this pool it is best to play a good fish from the bank, behind. Holding the rod high, all pressure removed, we use our free hand to scramble up the turf. The fish has now bolted to the tail and we hurry down, winding up as we go. We now get to work, pumping him in but letting him run when he must. Even so, it is nearly ten minutes before he lies beached and quiet.

Spinning: A great many sea-trout are caught every season in Britain by spinning with a 4 lb. monofil line, a fixed-spool reel, and a 7 or 8 ft light spinning rod made either of glass or of split-cane. Quill minnows about two inches long, small spoons of the revolving-blade variety, and devons are the most popular baits.

Fresh sea-trout have soft lips. Writers who assert that they have hard mouths have clearly only had experience with stale or semi-stale fish, for the mouths of sea-trout harden rapidly in fresh water and a big stale fish has a mouth like iron and teeth to match. Such fish are caught comparatively rarely by the spinner, since they feed mostly at dead of night. The spinner usually hooks fresh and active fish of between 1 and 4 lb., which will snap readily at a fast-moving bait. The speed of the bait and the rapid take of the fish mean that only a minority of takers are hooked. The others shake, jump, or kick their way to freedom.

This poses one of the strongest arguments against spinning, because it is obviously undesirable to spin down a river leaving a trail of frightened fish that have been pricked and lost. Yet one can see this happening all over the country.

There are various spinning techniques. When a strong current runs through a pool it pays to cast across and up, and allow the minnows to wash down on the current for a few yards. The angler then starts to tighten while at the same time he leads his rod round in a downstream direction. The minnow spins over in a sort of flattened parabola and the sea-trout, following, takes it on the turn.

Most sea-trout spin-fishermen are very mobile. They fan-cast systematically to every likely spot before moving up or down. This method is very effective when the river is full after rain and the fresh-run fish are scattered all over the water.

A natural preserved minnow is better than an artificial simply because it looks and smells like real food. Sea-trout are adept at cruising beside a bait and taking a sly nip, and if the bait is pliable and slightly oily they are emboldened into making a more determined attack. With artificial baits the sea-trout only takes once, and if the take fails to connect with the hook the fish sheers off in terror – 'put down' for the rest of the day, perhaps for several days.

Spinning is a good way of fishing estuaries if there is not too much fine seaweed in the water. Artificial eels made of soft leather are very effective, especially if they are left their natural drab brownish colour. Rubber sand-eels and plastic ragworms are also good. They should be fished across and down with a sink-and-draw motion.

Rolling Worm: The rolling worm is just as effective for sea-trout as it is for salmon although, naturally, the tackle must be scaled down to suit the smaller fish. A single worm fished on a Stewart tackle weighted by a drilled bullet is the best arrangement. The technique of fishing the worm for sea-trout is the same as for SALMON.

A deal of static worm fishing goes on in many rivers, usually during spates. Although this method fills baskets it is not, in my view, a sporting way of fishing, since, because the bait is usually gorged by the fish, everything that takes the worm must be destroyed – small trout, parr, and smolts. There is also a more serious objection to this form of angling. In some areas the use of salmon-ova paste to attract fish to the worm is still widely practised, despite its illegality. Much winter poaching for gravid salmon and sea-trout is aimed at obtaining a supply of 'jam' or 'paste' and the only possible customers for this traffic are static worm-fishers.

Static worming is quite distinct from rolling worm and clear-water worm fished upstream like a fly. These two methods are mobile in character, so that a ground-bait such as paste is of no use. There is a strong feeling that static worming ought to be either restricted or banned, for such a ban would abolish the winter poachers' market for prepared salmon ova. However – as we saw with salmon fishing – further restrictions on angling, whether justified or not, would be strongly contested on the grounds that, as long as men are allowed to catch fish in nets for private profit, the angler should be allowed full leave to use whichever method he thinks fit. This is the vicious circle that is ruining nearly all our fisheries.

Lake Fishing: Sea-trouting in lakes raises rather different problems from those encountered on rivers. In rivers, we usually have a fairly good idea where the fish lie; in lakes this is not so. A featureless lake can be a depressing sight to an angler who has tried for hours to contact a sea-trout and failed, for in the course of a day only a limited amount of water can be covered. Clearly it is of importance to fish through the right water.

There are various sorts of still waters holding sea-trout. There is the sea-loch which is flooded by salt water at each high tide. There are lochs drained by a channel which partially or wholly floods, depending on whether the tide is neap or spring. Then there are the freshwater lakes connected to the sea by a river up which fish run.

Sea-trout usually reach lakes in a shoal. On arrival, bursting with energy, they quarter the water, especially if it is small, but after a short period – perhaps half a day after arrival – they settle into well-used sea-trout lies. A typical lie might be at the end of, and alongside, a rocky headland.

The traditional method of lake fishing is to drift in a rowing-boat, casting the wet flies ahead of the boat and drawing them back. A fault with this method of angling is that it is sometimes hard for the angler to sink his flies deeply enough to catch fish, especially when the boat is drifting fast. Sometimes fish will rise all the way to the surface; at other times they want the fly deeply sunk. One solution is to mount a drogue or sea-anchor to the boat amidships so as to slow its drift. If the angler, in addition, casts his flies well to the side, it is possible to obtain considerable depth. If a gillie or a companion is in the boat then of course the flies must never be allowed to cross the half-way line, in case he should be hooked in the ear or in the hair.

Depth is very important in lake fishing. A surprising number of loch-fishers never seem to vary their tactics, but I am convinced that varying the swim of the flies from shallow to deep according to the mood of the fish makes all the difference to the bag.

Any fly-rod from 9 ft to about 11 ft can be used for boat-work. Longer rods offer the advantage of allowing the angler to dap or bob the topmost fly along the wave-crests – a deadly ploy, especially on windy days.

I prefer winged flies for this type of work, the size depending on local conditions. Flies dressed to hooks size H 12 to H 8 will be found suitable for most lakes and lochs. Patterns are a matter of personal conviction, but it is useful to have a bit of red in lake flies; a fly with a teal wing, yellow or green silk body, and a red tag at the tail (either of wool or fluorescent fibres) makes a good general-purpose pattern for lakes when tied in the above sizes.

Some anglers like to work their flies fairly fast, but speed of working really depends on the amount of wave. If there is a biggish wave, vigorous working certainly draws the fishes' attention to the lure; when there is no more than a ripple I feel that slow, steady drawing is the best tactic.

Dapping: Huge flies have been developed for sea-trout in lakes, their enthusiastic inventors using such descriptives as 'sparrow' and 'hummingbird'. Since visibility and secure hooking are the prime objectives, some successful dapping flies are dressed on a tube and incorporate a treble in the tail.

If sea-trout are lying in six or eight feet of water a fly dapped on the surface has to be pretty substantial before they will rise to it. A small wet fly, fished deep, would catch these fish.

Dapping has been described as a monotonous pursuit. It has one advantage, however, in that the angler clearly sees the fish coming at his fly. This is enormously exciting, so much so that one must constantly guard against the fault of striking too early.

General The British record sea-trout was a 22 lb. 8 oz. fish taken from the River Frome in Somerset.

F. W. H.

White-fish and Char

The whitefishes and the chars are members of the Salmonidae, although they are not recognized anglers' fishes in the popular sense. Few anglers fish specifically for these species, for reasons which will be outlined below. At the same time, angling is a progressive sport, whose methods and techniques are changing constantly. Pre-war fishing for big carp suffered from lack of suitable technique; fishing for flounders with a baited spoon has advanced from a freak method to something approaching a science. These two examples indicate that a technique suited to the catching of whitefish and char must not be dismissed as impossible. For this reason, some notes on these species may prove useful.

Whitefish: Powan, Pollan, Vendace.

The Victorian naturalists worked themselves into ecstasies over the whitefishes and divided them into so many subspecies that each lake might have been said to have its own form. Modern naturalists are wiser. They regard living things more as fluid expressions than as rigidly fixed types.

Whitefish are ROACH-like fish that inhabit deep lakes. They are modest in size, rarely exceeding a foot in length, and although related to the salmon family, they look and act more like coarse fish. They fall into three groups – the powans, the pollans, and the vendace.

The powan (*Coregonus clupeoides*), which looks rather like

a freshwater herring, is found in Loch Lomond and Loch Esk. Like all whitefish it inhabits deep water and is rarely captured on rod and line, probably because very few anglers present a bait at suitable depth.

The schelly (*Coregonus clupeoides stigmaticus*) is a variation of the powan and is found in Ullswater and Haweswater. Like the powan it is a deep-water fish and is captured, usually, by accident.

The gwyniad (*Coregonus clupeoides pennantii*) is the smallest of the powans and is found only in Bala Lake, Merioneth, although occasionally it appears in the River Dee, which drains the lake. After storms, hundreds of small gwyniad are sometimes found dead after being beaten against Bala's pebble beaches.

The pollans (*Coregonus pollan*) are the Irish branch of the whitefish family, and are found mostly in Lough Neagh, Lough Erne, and Lough Derg. They are silvery, oily, little fish with blue backs and rather large scales. Their presence in great shoals in the Irish lakes probably accounts for the large size reached by Irish pike, which feed on them.

Pollans too are deep water lovers and of course are adapted for living under pressure, which means that any fish brought to the surface will have had much of the fight knocked out of it by the rapidly changing pressure. Indeed powans are sometimes found on the surface of Ullswater. They have probably been hunted out of their depth by predators and have become 'depressurized' more quickly than their bodies can stand.

I feel certain that pollan could be caught on a rod if an angler had time to experiment and persist. Fishing into a hundred feet of water on Lough Erne I had several nibbles and plucks which I believe were caused by pollan. Striking a fish at these depths with the fine line and small hook in use, however, is very hard to time. In the autumn the pollan, like all the whitefishes, seek shallow water for spawning and late summer is the only time an angler is likely to catch them – always assuming they can be caught. Much information about pollan habits and locations could no doubt be gleaned from the professional fishermen who net them in large quantities.

There is scope here for enterprise and experiment. It is not suggested that these whitefishes are hard-fighting fish. But to catch an 'uncatchable' species in sufficient quantity to prove one's point would make an interesting achievement.

The vendace (*Coregonus vandesius*) is found in Scotland and in the Lake District. It is a small herring-like fish and, again, is almost never seen by anglers.

Chars: The chars (*Salvelinus alpinus*), too, provided a field-day for naturalists preoccupied with classification. Nearly a score of British chars have been described, although the small differences between each sort sometimes tax the resources even of professional biologists.

In appearance they may be described as colourful trout-like fish, their scales tinted with shades of pink and yellow. Confined to fairly deep lakes, the present-day British char would seem to be a land-locked form of a species whose ancestors were migratory; a migratory Arctic char indeed still exists. Like all land-locked races of fish the chars seem to have lost the qualities we seek in an angling species. Size and fighting vigour, alas, are absent. Yet it is possible that modern methods of fish-culture might raise the chars much higher in the esteem of anglers.

A foreign char – the American brook 'trout' (*Salvelinus fontinalis*) – has been introduced to Britain but with only limited success. Brook trout/brown trout hybrids are known as marbelled trout and are perhaps the most gorgeously marked fish of all the Salmonidae.

Chars are found in the deep lakes that geologists associate with the last ice-age. The Lake District, a few lakes in Scotland, the Western Isles, a few Irish lakes, together with four lakes in North Wales – this is the distribution of the char in Britain.

Welsh lakes such as Llyn Cwellyn, near Llanberis, used to be very famous for char and some heavy bags were made. However, comparatively few anglers specialize in these fish, probably because their season is limited, in practice, to late summer. Modern tackle and fine monofil lines may well make deep-water char fishing much more worth while.

It seems a great pity to me that this brilliantly coloured member of the salmon tribe should languish in a state of isolation in a few glacial lakes. One can only hope that one day it will be 'improved', introduced to new waters, and made a more important member of its distinguished clan. Instead of hurrying to stock our lakes and reservoirs with rainbow trout – which don't always do well – we might spare a thought for this native species.

Tackle and Fishing Methods

The best type of tackle for both whitefish and char fishing is a subject for experiment. A light cane roach rod fitted with a large-capacity fixed-spool reel seems the most useful outfit. The reel needs to be loaded with 150 yds of 6 lb. nylon. The hook links should be of finer nylon. The most useful type of float seems to be a peacock quill, 12 or 14 in. long, with a small ring whipped to one end. The line-stop I find best is a bit of thin rubber-band secured to the line with a clove-hitch.

Whitefish

When one is fishing in big lakes at these depths there is always a risk of hooking a big lake trout. Provided there is at least fifty yards of reserve line on the reel the angler stands a fair chance of landing such fish.

As with whitefish the paramount problem in char fishing is to contact the shoals in the deep water where they live. Deep trolling is sometimes successful. Occasionally, too, char rise to the surface in hot weather and may be taken on ordinary TROUT-flies.

September and October are the best months for char. They take a bait keenly when the previous night has held a hint of frost. Like whitefish they leave the deeps at the end of summer and come into the shallows. Worm or maggot is often killing, but the depth at which the bait is fished always presents a problem. An efficient sliding-float is essential if the char are rather deep.

General

Thoughtful anglers must wonder why the whitefishes and chars are scattered so curiously over the north and west of Britain, while none are found in southern England.

About 14,000 years ago, the great ice-sheet, which had ground its terrible passage almost as far southwards as the Thames, started to melt. The valleys, which had been ripped out of the land-surface by incalculable masses of ice and rock, filled with water. As the ice melted the land rose and in the course of time the lakes became isolated. The whitefishes and chars were probably sea-fish which became land-locked by this process. There is in fact a marine whitefish – the houting – which still ascends rivers to spawn, but it is rare. On this count, therefore, these two species are serious contenders for the title of Britain's oldest native fish species. No records are claimed for these species.

F. W. H.

Sea Fishing

Glossary

Backlash Over-run with drum reel when casting, resulting in a tangle or 'bird's nest'.

Baited spoon Spoon trailing a fish-strip or worm bait on hook at rear: used for flounder.

Centre-pin reel Free-running drum reel.

Drag Adjustable brake on reel, often called 'star drag'.

Drift-line Fishing from a boat, either anchored or drifting, in which weighted tackle streams out in the tide, but off the bottom.

Feathers Crude flies, fished one above the other, sometimes in considerable numbers, usually when mackerel are wanted for bait.

Fixed-spool reel Sea reels of this type are made in larger sizes with drums suitable for holding a great deal of heavy line. (See 'Coarse Fishing' glossary (p. 291) for full description.)

Ground The bottom.

Ground fishing Bottom fishing.

Jigger A weighted device, usually silver and armed with hooks, to resemble a small fish. This is jigged up and down above the bottom until a fish takes. Not of great sporting value.

Lask A strip of fish, often mackerel, mounted as bait.

Leger Weight for bottom fishing through which the line is free to run when a fish takes the bait.

Multiplying reel A geared reel, much used in sea fishing when it is made in larger sizes than for freshwater use. Multipliers are free-running for long-casting, have adjustable brakes or drags, and a device for paying the line back evenly over the spindle during the retrieve. In the largest sizes, they are used for big-game fishing.

Mark A known position on the sea bed where good fishing can be had, probably for one particular species. Marks are found by taking cross-bearings on points ashore.

Paternoster Bottom-fishing gear consisting of a weight at the end of a nylon or wire trace. Above this, at intervals, are wire, nylon, or Perspex booms on which baits are mounted.

Peeler — A crab on the point of changing its shell. When the shells are removed, these make deadly baits for many fish, including bass.

Priest — A small club used for killing fish quickly and humanely.

Pumping — Raising a big fish, perhaps a skate, off the bottom by winding the rod top-down towards it and then lifting the rod. The performance is repeated just as long as the fish will permit and line stand the strain.

Rubby-dubby — A method of ground-baiting, notably for shark, with chopped-up fragments of oily fish such as pilchards. The rubby-dubby, a mesh bag, is hung over the side of the boat so that it trails in the water and leaves an oily slick behind to attract the fish.

Schoolies — School bass, young fish of a pound or more which normally shoal together.

Snood — Hook-link of paternoster or leger gear when made of nylon or other line rather than of wire.

Surf-casting — Another term for beach fishing, often for bass.

Trace — The end portion of the tackle carrying the hooks, weights, etc. Sometimes of wire to prevent abrasion on rocky ground and to stop the fish biting the tackle through.

Tackle for Sea Fishing

In the last few years a revolution has overtaken sea tackle. Whereas the old idea used to be to fish with anything, no matter if it had the sensitivity of a broomstick lashed up to a one-inch hawser, the tendency now is to use the lightest gear possible. This, of course, improves the sport no end. The move towards fine tackle has also succeeded in attracting a great many freshwater fishermen to the sea during their own close season, where previously the old-fashioned heavy gear had discouraged anglers used to fishing with delicate equipment. Of course, there are limits to delicacy as far as sea tackle is concerned. Strength of current and power of surf often dictate the use of weights of between two and four ounces. Plainly the rod and line must be of test-curve loading (see pp.34–5) and breaking strain to cast weights. Even so, it is surprising what can be done within these limitations to produce suitably scaled rods. In many cases – for example, mullet fishing, black bream, bass spinning, mackerel spinning, and mackerel on the fly – light tackle is essential and rods comparable to their freshwater equivalents can be used. Just the same, the basic armoury of the sea angler needs to be tougher than anything freshwater requires. Here are some of the possibilities:

Rod	*Purpose*	*Reel and line*
9–11 ft fly-rod	Bass or mackerel	Fly reel and *old* fly-line (salt water ruins fly-line dressings)
8–9 ft light spinner	Bass or mackerel; flounder with baited spoon	Fixed-spool reel and monofil line
10 ft pier or jetty rod of fibre-glass or split-cane	All inshore species. Rod should be able to cast 4 oz. Must be strong, as in some cases fish will have to be 'lifted' from water. Hard to get really light gear for this	Large drum reel, multiplier, or sea fixed-spool loaded with 15–25 lb. b.s. line
7 or 8 ft fibre-glass boat rod	All off-shore species. Since long casting is not necessary, the rod can be reasonably light. A battle with a big skate or tope on a fibre-glass boat rod soon makes the equipment seem all too light	Large drum or sea multiplier loaded with monofil
10–12 ft split-cane or fibre-glass (sometimes, also greenheart) beach-casting rod	All inshore species from bass to tope	Sea multiplier mounted on top of rod for thumb control when casting. Line of 15–25 lb. appropriate to weight used
Big-game tackle	Tunny, big conger, really big sharks. Note that real big-game gear is only needed in Britain for tunny. Most sharks can be played on normal boat rods, though you may hook the exception	Big-game reel, line, trace, hooks, and harness

In choosing your basic rod you must, as always, be guided by the kind of fishing you hope most to do. If you live in an area of sandy shores where the local style is beach casting, you almost certainly need a beach-caster to get out to the fish. If you know that you are going out by boat most of the time, then the problem solves itself, but remember that a boat rod won't be much use for, say, pier fishing.

But a compromise is possible in the case of sea fishing with this first basic rod. A 10 ft rod with a fair amount of action will enable you to cast from the shore and also, at a pinch, to fish from a boat. If the rod is in two sections (a rule with all rods is the fewer the sections, the better the casting action) it is possible that the rod-maker can build a shorter, say 3 ft, butt to convert the rod for boat use without entirely ruining its action.

When buying a reel make sure that you have something big enough and sturdy enough. Simple drum reels of large capacity are all right for boat fishing, but if you intend to cast distances you will need either a free-running drum of the centre-pin sort, or else a multiplier or fixed-spool reel made for use in the sea. Do not contemplate a freshwater reel of the latter types. It will not be strong enough for the job, nor will it hold nearly enough line. Both these kinds of reel have a considerable advantage over the drum: they are geared to assist in the retrieve. They also have more sensitive braking devices. One useful compromise is the type of reel with a drum that sits in the normal attitude for the playing of the fish, but which, for casting, can be taken off and laid on its mount at right angles to the axis of the rod, thus becoming, temporarily, a fixed-spool reel. To avoid line kink which would result if the drum were always fixed for casting in the same position, the drum is placed on the casting spool with handles alternately facing front and rear.

Lines for sea fishing are cheap since, for most purposes, heavy b.s. nylon monofilament cannot be bettered. Landing nets and gaffs are sometimes necessary but these can be added later.

One thing must never be forgotten with sea-fishing gear, namely, that salt water is ruinous to lines, reels, and rods. Good sea rods and reels are proofed to a large extent against this corrosive action; nevertheless it pays to wash metal parts with warm, soapy water at the end of an expedition.

Finally, when buying a first sea rod – as with any first rod – the angler must not look on this choice as a stopgap. He should buy something which, no matter how he develops as an angler later, will always have a useful place in his collection.

C. W.

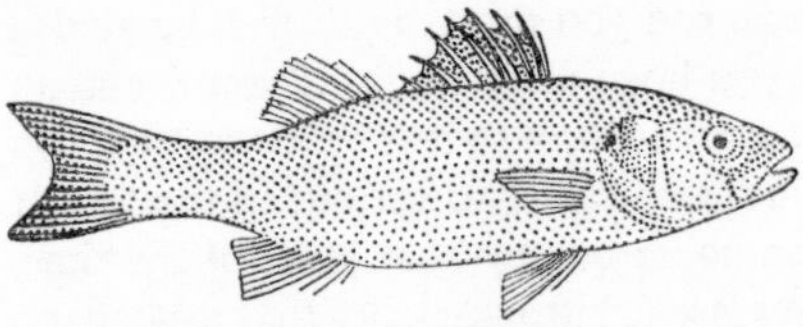

Bass

Early sea-fishing writers sometimes differentiated between what they called Channel bass and the ordinary variety. There is no scientific basis for this classification; in British waters we have only one member of the family of sea-perches (Serranidae) commonly distributed, and that is the bass (*Morone labrax*) itself, though the stone bass or wreck fish, an allied species, is sometimes taken in deep water off the West Country. Big bass look a little different from school bass (those up to about 2½ lb.); they are proportionally much thicker in the body and the coloration is different. Schoolies are brilliantly silver on the back and sides, white on the belly. The big solitaries are darker with a pronounced black lateral line, and the head has a bronze sheen. Some bass found in deepish water (five fathoms or so) have a brilliant blue colouring along the edges of the tail fin, very like the blue of the pectoral fins of tub gurnard. Presumably this is a variation caused by the depth or by particular diet.

The sharp spines of the front dorsal fin of the bass are well known, and bass fishermen take great care not to have them pierce their hands. Travis Jenkins states that they are nine in number, but I have caught many bass that had eight spines. In the West Country and in Wales bass are often called salmon bass, but there is, of course, no relationship at all with the Salmonidae. The bass is, in fact, a close relative of the PERCH.

In the opinion of most saltwater anglers who fish in the south and south-west of Britain, the bass occupies top place in the hierarchy of sporting fish. It is a handsome fish to look at; it fights hard on the hook; it is a fine dish at table; and it can be fished for in a variety of ways, from fly-fishing to legering in the surf with a heavy weight.

Bass are gregarious fish when they are young. When the big spring tides sweep myriads of herring and mackerel fry into the fast tideways, these are harried twenty-four hours a day by huge shoals of school bass which feed on the surface, ripping again and again into the tiny fish. By the time they have reached four or five pounds in weight, small companies rather than big shoals of bass are the rule, though there are exceptions to this where special circumstances concentrate the bass in a small area, as they do at the Splaugh shoals off Co. Wexford, where, on occasion, thousands of bass from three pounds up into double figures combine to harry shoals of fry. Very big bass are usually solitary in habit.

Bass are essentially inshore fish, which is the reason why they are seldom to be seen at the fishmonger's. Areas of low rock that shelter large numbers of crabs and small fish are a favourite haunt of theirs, as are tideways and tide races wherever there is a fast current. They often haunt the surf of sandy beaches, specially when the sea is dying down after a big blow. Sand and mud estuaries too are visited by bass, who show a great tolerance for, indeed are positively attracted by, brackish water. This is clearly indicated by the fact that very often the best spot to fish on a sandy beach is where a stream of fresh water crosses the strand, though it may be the merest trickle. Occasionally bass can be taken by the angler well out to sea when the fish are shoaling after fry or sprat. Usually, however, this will be in comparatively shallow water where there are rock formations which cause tide races and eddies.

Compared with such species as cod, bass are extremely slow-growing fish. Investigations by Dr Kennedy, Chairman of the Irish Inshore Fisheries Trust, showed for instance that a bass of 1 lb. 1½ oz. was five years old. He concluded that it takes about six years for a female bass to reach sexual maturity, by which time it may weigh perhaps a pound and a half. At the other end of the scale it was found that an 11½ lb. fish was twenty-one years old. Thus, as if to make up for the slow growth rate, the bass is a long-living fish compared with most saltwater species.

There is a moral in this, of course. Many inexperienced fishermen make their slaughter among the school bass without ever realizing that even small fish of a pound or so have taken five years to reach that weight. Bass, I am convinced, can be fished out to some extent by rod and line fishing in a particular locality, and I think angling clubs could do valuable work by suggesting a size and a bag limit to their members. There is no legal sanction to compel them, of course.

The spawning habits of bass remain a mystery. One authority simply says, 'The bass spawns from May to August either in the sea, brackish, or fresh water.' The consensus of modern scientific opinion is that most bass do their spawning off-shore in deep water. In British waters, only a very few young bass have ever been recorded. These were taken in a tow-net off the Eddystone and measured 4 to 7·5 mm. in length. Bass eggs have never been discovered in British waters, and the present assumption is that either they float too high for the naturalist's tow net, or else bass spawn in a very few restricted areas, the locations of which are unknown. There is no real evidence to support the old and very natural theory that bass come into brackish water to spawn.

The spawning period appears to be March to June. There also seems to be a strong possibility that spawning may be a long-drawn-out process, not being over and done with at once. Thus, fish which appear in estuaries in May after leaving their winter haunts in deep water are not always spawned out, so that while most spawn is cast in the deep-water environment of the bass, individual late spawners come into estuaries and beaches with unspent, or only partially spent roes.

In some favoured areas – the south-west coast of England, west Wales, and the south-west of Ireland – some bass remain close inshore throughout the winter. The general rule, however, is for the fish to move away from the shore in October or November, and not to reappear until the following May. Certain areas have an early run of bass which peters out after a couple of months, one such place being the Sussex coast in the neighbourhood of Beachy Head and Eastbourne.

The best months for the shore fishermen seem to be May and June, and September and October. Although there are always a few bass feeding inshore in July and August, it is often the case, particularly in hot weather, that the main body of the bass will be found off-shore chasing the shoals of MACKEREL and herring fry that feed near the surface in this period.

Bass are general predators. Schoolies feed on small crustaceans chiefly, slaters, sand fleas, and shrimps, as well as fry. Bigger bass feed on small fishes of all kinds, gobies and blennies and rockling if they are feeding close inshore among the rocks, mackerel and herring fry, sprats, and the young of other species in the tideways. A shoal of big bass may combine to play havoc with a school of mackerel averaging as much as three-quarters of a pound in weight. Crabs are taken in quantity by shore-ranging bass; nearly all the bass I have opened have contained a few. Prawns and sand eels are also taken avidly.

Bass seem also to be very fond of small flatfish of a few inches in length; one fish that I caught in Kerry last year contained twenty-four tiny flounders. In some seasons very large quantities of squid are washed inshore, and then bass become preoccupied with feeding upon them. (Incidentally, London bass fishermen have found their bait problems solved since the arrival in the city of immigrants from the West Indies: squid is a favourite fish with the West Indians and so fish shops have begun to stock it regularly.)

Bass also take razor-fish and lugworm when used by the angler, though no great quantities of these can be available to the fish in the normal course of events. Ragworms are more easily obtained by the bass; the big variety, known to sea fishermen as king rag, is a particularly killing bait in some localities.

Baits

Baits for legering for bass are thus fairly numerous. The bass fisherman's choice will depend on the kind of context in which he is fishing, the time of year, and the time of day (or night). Let us consider the best of them (in alphabetical order, *not* in order of efficiency).

Crab: I have had my best results with crab baits fishing near or among rocks where crabs may be found. This is not to say that crabs won't take bass fished in the middle of a sandy bay, but while in this latter context they are not specially effective, they certainly are in the former. As most sea anglers know, crabs periodically outgrow their carapaces and then shed them and grow new ones. Before the old shell is cast, a new one, very soft as yet, forms underneath it. This is the 'peeler' stage. Peelers are detected by gently pulling and twisting the lowest segment of one of the crab's legs. If the hard outer casing comes away, leaving the coloured flesh of the leg itself, the crab is a peeler. If the segment breaks off entirely and cleanly, the crab is a hard-back. When the carapace is shed naturally, the crab is quite soft for a short time; during this period it hides under a stone or in a rock crevice, where it is sought by the angler. The degree of softness will vary, of course; in my locality we grade them from 'jellies' to 'crispies'. Peelers have to be peeled, naturally, before they are used on the hook. Some anglers prefer a single-hook mounting for crabs, the bait being secured by a few twists of elasticated thread around it, while others use a treble hook so that the shank is pushed up through the crab itself. Then again there is a patent double crab hook which I am not altogether happy about myself since it seems to give too much of a margin of error in the strike.

In my experience, crabs are most effective for bass in fairly calm conditions when the fish are nosing about the rocks looking for what they can find. It should be noted that bass, especially big bass, often pick up a crab bait very delicately and nose it before moving off with it. It pays therefore to use a free-running leger so that the bass can move away feeling only a minimum of resistance.

It is vital that the rod should be held in the hand, so that as soon as the first tap is felt, the rod top can be lowered and slack line given.

Once the bass moves away confidently, an equally confident strike can be made.

Lugworms: These are widely used by bass fishermen. They are effective enough for small bass when fished on to sand or mud, but, although bigger fish sometimes take them, I feel that they are chiefly to be regarded as a second-string bait. I have found them to be more effective at night than in daylight fishing.

Mackerel and Herrings: These have accounted for some very big bass, especially in the autumn. Half a herring is by no means too small a bait for a good bass and the long fillet from the side of a mackerel is effective also. Small cuttings of fish bring little success.

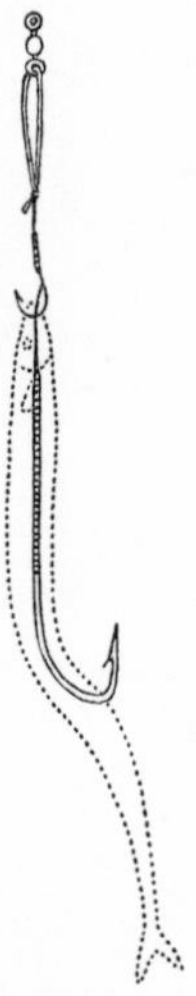

Baiting with dead sand-eel.

King Ragworm: A very killing bait, especially in daylight.

Squid: When they are inshore in large numbers these provide deadly bass bait. (For our present purposes, cuttlefish can be considered under the same head.) In fact, in these circumstances, big bass will scarcely look at anything else. A squid cutting has several advantages as a bait: it is attractive to the fish, it can (these days) be fairly easily obtained, and it is a very firm bait that will stand up to vigorous casting.

Razor-fish and Clams: Excellent bait fished over sand. Like king rag, they are especially effective in daylight.

Small fish of various kinds will take bass legered dead on the bottom. I have a distinct preference for the little three-bearded rockling that can be found in rock pools. Blennies and gobies, in my experience, are not so effective.

Among miscellaneous baits, prawns and sand-eels are better float-fished or used from a boat or projection on a drift-line. A useful bait is a small FLOUNDER of the kind that is often marooned in sand pools or can be scooped up in shallow estuaries. Many bass that I have opened, especially in the late autumn, have contained them.

Before leaving the subject of baits for bass, I should like to underline the efficacy of using a bait which is either unknown to, or unused by, the locals. This does not apply, for instance, to a rocky area which is clearly made for crab fishing; but the introduction of razor-fish or ragworm on a beach where they were previously unknown as bait is sometimes a killing tactic.

Tackle

Most bass taken along the British coast are victims of legering in one form or another, but the variety of contexts in which they are taken makes it difficult to generalize. Ideally, the bass fisherman would be equipped with a variety of tackle, but most of us are compelled to compromise. Let me begin then by describing tackle that will be satisfactory in most situations.

What is expected from a legering rod for bass fishing? Its first function is to throw a bait and a lead as far as possible. In most shore-fishing circumstances, distance casting is not required; bass may be taken within a few yards of the shore. But on many occasions, also, the bass may be feeding very far out, a hundred yards or more in storm beach conditions. Unless the bass fisherman is capable of using tackle that allows of a hundred-yards-plus cast he is often under a severe handicap. Sometimes even a few yards extra distance is all important when, for example, the angler does not happen to be equipped with chest waders, which would give him the extra yards necessary to drop the bait just beyond where the bass are feeding.

An 11 ft rod with a 3 ft butt, made of hollow glass-fibre, will be at its best throwing a 3 oz. weight, though at a pinch it will throw 4 oz. With it I suggest you use an American surf-casting multiplier of the kind that can be put out of gear so that a cast can be made on free spool. For a variety of reasons it is best to use a monofilament nylon line of about 20 lb. breaking strain; heavier line is unnecessary, and line much lighter than this is liable to part under the shock loading which sometimes comes about if there is a check to the cast. A detailed discussion of rigs can be left until later, but there are one or two points to mention. As far as hooks go, it is clearly vital that they be very sharp and fine in the wire; very often a strike has to be made when there is a distance of more than a hundred yards between fisherman and bass. For the last few years I have used only those eyed hooks that are sold for tying low-water salmon flies. They are expensive but very efficient. There is a multiplicity of shapes in which leads are available to the sea fisherman, but in legering there is no need for more than two (in various sizes, of course). The first is the simple bomb weight for running free above the swivel, the other the torpedo lead with wire grips for use in very strong tides, or when the sea is very rough.

Fishing Methods

Legering Techniques: The basic aim of the sea angler must be to put the bait where it will be discovered by the bass. On a shallow storm beach the fish will probably be working the line of the outermost breaker, and this, as we have seen, will entail a long cast. If the sea is very rough it will not be possible to use a running leger; a fixed lead will have to be used at the bottom of the trace, with wire grips if necessary. The bait or baits will then be fished paternoster style on short links (long links, in stormy conditions, have an unhappy habit of tangling with the main line).

At the other extreme, on a quiet lee beach where there may be scattered areas of weedy stones, a light running leger can be employed; the bomb-shaped lead runs freely on the line above a stopping swivel and below the swivel there is a trace of a few feet ending at the hook.

Whichever way of legering is adopted, however, it is of vital importance that the rod be held in the hand. Bass hit very sharply sometimes, and if the rod is in a rest there is a good chance that the strike will miss the fish. Bass bites vary, of course. School bass hit with an exciting rattle, but the bigger ones sometimes give no more than a gentle pluck, or even pick up the bait and move in towards the angler.

Playing a bass in the surf presents one or two problems if the fish is a good one, say over 6 or 7 lb. There are two danger periods. The first comes when the bass decides to head directly towards the fisherman. It is of the greatest importance that contact with the fish be maintained, otherwise slack line may allow the hook to fall out; no reel yet made will retrieve line fast enough to keep up with a determined bass. What the angler has to do is to use the beach for manoeuvre, retreating up it, running backwards if necessary, and winding at the same time. The second danger point is when the fish reaches very shallow water, when it may start kicking and floundering in a highly hazardous way. The presence of a companion who can gaff or net the fish is a great blessing at this point. If you are alone, try not to jerk at the fish but, if it is small enough, beach it with a steady motion. If it is a big fish that cannot be beached without hazard to the tackle, wade in and get on the *seaward* side of it before using gaff or net. Incidentally, the gaff is a much more reliable instrument in very shallow water.

Most anglers who fish the surf for bass are content merely to fish the tide in and regard fishing the ebb as a waste of time.

Unless the beach is a particularly shallow one, however, this is not necessarily the case. Especially in night fishing, so long as there is water for them to swim in, bass can hit the beach and start taking at any time.

Most bass fishermen would agree that sandy beaches fish best at night. Crab fishing amongst the rocks seems to be an exception to this. Very often, especially where they are not over-fished, crab-feeding bass will take as readily in daylight as they will in the dark. Bass are certainly less choosy in the matter of bait after dark; I would have little faith in lugworm bait in the light, for instance, but I am much happier with it as a night-fishing bait.

Very good fishing is often obtained after a good gale of wind that has whipped up a lively surf. It is often not of much use to fish during the storm itself; the time to be present is when the waves are dying back to fishable proportions, but when there is still some life in the sea. Calm, clear seas are generally considered to be the worst possible for bass fishing, but fishing after dark will often cancel out this disadvantage. I have taken some very good bags of fish from beaches in Ireland which had never seen a rod before, when the sea has been quite calm and so clear that bass could be seen moving near the surface off shore. I fancy that bass are made much more shy than we realize by our fishing activities.

A final word about legering. Find out the date of those monster fishing competitions. Hardly anything is ever caught in them, but large quantities of bait gets discarded after the match, much to the benefit of the angler who fishes quietly on the following day at that spot. He will almost certainly catch as many fish as were caught in the match by all the competitors put together.

Float-fishing: This is most useful for covering rocky areas that could not be fished with a leger because of the foul bottom. The tackle used can be lighter than that recommended for legering, the sort of gear that is used for live-baiting for pike being ideal. The size of the float used will depend on the size of the bait and the turbulence of the water. A pike float is necessary to hold up a big soft crab and the lead needed to hold the latter down in the water; but an Avon float may be all that is wanted to fish a couple of prawns.

The kind of float-fishing I should recommend is covering narrow gullies between the rocks, letting the float swash around in the white water almost up to one's feet. It is vital, of course, in this game to keep out of sight, or at least low down on the horizon; a long rod is a great advantage here. In most circumstances, bass take the float away very positively and quite often a good fish will hook itself.

Because of the absence of a heavy lead, bass are a much tougher proposition on float tackle than they are on the leger rod in the surf. They will indulge in a variety of tactics, as a rule heading out to sea at great speed, but occasionally diving for the weedy rocks. Float-fishing areas are usually full of hazards, and it is a good idea to use a light wire trace and avoid the risk of having the line cut on a jagged rock.

The standard baits for float-fishing for bass are soft crab and prawn, but as substitutes for these, sand-eels and king rag may be used, though I prefer to use the former on drift-line tackle from a boat.

Spinning from the Shore: This can be very productive of big fish if the right spot is found and if it is fished at the right time. This sounds a tall order, but the following advice might be helpful. The most likely place is where a headland of rock forms a miniature tide race, or where the sea is channelled fast between, say, a couple of rocky islets. Deep water is good (though the bass may not be feeding deep). In calm clear seas, bass will sometimes follow a spinner but fail to take it. In these circumstances, they are occasionally willing to take a plug bait, but it is usually better to substitute a very narrow lask of fish hooked on at the extremity of the broad end. With a medium-fast retrieve this will prove to have an attractive, fluttering motion; and bass seem much more inclined to take this than an artificial.

An 8 ft glass spinning rod with a standard-sized fixed-spool reel is the best outfit for this work. Since it often involves a good deal of rock scrambling, a light gaff which hooks on to the belt is a blessing. For artificials, apart from plug baits, I favour long, narrow, Swedish-type spoons in various sizes from 4 ins. down to 1½ ins. Sometimes bass, feeding on mackerel and herring fry, will refuse a spoon longer than 2 ins. in length. At other times they will be on sprats or small mackerel and want the big spoon.

The most productive time to spin is when this tide is going at its fastest, that is to say the middle two hours of either the ebb or the flow. Spring tides are preferable to neaps.

Boat Fishing: The great majority of bass are taken from the shore, but superlative fishing can be had at times from boats. Large estuaries are best commanded from boats in mid-stream.

Drift-lining with a live sand-eel can be recommended, especially in sandy bar-estuaries, while in others 'whiffing', that is to say trailing a sand-eel, brings good results (Salcombe in South Devon is a centre for this kind of sport). *Bass*

Sometimes bass shoal off shore in large numbers, and then light spinning from a boat can be magnificent. The real secret of this kind of fishing is to get a good boatman who will work hard getting you up-tide of the fish, cutting the engine and drifting into them, then repeating the process as the fish scatter and re-form, their whereabouts being revealed by the shrieking terns, the 'fowl on the water'. Magnificent fishing of this kind is to be had at Rosslare, Co. Wexford, and Dungarvan, Co. Waterford.

General

In British waters, bass may be said to occur south of a line drawn between Anglesea and the Wash, though of course occasional fish are taken north of these limits. On the west coast of Ireland, Connemara is the northernmost limit of consistent bass fishing, and on the east of the Boyne estuary. If we are talking in terms of most favoured areas, the following list covers the best fishing: Devon and Cornwall; the Gower coast of Glamorgan, Carmarthenshire, Pembrokeshire, and Cardiganshire in west Wales; the south coast of Ireland from Wexford to Kerry and north to Co. Clare. The English Channel is patchy; parts of the Sussex coast have a good run of bass early in the season, the long reefs off Beachy Head being one obvious attraction.

Fringe areas include the Suffolk coast and North Wales and the coasts of Co. Down and Antrim. The curious thing about these places is that although the arrival of bass is spasmodic and the fish do not occur in the very large shoals that sometimes assemble in the south-west, the average size is high. Indeed the record fish (Felixstowe, 1943, 18 lb. 2 oz.) came from one of these fringe areas. The Menai Straits, each year, produces some double-figure bass. The biggest bass I ever saw was displayed in a Swansea fish shop (it was net caught) and weighed 22 lb. Many excellent bass fishermen go right through their careers without taking a bass of double figures, and in my opinion anything over eight pounds must be considered a very good fish indeed.

The best bass fishing is undoubtedly to be found where fishing pressure is light or non-existent. Very little rod fishing for example has been done in the west of Ireland and splendid fishing may be had, particularly in the autumn, in Cos. Kerry and Clare.

C. G.

Bream

1. Black Bream (*Spondyliosoma cantharus*). The black species is highly localized, at least as far as the British coast is concerned. Black bream are encountered mainly at the eastern end of the English Channel, notably in the Littlehampton area. Their name describes them accurately. In colour they are bluish-black. They have the typical deep thin look of the BREAM family but are far stronger and more powerfully built than their freshwater counterparts. The dorsal fin is spined, the eye large, and the tail forked.

Depending on the warmth of the season, the black bream arrive at the English Channel reefs at the end of April or in May. The time of their arrival may vary by several weeks. In 1960, for instance, I made my annual trip to Littlehampton in late May, to find that the brief season before the fish split up into smaller groups over a wide area was almost over. In 1961, I made the same trip at the same time of year and found that because of the late spring the fish had not yet arrived. The fish stay over the reefs in big, concentrated shoals for the purpose of spawning for about six weeks. The shoals then seem to break up and the fish are scattered over a much wider area, so that although fish may be taken well into August, the very big bags characteristic of the beginning of the season are unlikely to be repeated. After they have spawned, the fish are not all necessarily to be found on rocky ground but may disperse over broken, rubbly bottoms.

Towards the end of the summer, odd fish are caught miles away from the reefs where spawning took place and in some areas the small one- or two-year-old fish are present right through the year.

As indicated, the black bream show a decided preference for reefs. One point of interest is that they assemble in rather shallower water than the red bream. The principal reef over which they are found does not have much more than five fathoms over it. Like the red bream, they feed principally at the bottom, but, depending on the state of the tide and the time of the day, they may be found just off it or at mid-water. Later in the season small fish will be found inshore, feeding around the piles of piers and such places.

It is possible that the black bream is not so much of a fish-eater as the red, although herring strip is a favoured bait. Shrimps, worms, and cockles are suggested by Minchin, who claimed to have investigated the stomach contents of rod-caught fish.

Many anglers believe that there is an annual migration of black bream through the Straits of Gibraltar from the Mediterranean where the fish winter. How much truth there is in this it is difficult to say. Certainly it is nothing like a scientific certainty.

What is undeniable is that black bream turn up year after year at the Kingmer reef off Littlehampton and at another mark near by known as the Ditches. If you are going to fish for black bream, it is essential to go either to Littlehampton or Bognor Regis at the right time of year.

The boatman there are well experienced in the way of bream, and, other things being equal, they will find you the fish. A word of warning: weekend bookings for boats during the black bream season have to be made months ahead – before Christmas if you want to fish the following May. But if you do go to this trouble, I think you will agree that it is worth it.

2. Red Bream (*Pagellus centrodontus*) These fish are found mainly on the rocky south-west coast. In shape they are much the same as the black bream. Their colouring varies from crimson along the back to silvery-red on the flanks. There is a large dark spot on the lateral line just behind the head. They are also known as common bream.

They have suffered considerable diminution in numbers since the First World War. There are two possible explanations of this. The first has to do with the disappearance of the eel-grass (*zostera*), as a result of a world-wide disease. Some authorities claim that the bream depended on this rich weed and suffered from its going. Another theory has it that the development of trawls which could fish over the foul ground that bream loved was responsible for their thinning out, and adherents of this theory can point out that, after the lapse in fishing during the Second World War, red bream numbers increased for a time. It is interesting to note that the eel-grass is reappearing, so that there may be better news to come. Anyone who has caught red bream will pay tribute to the fighting qualities of this handsome fish, and express the hope that it will soon be fully re-established.

Red bream spend only a limited time inshore – the warmer summer months. It is not known with any certainty what their spawning habits are, but there are indications that spawning might take place over a quite protracted period, from as early as January until October. The fry may reach three inches in length in their first year and perhaps six or seven inches in their second. (These are the 'chad' which can be such a bait-robbing nuisance to fishermen in Cornish waters.)

Bream show a decided preference for rocky ground, and while small specimens may be taken well inshore, the bigger fish seem to prefer a depth of fifteen fathoms or more. For most of the day, the tendency is for them to feed near the bottom, but towards evening they will rise and may be taken at mid-water. As we shall see when we come to discuss angling techniques, this is something that will have to be taken into consideration in rod fishing.

Red bream are not particularly choosy feeders. Big specimens may feed on small fish but they will also take brittle stars, anemones, worms, and crabs, and may well browse and crop at the weeds. They are pretty well omnivorous. It is recorded that on one occasion when a wheat ship went down off Cornwall, bream taken in the vicinity thereafter were found to be crammed with wheat.

The red bream occurs from the Mediterranean and the Canaries in the south to Scandanavian waters in the north, but around the British Isles it certainly favours the rocky south-west. In the days when it was an abundant fish, it was very common all round the coast of Ireland, around Devon and Cornwall and the west coast of Wales. Nowadays the best place to look for a specimen red bream is in some western area where the ground is too foul for the trawls, or too remote. In the last few years I have taken bream off Ballycotton, Co. Cork, Valentia Island, and in Milford Haven, Pembrokeshire. Old fishery maps are still full of 'Bream Rocks' and marks with similar names, but very often it will be found that the fish have deserted them. The coasts of Cornwall and Devon still produce red bream.

Tackle Bream are among the gamest fish I have encountered, but they are small fish, and the worst possible crime in my opinion is to fish too heavy for them. At Littlehampton, old-timers still go out with heavy boat rods, big leads, and paternoster tackle, and haul up bream three at a time, for they are not difficult to deceive at the beginning of the season. But tides at Littlehampton are comparatively slack, and sometimes as little as a ¼ oz. of lead is sufficient to get the bait down to the feeding fish. With fine line, even the fastest tides require no more than 3 oz. at the outside.

When fishing for red bream in deeper water, in tides that are

Red Gurnard

Trigla cuculus
Record 3 lb 1 oz

Yellow Gurnard

Trigla lucerna
Record 11 lb 7½ oz

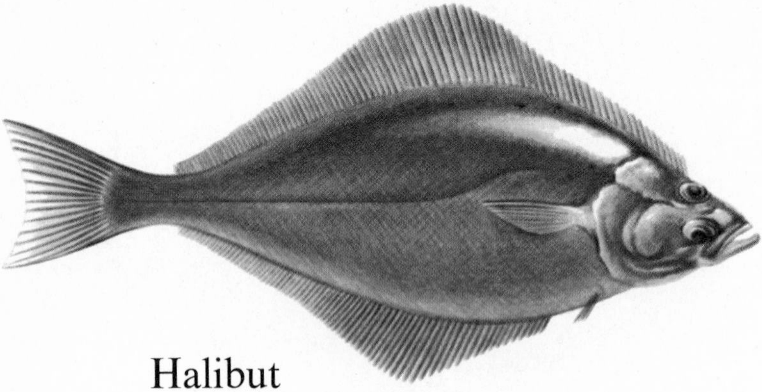

Halibut

Hippoglossus hippoglossus (page 293)
Record 161 lb 12 oz

Turbot

Scopthalmus maximus (page 346)
Record 29 lb

John Dory

Zeus faber (page 295)
Record 10 lb 12 oz

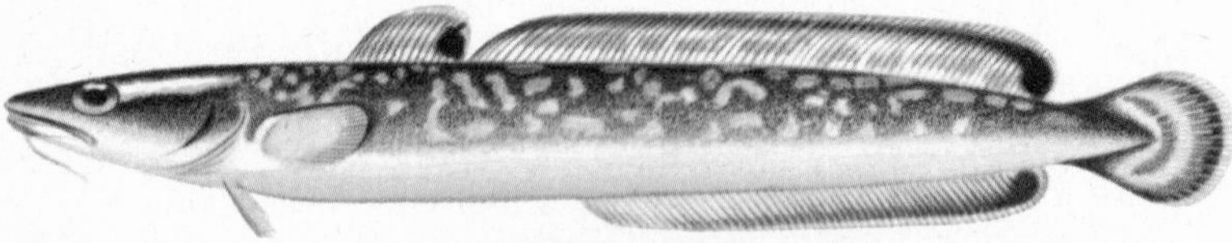

Ling

Molva molva (page 296)
Record 45 lb

Hake

Merluccius merluccius
Record 25 lb 5 oz 8 drams

a good deal more fierce than those encountered off the Sussex coast, it may not always be possible to use light tackle. But the fish pull just as hard as their black cousins. I remember one day catching fair pollack on the drift-line off Ballycotton – the fish were going, I suppose, 6 or 7 lb. apiece. Then I hit another fish. 'Here's a really big pollack', I told the boatman. But I was wrong. It was a 4 lb. red bream.

The best rod to use is a light spinning rod. I would have said fly rod except that bream are faster and tougher than trout and a smash would be quite likely. A free-running drum reel of the centre-pin type is the next item – preferably a long-trotting coarse fisherman's reel. Line of 4 lb. b.s. is just right under neap tide conditions. A light bomb weight is mounted well up-trace, stopped by a small swivel. The length of the trace should be as long as you can comfortably manage, and should end in a small, long-shanked hook.

Bait could be MACKEREL or herring strip (cut very fine), lugworm or mussel, or a combination of any of these.

Two methods of baiting with mackerel or other fish strips.

Fishing Methods

The trace is lowered into the water and the weight sinks until you feel it just tip bottom. You should choose your weight so that when you lift the rod point and give a little slack it is light enough to trundle down with the tide, but not light enough to be swept away quickly. If you search the bottom some distance away from the boat and find that there are no fish there, a very gentle retrieve can be made in order to find any fish that may be swimming higher up in the water.

On this tackle red and black bream fight magnificently. Their style of play is unique. You hit the fish and think you have him well under control, if sullenly resisting, as he is drawn to the top. But then, without warning, he will crash-dive, quite irresistibly, and unless you are expecting this there will be an almost certain break, sometimes of the trace, sometimes of the rod point. And the fish will do this four or five times on the way up. A landing net is absolutely essential in this game, by the way. And make sure your boatman knows how to use one.

General

Judging from personal observation and from reports in the angling press, any black bream over four pounds must be considered an exceptional fish. A big fish is most likely to be caught at the beginning of the season when the bream arrive on the reef and are full of spawn. I know that if I were fortunate enough to catch a black bream of between, say, 4½ and 5 lb., I should immediately claim the record, since the fish which now appears on the record list should have been subjected to investigation long ago. It weighed 6 lb. 5 oz. and was taken in the Menai Strait. Now this is a remarkably large fish, much heavier than anything which has been reported for years. Black bream, moreover, are unheard of the in Menai Strait. But WRASSE have been called 'bream' there since time immemorial. The possibility of an honest mistake is obvious. All claims are now verified by the British Record Fish Committee.

Red bream, on the other hand, regularly reach weights of 6 or 7 lb. The record red bream, a 7½-pounder, was taken off Fowey, Cornwall, in 1925.

Incidentally, a word of warning. If you happen to be fishing in Ireland or in west Wales and you are told that 'bream' are plentiful at such and such a mark, do not be too hopeful. Bream as I have mentioned is a name that is given quite widely in these parts to the wrasse – the real bream being sometimes known as carp, just to complicate matters.

C. G.

Cod

The cod (*Gadus callarias*) is hardly likely to be mistaken for any other species encountered around these islands. It is not a particularly beautiful fish to look at – the seemingly disproportionate size of the head and jaws and the characteristic pot-bellied look are enough to rule out such a judgement – but it is not an entirely ugly fish either, with its greeny-brown sides marked with yellow and brown spots and the distinctive broad white lateral line. Let it not be thought that it is repulsive in the way that dogfish and similar 'animals' are. Maybe it is something to do with the wintry environment in which we catch them, but a good cod always looks clean and cold to me, and a worth-while prize. Other characteristic features are the triple dorsal fin and the single barbule on the jaw.

In British waters, cod spawn in the spring, in March and April. After spawning, they shoal in water of considerable depth, well off shore, and, except for the occasional big 'rock' cod taken by deep-water fishermen, do not come into the inshore angler's programme until late October or November,

Cod

when there is a general movement of fish towards the littoral shallows.

From November on, cod are taken from the shore in favoured localities, from piers and sharply shelving beaches. They are also taken by boat fishermen operating close inshore. November and December are the best months, with a gradual falling off in the New Year until the cod leave once again for the banks on which they spawn.

The seasonal movement inshore may depend, for the particular direction it takes, on movements of shoals of fish on which the cod feed – sprat and herrings in particular. Generally speaking, however, they turn up at the same places year after year, though some years, undeniably, are better than others.

Most cod are taken over clean ground, sand or mud, or over patchy, stony ground. They are bottom-feeders – this may be stated axiomatically – and for any success at all the angler must ensure that his bait is on the bottom. The big 'rock' cod, however, are occasionally to be found over a reef in deep water. These fish are much more reddish-brown in appearance than normal cod, and so far as I can make out they are rarely present in the big shoals one expects in the winter.

Cod have a marked liking for estuaries, especially ones which have a strong run of tide. As a rule they do not penetrate far into the brackish water.

At most places where the cod fishing is good, there is usually a 'cod corner' which is a particularly good mark, and this, I've noticed, is often a patch of weedy stones adjacent to clean ground. It is very important for the anglers to locate these cod 'patches', since the movement of cod may be very localized, so that even though you may be only a few yards off the mark you may miss the fish altogether.

Baits

To quote Dr Michael Kennedy: 'The cod is a voracious fish, with a mouth like a trawl and a swallow like a vacuum cleaner, and its stomach contents are usually a pretty fair cross-section of the marine life in the locality in which it is captured.' In British waters, most of the cod's diet is made up of crustaceans and worms, except when shoals of sprat or herrings are being followed.

The cod has a hearty appetite, but it would be a mistake for the angler to take this as meaning that choice of bait does not matter. When they are feeding inshore cod can be extraordinarily pernickety. On some days a good bunch of lugworm is all that they will look at; on others a fish bait is necessary for success. A sprat fished whole will often account for big cod.

One cod expert, Leslie Moncrieff, claims that one of the best of all cod baits is the sea mouse (*aphrodite*). This claim is borne out by the fact that this marine worm figures large in an analysis of the stomach contacts of large numbers of cod, and by Moncrieff's own success. I myself am very fond of mussel as a cod bait – for boat fishing particularly, since it is very difficult to cast from the shore. Sometimes a sandwich bait is very tempting to cod – a lugworm is threaded on the hook first of all and a mussel follows it. It very often happens when fishing with this bait that the mussel is snatched off first and then the cod returns for the worm. However, not long ago I found that the cod preferred the mussel so strongly that they would not come back for the worm at all, and it soon became clear that the latter was a waste of time.

One thing is axiomatic in cod fishing: use a very big bait. A couple of years ago, I watched Sam Hook, the holder of the present cod record, bait up for a session on Lowestoft Pier, Suffolk. He used a large hook, and threaded on no fewer than six lugworms!

Cod, of course, *will* take the most extraordinary things on occasion. It is recorded that among the odd things found in cods' stomachs have been a hare and a bottle of whisky.

Tackle For *beach casting*, very much the same sort of gear as that recommended for surf fishing for BASS will do. Some cod beaches, however, particularly those on the east coast, are very steep, with a powerful undertow, so that there is a case for using heavier gear than on a shallow, sandy bass beach. Some cod experts prefer a lead as heavy as 6 oz., since this will hold well out in heavy winter seas. I leave it to the individual angler to decide whether this sort of fishing is worth the candle. At Dungeness, a cod beach which has produced some good catches in the last few years, long casting is said to be required to reach the fish, which may be feeding as much as 150 yards out. Recently a beach-casting rod has come on the market, designed by a Dungeness cod specialist, which is more than 13 ft long and made of hollow glass. This is certainly the weapon if you wish to make long casts. As for the fishing itself, it is unlikely to answer as well. It certainly could not be held comfortably through a tide and is presumably meant to be used in a rest. I am never happy when fishing a rod in a rest, and it seems quite clear to me that many fish are lost this way. On most beaches it is not necessary to cast as far as this, and a lighter, shorter rod is a more practicable proposition, as well as being productive of more sport.

For shore cod fishing, a multiplier loaded with 24 lb. b.s. line will do all that is required, and there are many circumstances in which a lighter one could be used. A supply of spiked leads is essential for winter cod fishing. A useful average size is 4 oz., but circumstances will dictate what the angler must use. Hooks should be large – look at the size of a cod's mouth – and, as indicated above, they have to carry a good-sized bait.

Cod

If you are using a spiked lead, a very useful thing to have is a detachable French boom in light metal. This can be fixed on to the trace just above the lead so that the hook link will be well clear of the spikes which would otherwise foul it. Fishing this way some anglers use two hooks below the weight.

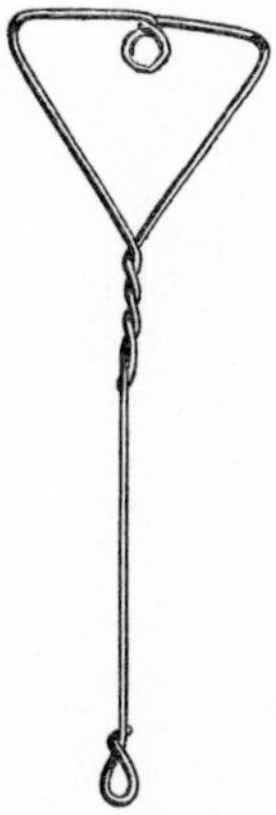

Detachable French boom

Boat Fishing: Boat-fishing rods have improved in design a good deal since the introduction of fibre-glass and it is possible to buy one quite cheaply that will give excellent service. For a short boat rod, the ordinary objections to whole glass, which are principally concerned with its curve under pressure, do not apply. If you are buying a cheap rod, however, make sure that the rings are of good stainless steel. Sometimes the reel fittings on a very cheap rod are not particularly satisfactory either.

I always use my surf-casting multiplier for light boat fishing and, in most areas, there is no need to put on a heavy line simply because one is boat fishing. An exception is the fishing at Deal, on the 'heel' of England, where very heavy tides make it necessary to use very large weights and correspondingly heavy tackle.

Where possible, use a running leger from a boat. The old-fashioned 'banker's' lead, much used by professional line fishermen, is still very effective. With it two hooks may be used below the weight.

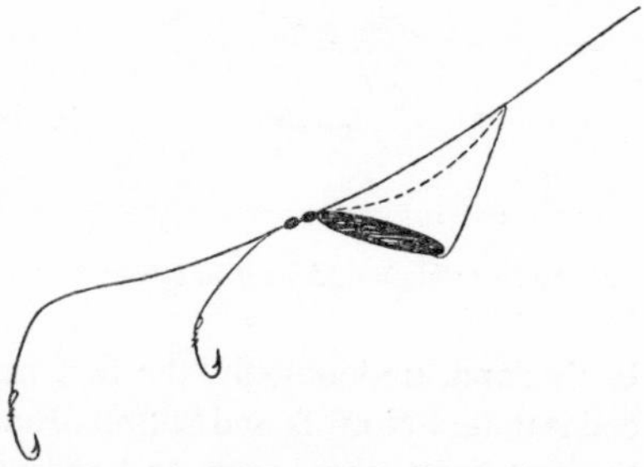

Banker's lead

Fishing Methods

Now that the technical side of the subject has been discussed, there is little to add, except that knowledge of the ground is all important. From piers and beaches one can usually expect a good knock from a taking fish. Try to arrange it so that your bait is well on the bottom. Apart from the baits that have been mentioned already, soft or peeler crab is an excellent bait to use from the shore. If your crab is a really large one, it will be all the better.

As with bass fishing, much of the best cod fishing is at night. It may seem superfluous to point this out, but make sure that you are very warmly clad. If you are warm and comfortable you will fish better. Even if you don't feel hungry when you set out, carry some food and a hot drink in a Thermos. Some people are addicted to all-night fishing sessions. I enjoy one from time to time, in good company and with a fire going, but I have rarely found the actual fishing results to be worth the effort. For serious night fishing I prefer to select three or four hours when the best part of the tide coincides either with the first few hours of darkness or the pre-dawn hours. It's better to have a couple of hours concentrated fishing than spend the night fooling about with barbecues on the beach.

Boat Fishing: In boat fishing, a great deal depends on picking up the right marks. If you are visiting a strange fishing station you will have to rely on your judgement of the boatmen, and it is always worth trying to find out which of them is best regarded locally before you make a firm booking.

If tides are slack, ground-baiting will bring the cod to you, and, as in so many other forms of boat fishing, it is enormously worth while. I've noticed that in boat fishing the bite is not always as positive as one might expect, even where quite large fish are involved. Strike at every little 'pick'. It may be that you will merely hook a pouting – but it may be a 40-pounder!

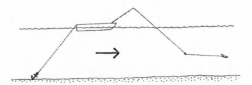

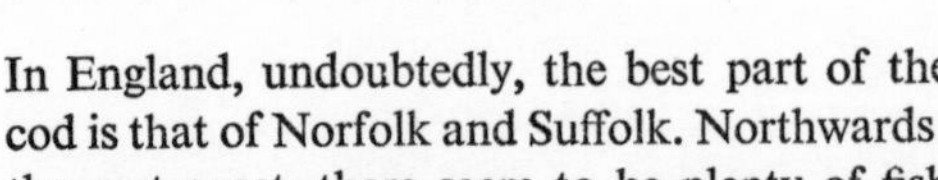

Fishing from anchored boat in strong tide.

General In England, undoubtedly, the best part of the coastline for cod is that of Norfolk and Suffolk. Northwards of there, along the east coast, there seem to be plenty of fish, but they run smaller on the average. On the East Anglian coast, the area around Lowestoft is productive of good fish every year, and beaches like Shingle Street are also worth visiting. The estuaries of the Deben and the Orwell provide useful boat fishing when the weather is too rough to get outside.

The Kent coast offers good cod fishing too. Dungeness Beach, a desolate shingle ridge which no one would visit for any other reason than cod fishing, I imagine, has come into a good deal of prominence in the last few seasons. Deal is noted for its cod fishing, both from the shore and from boats a little off shore. Like Lowestoft, it has a pier which transcends the usual low level of pier fishing.

Cod do not seem to be so prominent in the western end of the English Channel, nor may they be expected in any quantity on the Atlantic coasts of Cornwall and Pembrokeshire, although in the Bristol Channel, east of Swansea, there is some good cod fishing. The North Wales and Lancashire coasts are notoriously bad for all kinds of sea fishing, but some codling are taken. What the Scottish picture is remains obscure, but, from the geographical position of the country, there should be good cod fishing, especially in the north east.

In Ireland, the easterly pattern is repeated. The Irish Sea coast, particularly in the neighbourhood of Dublin Bay, provides good cod fishing in the winter. Individual rock cod of good weight turn up off the south coast in the summer – the Irish record cod, a 42-pounder, was one of these, coming from Ballycotton. What the winter situation is I do not know. The only well-established fishery for cod on lines is at Youghal on the estuary of the Munster Blackwater. Here, small codling in their first and second years ('pickers', as they are called) are present throughout the year. In November come the bigger fish, 5-pounders to 7- or 8-pounders ('tamlin') and after them the big fish of anything up to 40 lb.

I have a theory, which I expressed fully in *Shore Fishing*, that cod have a preference inshore for water that is less saline and 'weaker' than the 'rich' Atlantic water brought in by the North Atlantic drift. Thus, areas like Cornwall which provide excellent all-round fishing as a rule may not provide good cod fishing, while an area of sea like the upper Bristol Channel where the fishing is usually mediocre will attract good cod because of the lower salinity of the water. The whole question is too detailed to go into here, but two maps drawn as a comparison made the theory very feasible. One showed the areas of cold, 'enclosed' water of low salinity around the British Isles, the other marked places from which cod were consistently reported as having been taken. These areas coincided almost exactly. To give a simple example, both the Irish Sea and the

North Sea, areas of low salinity, produce good cod fishing. The presence of such good cod fishing at Youghal is difficult to fit into the theory, but it must be remembered that into this estuary goes the fresh water of one of Eire's major rivers – the Munster Blackwater – and the diluting effect of this may well be the factor that draws the cod.

Growth Rate: Quite a lot is known about the natural history of cod, which is not surprising when you consider that the species is the most important food fish in the world. They are fast-growing fish, and, of course, very prolific. They have to be to survive – consider the millions of tons of cod landed each year by the trawlers. The figures we have for North Sea cod show that a year-old cod weighs nearly a pound and measures a little more than 7 ins. Second-year fish are 2-pounders. By its sixth year, a cod may have reached a weight of 15 lb. Cod probably become sexually mature in their third year. The maximum weight a cod may reach is very great indeed. The present British record fish is not much more than 30 lb. (a new record claim for a 40-plus fish is under consideration at the time of writing), but very much bigger fish are taken by commercial fishing vessels every year. Occasionally 100-pounders turn up from Arctic waters, and the world's record (commercial) catch was a 211½ lb. fish taken off the coast of Massachusetts. So there is plenty of scope!

C. G.

Conger

The conger (*Conger conger*) is one of those fish, like the pike, that assembles legends around itself. For one thing, unlike most sea fish, congers tend to keep to one place, so that the presence of a monster in a local reef or in the crevices of a harbour wall may be known to anglers over a number of years.

Naturally, the fish's fame grows in proportion to the amount of tackle that it smashes. Fearsome tales are told of the power of congers, how with a blow of the tail they smash the thwarts and gunnels of small boats, and how their jaws are capable of reducing to pulp the unwary hand or foot.

It has to be admitted that the conger *is* a dangerous and tough customer to have in the boat. It is a very strong, muscular fish, and when one considers that conger of more than eighty pounds have been landed on rod and line, and that many bigger fish remain unlanded, it is easy to believe the strangest stories. Many anglers have developed a healthy fear of the conger. A friend of mine believes that one of them actually *chased* him up a slipway after coming off the hook. I myself would certainly be disinclined to go conger fishing after dark alone in a small boat.

This aura of evil which congers seem able to produce is intensified by the kind of place where it is necessary to fish for them, particularly from the shore. One spot I know, very productive of good conger, is near an old hulk, far up a deep inlet of the sea, where there is scarcely ever any rough water, and where the sea seems to take on a hue of deep bottle green from the trees on the shore which overshadow it. The water is very deep, and at night the atmosphere of this 'conger pit' is almost palpable.

There is little likelihood of mistaking a conger for any other fish, even the common eel. Proportionately, the conger is very much thicker than the common eel, its eyes are much bigger, and above all its jaws are plainly much more formidable, both in size and in muscular power. They are equipped with a fearsome set of cutting teeth, and once the fish has made up its mind to hang on they are almost impossible to separate. If you catch a conger over rocky ground he is likely to be a darker fish than one which is taken on sand, brownish-black as opposed to a slatey tinge in the latter case. The belly is usually whiter in the case of a conger caught over sand.

Most authorities state that the conger migrate to deep water once the hard weather starts, and this is probably true in many localities. However, in south Pembrokeshire, where most of my conger fishing has been done, the fish seem to remain inshore right through the year. This might well be true of other localities where mild winters are experienced – the West Country for instance, or the west of Ireland. A spell of very hard weather may possibly drive the fish off shore. There are many recorded incidents of conger being washed up dead in very cold weather.

This lack of seasonal movement may be due to the fact that congers make a spawning journey only once in their lifetime. This is a formidable undertaking, for the goal is the abyssal depth of the Atlantic where the spawning ground may be more than 1,600 feet deep (Travis Jenkins). The behaviour of congers ripe for spawning has been observed in aquaria. The development of milt and roe is accompanied by deterioration in the fish itself, affecting the teeth and bones, as calcium is withdrawn from the body. Male congers seem to become sexually mature when they are around two feet in length; all big congers caught are female. The females may be twice this length, or very much larger, before they begin their spawning journey. It is an interesting fact that the biggest fish to be found inshore – fish of more than 100 lb. in weight – are unspawned maiden fish. The conger does not return from its spawning journey, but dies once it has been accomplished.

As far as fishing is concerned, late autumn is the best time of the year for congers. Possibly this is due to the fact that they feed extra well at this time against the leaner time to be expected in the winter and the spring. Settled weather seems to induce them to feed with confidence, and the traditional idea that eels are stirred up and ravenous during thundery weather seems to be borne out by experience.

Congers are certainly night-feeding fish for the most part, and the angler must fish at night if he hopes to get among the big ones. Small congers up to ten pounds or so will feed during daylight, however, and it seems possible that when very deep water is fished there is no significant difference between daylight and night fishing.

There has been little modern investigation into the growth rate of congers. However, it would seem that the fish is very fast-growing and short-lived – an idea rather at odds with the traditional one that these mighty congers are ancient fish. J. T. Cunningham, a nineteenth-century authority on marine fishes, declared that a conger in Southport aquarium reached a weight of 90 lb. in five and a half years.

Congers are chiefly found on rough ground, wherever there are crannies where they can lie up during the day, and from which they can ambush passing fish. Harbours and piers usually have a few resident conger, particularly where fish are landed and possibly gutted. These harbour conger will often take up residence in a cranny in the harbour wall which dries out at low water of spring tides, but they don't seem to mind. Conger are also left high and dry occasionally amongst the rocks of the foreshore, where they are sometimes come upon by men out for crabs and lobsters. Once you have observed how congers can conceal themselves in the rocks you will be reluctant to put a hand 'blind' into a rock crevice.

Although most congers spend all the daylight hours concealed in rocks or stonework, at night they will often venture out across the sands in pursuit of fish. Sometimes it is a good idea, when night fishing, not to fish right on to the reef itself but to drop the bait a short distance away on to clean ground. As we shall see, this gives the angler a considerable advantage in landing the fish.

Sometimes congers will venture far up estuaries, presumably in pursuit of shoal fish, but they are unlikely to take up residence unless there is rocky ground for them to lie up in.

Conger

Although quite large conger can be taken close inshore – specimens of up to 60 lb. have been caught in harbours – the bigger fish seem to prefer off-shore reefs where there is a good depth of water, and presumably a better food supply.

The conger's diet is mostly made up of fish. I do not know what species form the basic diet of conger, but presumably fish that frequent the rocks are the most likely. Rockling, POUTING, and POLLACK clearly comprise a good proportion of the conger's food supply, and at night, when the big eels venture out over the sand and mud, they undoubtedly eat other species such as DABS and gurnards. Crustaceans must figure in the diet as well, and many crabs fall victim, as do squid and cuttlefish when they are available. Conger usually feed at the bottom, but there are times when they will cruise in search of food along the weeds which skirt the rocks. This is particularly true of harbour conger, which sometimes patrol the walls near the surface.

Baits

Traditionally the conger fisherman is advised always to use fresh bait, and many conger experts would not dream of going fishing with stale bait. In recent years, however, this view has been challenged. Dr Michael Kennedy, for instance, states that he has caught conger of up to 45 lb. on very stale mackerel, and is of the opinion that it simply depends upon how hungry the conger is. Stale bait has no advantage over the fresh stuff, apparently, so the best advice is to use bait as fresh as can be managed, though the fact that it is unobtainable should not be taken as ruling out all possibility of fishing.

Oily fish like herring and MACKEREL make attractive conger baits. Congers seem to hunt by smell, and the traces of oil given off by the fish mentioned will undoubtedly draw the eels into the vicinity. In Cornwall another oily fish, pilchard, is much in use.

Of the other fishes likely to be available as bait, a small POUTING or poor COD makes a very good bait indeed. In fact, a small pouting fished whole is the bait that I prefer above any other for conger. Conger take small POLLACK, but not, I feel, so readily as the other fishes mentioned. Rockling can be used, and if squid is plentiful in the neighbourhood it can be a deadly bait. Conger have been caught on such unlikely baits as rabbits' guts, but it will probably pay the angler to be more orthodox than this.

Tackle There is a strong case to be made out for using nothing but a handline for big conger. The fight is usually one of brute strength, and the rod, unless it is very strong, tends to be more of a hindrance than a help. But since it is one of the basic tenets of sporting sea fishing that a rod should be used, we had better start thinking in terms of one that will do the job. A short boat rod of the toughest kind is the only one to use where big conger are expected. A big conger is a much tougher proposition than a blue shark, but usually a shark rod is heavier than one used for conger. In my opinion, a big game-rod, test curve somewhere around 25 lb. or even more, is the only weapon that will give you half a chance with big conger fished for over an off-shore reef. The line should be 100 lb. b.s. of Terylene or Dacron, not monofilament, for a reason which will emerge in a moment. The trace should be in proportion as regards strength, and of cable-laid steel wire. The swivels must be carefully tested for strength before being used. The hook should be very sharp – many conger are lost quite mysteriously at the boatside when they spit the hook out. The lead, arranged to run on the line above the swivel, should be heavy enough to hold bottom in the kind of tide that you are fishing. A pear-shaped lead is less likely to foul in the rocks than one of any other kind. Some anglers use several swivels on the trace since the conger has a habit of spinning round. This tactic, without the relief of a swivel, can weaken the line. The gaff head should be very strong and lashed on firmly. A screw-head gaff is not of much use in conger fishing, once again because of the twisting tactics of the fish. A big-game belt with a socket for the rod butt is an advantage in fishing where congers run big.

It should be realized that in these directions I am visualizing the possibility of a 50 lb. plus fish turning up. Most congers, of course, will be below this weight, and sport with them will be largely lost on heavy tackle. But it is the really big fish that have always fascinated sea anglers and there is no chance at all of landing these unless really formidable tackle is used. If you are daylight fishing some harbour or pier where only small conger are expected, then it would be sensible to scale tackle down, but for serious conger specimen hunting only the toughest gear will do.

Fishing Methods Congers very often mouth the bait a good deal before taking it properly. Some conger fishermen strike on the first knock, on the grounds that if the fish is hooked it is easier to keep it clear of the bottom, but most judge it better to wait for a positive, slow run and hit that.

Hit the fish hard, and try to gain as much line as possible in the first few seconds, knocking the fish off-balance, as it were. The instinct of every conger is to regain its lair in the rocks, and once it has managed to get its immensely muscular tail around an obstruction it becomes almost impossible to move. *Conger*

This is why a plaited line, rather than monofilament, is recommended. There is a measurable amount of stretch in monofil nylon which may be all that the conger needs, especially in deep water, where several feet of stretch may be involved. If you can keep the conger away from the bottom for the first few minutes of the fight, the worst is over and the remainder is an up-and-down fight. A big conger is immensely strong, but eventually a continuous strain will tell, though there will be moments when it will seem problematical whether you can outstay the fish.

Once you have the conger on the surface, it is desirable to get the gaff in as swiftly as possible, and to keep the surface splashing down to a minimum. In the case of a really big conger, two gaffs are better than one; in any case be prepared to put the rod down and go to the aid of the gaffsman to haul the fish inboard as swiftly as you can.

Once in the boat, the conger can still be a menace. A heavy blow over the vent will keep it quiet for a time, but do not try to regain the hook until the conger is certainly dead – it's better to put on a new trace and recover the other at your leisure much later on. While the fish is still stunned, get it into a sack, where the harm it can do is minimized.

General

A big conger can turn up almost anywhere, but the rocky Atlantic coasts of the south and south-west seem to be the most productive of big fish. By and large, the east coast of England, sandy and low-lying for the most part, is not a particularly good area for conger. Off-shore wrecks, however, are clearly an exception to this rule. Devon and Cornwall provide good conger fishing from the rocks and harbours; the best harbours are those that still maintain a fleet of small trawlers and where fish may be gutted on the quayside, or fish waste thrown overboard. The sea inlet at Dartmouth, in South Devon, offers good conger fishing. The west coast of Britain generally is good for conger, particularly where there are rocks. There are huge conger in Milford Haven, but they are difficult to fish because of the big tides. When the big holes can be fished, however, a really monster conger – i.e. 50 lb. plus – is always a possibility. The present record fish was an 84-pounder taken off Dungeness by the redoubtable H. A. Kelley in 1933.

This record is one which, in the opinion of many sea anglers, could be broken any season. The hazards of landing a very big conger on rod and line from a characteristic rocky conger haunt are pretty intimidating, however.

There are excellent possibilities of specimen conger on the Scottish coast, particularly on the west coast, and the species is present in most Irish waters. There must be some huge conger lurking, for instance, around the wreck of the *Lusitania*, from which such splendid catches of ling have been made. Some of the biggest conger I encountered in Ireland were in small harbours like Ballycotton, where I shall never forget being broken one evening on shark tackle!

Fishing for specimen conger offers great scope to the keen sea angler at the moment, especially in view of the possibility of a new record. One day, perhaps when you are fishing well off shore, the pouting will stop their nibblings and there will come a long, powerful draw at the rod tip that will announce the first 100-pounder to be landed on rod and line.

C. G.

Dab

The dab (*Limanda limanda*) is one of the smallest flatfish. It is usually a lightish sandy colour on the back but can best be told from other finny 'flatties' by the lateral line which curves sharply upwards above the pectoral fin. The scales on the back feel rough to the touch; on the underside, they are smooth.

The dab lives over sandy ground foraging for marine scraps, worms, crustacea, and so on. It is found inshore all the year round but not so often in deep winter. Large numbers are caught from piers at the various seaside resorts ranging from Blackpool southwards. They are also taken from many beaches on the south-coast and the Bristol Channel. Normally they are in their best condition during the autumn period, September to November. As a rule those taken from the shore run up to about $\frac{3}{4}$ lb. with the occasional bigger specimen. The record fish, 2 lb. 9$\frac{1}{2}$ oz., was taken from a beach at Port Talbot in 1936.

Tackle and Fishing Methods

Dabs are usually fished for with a light three-hook paternoster on the bottom. Baits include ragworm, lugworm, mussel, and shrimp. I have seen them taken on a piece of sprat. The dab is a fish that often takes the bait well down, hooking itself in the process. Hooks should be of fine wire and long-shanked. Anglers who regularly fish for dabs state that the bait should not be left stationary but should be moved a yard or so at intervals. Dabs are taken in number at times in what is known as a skim net. This is a triangular net on a frame, usually 11 ft across the mouth. It is worked in the sea from about a foot or so of water to the last 6 ins. Catches in excess of 20 lb. of dabs and other flatfish are made at times.

Dab

General

The record dab of 2 lb. 9½ oz. was caught at Morfa beach, Port Talbot, by M. L. Walls in 1936. The south coast from Hastings to the Isle of Wight has produced several dab over 2 lb.

Derek Fletcher

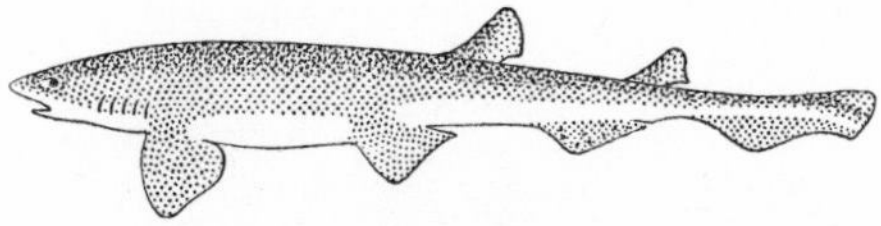

Dogfish

There are three types: the lesser spotted (*Scyliorhinus caniculus*); the greater spotted (*Scyliorhinus stellaris*); and the spur (*Squalus acanthias*).

None of the dogfish is of great interest from a sporting point of view. Nevertheless they are caught with such frequency when one is fishing for something else that they must, at least, be mentioned.

The lesser spotted dogfish, sometimes called 'rough hound', has a skin of sandpaper texture. As a small relation of the SHARK it has the characteristic underslung mouth which in this species is crescent shaped. The skin is generally sandy coloured but marked with numerous dark spots.

The greater spotted, or bull huss, is a slightly better angling proposition. It is usually darker and bigger, and the spots are larger. It can be told from the lesser spotted dog by its nasal flaps. In the latter the flaps have a simple curved edge; those of the greater spotted are lobed. The British record for the greater spotted is 21 lb. 3 oz. from Looe.

The spur dog is dark grey or brown above and white below. It puts up a better fight than the other two varieties of dogfish. The spurs, one in front of each dorsal fin, are capable of giving a nasty wound which often turns septic. The best thing is to pin the fish down, knock it on the head, and nip off the spurs with heavy pliers.

Dogfish is good to eat and when skinned and beheaded appears on the menu as 'rock salmon'.

The lesser spotted is usually found over sandy or muddy ground feeding close to the bottom. Crabs, small fish, and starfish feature largely on its menu. It is found round the coast most of the year.

The greater spotted is more likely to be found over rough or rocky bottoms, otherwise its habits are much the same. The spur dog is more inclined to wander but is usually met in numbers in the summer months when one is boat fishing.

Since few people fish deliberately for dogfish, they are usually caught on whatever tackle the angler is using at the time. Strips of fish, lugworm, mussel, or almost any smallish bait will lure them.

D. F.

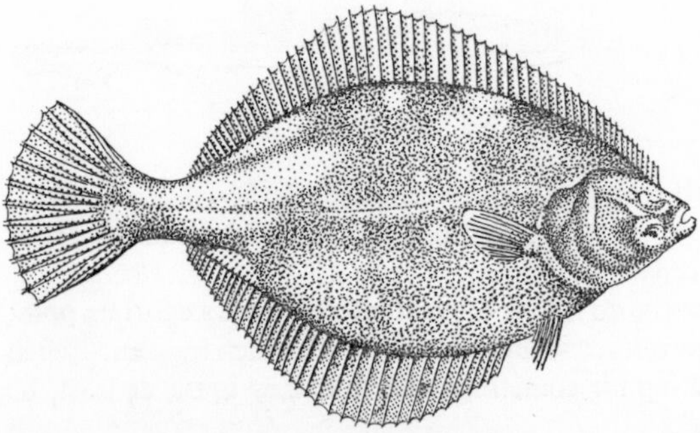

Flounder

The flounder (*Pleuronectes flesus*) starts off its life with its body in a vertical position (i.e. like a MACKEREL and not like a flatfish), but a few weeks later the body tilts to one side until one of the eyes moves round to meet the other, and the fish sinks to the sea-bed – a true flatfish.

The colouring of the flounder often varies from coast to coast, according to the bottom it frequents. The upper surface may be a brownish-black, or a light brown. Sometimes there are almost plaice-like spots on it, but these fade pretty quickly on capture. The underside is white, except in the occasional freak which has the same brownish colouring all over.

Sometimes the flounder, or fluke as it is called in many areas, is confused with the DAB. An aid to identification is the fact that the flounder feels smooth, except for small tubercles at the base of the spine, when you run your finger along its back from tail to head. The dab feels rougher to the touch, like very fine sandpaper.

Flounders run to a good size, the best being caught in spring before the spawning period.

Lumpsucker

Cyclopterus lumpus
Record 6 lb 3 oz 4 drams

Opah

Lampris luna
Reaches 100 lb or more
No record

Mackerel

Scomber scomber (page 300)
Record 4 lb 11 oz

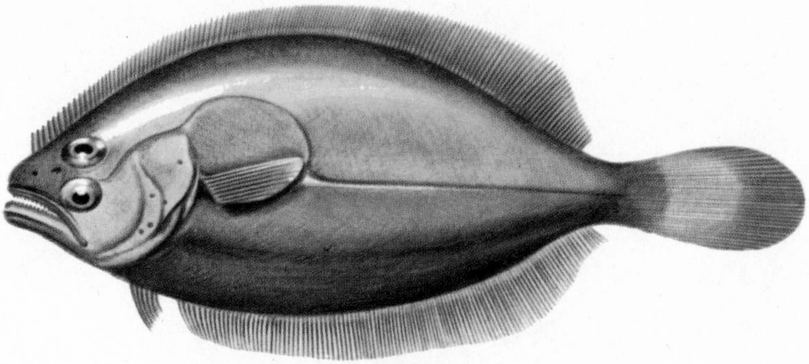

Megrim

Lepidorhombus whiff-iagonis
Record 3 lb 10 oz

Brill

Scophthalmus rhombas
Record 16 lb

Angler Fish

Lophius piscatorius
Record 68 lb 2 oz

Monk Fish

Squatina squatina
40 lb is a good fish
Record 66 lb

Flounder

Flounders are an inshore fish and can be caught from piers, harbours, muddy creeks, or inshore boats; they are often found well up rivers. They have a liking for fresh water and good catches are often made where fresh water enters the sea.

Tackle and Fishing Methods

There is a big list of baits with which to lure flounders, varying according to the area being fished. Ragworm, soft crab, slipper limpets, lugworm, and pieces of sand-eel or sprat are all useful hook-baits.

Observation pays in this kind of fishing. Flounders like to lie in gullies, waiting for food to drift into them. These gullies are often only a few yards from the shore, so it will pay to survey the beach at low water to note them.

While beach fishing do not be in too much of a hurry to strike. Many fish are lost by hurried striking. Flounders are noted for the time they take in mouthing the bait, and it is some time before they take in the lot. Use a single hook and a flowing trace rather than a paternoster with several hooks and a heavy weight. A weight sinks slowly into the sand and becomes buried. A trace will move around with the tide, attracting the fish by its free movement.

Flounders are very inquisitive fish and quick to investigate any disturbance on the sea-bed. In some estuaries anglers attract them by 'mudding' – raking the bottom with a fork. This is the theory behind the wander tackle devised by Mr P. Wadham, who fished the many Hampshire creeks with great success. It is a light-gear method of taking fish and is easily set up.

At one end of a long nylon trace tie a small swivel for attaching to the main line. A foot away from this fix a plastic boom with a small trace to a No. 4 hook. Add a tiny spiral lead 6 ins. along the main trace. Between this and the final hook have a small ball-type lead, stopped by a lead shot.

In practice, the lead moving along the bottom will stir up sand, etc., attracting the fish. It is a particularly good idea to use this method in crab-infested areas.

The 'bounce' idea is another popular method, especially from inshore boats. It was once thought that flatfish were slow-moving fish and one had to leave the bait where it was first cast. This is not the case. With this style one uses a single-hook trace which is retrieved with a series of jerks. The principle is similar to that of wander tackle – to disturb the sea-bed and lure the fish to the disturbance.

A baited spoon is a wonderful way of taking flounders. Often the problem is just what spoon to select. There is a

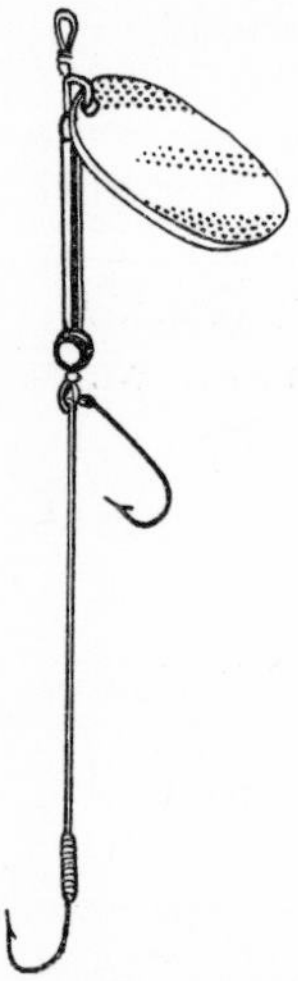

Baited spoon rig for flounder.

varied assortment on the market and it is important not to buy one too small. A 3 in. plated or white enamelled spoon will do nicely.

Some anglers have been disappointed when they first tried spoon fishing because they have presented the tackle in the wrong way. It is essential that only the spoon spins. If the hook goes round as well, the flounder will have no chance to mouth the bait and the fish will be lost. The hook behind the spoon should be baited (ragworm is good), the idea behind the method being that the flounder should think the fluttering spoon is another flatfish following up food, so it decides to investigate and seizes the bait.

Spoon fishing is best done from a boat and accounts for big bags in places such as Poole Harbour, Dorset. It is preferable to operate from a rowing boat with the rod out over the stern. Watch the rod carefully as the tip beats with the revolving of the spoon. When the beat changes to a twitching it is a sign that a flounder is interested. A tightening of the line follows as the fish dives with the bait. See that the tackle does not snag a weed-bed, for a small wisp of weed is enough to upset the smooth operation of the gear.

Another sporting method is fishing with a roving float. This is useful for fishing from piers, harbour walls, and occasionally boats. The bait should be arranged just to trip the bottom and allowed to roam unhindered in the current.

Anointing the worm with pilchard oil can help a great deal. The oil gives off an attractive trail on the sea-bed. Again, hesitate in making the strike. Let the float go well down and don't act on a mere bobbing which only means that the fish is giving the bait a once-over.

General The record, 5 lb. 11½ oz., was taken at Fowey in 1956 by A. G. L. Cobbledick. Most of the really big fish have come from the West Country. D. F.

Garfish

The garfish (*Belone belone*) is a long, silver-green, rather eel-like fish which is known by various local names such as sea-needle, gorebill, garpike, long-nose, greenbone, mackerel guide, old wife, snipe eel, hornfish, and numerous others. The garfish bears a strong resemblance to the skipper or saury pike, which is, however, a shorter fish, having a maximum length of about 18 ins.; the pike's beak-like mouth, also, is shorter than that of the garfish.

Garfish

The average weight of garfish seems to be about 12 oz. One specimen in particular which I had for examination and photographing weighed just under 1 lb. – but it measured 20¾ ins. (extreme length) and of that length its long beak measured 3½ ins.

The approach of spring and a warm spell of weather brings in the garfish, which then move into shallow water to spawn. Garfish provide lively sport while they remain inshore and do not move out to deep water again until the late autumn or early winter. They can be caught from rocks, piers, breakwaters, and boats; they are occasionally taken in the brackish water of estuaries.

Baits

Almost any of the usual sea-fishing baits will take gar, but a short list would include live prawn, sand-eel, and herring and mackerel strip, or even a strip from another garfish. The bait strip can be 2 to 4 ins. long and about ½ in.– 1 in. wide. Present the bait and keep it working in the top layer of water.

Tackle and Fishing Methods

During the season specially designed garfish tackle is used by many pier anglers. This consists of a sliding float arrangement which is attached to the line by a quick-release clip *after* the weighted line has been cast out; the float is then allowed to slide down the reel-line to the water. The weight on the end of

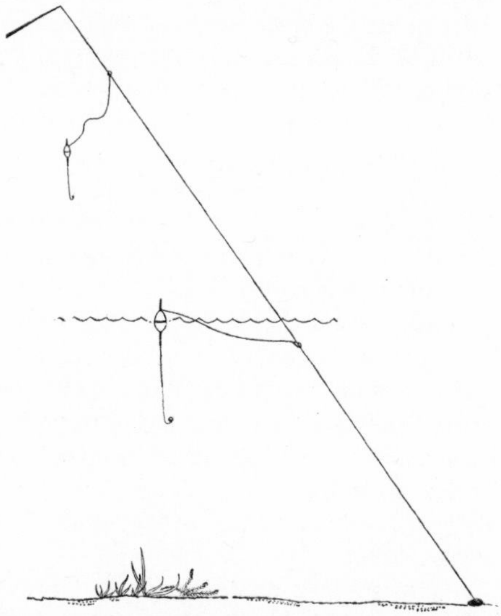

Pier rig for garfish. At top, float is shown sliding down line. Below it is sitting on the water.

the taut reel-line holds this float in position and thus presents the bait between mid-water and the surface. Line of about 5 lb. breaking strain is about the best for this tackle.

In addition to sliding-float tackle some anglers have two or three feet of nylon trace with baited hook tied a few inches above the bottom weight: this takes the odd FLOUNDER, PLAICE, or other fish which may be feeding on the bottom. Garfish, along with mackerel, often attack the shoals of brit or whitebait.

Spinning is a sporting way of fishing for garfish, but to get the best sport use a light spinning rod and the lightest of tackle. A mackerel spinner will sometimes take large numbers of garfish. In fact, almost any small, silvery spinning lure will catch them. The line may be of nylon with a breaking strain of some 4 lb. to 5 lb.; use a swivel to prevent the line from becoming twisted. On the reel line, above the trace and swivel, an anti-kink lead should be fitted.

Drift-lining from a boat is another successful method. You'll need a light rod, a centre-pin reel, and about 100 yds of 5 to 6 lb. b.s. nylon monofilament line. A 3 to 4 ft nylon trace (of slightly lower b.s.) may be attached to the end of the reel line by a small swivel. To the end of the trace is tied a No. 5 hook. As the garfish are usually swimming in the surface water, a very light weight should be all that is necessary unless the current is very strong. Then it will pay to experiment in order to get the exact weight of lead needed.

Bait by hooking a prawn or sand-eel lightly through the back, or with a lask of fresh mackerel – say 2 ins. by ½ in. wide. The hook is inserted at the broadest end of the mackerel lask, which should then wriggle attractively in the current. Lower the drift-line into the water and allow the current to carry or drift it along while the bait sinks slowly and naturally. Pay out line as the baited hook drifts with the current.

A float tackle can be fished in similar fashion. The tackle is the same, except that a float and the extra weight needed to balance it are added. Weight the tackle so that you leave sufficient float protruding above water for it to be clearly visible. Simply let the float tackle trot with the current, but when a bite comes you must strike quickly, especially if you've let the tackle drift some distance, for there will then be many yards of line lying on the surface which the rod must pick up on the strike.

A firm strike is needed because, if only lightly hooked, a garfish will probably shake itself free. Moreover, because a garfish moves at such speed, it is almost impossible to keep it on a tight line. It fights well and often goes wriggling along the surface then leaping a couple of feet out of the water. Let the hooked fish tire before you start to reel in.

Garfish

General

Garfish rarely figure in the lists of notable fish, but the British record is held by a 2 lb. 9 oz. fish, taken at Coverack, Cornwall, in 1935. There is every chance of bigger specimens being taken.

W. H.

Halibut

The halibut (*Hippoglossus hippoglossus*) is the largest of the world's flatfish; fish up to $7\frac{1}{2}$ ft in length and weighing 320 lb. have been recorded. It is smooth-skinned, dark olive in colour, and lightly marbled. The lateral line is curved over the pectoral fin and the eyes are on the right side of the head.

The halibut is generally associated with Icelandic waters and other very cold seas, and big specimens are rarely taken in British waters. In California, however, great numbers are caught close inshore, especially in the Malibu Beach area, where they are fished for from a drifting boat, in twelve to fifteen fathoms, using live sardines as bait.

Halibut spawn in the early summer (May to July) and are to be found at all times in deep water.

Baits

Whole live-baits – young WHITING, CODLING, WRASSE, or POLLACK – are the best. If dead-bait is used it is important to present it to the fish in as lifelike a manner as possible. Thread the trace through the fish from vent to mouth, binding the fish to the line by means of a light piece of line passed through the head and tied on to the main line. In this way the bait will move through the water like a swimming fish. With live-bait it is advisable to use two hooks, one of them through the body beneath the dorsal fin, and the other through the lip.

Tackle

You need the heaviest boat rod short of big-game gear, for, like the skate, the halibut has to be pumped to the surface by brute force. The rod should have a tip ring fitted with a revolving steel roller. Use a big sea multiplier reel loaded with 80 lb. Terylene.

Fishing Methods

Normally the halibut prefers a moving bait. In Iceland in particular a large, heavily weighted lure is used with great success by the professional fishermen. This is worked in much the same way as a jigger, a chromiumed weight incorporating hooks, which is lowered to the bottom and snatched up and down. The glistening of the spiralling lure attracts the fish, which grabs at what it thinks is moving prey.

Drift fishing for halibut is done by much the same methods as are used by the SHARK boats out of Looe, only instead of having the bait near the surface it is fished near the bottom. In drifting for halibut, a very useful method is to tie a very large silver spoon to a trace of 6–8 ft and attach to it a 9/0 or

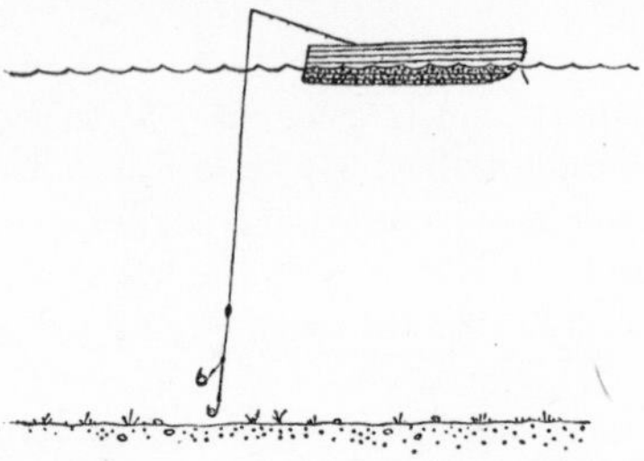

Drift fishing from a boat.

10/0 hook. The trace is made fast to the line by means of a 6/0 swivel with a running boom above it. Naturally a very heavy weight will be required, depending on the speed of drift, for the bait must at all times be moving along just clear of the bottom. The bait must be a newly caught whitefish.

Halibut fishing is hard work, for with a drifting boat it is necessary to let out line all the time, but at the same time it is imperative to maintain contact with the weight so that, in the event of its hitting against rocks, enough line can be retrieved to raise it clear before dropping it once more to the bottom behind the obstruction.

In drift fishing, the fish will be found in the sandy or muddy ground among the rocks and stones, and will only go for the bait as it passes overhead or alongside. The bait is taken from below. The usual indication of a bite is when you lose the feel of your weight as the fish swims upwards. Immediately following this the halibut dives straight for the bottom once more, where it sinks into the mud or sand and requires considerable purchase to move again if it is a large specimen.

General Recently a halibut of 600 lb. was landed at Dieppe by a French trawler returning from the deep-sea marks off the Westmann Islands in south-east Iceland. During recent international festivals fished in Icelandic waters, several halibut of up to 100 lb. have been taken on rod and line, using dead-bait (herring) from a drifting boat.

Halibut

In pre-war days Valentia Island off the west coast of Ireland produced some magnificent fish, but in recent years very few have been boated. In 1926 E. C. Henning landed three fine specimens in one day's fishing there. They weighed 152¾ (the present European and Irish record), 128¾, and 120 lb. respectively. Ballycotton, on the south coast of Ireland, also had at one time a reputation for large fish, but as at Valentia few have been seen in recent years. There is little doubt that the fish are still in the vicinity, but their new feeding grounds have not yet been located. The mark where Henning took his fish has altered entirely, for the rough ground has given way to a sandy bottom.

Leslie Moncrieff, the well-known casting expert, fishing the marks mid-way between Puffin Head and the Skerries Rocks south-west of Valentia in July 1962, hooked and landed an 80 lb. halibut from the thirty-fathoms mark. This particular spot has rarely been fished by rod and line anglers and could well be the new feeding ground. Fishing these same marks in September 1961, Leslie Norman of the City of London Piscatorial Society was smashed by a very large fish that was probably a halibut. His tackle consisted of Hardy Big Game rod, Fortuna 9/0 hook, and 130 lb. breaking strain line.

The deep waters of Cornwall and the whole of the west coast of Scotland are comparatively unexplored regions. It is from these places that big fish will be taken. Scotland in particular offers great possibilities, for the nature of the ground is much like that off Iceland.

S. Norton-Bracy

John Dory

The John Dory (*Zeus faber*) is a sad-looking fish and is not taken in large numbers by anglers, although it is often brought in by netsmen off the south and west coasts.

It has a deep, narrow body, with a large head and mouth, and when first captured is usually a golden colour, which however soon fades to olive-brown. There is a large round black spot on either side of its body. It is a small-scaled fish.

Anglers who catch the Dory for the first time are usually puzzled by the identity of their catch. A number of local names add to the confusion. One popular alias is golden bream; the Dory's body at a first glance is not unlike that of the sea BREAM.

Small fish, such as sand-eels, smelts, and pilchards are the John Dory's main diet. But prawns and limpets have been found inside some specimens.

Sea Fishing The Dory is a slow-moving fish, relying on its large mouth to engulf its prey. This shoots out like a funnel, and small fish are sucked in quickly. John Dory observed in aquariums have sucked in food up to 18 ins. away from their mouths.

In really warm weather the Dory is known to drift on the surface, striking now and again to feed off brit and sand-eels. Back in 1956 several were found washed up on Chesil Beach, Dorset, and it was thought they must have become stranded when the professionals were netting mackerel inshore. The Dory were probably feeding off small mackerel at the time.

Anglers seldom, if ever, deliberately fish for this species. Dory are usually taken when fish baits are being floated for bass and pollack from boats and rocks. The larger fish do not swim in shoals, but occasionally one can catch a number of the smaller fish from rocky points, particularly during late evening in the summer.

Those who do fish for Dory are mainly anglers who have realized their good table qualities. Although one rarely sees them on fishmongers' slabs in this country, they are something of a delicacy on the Continent and fetch a good price.

Dory can be fished for from boats by drift-lining with a live sand-eel as bait. Tackle is simple: a light rod, free-running reel, trace, and hook. Only if a strong current is running is it necessary to add a small spiral weight to get the bait down to the fish.

From rocks surrounded by deep water, the best method is float-fishing. Arrange the bait mid-water and let the float move around with the current, near weed-beds if possible, for the Dory will be nosing around after the small fish that feed in seaweed.

General John Dories grow to a good weight, and fish of 12 lb. have been netted, although the largest rod-caught Dory (in 1922, off Mevagissey) was 8 lb. 8 oz. One of 7 lb. was taken in Brixham waters during 1960, and it is along the Devon and Cornish coasts that one is likely to catch the largest of this species.

D. F.

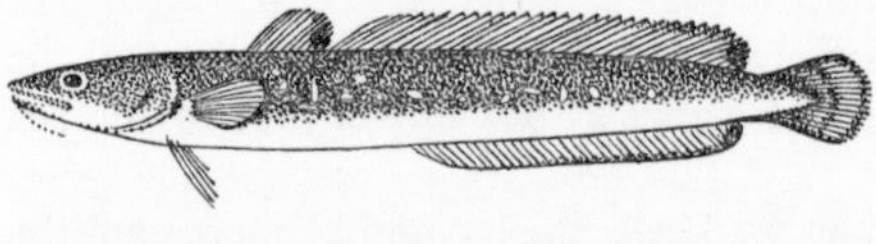

Ling

The ling (*Molva molva*), a near relative of the COD, is a deep-water fish. Although it has a broader head than the cod, it resembles that fish considerably. The placing of the barbule below the jaw is identical and the ling has the large eyes of the cod and the same colouring of body. From its dorsal fin to its tail it resembles the CONGER. The tail, however, is fan-shaped in comparison with the tapering of the conger's.

Ling

The ling is nearly always found where there are heavy rock formations or big wrecks, lying at a depth of from fourteen to thirty-five fathoms. Unlike the conger, it does not live inside the wrecks or in a hole in the rocks but lurks amidst the seaweed and marine growth, where it blends with the colour of the rocks.

Undoubtedly the ling prefers clear water to cloudy conditions. This must be qualified by the fact that the best fish so far landed have come from the deeper waters of Cornwall and Ireland, and from even greater depths off Norway and Iceland.

During the summer months a few small ling, ranging from a few inches to a foot in length, are caught inshore, especially on the south coast. This indicates that the spawning grounds are not very far away, probably in the region of the Channel Islands. From these the young fish are swept up Channel by the strong tides.

Baits

The ling is a voracious feeder on all kinds of fish but will rarely, if ever, take a hook offering anything other than fresh whitebait. Pilchard, MACKEREL, BREAM, and POLLACK have all been found inside its stomach. In the northern waters ling certainly eat haddock. One thing is essential – the bait must be freshly caught.

Tackle

For drift fishing, the 6 ft 6 in. solid glass or tubular fibre-glass rod, used in conjunction with a multiplying reel, is ideal. For bottom fishing from an anchored boat, a centre-pin reel is as good. Line should be of Terylene or nylon with a breaking strain of from 23 to 27 lb. Bear in mind that bottom tackle must be strong and capable of withstanding constant friction against rocks and wreckage.

Wire traces are far from ideal under these conditions and do not allow a bait to work freely; therefore use a heavy nylon of at least 50 lb. breaking strain at the end of your line.

For drift fishing a long, flowing trace is best. This should be broken into two 6 ft lengths, swivelled in the centre. One end is attached to the swivel on the main line and the other to the hook.

A spiral weight is now added to the section between the main line and the centre swivel, so that you have a heavy section of line above the weight and also between the weight and the hook, affording a certain amount of protection from jagged edges. The amount of weight to be used depends largely on the rate of drift. Ideally it should be enough to allow your bait to work through, or just above, the marine growth over which you are drifting.

With an anchored boat this tackle is virtually useless, as the long trace very soon becomes entangled. This applies equally to booms or paternosters. Instead of a wire paternoster, therefore, take a length of heavy nylon about 6 ft long and make three short snoods at equal distance along its length, leaving enough at each end to make a loop. One end should now be made fast to a swivel which in turn is tied to the main line. The other end should also be armed with a swivel. To this you fix the weight. Next attach three hooks to the snoods by means of the eye, in much the same way as for MACKEREL feathers (see p. 302). You now have an excellent paternoster. If the hooks are well baited so that the barb is covered, there should be little risk of their getting caught up below.

The weight should be attached to the bottom swivel by means of a very light line of lower breaking strain than the main line. Then, in the event of its becoming lodged between two rocks or other obstructions, it will break free and save you loss of tackle.

Always check your bottom tackle when bringing it inboard, for the continual friction against rough edges is bound to fray it. As soon as you find any signs of fraying, replace the piece concerned.

Fishing Methods

The ling prefers a strongly flowing run of water to a slack tide for feeding. When you are drift fishing in a strong breeze which draws the tackle through the water at speed, the ling are quite likely to grab the bait.

There is little doubt that a brightly coloured bait attracts this fish best, and a very effective method is to fish a large silver spoon as a lure with a strip of white bait attached. This will usually be taken almost as soon as it reaches the bottom, more often than not as it is spiralling down on the last fathom or so.

Do not hesitate to move the bait up and down in the water when anchored; the ling goes for a moving bait. Raising it a couple of fathoms and then letting it go again often produces a strike.

Ling

There is no mistaking the bite of a ling and there is little need to strike when fishing from a moving boat. As the fish takes the bait – usually a few feet from the bottom – it stops dead and holds firmly. Once it feels the drag it will shake its head from side to side like the conger in an effort to get rid of the hook. Once it realizes that it cannot get away, it bores for the bottom and tries to get among the rocks or wreckage. Unlike the conger, it makes no effort to whip its tail around a rock or any handy underwater obstruction.

Ling are hard fighters, especially for the first five fathoms after getting them off the bottom. However, as they approach the surface, particularly when caught on the deeper marks, the fight goes out of them, possibly because of the change in pressure. A fish of 30 lb., when light tackle is used, should be boated within five minutes of the strike.

It is always advisable to 'pump' a ling to the surface, for you can never be certain when it is going to refuse to budge and start shaking its head again. It is during these spasms that the heaviest strain is imposed upon the tackle.

It is probable that many pollack fishermen hook a ling, but with their light tackle they are unaware that they have a ling on, and they return home with a story about the monster that got away. For it is around pollack and coalfish grounds that ling are most likely to be taken.

General

The ling is probably far more common in our waters than most fishermen realize. However, during the past fifty years only two specimens really worthy of mention have been landed. The largest ever recorded, a magnificent 45-pounder, was taken by H. C. Nicholl in 1912 at Penzance. The only other notable specimen, one of 35½ lb., was landed by Gurney Grice at Falmouth in 1957.

Most British sea anglers have an aversion from drift fishing, and this probably accounts for the very small number even of immature ling recorded each year. In southern Ireland at such centres as Ballycotton, Kinsale, and Valentia, some magnificent catches have been recorded, and nearly all were taken from a moving boat. The same applies to Iceland and Norway, countries whose anglers believe that better fishing is obtained by drifting than from an anchored boat

Ling make excellent eating. They taste very much like cod, and, in fact, should be cooked in the same way.

S. N.-B.

Mackerel

Streamlined, iridescent, fast, and strong, the mackerel (*Scomber scomber*) is among the most beautiful fish in the sea and, weight for weight, the hardest fighting. Unfortunately, it reaches an average size of no more than a pound, so only ruthlessly scaled-down tackle will do it justice. It shoals in vast numbers and few parts of the British coast are not visited by it at some time in the summer or autumn. It provides generous sport for many anglers, sport that is generally undervalued because the fish are available in such quantity. It is closely related to the tunny.

Identification problems should not arise. Occasional variations occur in coloration, producing the so-called 'spotted' and 'scribbled' varieties, but these are merely varieties, not separate species, in the eyes of the ichthyologist. Scad, sometimes called horse mackerel, are different in body structure and colour. Very rarely a bonito may turn up in a catch of mackerel, especially in coastal areas of the Celtic sea, where a number of occurrences have been noted. This fish (the 'plain' bonito) is larger than our mackerel and rather more stoutly built, and largely lacks the typical marblings that are so characteristic of the native species.

It seems fairly certain that the little 'joey', or harvest mackerel, is a fish in its first year, attaining a length of 7 or 8 ins. The great majority of mackerel taken around our shores are in their second year or older, and average slightly more than a foot long. Most of the growth seems to take place in the first two years, so that G. A. Steven (who investigated the habits of mackerel in the Channel and in the Celtic Sea) writes of a thirty-year-old fish that reached 18¼ ins. in length and weighed 2¼ lb. There is a class of mackerel, however, not very numerous but certainly present in our seas, that may attain a weight of 4 lb. or more, so that it seems likely that some factor of which we are not yet aware may enter into the life history of these exceptional fish, of which more will be said later.

The October storms usually see the last of the mackerel, which then leave for deeper water. Recent research has shown that they make for certain quite precise locations that may be separated from each other by many miles; the Hurd Deep, for example, north of the Channel Isles, and the area of the Smalls, off west Wales. In these depths they winter, huddled together in great numbers, feeding very little because there is little for them to feed on. The first fish leave the winter quarters in January, beginning a migration that will end with the spawning period, which reaches its peak in April but may be prolonged into June. Mackerel from the southern and western coasts of Britain and Ireland concentrate in vast numbers on the 100-fathom line of the so-called Celtic Sea (the portion of the Atlantic adjacent to Wales, south Ireland, Cornwall, and Brittany) for spawning.

Once spawning is over, the shoals make for the littoral shallows. Until this happens they have fed chiefly on plankton. But from this point on fish play a larger and larger part in their diet. According to Dr Kennedy, rockling fry preoccupy them at first. Then, as they move inshore, larger fish – sand-eels, sprat, the fry of species like herring and pilchards – become their staple diet.

Once they are inshore, mackerel become roving fish. The shoals may be found almost anywhere. They will enter harbours, especially in the evening; they will shoal on beaches within casting distance of the sands; they will suddenly rip through placid water near rocks in search of food fish. Mackerel can turn up almost anywhere without warning, churning up an acre of sea or more as they break surface in pursuit of fry, and many an angler who has been bottom fishing from the rocks for other species has cursed his luck for being without spinning gear when they arrive.

Baits, Tackle, and Fishing Methods

Most boat fishing for mackerel is undeniably crude. Summer visitors who are sea fishing for the first time go out with longshoremen at holiday resorts, are handed a line furnished with a very heavy lead and a spinner, and trail this behind the boat until a mackerel attaches itself. If mackerel are present in quantity, the visitor will catch them in fair numbers and when he steps out of the boat will be faced with the problem of what to do with his catch, since mackerel will be so plentiful that he will not be able to give them away. Or he may be permitted to work the 'feathers' (very crudely made artificial flies that resemble small fish) and load the boat that way. Most holidaymakers' mackerel fishing is devoid of sport and the participant often sickens of it before the day is through. It need concern us no longer here.

Crude methods are permissible when mackerel are needed as bait in deep-sea fishing. Some can be picked up on the way out to the fishing grounds by trailing a spinner. Usually this means a heavy lead which is tedious to haul, but there is now a device available which, attached to the line, acts as a paravane and goes deeper the faster it is trailed. When a mackerel hits, it comes to the surface and the fish can be easily hauled aboard. More effective, perhaps, are the feathers. These are chicken feathers dyed in bright colours and mounted on hooks in the manner of crude flies. Seven or eight of them are fished on a trace, to the end of which is attached a lead heavy enough to reach the bottom quickly. The feathers are usually 'jigged', that is to say worked up and down by moving the rod top. Once a shoal is located it is possible to haul a 'full house' of mackerel at nearly every drop. Needless to say the rod has to be pretty stout to do this work.

Crude as it may be, there are certain tricks of the trade even in this. When you feel the first mackerel hit, for instance, do not haul up at once. Wait until you feel the other vacancies being filled! It is noteworthy that new feathers work best, and this is due, I think, to the fact that with a new trace the hooks are bright and silvery. It is possible, by using a rod, to beat professional mackerel fishermen (who use stout handlines) at their own game; you can work faster, and the comparative sensitivity of the rod will tell you when you have a worthwhile load of mackerel to haul.

A word of warning isnecessary here. A trace of feathers can be a very dangerous thing in the hands of a novice. If the lead slips overboard inadvertently when you are holding the trace, it is quite easy for its weight to drive one of the hooks into your hand – and a hook driven in this way really stays driven! (If this ever happens to you, you may have to nip off the eye of the hook with pliers and thread the hook out shank last.)

Latterly, plastic feathers have begun to replace the real thing, but so far there have been conflicting views on their effectiveness. Commercial fishermen use barbless hooks on mackerel traces when the fish are very numerous, so as not to lose time in unhooking fish.

I should stress again that I do not recommend feather fishing for mackerel in the ordinary way, but simply to catch fish for bait. A party of half a dozen anglers out for a day's deep-sea fishing might get through a couple of dozen mackerel baits apiece, so there is a need for some method whereby mackerel can be amassed quickly and in quantity. In this respect, incidentally, an echo-sounder in the boat is of great value in locating mackerel shoals. It will not pick up individual fish, naturally, but a large shoal will show up clearly, as will the depth at which it is swimming. Sea-birds also indicate the presence of mackerel shoals. Gannets are the best indicators;

if they are seen massing to feed, it is certain that there are mackerel beneath.

Mackerel fishing from a boat for sport is usually an inshore game and very light tackle can be used. First the fish have to be located and the best way to do this is to trail a spinner on a handline until the contact is made, when the fish can be kept together by trailing a fine rubby-dubby – a net full only of oily fish scraps. A trout spinning rod and a small fixed-spool reel loaded with 4 lb. breaking strain line makes a useful outfit, and I favour a small, heavy lure like a silver devon or the Swedish 'Little Tilly' bait. Some of the small Continental bar spoons are very effective as well. The conventional mackerel spinner sold in shops is not very satisfactory; it lacks weight for casting and has a marked tendency to kink the line, and the flanges sometimes prevent the hooking of a fish.

Mackerel usually take very firmly. There is no need to strike as a rule; it is enough to hold the fish for a second or two when it takes. Sometimes a mackerel will kick off in mid-fight, but there is little you can do to prevent this happening. A landing-net will be useful to cut down the strain on your rod.

Bait fishing from a boat usually involves float-fishing. The mackerel are gathered by the use of ground-bait (it's incredible how most sea anglers completely neglect this aid to fishing) and the float is set between mid-water and the bottom, depending on where the fish are feeding, which is something to be found out by trial and error. A 1/0 hook is about right and the float should be as light as you can make it in the circumstances. Once again, floats labelled in the tackle shop as intended for mackerel are not often suitable – they are a good deal too big, and large mackerel, which become quite shy towards the end of the season, might well be put off by them. Sand-eels make wonderful bait, but most sea anglers are reluctant to use them on fish which are not as discerning as they might be about food. They'd rather use sand-eel on bass. A fish bait is ideal, preferably an iridescent strip from the side of another mackerel. Notice that a cleanly cut strip, long and narrow, is very much preferable to a jagged lump of fish cut anyhow.

As befits a member of the tuna family, the mackerel is a splendid little fighting fish. It is incredibly active on the hook, boring down one minute, then changing direction with extraordinary speed and making for the open sea. The fight is possibly a little harder and certainly faster than with a sea-trout of the same size.

There seems very little to add. In boat fishing, if you can

find the mackerel you will nearly always find no difficulty in getting them to take. I suppose that the one drawback with mackerel is that they are usually an easy fish to catch, and this detracts somewhat from their quality as sporting fish.

Now to consider shore-fishing.

Spinning from the Shore: There are two distinct patterns in the behaviour of mackerel feeding within casting distance of the shore. There are certain places which, during the season, will nearly always hold some mackerel at a certain time of the tide. Rocky headlands which impose a race on the tide often fall into this category. So long as the weather is warm and settled the angler who knows his ground will be able to take a few fish from such spots on any evening, though he will not always make a great bag, numerically speaking. The second pattern involves the arrival, often in an enclosed space such as a small harbour or a rocky cove, of a large number of mackerel out of the blue as it were. The shoal may stay in the vicinity for a couple of days, or the visitation may be only for the space of a couple of hours at the top of the tide.

Settled weather is an important factor in either case. A storm will drive the mackerel off shore very quickly and they will not return until anticyclonic conditions are restored. The best time to fish is in the evening, best of all when high water coincides with dusk. It has always seemed to me that half a dozen fish taken from the rocks from little companies of mackerel that are passing through makes a more satisfying bag than several score taken from a mass of shoaling fish that are almost jostling each other out of the water in their eagerness to get at the food fish jammed between mackerel shoal and shore. The tackle is the same as used from a boat for spinning – a short, light spinning rod and a fixed-spool reel loaded with light (6–8 lb.) monofilament. There will be occasions when you find yourself underpowered with this gear – when a good BASS or POLLACK takes the mackerel spinner – but this is all in the game. It might be worth mentioning here that very heavy bass will sometimes come in to feed on shoaling mackerel in a tide race near the shore. They seem to work *underneath* the mackerel, possibly picking off odd fish. If you suspect their presence – and I have had large bass take mackerel off the hook as I was landing them – put up a larger spinner, or a good lask of mackerel, and, if the race is strong, lead enough to carry the bait down quickly and prevent the mackerel from getting it before it reaches the bass. If they are there and taking, you will not have many under 5 lb. weight.

Horse Mackerel

Trachurus trachurus
Record 3 lb 3 oz

Plaice

Pleuronectes platessa (page 314)
Record 7 lb 15 oz

Pollack

Gadus pollachius (page 316)
Record 23 lb 8 oz

Coalfish

Gadus virens
Record 23 lb 8 oz

Pouting

Gadus luscus (page 322)
Record 4 lb 10 oz

Whiting

Gadus merlangus (page 348)
Record 6 lb

Bait Fishing from the Shore: In the autumn, not long before the annual migration of mackerel to their winter quarters begins, small companies of big mackerel may be picked up on the bottom on fish bait. I became aware of this for the first time a few years ago when the large tope bait I was legering from the rocks was picked up by fish that ran a few yards with it. Striking produced no result; the hooks were evidently too large for whatever it was that was causing the runs. The tope fishing was slack, so I changed down to a smaller hook and a small strip of herring. The first fish I landed was a mackerel of 2 lb. 5 oz., a good one by any standards. Thinking that if the mackerel were there they'd take a spinner anyway, I set up a light rod and attached a narrow spoon. The mackerel were interested enough to follow the spinner, but not enough to take it. Only a fish bait would do.

Mackerel

Since then I have heard of big mackerel being taken in similar circumstances by other anglers. Des Brennan, for instance, has had similar encounters in Irish waters.

The kind of place in which to find these large autumn mackerel is probably in fairly deep water (by shore-fishing standards) – five fathoms or so. The most likely approach is to fish on to sand from the rocks in the vicinity of a fast tide race.

Clearly, some kind of rubby-dubby or ground-bait would be a great advantage in this kind of fishing. Lately, concentrated ground-bait in cube form for sea fishing has come on the market. It is made of biscuit meal and pilchard oil and I have found it especially effective for fishing over sand on slack tides for TOPE. I have no doubt that it would be equally effective for other ground-feeding species, including mackerel.

General

Mackerel are taken in the summer-time right round the coast of the British Isles, and a big specimen could turn up almost anywhere. The present record fish was taken off the Isle of Man by Flight Lieutenant P. Porter in 1952 and weighed a fraction over 4 lb., though bigger specimens have been reported by commercial fishermen. Certain localities are noted for large mackerel; the Gwingeas Rock off the Cornish coast is one, and so is the Splaugh Shoal off Co. Wexford. Generally speaking, south-western coasts produce the greatest numbers of mackerel. Dr Michael Kennedy notes that there is a significant difference in size between the mackerel taken off the east coast of Ireland and those taken off the west coast.

C. G.

Monkfish

Few anglers fish deliberately for monkfish (*Squatina squatina*), except in such places as Clew Bay, Co. Mayo, where they are particularly numerous. Outwardly, they are unprepossessing creatures. The monkfish (some sea anglers and many professional fishermen call it the angel fish) is the only representative we have around our shores of a family called the Rhinidae. In body structure it looks like a cross between a SHARK and a SKATE. The trunk, so to speak, is flattened, but not to such a degree as it is in a skate. The characteristic skate 'wings' are there, much foreshortened. As with sharks and skate, the mouth is 'anterior', that is set under the head, so that food is swept up off the sea-bed in a shovel-like manner. The coloration is typical of cartilaginous fish that haunt inshore waters – a drab brown with flecks and patches of white.

Monkfish approach inshore waters in the spring and summer and are caught fairly frequently by shore anglers, sometimes even right in the surf within a hundred yards of the shore. They appear to be commoner in the south-western waters of the British Isles and are particularly numerous off the west coast of Ireland. They are usually taken on clean ground.

Baits Little is known of the diet of monkfish. It seems pretty certain that fish supply a large part of it, and since the monkfish is not a fast swimmer, a reasonable guess would be that flatfish of various species predominate. Undoubtedly crustaceans too are scooped up from the sea-bed by that intimidating mouth. Dr Michael Kennedy gives mullet as an important item of food for monkfish. From all this the angler may gather that a fish bait is probably the best to use, a cut of fresh MACKEREL being as good as anything.

Tackle and Fishing Methods If you are going out specifically for monkfish, your tackle had better be substantial, though monkfish are more inclined to move about and do not have to be hauled in the manner of big skate. On the other hand, tackle need not be very complex. The kind of boat rod you would use for medium CONGER would do nicely, and a multiplier armed with 30 or 40 lb. b.s. line should kill any monkfish going. A big hook, fished on a few inches of wire for safety's sake, should carry a good-sized bait of fresh MACKEREL or herring. Monkfish feed on the bottom, so a running leger with enough weight to hold it down meets the case.

Monkfish

It is much more likely, however, that you will pick up your monkfish while after other species. If you have not a great deal of line on the reel, you are likely to find yourself in some difficulty. The usual tactic of monkfish is to move inexorably out to sea at a dignified pace. This habit is a good clue to what you have on if you hook a big fish unexpectedly. A SKATE would go to the bottom and hold on; a TOPE would run very fast. But the old monkfish just keeps a-going. All you can do is to keep a steady pressure and hope that he will turn before your line runs out. Eventually you will be rewarded by the sight of something that looks like a double-bass that has been left out in the damp wobbling slowly to the surface.

General

It is perhaps unfair to be facetious about the odd appearance of the monkfish, for it can put up a thrilling fight. I remember one occasion when a monkfish was hooked from a high rock just at nightfall. The angler was tope fishing with the light tackle that is frequently used from rock stations – 18 lb. b.s. line and a light surf-casting rod. The run that the monk gave was much slower than that of a tope, and when he struck the angler was thinking in terms of greater spotted DOGFISH. He expected a dead weight to come through the water. Instead his rod was forced firmly down and the fight was on. By the time he had turned the fish (since he was tope fishing he'd been using more than 300 yds of line), darkness was falling and a big swell had begun to run. In the dark, with the constant possibility of a big roller coming in, this was no joke. To add to the complications, each time the fish was brought close in it dived for a submarine ledge. On each occasion it had to be hand-lined out. The fish was finally landed by torchlight three-quarters of an hour after it had been hooked. It weighed 40 lb., like most monkfish!

If you are positively determined to catch monkfish, the best place to fulfil this ambition is Clew Bay, in the neighbourhood of Westport, Co. Mayo. Why it should be so I cannot say, but numbers of specimen monkfish have been taken from boats fishing a little off shore there. If you prefer to fish from dry land, Fenit Pier, Co. Kerry, has produced numbers of large monkfish. Work from the viaduct, choose the biggest spring tide you can, and fish the fastest part of the ebb. These are two places from which consistent catches of monkfish have been obtained. But a big one could turn up almost anywhere. I'd venture a guess that very few monkfish that have been landed were ever caught deliberately. The average size of monks seems to be around 40 lb., but the record fish, which came from Littlehampton in 1919, weighed 62 lb.

C. G.

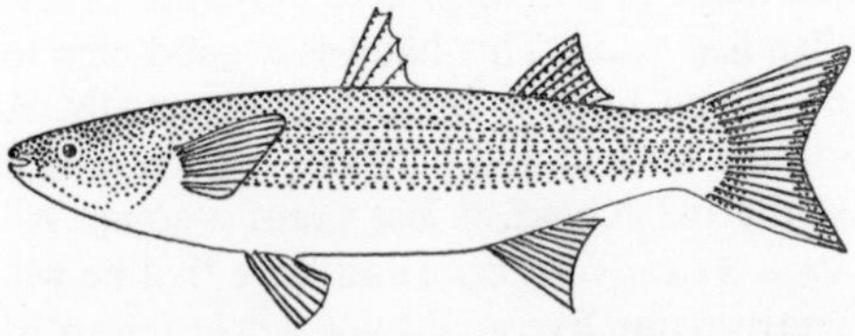

Mullet

Mullet (thick-lipped, *Mugil chelo*; thin-lipped, *Mugil capito*) are notoriously the most exasperating of sea fish, yet they exert a strong spell over sea fishermen, sometimes to the point of becoming an obsession. One reason, I suppose, is that they *look* so attainable, lazily swimming near the surface of very shallow water so that every detail of their scaling is visible. Then very light tackle can be used for their capture, the kind of gear that a freshwater man would use for CHUB, or even ROACH, though no roach or chub that ever swam could approach the verve and strength of the mullet's fight. Finally, they are such a challenge. At first it seems absurd that fish that can be seen so easily, that are so plainly feeding, should be such a difficult proposition. But that's what they are and sooner or later the mullet haunt requires a different approach and a different technique if the fish are to be caught. One really obsessed mullet man has told me that as soon as he has discovered the way to catch mullet in one particular place, he loses interest and searches for another estuary or harbour where fresh problems arise for him to worry about.

We can begin our discussion of the British mullets by dismissing altogether as a serious angling species the so-called red mullet. This fish is very rarely taken by sea anglers in this country and is insignificant in size. Furthermore, it is not at all closely related to the grey mullets, in spite of its name, belonging to a quite different family of fishes. The only point worth noticing, perhaps, is that it was to this fish that the ancient Romans were referring when they wrote of the gastronomic excellencies of mullet – and how right they were.

Of the three grey mullets, one can be disposed of quickly – the golden-grey mullet (*Mugil auratus*), distinguished from the others by the two pronounced gold spots on its head, one on the cheek, and a larger one on its gill-cover. Although Dr Tate Regan claimed that it was sometimes plentiful on the Devon and Cornwall coasts, no specimens have been reported in recent years, so that the angler who captures one may congratulate himself on having a considerable rarity in his fish bag. We are left then with the two chief species of British grey mullets, the thin-lipped and the thick-lipped – species, note, not varieties. No precise study has been made, but it seems likely that the thin-lipped fish are commonest along the Cornish coast and around the Channel Isles, where they probably outnumber the thick-lipped species. Some writers in the past have referred to this species as the 'greater grey mullet' and there is a record by the British Sea Anglers' Society of a 16¾ lb. specimen netted at Pagham Harbour, Sussex, but there is little indication that there is much to choose between the two species in average size. I have myself observed very large grey mullet of around the 15–16 lb. mark feeding in very clear water close to the wall at Milford Fish Docks and it seemed to me then that they were the thick-lipped species, though it is impossible to be absolutely certain without a close examination.

Both are solid in the body and rather blunt-headed, and have two barbules below the chin. Briefly, the difference lies in the relative smallness of the fins on the thin-lipped mullet and, as the name suggests, in the difference in thickness of the upper lip. There are also certain differences in fin-ray formulae, so that the angler who is really in doubt about the species of the mullet he has caught should take his fish to an expert ichthyologist, or, failing that, should consult one of the reliable reference books like those by Kennedy or Travis Jenkins.

The thick-lipped species is undoubtedly the most widespread in British waters and is the fish we see moving in stately fashion up saltwater creeks and into little harbours, turning indolently from time to time so that a heart-stopping bronze-silver flash signals through the water. This is the one that causes all the trouble, and hereinafter, when I refer to mullet, this is the fish I am writing about. So far as I know, no one has ever suggested that different fishing techniques are necessary for the two main species, though it is just possible that the thin-lipped fish are more likely to take larger forms of life as food than the thick-lipped. Thin-lipped mullet are predominant in the Mediterranean and seem easier to catch there, so that this may be true of British thin-lipped mullet also.

On most parts of the coast, mullet are not found inshore in winter, though, as we shall see, there are certain favoured localities where they do spend the winter near the shore and can be caught throughout this season – which may well be the best part of the year for angling. If it is a warm spring, the fish will generally show up in March or early April, and remain inshore until late October or November, when they seem to migrate into deeper water.

As with other sea fish which have little commercial importance, very little research has been done into the spawning habits of mullet. Spawning probably takes place a little after the annual inshore migration in the spring, but it is not known for certain whether it takes place in brackish or in salt water. It is quite possible that it takes place in both.

Growth Rate: Once again, no detailed observations have been made of mature fish. Scale reading is difficult in the case of mullet. However, fry and small fish have been collected which seem to indicate that the mullet is a slow-growing fish. Second-year mullet, for example, measured only 3 ins. long.

It remains to be remarked in this section that mullet are markedly gregarious in habit, and they seem to shoal according to size. Even fish of specimen size (5 or 6 lb. class), keep in small companies. Mullet do not seem to feed at night, though they may sometimes be taken in the strong light of harbour lamps.

Mullet have a very strongly marked preference for the brackish water provided by river estuaries and will ascend as far as fresh water, farther than any other strictly marine fish. I have noticed that in the upper reaches of Milford Haven mullet will press even farther up the estuary than school bass. Perhaps my statement will be thought a little too dogmatic when flounders are considered, but it is doubtful whether they can strictly be regarded as purely marine fish. Incidentally, the thin-lipped mullet seems to have an even greater tolerance for fresh water than the thick-lipped.

Mullet also enter harbours, lagoons that form behind sandy beaches, mud creeks, and sheltered bays, and they frequent open-sea rocks when conditions are calm. They are probably a good deal more catchable under open-sea or harbour conditions than they are in estuaries, especially when they appear to be travelling on their way to a feeding ground. Mullet, incidentally, nearly always reveal their presence by producing characteristic V-shaped ripples in the water or by flashing. As the tide makes up the creeks of a small estuary, it is quite easy to tell the gentle, leisurely swirls and ripples made by mullet. Bass are much more splashy and dramatic.

With that we come to the basic angling problem regarding mullet. There seems to be no doubt that the staple diet of inshore mullet consists of microscopically small plants and organisms. They may be observed sucking at weedy stones or at harbour walls, seemingly feeding on the weed, though the soft weed itself may be supplemented as diet by the tiny creatures that live in it, such as very tiny snails, amphipods, and chironomid larvae. Clearly, this is impossible to use as hook-bait, which is why ground-baiting is so important in mullet fishing.

Mullet that come into harbours, however, may adopt a very different diet, one imposed on them by the variety of food that is available because of the presence of man. For instance, mullet taken at Ballycotton, Co. Cork, contained, among unidentifiable matter, the following: maggots, blue-bottles, bread, curd, fish guts, bacon rinds, and peas. Dr Kennedy has observed mullet at the fishing port of Kilmore Quay nosing at the livers in the carcases of rays and skates that had been jettisoned over the side of the harbour wall.

Baits

Mullet are often reported as being caught on the oddest of titbits, and presumably it is the kind of very mixed feeding to which they become accustomed in harbours that makes them susceptible to such baits. What these baits have in common, it is worth noticing, is that they are usually soft and often light in colour – banana and macaroni are two often-quoted examples. It is extremely doubtful, however, whether mullet cruising far up an estuary and feeding on a natural diet would take much notice of one of these exotic baits unless a huge programme of pre-baiting had been arranged.

Used in the right conditions, a wide variety of baits will take mullet. Apart from the two mentioned, bread paste, worm, cheese, and partly boiled cabbage stalk are among the most effective. Ragworms are probably the best of the worm baits.

Mullet will often suck at the hook-bait and tease it until there is nothing left. This can be most exasperating when you are using a tender bait like ragworm. Bread paste or cheese will often stay better on the hook if a twist of cotton wool is added.

Tackle

Since mullet are nearly always taken in calm water of no great depth, in sheltered places, very light tackle can be used and indeed is advisable since the fish are often shy and the bait has to be presented to them perfectly.

One of the best rods for mullet is that known to coarse fishermen as an Avon type, of the kind first used by F. W. K. Wallis and designed by him. It consists of a whole bamboo butt piece and two top pieces of built-cane, the whole thing being about 11 ft long. The Avon rod is ideal for several reasons. It is light, for a start, being much lighter than the glass spinning rods that many sea fishermen think adequate for mullet. Its length is important also. Very often the fish are feeding close to the angler and a long rod helps him to keep out of sight. For mullet, also, it is advisable whenever possible to fish right under the rod point. Mullet are difficult fish to strike and I find that the best way of making a successful contact is by means of a direct lift of the hook, which implies a gentle upraising of the rod point. Finally, although this rod is light, it has a lot of power in it, which is often necessary to turn a mullet away from an obstruction.

The best reel to use is, I find, a centre-pin of the sort designed for long-trotting in river fishing. The Speedia is an excellent mullet reel. A fixed-spool reel is a possibility, but its main advantage – being able to cast a light line a good distance – rarely comes into play in mullet fishing. There are its disadvantages, chiefly in loss of directness when playing the fish to be overcome. In either case, the line need not exceed 6 lb. b.s. monofilament nylon, and should not be less than 4 lb. Mullet are very strong fish, and even on 6 lb. line have to be played very carefully indeed.

Most mullet fishing is float-fishing, and here an interesting point, and something of a paradox, arises. We are told to fish as light as possible for shy-feeding fish, and in ninety-nine per cent of cases this is good advice. One's instinct in mullet fishing is to use as fine a quill as possible, for the good fishing reason that it will be less conspicuous and offer less water resistance. However, I have found on using such a quill that it is too sensitive. With a mullet bite it is always best to delay the strike until the float is moving firmly away, and it takes so little to pull a light quill under that there is a tendency to strike prematurely. A light, cork-bodied Avon type is probably better; when this goes firmly under it is time to strike, and the mullet don't seem to mind the extra resistance. Unless the water is very clear indeed, therefore, and the mullet particularly shy, there is no need to use an ultra light float. Hook size will depend of course on the bait being used, but an 8 or a 6 will usually be adequate, though you can fish smaller if you like.

Fishing Methods

Generally speaking, ground-baiting is absolutely essential for success in mullet fishing. If the fish are feeding in completely natural conditions on diatomic life, it may take a week of massive ground-baiting to persuade them to look at your bread or your ragworm. In most circumstances there may be no need for this long siege, but some ground-baiting will nearly always have to be done.

Most successful mullet ground-baits have a base of bread or bran, with which are mixed bits of oily fish, like herring, or pilchard. A cloud-bait effect should be aimed at. (This is the stuff known in the Channel Isles as 'Shirvy', only there it is made principally from ground-up shrimps.) The ground-bait is most effective when you can see the mullet in the water and can feed it directly to them. All mullet fishing, for that matter, is better when you can see the fish, and for this Polaroid sunglasses are most effective. I have known occasions when it has been necessary to lower the bait right under a mullet's nose before it would take; if it was three inches away to the right or left it wouldn't look at it.

Timing the strike will come by experience. The commonest mistake is to strike too soon. Once the fish is hooked it is important not to try to 'horse' it in. The hook hold will often be a weak one and many mullet come off the hook before they are landed. A good-sized landing-net is useful.

As an alternative to float-fishing where deepish water is involved a very light paternoster may be used. Such a paternoster should bear little relation to the ones used in boat fishing or surf casting. A quarter-ounce pear-shaped lead is all that is necessary. Bites are much harder to judge by this method and I prefer to use a float whenever possible.

Big mullet are occasionally taken by surf fishermen on quite large hooks. This occurs so infrequently that it is certainly not worth while making a special fishing method out of it.

Mullet are not really worth carrying home to eat and I make it a practice to release them as a rule. A comment on their culinary value is made by the fact that the only commercial market for them is provided by zoos which have seals to feed!

General

The present British record was a 10 lb. 1 oz. fish taken off Portland Bill in 1952. Whether thick- or thin-lipped is not known.

The Channel coast of England has always been productive of good mullet. Most piers and harbours are visited, and so are the estuaries. The Arun estuary at Littlehampton has a good reputation, as has that of the Cuckmere, also on the Sussex coast. In the West Country there are many small estuaries and harbours which give good mullet fishing and there is open-sea fishing from the rocks as well. Portland Bill, which produced the record mullet, has also supplied many other specimens. Some of the most unlikely places offer excellent mullet fishing – a large commercial dockyard such as that at Swansea, for example. In winter, huge catches of fish are sometimes made at Sennen Cove in Cornwall, and the Channel Isles are particularly noted for great mullet catches. The range of mullet extends beyond that of bass in a northerly direction, but detailed information is scarce. The vast complex of creeks that feed Milford Haven are full of mullet most of the year, and as I have already mentioned some of the biggest mullet I have ever seen were in the fish docks at Milford itself, gorging themselves no doubt on the vast quantities of fish scraps and offal available to them there. Alas, fishing is forbidden.

Mullet are plentiful around the coast of Ireland. The places which are particularly well stocked with catchable mullet include the estuary of the Colligan at Dungarvan, and that of the Ilen at Skibbereen, Co. Cork, Courtown Harbour and Kilmore Quay in Co. Wexford, and Ballycotton and Kinsale Harbours in Co. Cork. Dingle Harbour in Co. Kerry can be excellent.

C. G.

Plaice

The plaice (*Pleuronectes platessa*) is a common flatfish, well known from the fishmonger's slab. It is brown on the upper side, with red or orange spots, and completely white on the underside.

At times odd-coloured plaice are caught. These are known to professional fishermen as flukes, confusingly, because this is another name for flounders. The odd colouring can be a greyish-green or even orange all over the top side. One large fish taken off Bournemouth a few years ago had reverse colouring, an orange body with brownish spots. Reasons for colour variation are not definitely known, although some fishermen believe it is due to the habit of some plaice of keeping to heavily weeded areas, with the result that they eventually take on the colour of the weed.

Plaice do not grow to any great size. A 3½ lb. fish is a specimen, although weights of 7 or 8 lb. are sometimes reached.

The plaice is caught over sandy ground. It spawns in the early months of the year, coming shorewards in April or May. Sport is often enjoyed until quite late in the year, although the length of the season varies on different coasts. In some areas plaice can be caught in harbours and estuaries all the year round.

Growth rates vary according to the feeding grounds frequented; often the heaviest fish are captured in estuary waters. Research on their migratory habits shows that some plaice travel large distances. But not all roam far. A batch of plaice netted from a mark on the south coast were tagged and released about five miles away. Within a week some were re-netted over their home mark; one was caught there two years later.

Generally, calm seas are most suitable for plaice fishing. A sudden rise of wind that makes the sea choppy will often make bites go right off. Small plaice are often found in the warm waters around power stations, but such spots are usually nursery grounds for very young fish and should be left well alone.

Plaice are mostly bottom-feeders, although they will rise on occasion to an attractive moving bait. Generally they stay put on the sea-bed, where they cover themselves with sand by quickly flapping their bodies. They can move quite fast when the occasion arises, however, turning into the vertical position to do so.

The largest fish are caught from boat marks, but one has to find spots which act as larders of food. These are the deep holes and hollows into which shellfish and other food is likely to be washed.

Baits

Shellfish is a favourite diet for plaice, a fact which many anglers ignore when choosing their bait. Ragworm and lugworm do account for a number of catches, but more fish would be taken if baits like razor-fish, slipper limpet, and soft crab were used. Sand-eels are taken on some coasts.

Plaice are changeable in their diet. A mark may be fished where razor-fish is readily taken on one day and completely ignored the next. For this reason it is always wise to take along a selection of baits.

Tackle

Keep your tackle as light as conditions allow, remembering that a large-sized plaice over a boat mark will provide a much better fight than the same fish reeled in from the beach.

A running leger can be used to good advantage. Some anglers prefer float gear while others use nylon paternosters. But it is hard to beat a single-hook nylon trace. Make a trace of 8 lb. b.s. nylon, 6 ft long, and tie on a No. 2 long-shanked hook. Attach the trace to the main line with a half-ounce double-swivelled Wye lead. Use a centre-pin reel in preference to the fixed-spool type.

Fishing Methods Ground-baiting will improve catches a great deal and help prevent the plaice wandering too far away if disturbed. Anglers have their own favoured mixtures, ranging from fish cuttings and crushed crabs to mashed mackerel mixed with bran and pilchard oil. Put the ground-bait of your choice into a fine-meshed net bag and attach it to the anchor rope. Or alternatively have it on a separate rope, let it down to the bottom and jog it up and down every so often.

Very often in boat fishing striking is unnecessary. A large fish will take the bait with gusto, but a smaller one will be inclined to suck the bait for a while, finally indicating that it has really taken by a series of thumping tugs.

From the shore still keep to the single-hook tackle, although this can be run off a boom if conditions require a heavier lead. A good place to cast is into that dark stretch of water between the waves and the shore. The breaking waves mean a sand-bar and the darker water indicates a gulley inshore from it. Here plaice lie in wait for food washed from the sand-bar by the waves and the tide.

A number of dodges can be used to improve shore fishing when sport is dull. A coloured bead threaded on the trace above the hook is often useful. An old but useful trick is to put a button on the trace about three inches from the hook to stir up the bottom. After the cast is made, reel in slowly every few seconds. The button stirs up the sand, and plaice often come to see what has caused the disturbance, in case it should be food. The addition of a few strands of red wool hanging above the hook sometimes helps.

The best time for beach fishing is usually from about two hours before dusk, rather than full daylight. Anglers rarely agree about which is the best state of the tide for productive fishing, which suggests that in some places reasonable fishing can be expected at all states of the tide.

General The British record plaice was a 7 lb. 6 oz. fish taken from the Skerries Bank off South Devon.

D. F.

Pollack

The pollack (*Gadus pollachius*) is a handsome, streamlined fish, and, unlike many other species of our inshore waters, has scarcely been affected at all by over-fishing by commercial vessels, since the kelp-covered underwater reefs that it haunts can never be trawled. No one who has seen a good pollack fresh from the sea will deny its beauty, with its large, dark blue eyes, olive sides, and perfectly symmetrical shape, and the impression of speed and power that it gives. The pollack is a gadoid fish – a member of the cod family – but bears little family resemblance to the squat little POUTING or the heavy-bellied, big-mouthed COD. There is something thoroughbred about the look of a pollack.

The only fish with which it might become confused is its northern relative the coalfish, and this is a convenient place to mention the chief points of difference between them. The lower jaw of the pollack protrudes quite markedly beyond the upper; only in the larger coalfish does the lower jaw protrude, and then nothing like so far as in the pollack. The pollack has no barbel at all beneath its chin; the coalfish has a rudimentary one (which has to be looked for, incidentally). The lateral line of the pollack is black, very distinct, and positively curved; the lateral line of the coalfish is almost straight and nearly white against the background of the flank. Coloration is a guide as well, though not such a sure one. Pollack are usually reddish-gold on the back and olive on the sides. Coalfish are greenish-black on the back, shading to pure white on the belly. Sometimes, however, pollack from the northern end of their range are greener on the back. Generally speaking, the coalfish is a more portly-looking fish than the pollack.

Spawning takes place in the spring, before the fish move on to the inshore reefs, in deep water of fifty fathoms or more. Pollack swim into the angler's orbit around April and May and at this time of year keep strictly to the reefs. In the summer they are willing to move away from the rocks to pursue shoals of smaller fish, but they rarely desert them for long. It is always over the reefs that the angler expects to take his fish. These reef pollack seem to vary in size according to location. In some areas of coast, they may average only, say, 2 lb., while in others the average size may reach 5 or 6 lb. with a sprinkling of much bigger fish. In my experience, reefs close inshore tend to produce smaller pollack than those a couple of miles out.

During the day, the pollack seem to feed near the bottom, and it is there that the angler must look for them – and inevitably lose tackle. Fishing at first and last light is the most profitable as a rule, for then the pollack rise up in the water and begin feeding close to, or right on, the surface. The bigger fish seem to lose much of their daytime caution then. Not for nothing is the last hour of light known to anglers in the West Country as the 'suicide hour'. But more of this later.

The pollack leave the reefs in the late autumn after the first big storms, but some of the very largest fish turn up in the winter over clean ground. This unusual behaviour is accounted for by the shoals of herrings which are inshore in the late autumn and winter. Large pollack will travel many miles in pursuit of them. Minchin records instances of big pollack taken on trailed lines well out to sea in St George's Channel at this time of year. In the winter of 1961–2, a very large pollack was caught by a surf-caster fishing at Dungeness, Kent, many miles away from any recognized pollack reef. It is very likely that this fish, probably a solitary, was ranging far from its usual haunts after herring or sprat.

The growth rate of pollack is very much linked to the food supply of the area of rocks it haunts. Growth, as with most sea fish, is rapid in the summer and autumn and slows down in the winter. A pollack might reach a length of about 8 ins. at the end of its first year, while a ten-year-old fish could be over 3 ft long. Pollack seem to reach sexual maturity in their fourth season, though this may not be the case with slower-growing fish from less favoured locations.

In many harbours, the weeds at the wall's edge are the haunt of very tiny pollack indeed – fish of the year's spawning. They feed at this stage on amphipods and the like, but the voracious quality of their species is shown in the dashing way they will attack a morsel of fish or mussel lowered over the side. The little fish stay inshore for their first winter but by next spring they have begun to feed on small fry, and in their second summer will be tackling sand-eels and small fish of various kinds.

Baits The food of mature pollack consists chiefly of fish, and it is these that the angler will use or imitate in his pollack fishing. In the spring, however, when the ragworm are spawning and therefore free-swimming, large quantities of these worms will be eaten as well. The summer fish that make up most of the pollack's diet are sand-eels, herring and mackerel fry, and sprats. The pollack has catholic tastes and few small swimming creatures come amiss.

Sometimes in the spring big pollack will move into the estuaries of salmon rivers and feed on smolts that are migrating to sea. This has been especially noted in the estuary of the Munster Blackwater at Youghal, in Devon estuaries, and in the Teifi estuary, Cardigan Bay. Incidentally, large BASS are of the same habit. Far be it from me to suggest drift-lining a salmon parr down to them.

Artificial baits for pollack are many, but perhaps the best of all is one of the most traditional – the rubber eel, in various colours and sizes. Every angler has a special weakness for a certain colour, but amber, black, red, and white eels are all killing at times. Feathered lures will kill pollack, but the hooks on the ones sold on traces are too small and too weak. One or two feathered lures on the trace are plenty. It is perfectly easy to make up one's own feathered lures, but the big lures used by Irish commercial pollack fishermen are very effective indeed. A chromium spoon makes an effective pollack bait, but losses are heavy, and sooner or later it becomes too expensive.

Natural baits are usually more killing than artificials, though more of a bother to use.

Tackle

A SALMON spinning rod is excellent for pollack fishing, though traditionally a much stouter weapon is used. A salmon rod will give full value for the weight of the fish, though there may be times when you will lose a good one when it is able to dive for the kelp tangle and reach it. The take of a good pollack on such a rod is a thing of joy as the point is dramatically pulled under the water. This rod also gives the smaller fish a chance to acquit themselves well. A light multiplier is a good choice for a reel. A centre-pin is pleasant to use, but the suddenness with which a pollack takes sometimes pulls one's fingers away from the reel handles and an over-run results. If you are fishing an area where the fish are known to run large, a 15 lb. b.s. line is not too heavy. You may want to go heavier over unfamiliar ground where tackle losses could be heavy.

Apart from rod, reel, and line, the pollack fisherman needs a selection of artificial baits, and some spiral or bomb weights in various sizes. The size of hooks chosen will depend on the size of pollack expected, and the kind of bait used.

Fishing Methods

It must be admitted at the outset that the best pollack fishing is not to be obtained by the shore fisherman, though some interesting sport is to be had on light tackle. Pollack that are likely to be caught from the rocks rarely exceed a couple of pounds, though a better fish can come along at any time and test light gear to the uttermost. My best pollack from the rocks was only 6 lb., but I have seen a 12-pounder fall to the rod of a shore fisherman. These odd big fish probably find themselves inshore after pursuing shoal fish.

Rock ledges from which it is possible to command a tide race are best suited for shore pollack fishing. Spinning is the best method, of course, and it is always worth while to examine the ground at low tide so that you can avoid the more obvious obstructions. One of the best baits for pollack in this situation is a slender, slightly dished silver spoon, but if conditions are very calm a rubber eel will be a better fish killer. As in boat fishing, early and late expeditions will bring the best results.

Float-fishing is also a possibility from the rocks. A good bait in this respect is a lask of mackerel, the hook nicked into the broad end. If you are very sure of your ground it is sometimes possible to drift a light bait on a long flowing trace away from the rocks, but breakages are liable to be frequent. This is more a method to be used around the piles and projections of a pier or from a harbour wall. Pier and harbour pollack, however, are generally insignificant fish, though the odd two-pounder may be taken.

Rubber sand-eel

To give an idea of the possibilities for sport which boat fishing a distant mark may produce, the following might be of interest. Two years ago, a friend and I managed to persuade the skipper of a 35 ft boat to take us twenty miles out into the Atlantic to fish a reef called the Smalls which showed at low tide. When we arrived at the mark we decided to put up some feathered lures, seven to a trace, to see what the water held. We found a depth of less than two fathoms near the reef; the leads touched bottom simultaneously and seemed to foul in the rocks. But the 'rocks' were alive, thumping heavily away, and we realized that we were into a full house of pollack that we could not haul. The hooks were small, and after a moment or two we felt some of the fish kick off so that with a great strain on the rod top we were able to haul the remainder. They weren't specially big pollack – five- and six-pounders – but there were a lot of them. In the hour that we stayed at this mark we boated over three hundredweight of fish. The feather traces were abandoned at the beginning, of course, and single rubber eels substituted. The odd thing was that we should have done better. In case this sounds greedy, I should explain that, instead of looking for rather deper water a little away from the reef, we continued to fish the same spot, for reasons which all anglers will understand. It's difficult to persuade oneself to move when fish are taking. But we caught only five- and six-pounders when we might have had double-figure fish. It's worth making the point here that the better-quality fish are usually found over rock in depths between ten and twenty-five fathoms.

Trailing a bait behind the boat is the commonest kind of pollack fishing. The most vital factor for success is that the boat should travel at the right speed, so that the lure works

Blue Shark

Carcharinus glaucus (page 324)
Record 218 lb

Tope

Eugaleus galeus (page 340)
Record 74 lb 11 oz

Mako Shark

Isurus oxyrinchus (page 324)
Record 498 lb 8 oz

Porbeagle Shark

Lamma cornubica (page 324)
Record 324 lb

Thresher Shark

Alopias vulpes (page 325)
Record 280 lb

Twaite Shad

Alosa finta
Record 3 lb 2 oz

Allis Shad

Alosa alosa
Record 3 lb 4 oz 8 drams

Thornback Ray

Raia clavata (page 334)
Record 38 lb

Common Skate

Raia batis (page 336)
Record 214 lb

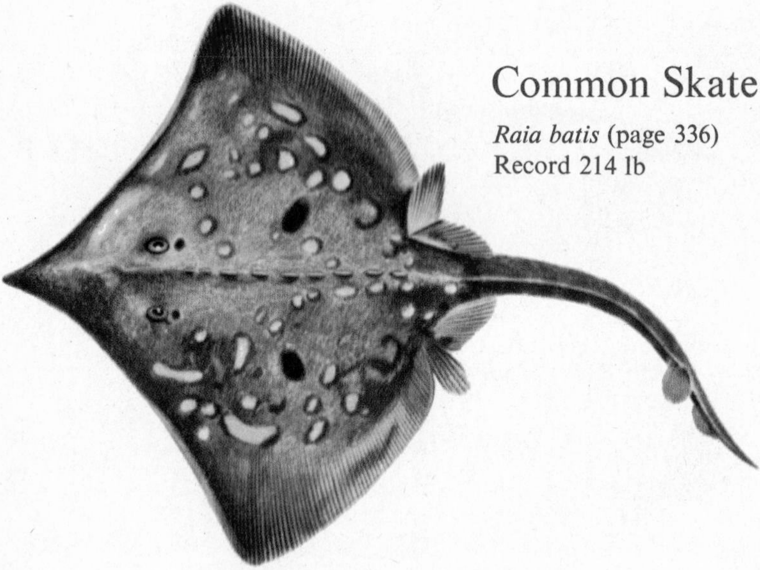

just as near as can be managed over the reef. If the boat is going too fast, the lure will sail much too high over the heads of the fish. Go too slowly, and the lure is constantly fouled. One ot the advantages of the eel is that it is less likely to snag than a metal spinner. A second very important requirement is to know the ground and to be sure that you are working over fish-holding reefs and not over barren sand. Clearly a great deal will depend on your boatman's putting you right in both these respects. In pollack fishing, as in so many other kinds of sea fishing, a good boatman is a jewel. If he is experienced, he will know enough to stop rowing or stop the engine as soon as you hit a fish and to take you back over the same ground as soon as it is landed.

Drift-lining is perhaps a more interesting form of the sport. A long rod is useful for this game and a spiral lead should be attached well up-trace (its weight depending on the kind of tide that is running). The bait is usually a natural one, a sand-eel for choice. The idea is to let your lead just tip the rock, then come up a little so that the trace flows out. You can let more line out and fish farther away from the boat, or you can retrieve very slowly. I have found the latter method more effective. Sometimes the first bite is quite minor, even when a big fish is involved, and a small knock should be the signal to give a little slack.

Drifting is practised when the boat drifts with the tide over likely ground. It is a very useful method over an extensive reef. The bait is fished up-trace of the lead. The best plan is to let the lead bump the bottom and then come up a few feet. The rod top can be used to give a jigging motion to the bait. Feathers are usually fished in this manner, though a natural bait is better.

When the fish move up in the water in the late evening, orthodox spinning tactics can be used, especially when the fish can be seen breaking the water. I am told, though I have not tried it myself, that fly-fishing also pays exciting dividends in these conditions.

General

The angler must travel south-west for much of the best pollack fishing. Small pollack are to be had as far up the English Channel as Dover, but they *are* small, and not until well west of the Dorset coast does the size begin to improve. Devon pollack are worth catching, but for specimen fish there is no doubt that Cornish waters are unsurpassed. For the holiday angler, there are boats and professionals available at such places as Fowey and Looe. The marks are well known, and to book a boat at one of these resorts is perhaps the best guarantee of getting among good pollack. Fish of between 15 and 20 lb. are taken each year, and it was in this locality that the record fish (23½ lb.) was caught. The Channel Isles also offer good pollack fishing, and it has always struck me that the Scillies might produce magnificent sport for an experienced angler. However, like so many of the best pollack fishing grounds, these islands are very much off the beaten track.

In Wales, there is excellent pollack fishing from the Pembrokeshire coast and the fish run very large on the off-shore reefs. It is very difficult to get hold of a suitable boat there, since the best marks are well out to sea in the open Atlantic; in particular, the reefs in the vicinity of the islands of Skomer and Skokholm. Ramsey Sound is another first-class spot. Once into the Irish Sea, the fish tend to run smaller. The west coast of Scotland has every indication of being an excellent pollack ground but little is known of it from the rod and line point of view.

The Irish coast yields magnificent pollack and, since many of the reefs are fished with lines by professionals, most of the good pollack marks are well known. Working from the east, the reefs around the Saltee Islands out towards the Conningbeg Light are excellent, but it can be said that right round the coast of Ireland, right up to Donegal, there is good pollack fishing everywhere.

Much of the fascination of pollack fishing stems from the magnificent surroundings in which it is carried out. Fishing in a small boat right up into the white water that surges back from a showing reef like the Smalls is a thrill which is scarcely to be equalled in any other form of fishing. The record pollack of 23 lb. 8 oz. was caught at Newquay, Cornwall, in 1957.

C. G.

Pout Whiting or Pouting

The pout whiting or pouting (*Gadus luscus*), a small member of the great cod family, is only too easily caught. When it comes out of the water it has a beautiful iridescent, almost copper colouring, with dark bands across its body and a black spot at the fore-end of the pectoral fins. There is a single barbule beneath the lower jaw. It is also called 'bib'.

As a rule it is the small fish that come close inshore, the larger specimens being found in deeper water. Piers, harbours, rocks, and beaches all provide their quota. Most of the fish taken from the shore range up to the ½ lb. mark, with the occasional specimen over 1 lb.

Pout whiting are found in the greatest numbers all along the south coast, but they are also present in other areas such as the Bristol Channel. It depends on locality, but as a rule they make their appearance during the warmer period of the year, earlier than their more slender counterparts, silver whiting.

Pout Whiting

The tackle required is similar to those used for WHITING – in other words, the lightest possible consistent with tide and currents. Baits are also similar – ragworm, lugworm, and mussel. Pout whiting are usually taken on paternoster gear.

Baits, Tackle, and Fishing Methods

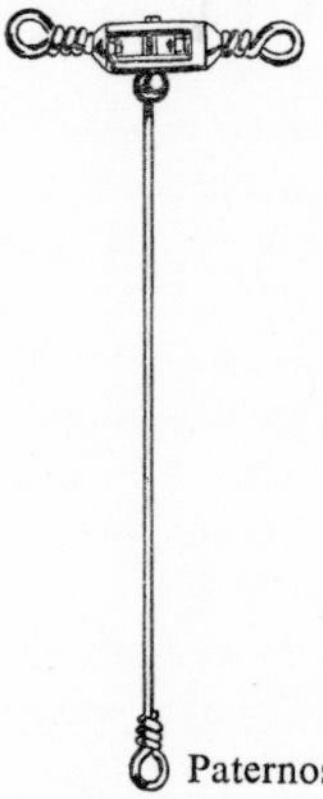

Paternoster boom

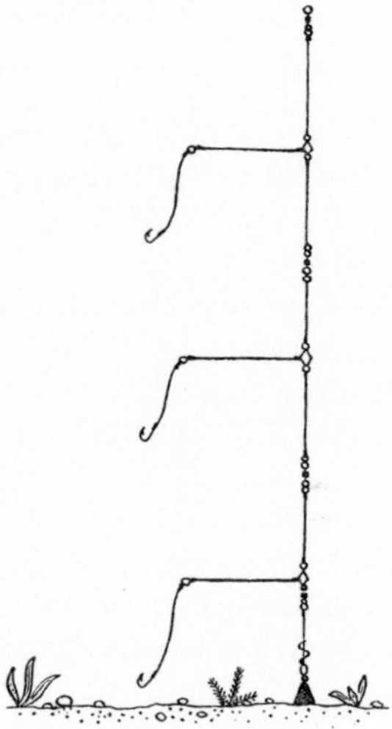

Paternoster gear

The best sport is usually around dusk, but this fish will also bite well after dark. The most suitable state of the tide depends on the area fished, but as a rule the best time is near and after the top of the tide.

The record fish, 4 lb. 10 oz., was taken at Coverack in 1935.

General

If you can cook the pout whiting soon after capture, it is delicious, but it goes off more quickly than practically any other fish.

D. F.

Sharks

Five species of shark are fairly common in our waters. They are the basking, blue, mako, porbeagle, and thresher sharks. However, other species have been reported, such as the hammerhead, humantin, and six-gilled, and there is one isolated instance of the man-eating white shark.

Of the five species mentioned, only four can be caught by rod and line, for the basking shark feeds solely on plankton and cannot be hooked by means of a bait.

Commonest of all sharks in our waters is the blue (*Carcharinus glaucus*). It seems to appear in large numbers west of

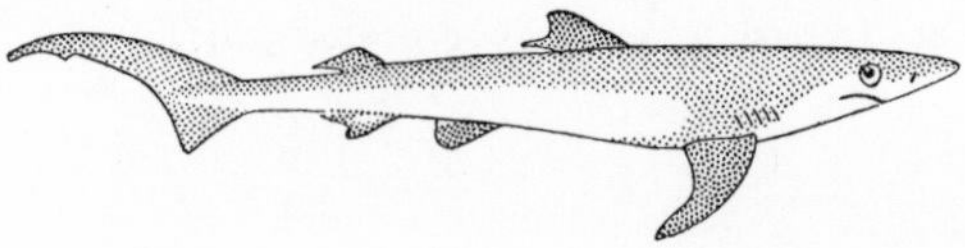

Blue shark

Portland Bill but rarely appears farther up the Channel. This species is also common on the south and west coasts of Ireland and has on occasion been seen off the west coast of Scotland. The blue is the shark which has made the sport of shark fishing so popular in Britain. Its general colouring is blue and its underparts are white. Though it is known to reach 25 ft in length, a 4- or 5-footer is more likely to be encountered by the angler. Fish of 75 lb. and upwards are certainly specimens.

The blue shark is very common throughout the entire western seaboard of Europe and is found in great numbers in the Mediterranean, certainly as far east as Cyprus. It is a poor fighter compared with other species, although if taken on light tackle it will provide far more sport than most people anticipate.

Nearly all blue sharks are hooked near the surface, where they prey upon the schools of pilchard, mackerel, and herring. Occasionally the odd one will be found in deep water, but more likely than not it has followed a bait down.

The mako shark (*Isurus oxyrinchus*) is a real fighter and will very often leap high in the air when being played. In New Zealand, where it grows to a very large size, it is often referred to as the leaping shark. This fish is found in most parts of the world, and, although it has never been established, there is a distinct possibility that there are two entirely different species in the Pacific and the Atlantic.

The mako is a mid-water feeder and is often found near rocks, where pollack, pout whiting, and possibly cod provide it with a very much larger meal than smaller fish such as pilchards.

The porbeagle shark (*Lamma cornubica*) is very similar to the mako in appearance and in habits. Although several methods of identification, such as examination of the positioning of the fins, are reliable, without any doubt at all the easiest and most accurate method is to examine the teeth. The teeth of the mako are long, large, and irregular and assume a criss-cross pattern; the porbeagle's are regular with several rows one behind the other. Occasionally one comes across a porbeagle with a tooth out of line, midway between two rows.

Sharks

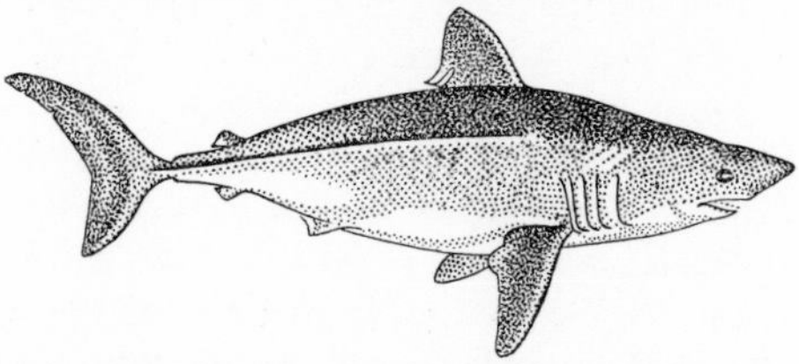

Porbeagle shark

This is caused by the loss of a tooth from the front row and the forward movement of the teeth behind. A porbeagle may have as many as seven rows of teeth, and every time one of the front ones comes loose a new one moves forward to take its place. In turn all seven teeth shift into their new positions.

Generally speaking, the porbeagle is larger and deeper in the body than the other species. It appears to be an Atlantic fish, for there are few reports of its being caught in any other part of the world.

The porbeagle thrives on mackerel and in fact is also referred to in some countries as the mackerel shark. However, it is not averse to any other bait, provided it is fresh. In the Mediterranean, especially around Malta, where this species is caught in great numbers, the professional fishermen bait their hooks with live bream and fish at thirty to forty fathoms in an overall depth of three hundred fathoms.

The porbeagle, like the mako, is to be found in mid-water and close to rocks. Usually it likes deep water and when hooked will make a very fast and strong run in a downward direction. Again like the mako, it needs to be fully played out before bringing to the gaff.

Far and away the rarest visitor to our shores is the thresher shark (*Alopias vulpes*). This vicious monster can sometimes be seen on the surface in fine weather flaying the water into foam with its scythe-like tail as it rounds up a shoal of mackerel or other fish. In comparison with the tail, the second dorsal and anal fins are small. The thresher, like the porbeagle, grows to great size.

Tackle

Looe, Cornwall, where British shark fishing was developed, is as well organized for this sport as any of the American big-game fishing centres. Over twenty boats are available for charter daily.

The boats are all around the 36 ft mark and have a wide beam of up to 12 ft. The forrard portion is decked in with a wheelhouse set about a third of the distance back from the bow. The wheelhouse extends from gunwale to gunwale, allowing ample protection for passengers and crew when driving into heavy seas.

Aft of the wheelhouse is a large area clear of all obstructions except for a fighting chair and the rubby-dubby bins. Deck planking has specially designed handles so that sections can be lifted up in order to get the shark into the compartments below as quickly as possible after it has been brought inboard. Not only does this prevent the fish from lashing around with its tail, thereby causing damage to the boat and possibly the boatman, but it also keeps the decks clean and safe to tread on.

The fighting chair is in effect very much like the normal office chair. It can be swivelled to adjust height and direction as required and is bolted to the deck firmly enough to take the strain of a 1,000 lb. fighting fish, plus the strain put upon it by the angler. On the front edge of the chair is fitted a pintle, into which the butt on the rod is dropped. This swivels, allowing the angler to work his rod up and down to 'pump' his fish.

Tackle for shark fishing must necessarily be much heavier than for ordinary boat fishing. Until recently, when the American Penn multiplier reels became available for the British market, the Fortuna reel was looked upon as the only reel really capable of coping with these fig fish. This was fished under the rod. With the advent of the Penn multipliers, the whole outlook on fishing changed. Instead of fishing the line beneath the rod, the reel was now carried above, allowing a far easier action when pumping a fish. In both cases, however, it is necessary to use a harness, for the weight of rod, reel, line, and fish make it virtually impossible to hold the tackle for long by hand alone.

With the Fortuna, a ring was normally fitted on the rod to which the quick-release of the harness was attached. On the multiplier there are two harness lugs, one on each end of the reel, facing upwards towards the angler.

Today the accepted size for either reel is 9/0, capable of taking a minimum of 300 yds of line of 100 lb. or more breaking strain, or 500 yds if using a lighter line.

The harness, which can be of leather or webbing, is nothing more nor less than a waistcoat which is fitted over the shoulders and around the waist, then strapped tight to prevent movement when fighting a fish. Straps lead from the shoulders to a quick-release snap and thence to the rod or reel. The quick-release snap is solely a life-saving device in case you should slip and go overboard. Fortunately it has never been required in this country, for the boatmen are experienced and keep a watchful eye on the anglers from the moment they hook their fish. It is, however, wise to use this precaution, for if anybody did go overboard attached to a fighting fish with the weight of rod and reel dragging him down he would have little chance. By merely pulling a toggle on this equipment he is immediately freed.

Although most of the modern lines are much the same in quality, braided Terylene is the most popular. Some anglers appear to think that the stretching of nylon lines prevents a good strike being made. However, when over a hundred yards have been stripped off a reel, there is bound to be a certain amount of 'belly' in the line. Whether it is of Terylene or nylon the results will be the same.

Since the advent of glass rods, selection of the right weapon has become easier. In fact any solid glass rod with a test curve of 30 to 35 lb. suffices.

Hollow glass-fibre rods, although reputed to be extremely strong, have on several occasions snapped near the top at a critical moment. Hardy Bros. split-cane game rods are, of course, ideal for the job, but as with any hand-made rod the price is high.

In buying a rod for shark fishing, it is essential to check that you have one with a correct winch fitting, capable of taking the reel you intend to use. Many rod manufacturers overlook the size of the reel stand on the larger types of big-game reel, so always check to see that the reel fits snugly into the housing and can be screwed down, allowing no movement whatsoever once the reel is securely in position.

The bottom tackle must be extremely strong, for a shark's skin is rough and will cut through any ordinary lines. Experience has shown that a light rustless wire trace with a breaking strain of around 200 lb. is ideal. This should be from 12 to 16 ft in length and swivelled at one end and in the centre. Stainless-steel wire is not recommended for traces, plaited or braided wire being much better. Cable like that used for motorcycle brakes is cheap and excellent for the job. Blue sharks in particular have a habit of rolling in the wire traces when hooked, hence the necessity for this heavy gear at the end of your line.

Swivels must be the best obtainable and capable of working when a heavy fish is on the line. Small ones are useless and invariably snap or draw out under pressure. Shark tackle dealers around the coast and in some of the larger inland towns can recommend the correct type to use, and do in fact supply swivels that are guaranteed by the makers. A guaranteed loading of 100 lb. is necessary.

The hook must be of forged steel, size 9/0 to 10/0, and soft-welded to the end of the trace without a swivel. It is therefore necessary to have a brazed eye on the hook through which the trace can be put before welding. Always keep the point of the hook sharpened, for the mouth of a shark is hard and the hook must be driven well into it when striking.

The only other item of equipment is a float. Although some anglers like to see a brightly coloured float dancing on the water, it is equally effective to use a piece of cork with a slit down one side into which the line is slotted and a sliver of wood inserted to hold it in position at the required depth.

Most boats employed on shark fishing have an adequate set of gaffs capable of dealing with the largest fish likely to be taken. Most are powerful weapons capable of handling fish of 400 and 500 lb. The best type of gaff is that with a detachable head and ring to which a line is attached.

Fishing Methods

Although sharks have been caught on rod and line in Great Britain only during the past ten years, many books published prior to the turn of the century contain accounts of the epic battles between professional fishermen and these monsters. Nowadays, over six thousand sharks are landed annually by rod and line sportsmen, the majority of them in Cornish waters. Brigadier J. A. L. Caunter of Looe first attempted to take shark in the early 1950s. His experiments over the years with new tackle and methods finally produced a means of attracting the fish to the angler which is now accepted as common practice throughout Great Britain.

The method employed in this country is to drift with tide and wind so that, in effect, one is playing the fish from a stationary position and must fight it from the initial strike. Occasionally, of course, when a boat is fishing on its own and well clear of the others, the boatman will use his engines in order to run up on a big one, but this is exceptional.

It can easily be seen that in these circumstances heavier tackle is required than would be necessary with a boat that is capable of going as fast as, if not faster than, the fish that is on the line. For example, if the boat is drifting with tide and wind at, say, four knots and the fish takes off in the opposite direction, it is obvious that his run has to be stopped quickly, otherwise there would soon be no line left on the reel.

Furthermore, one never knows just what species will take the bait next. Experienced shark anglers have on many occasions tried to get their fish with light tackle, but invariably something really big has come along and snapped their lines as if they were cotton.

Most anglers agree that it is far more fun to catch a blue shark on tackle with a line of around 30 lb. breaking strain than on tackle of 130 lb., yet experience has proved that if one is to succeed in landing a really big fish from a stationary boat, it is essential to use the latter. The whole story would of course be altered if the fish were caught from a moving vessel.

One of the most important elements in the method employed in this country for shark fishing is the rubby-dubby. This is a pulped up mass of pilchard, herring, or mackerel. The first of these is the best attractor of all, for the pilchard has a very high proportion of oil content compared with the others.

It matters little whether the pilchard or other fish is stale, for by the time it has been pulverized into minute portions, little remains but a squelchy mass of bones and juice. The mashing is usually done in a dustbin on the way to the fishing grounds.

Abroad, the word 'chumming' is employed to describe ground-baiting, but more often than not this entails using scoops of live fish, which are thrown in the water around the boat in order to attract fish into the vicinity.

On arrival at the area to be fished, two small meshed bags are filled with the rubby-dubby and tied at water level, one on the stern, the other at the bow. As the boat rolls, the bags go in and out of the water, each time sending out a stream oι minute portions of fish. Very quickly the effects of the oil from the fish begin to tell on the surface, and before long a long, oily slick will be showing up on the weather side as the boat drifts.

The oily slick serves a dual purpose. Firstly, it enables the boatman to see in which direction the tide and wind are taking the boat, thus helping him to adjust his jib so as to keep the boat beam on to the sea. Secondly, in rough weather it helps to keep the sea flattened out around the boat.

Unlike other forms of sea angling, shark fishing is better in rough weather than in calm seas. Once the engines are shut off and the boat is left to the mercy of wind and tide, the stronger the wind the better, for it allows the boat to move at a greater speed through the water, thereby covering a far greater area.

Usually it takes from an hour and a half to two and a quarter hours to reach the sharking grounds. Even hazy weather creates no problems, for each boat is fitted with an echo-sounder and the boatmen know every inch of the bottom. As the boat leaves harbour, watches are checked, and at the end of the allotted steaming time the echo-sounder is switched on. Immediately it shows the depth that the boatman expects, the engines are switched off and the drift begins.

Although some sharks are taken very soon after fishing commences in the morning, most are hooked during the afternoon. It appears that the fish take some time to follow the rubby-dubby trail to its source and more often than not it is an hour and a half to two hours before the first strike occurs.

The first step is to put the two rubby-dubby bags overboard, in order to get them working as quickly as possible.

Next the rods are baited with whatever is available. Live MACKEREL are excellent, but often these are not obtainable and then dead pilchards or herrings are used in their place.

When fishing with live-bait, the normal procedure is to hook the fish through the body under the dorsal fin, or through the mouth. This way there is little interference with the swimming ability of the fish, which can move around and will attract greater interest than motionless dead-bait.

When dead-bait is used, in view of the fact that sharks usually take the bait head first, the best method is to thread the trace through the fish by means of a baiting needle, leaving the hook protruding from the mouth, eyes, or gills.

Most people prefer to use one hook, but up to three are allowed, a triangular counting as three. When two separate hooks are in use one should be threaded through the mouth, the second farther back behind the dorsal fin. This ensures that when the fish takes the bait one of the hooks strikes home.

Generally the baits are set to fish between three and ten fathoms. The line is measured off the reel to the required distance, and the float is attached. Line is then paid out again until the float is in position from three to four fathoms from the boat. (If two rods are in use one float will be set for fishing one depth and the second a couple of fathoms deeper.) The rods are then placed against the gunwales, with the reel in the free position and on the check or ratchet, so that the moment a fish takes the bait it is free to run without hindrance, but the angler has time to get his harness adjusted and ready for the strike.

Experience has shown that if a strike is made on the initial run, the fish will throw the bait. To be certain that this does not happen, no effort should be made to stop the fish on this first run. When the reel ceases to revolve, indicating that the fish is swallowing the bait, the rod should be hooked into position. As soon as the shark moves the second time, the strike should be made by lifting the rod straight up, driving the hook home.

From now onwards it is a case of angler against shark. Once the fish is under control, but lying deep in the water, it will be necessary to pump it surfacewards. The end of the rod is lowered to a point just above the gunwale – it must not touch the boat or any person in it other than the fisherman, or the catch will not be recognized for record purposes. Then, exerting pressure, the angler forces his fish to the surface. Under no circumstances must it be jerked, otherwise the hook will come away or the line will snap. If the rod is worked in exactly the same way as a pump there should be no great difficulty in eventually bringing the fish to the gaff. The pumping process may have to be repeated two or three times before the fish is brought in.

It is of course highly probable with a fish of 400 to 500 lb. that the combined efforts of boatman and anglers would not be enough to get it into the boat. It is much easier to sink a barbless hook into the fish and haul the line taut, thereby depriving the fish of much of its fighting power, than to try and haul it inboard.

Most fish are gaffed in the region of the vent. With a detachable gaff head, it is fairly easy to get a good purchase around the mast and lift the tail of the fish from the water. This deprives it of most of its fighting power. A second gaff can then be sunk into the mouth of the fish and made fast forrard. If there is much fight still left in the fish and it is possible to steam ahead, a quick method of killing it is to keep the head level with the water and go ahead at full speed. With a very large specimen, it is far better to leave it outside the boat for the journey back to port. The accepted way to do this is to haul the head clear of the water from the bow and the tail from the stern, so that the rest of the body skates over the water, causing minimum drag.

All boats employed in shark fishing carry a 'priest' or cosh. This is a very important piece of equipment, for once a shark has been brought inboard it begins to flail around with its tail, and, if not brought under control at once, could do serious damage to those aboard and to the boat itself. The priest usually weighs several pounds and is brought down in no uncertain manner on the head of the shark.

General Returning to port in the evening, each boat flies pennants from the yard-arm indicating the number of sharks on board. In order to give notice to the official weigher that the boat has sharks over 75 lb. in weight, which is the minimum required for membership of the Shark Angling Club of Great Britain, those estimated to be under 75 lb. are shown below and those over 75 lb. above a blue pennant.

The Shark Angling Club of Great Britain was founded by Brigadier Caunter in 1953. This club is now looked upon as the leading authority on shark fishing in Europe and the Brigadier as a world authority. The Club has a strict set of rules that must be adhered to when catching sharks, based more or less on those of the International Game Fish Association of Miami, Florida.

Records of all sharks caught in British waters are held by the Club, and when a claim is made for a new record, a thorough investigation is carried out to see that the fish has been caught by fair means, and is in reality of the species claimed.

Until 1961, the world, European, and British porbeagle record was held by Mrs Hetty Eathorne of Torquay, who in 1955 landed a 271 lb. fish at Looe. In 1961, however, a fish of 388 lb. was landed at Montauk Point, U.S.A. Mrs Eathorne still retains her European and British records together with the ladies' world record.

The world record for mako is held in New Zealand with a fish of 1,000 lb. landed at Mayor Island. A 745 lb. fish was landed from Shinnecock Inlet, U.S.A. The British and European record is now held by Jack Sefton with a fine specimen of 428½ lb. caught at Looe in 1961.

The world record for thresher is held with a fish of 922 lb. taken in New Zealand in 1937. The largest ever recorded in this country was a fish of 280 lb. caught by H. A. Kelly at Dungeness in 1933. This holds the European and British records. In recent years Brigadier Caunter, fishing out of Looe, landed a fine specimen of 268 lb. which captured for him the European and British record for an 80 lb. breaking-strain line.

The largest blue shark caught in European waters by rod and line was by Nigel Sutcliffe at Looe, Cornwall, in 1959. This fish weighed 218 lb. and holds both the British and European records. A fish of 212 lb. was landed from Achill Island in the same year. Recently, another fine specimen of 200 lb. was landed by a Parisian angler at Dieppe.

Sharks

The cost of a day's shark fishing is very reasonable, considering that you can have the exclusive use of a deep-sea fishing vessel and crew. At Looe, the charge for a boat is £8 per day including bait and rubby-dubby. Each boat is equipped to fish two rods. One can either have the boat alone, share it with another, or make up a party of four and fish in turn.

Jack Bray who runs the fishing tackle shop on the East Quay, Looe, undertakes the booking of all boats, and will provide big-game tackle for 30*s.* a day. The cost of buying a set of sharking tackle varies considerably. Here is a reasonable budget: a 'Pegley-Davies' 'Mako de Luxe' rod, a Penn 9/0 reel, filled to capacity with braided line, and the necessary bottom tackle – the complete set costs around £40.

S. N.-B.

Skates and Rays

There is no scientific distinction to be made between skates and rays. They are all members of the family Raiidae, the smaller species tending to be labelled as ray by fishermen, while the larger are usually called skate. Since we are not ichthyologists but anglers, the unscientific distinction might as well be retained here.

Rays and skates are flattened, but are not flatfish. There is still confusion amongst fishermen on this point, so it seems as well to state now that while skates are flattened from above, so that they swim belly down, and their eyes are symmetrically

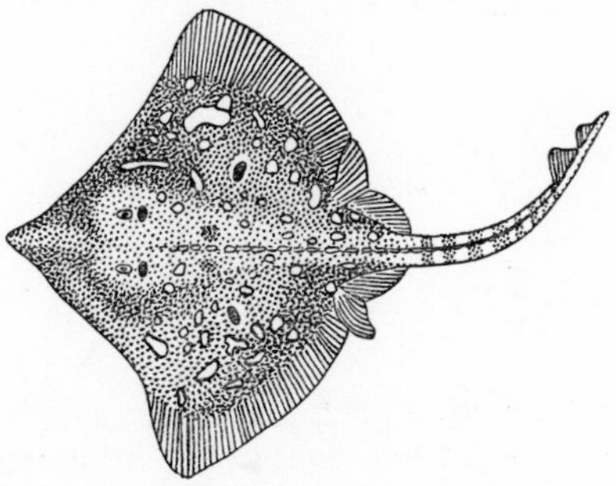

Skate

placed on top of their heads, 'true' flatfish like plaice and flounders are flattened sideways, so that they swim on their *sides*, and have both eyes on one side of their bodies. Furthermore, skates and rays are of that great family of fish, including MONKFISH, DOGFISH, and SHARK, which have no true backbone – the cartilaginous fish.

They are odd fish in appearance. The development of the pectoral fins into 'wings' is characteristic, and these wings together with the central body form the 'disc', to which is appended a long tail. The mouth is situated underneath the head and is clearly well adapted to feeding right on the sea-bed. It is a curious fact that, since the mouth is usually pressed against the bottom of the sea, breathing is by means of valves set behind the eyes, 'breathing' in this case of course meaning the intake of sea water.

The skin is rough and scaleless, as in other members of this family, and many species have sharp spines set in the disc and in the tail. Most species also have rounded, crushing teeth, though occasionally, as in the case of the male thornback, they may be pointed.

Distinguishing between the various species of ray that inhabit British waters is something of a nightmare. No indication of species is given by fin-ray count, for there are no true bones in the fish. Nor are there any differences in the arrangement of the fins. Differences in the shape of the disc are the result of differences in age and sex; so are those of coloration. The sharp spines which are carried by many of the rays do not guarantee identification either. Some degree of differentiation is possible however between long-nosed and short-nosed species (the former are the bigger species referred to as skate, the latter the rays). Dr Michael Kennedy makes this distinction: 'If the distance of the eyes from the tip of the snout is at least fifty per cent of the width of the disc at the level of the eyes, the fish may be regarded as long-snouted. If, on the other hand, it is not more than forty per cent of this measurement, the fish may be regarded as short-snouted.'

The following points may be useful to the angler as an *indication* of identification. If you are firmly convinced that you have broken, let us say, the blond ray record, make certain that you keep the body for expert investigation.

Thornback Ray (*Raia clavata*): This is the commonest ray to be met with in British waters. As its name suggests, it wears an armoury of sharp spines, but the ones that distinguish it from other spine-bearing species are the large spines situated right in the middle of its wings. In the male fish (distinguished by the 'claspers', the two roughened flaps at either side of the tail) the teeth are pointed. The disc is more angular than in other small rays. Like most other rays, the thornback is patterned with light spots on a dark ground.

Blond Ray (*Raia brachyura*)*:* The disc is more inclined to be heart-shaped and carries fewer spines than the thornback's. The colour is rather light. An identifying characteristic is that the spots extend right to the edges of the wings. On the *under-side* there is an edging of small spines along the wings.

Spotted Ray (*Raia montagui*)*:* Very similar to the blond ray. The spots are fewer and larger and do not reach the edges of the wings as in the above species. There is no border of spines on the edges of the under-surface of the wings.

Cuckoo Ray (*Raia naevus*)*:* This has large spines. The disc is heart-shaped. The chief characteristic is a notably large dark spot on each wing, like an eye, 'superimposed upon which are yellow, hieroglyphic-like markings' (Kennedy).

Sandy Ray (*Raia circularis*)*:* Very similar to the cuckoo ray, but the nose is rather more pointed and the tail is shorter. It is light brown above with a symmetrical pattern of yellow spots on each wing.

It will be clearly seen that there are many problems for the angler who wishes to identify his catch. In some cases only physical comparison of similar species will be of any help.

The Sting Ray (*Trygon pastinaca*)*:* Every season a few sting ray are caught by sea anglers in this country, though it is doubtful whether anyone fishes for the species deliberately.

The sting ray is easily distinguished from the other rays by its elongated spine and long whip-like tail. There are no markings on its brownish disc, as there are in the case of the other rays.

This fish seems to come inshore in the late summer, particularly favouring the east coast. Two of the biggest specimens recorded were the 52½ lb. fish taken on the Hampshire coast in 1938 and the estimated 70 lb. fish from Clacton pier in 1952. (Clacton pier seems to produce these creatures!) Unlike the rays we have been considering the sting ray is viviparous, and seems to be less of a fish eater than the others, taking for preference molluscs and crustaceans.

The spiny tail of the sting ray is capable of inflicting an unpleasant wound in its own right, but its long spine can cause severe pain and possibly a fatal wound by reason of the venom it secretes. Immediate medical attention is necessary should you be unlucky enough to receive a sting. On landing a sting ray, the best plan is immediately to cut off the tail where it joins the body.

The long-nosed species, the skates, do not present quite such formidable identification problems as the rays. Three of them come within the scope of the British sea angler.

The Common Skate (*Raia batis*), the 'big skate' species most commonly taken by British sea anglers, is a drab, browny-grey above, and there may or may not be small light spots on it. Beneath it is greyish – not white – with possibly a number of black 'pores'. It may weigh as much as 200 lb.

The White Skate (*Raia marginata*) is distinguished from the above by its pure white underside and the distinctive 'bottle nose' that has caused it to be known in some quarters as the Burton skate. It is the largest of the British skates.

The Long-nosed Skate (*Raia oxyrhyncus*) is easily distinguished from the other skates by reason of its particularly long snout. It is greyish on both sides, with spots and streaks on the upper.

No precise information is available at the moment as to how fast skate and rays grow, but the impression is that they are a fairly slow-growing race, as well as being not particularly prolific. As far as thornbacks are concerned, anything over 15 lb. is a good fish; the record is 38 lb. (Rustington Beach, 1935). Blond rays grow bigger – up to three feet and more – as may the spotted ray. The cuckoo ray is quite a small fish, with a suggested maximum length of two feet. The sandy ray may reach twice this size.

The skates grow to a mighty size; indeed they are the biggest fish to inhabit British waters, if basking shark, of no interest to anglers, are excepted. The biggest rod-caught skate was taken off Ballycotton in 1913 and weighed 221 lb., but fish in excess of 400 lb. have been taken by trawlers. The white skate may attain a weight of 500 lb. The long-nosed skate runs considerably smaller.

Once again I should like to stress that expert identification is necessary if you want your ray or skate considered for record purposes. I should also say here that I am indebted to

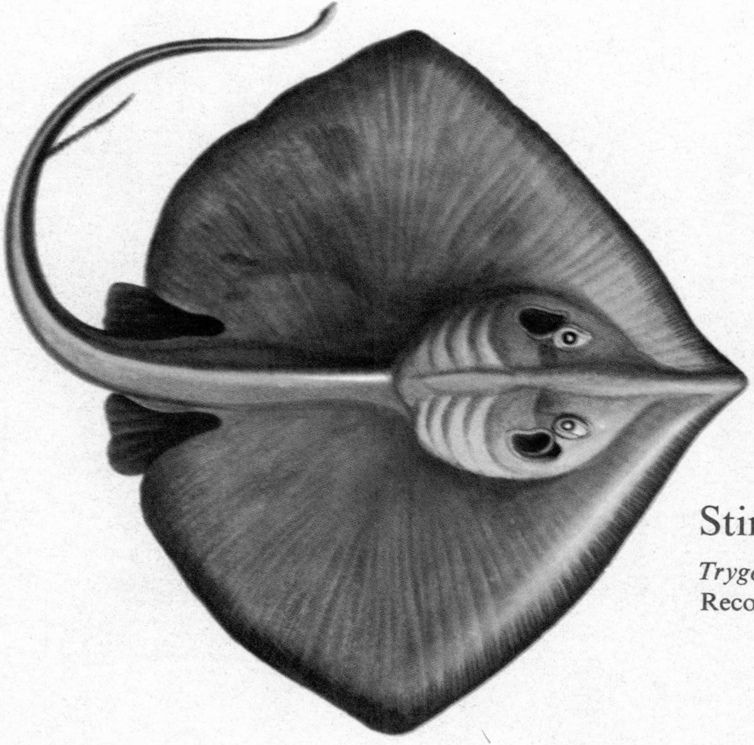

Stingray

Trygon pastinaca (page 335)
Record 59 lb

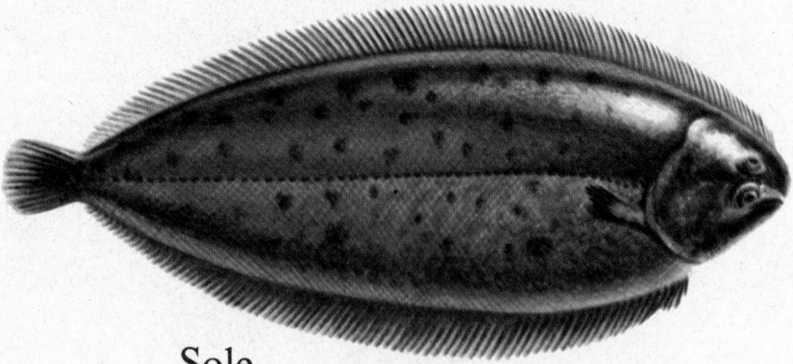

Sole

Solea Solea (page 339)
Record 4 lb 1 oz 14 drams

Solenette
Microchinus boscanion
No record

Tunny

Thunnus thynnus
Record 851 lb

Ballan Wrasse

Labrus bergylta (page 350)
Record 12 lb 12 oz*

Cuckoo Wrasse

Labrus mixtus (page 350)
Record 1 lb 3 oz 10 drams

Corkwing Wrasse

Crenilabrus mixtus (page 350)
No record

Dr Michael Kennedy of the Inland Fisheries Trust, Dublin, for these points of identification.

The spawning period of skates and rays may extend over several months. The fish 'lay' eggs in horny purses, rather like those produced by the dogfish, which are generally buried in the sea-bed. Failing this, they carry sticky threads which pick up fragments of marine rubbish – bits of stone or weed – causing them to sink. The young skate remains for a very long time in the capsule; when it finally becomes free very little of the egg yolk remains attached to it, as it does in the case of most young fishes. The process of incubation may be extended over a very long period – six or seven months.

It is not known with much certainty what migrations these species undertake. Certainly, however, from one's observation as an angler, it can be noted that the fish are more plentiful at some times of the year than at others. Thornback rays seem to be particularly common between May and November – they do not seem to be active inshore in the colder months of the year.

Sometimes there are mysterious movements of skate from one locality to another. I remember seeing one of these migrations at Tenby in 1960. From the boat it was possible to see thornback ray swimming on the surface on all sides. Where they were going or for what purpose it was impossible to tell. Very big skate, incidentally, are always taken in the summer, but there is little significance to be attached to this, since to my knowledge the marks over which these fish are taken are only fished in the warm months in any case.

Rays are often taken in shallow water, sometimes by anglers casting out from surf beaches. This applies particularly to thornbacks. Blond rays prefer deeper water, ten fathoms or over. Spotted and cuckoo rays are often shallow-water dwellers, but the sandy ray is certainly a deep-water species. Big skate are chiefly found in depths of fifteen fathoms and over, though occasionally they may be encountered in shallow water; I once hooked a very large skate at a depth of a couple of fathoms, and the Latchford brothers of Tralee took five notable skate of over a hundred pounds apiece fishing in five fathoms off Fenit Pier in one tide's fishing.

All the species we are considering prefer mud, sand, or gravel, but it is noticeable that the big common skate are chiefly taken on patchy ground, where sand and gravel are broken up by areas of weedy stones. Generally speaking, while thornbacks and some of the other rays come within the shore angler's range, a boat anchored well off shore is needed to come into contact with the big skate.

Baits The smaller rays seem to be pretty much omnivorous, but thornbacks are particularly partial to sand-eels, which in fact are the best bait for most rays. Crustaceans like hermit crabs are important; lugworm, sand shrimps, and bivalves are also taken. Small fish, in particular the bottom-dwelling ones like DABS and small PLAICE, are picked up as well. A strip of an oily fish, such as MACKEREL, is another useful bait.

The big skate are almost exclusively fish eaters, preying chiefly on the bottom-swimming species. A ten-pound DOG-FISH is not too big to be taken, while gurnards and WHITING, POUTING, small skate, and various species of flat-fish undoubtedly figure prominently on the menu.

A whole mackerel is by no means too big a bait, and if bait fish are plentiful this is what to use. A half mackerel, split from head to tail is more usual, however.

Tackle – Ray If you are fishing especially for ray – and in ninety-nine cases out of a hundred it will be thornback that you have in mind – abandon the heavy boat or pier rod and fish with surf-casting gear. Thornbacks can fight very well, running and boring in a manner that one does not usually associate with skate, and the surf-casting tackle gives them a chance to show what they can do.

Tackle – Skate Big skate vie with CONGER for the credit of being the toughest of all British sea fish to bring to the gaff. If you are fishing for big skate on one of the classic marks, do not risk the disapproval of the boatman by bringing light gear. The heaviest grade of saltwater rod with a roller tip ring is needed, and your reel, either a deep-water multiplier or a big single-action model, should be loaded with 80 lb. Terylene. (I am assuming you are serious about catching a big skate.) The lead should be fished above the hook (a running arrangement is preferred). The hook should be on a wire link and should be very strong; the crushing teeth of a big skate are formidable. A swivel should connect the trace to the main line.

Fishing Methods – Ray If the fish goes to the bottom and stays there, using the pressure of its wings to keep it down, there is no need to strain the rod tip. Get hold of the line between the first ring and the reel and pull it backwards and forwards in a sawing motion. This hardly ever fails to shift the fish. Watch out for the spines when you have landed it.

Fishing Methods – Skate

Skate-fishing does not require much finesse; it is largely a matter of strong tackle, brute strength, and staying power. Since skate are almost exclusively bottom-feeders, it is essential that the bait be on the bottom. For this reason, it is much better to fish from a boat than on the drift. Generally the bait is legered or paternostered (see p. 30). Men who have never caught one sometimes refer to landing a big skate as if all one had to do was haul it up from the bottom. It is true that a skate does not usually run, but it uses the great spread of its wings in conjunction with what tide is flowing to get down to the bottom, and once it is there it is very difficult to shift. A big skate can give a prolonged, exhausting, and exhilarating fight.

General

Thornbacks are pretty generally distributed around the coasts of the British Isles. There are some places where they can be taken in numbers however. I have usually struck these a couple of hundred yards off a sandy shore. Carmarthen Bay, near Tenby, can give excellent fishing for thornback, as can the waters off the Burrow Shore, Kilmore Quay, Co. Wexford. There are probably dozens of other spots where local conditions favour the presence of these fish in large numbers.

As for the other species of rays, it is difficult to know what advice to give, since they do not figure much in the angler's catch – or possibly are not always distinguished from thornbacks. However, one place from which blonde ray are reported fairly regularly is the Isle of Wight.

Common skate could, I suppose, turn up in most places but specialist fishing for them is almost entirely restricted to Irish waters, and if you want a big skate very badly, you should go to Kinsale, Ballycotton, Dingle, Valentia, or Westport. There are undoubtedly big skate in Cornish waters, but little real fishing for skate is done there – the visitors are more interested in blue shark. Lately some interest has been aroused in the possibilities of Scottish waters for big skate; a few very big specimens were taken in the summer of 1961, but so far not enough has been done in these waters to give a clear idea of their potential.

If you are even harder to please and insist on a white or a long-nosed skate, Westport, Co. Mayo, has produced most specimens in recent years.

C. G.

Sole

The common sole (*Solea solea*) is too well known from the fishmonger's slab to require much description. It is oval in

Sea Fishing shape and a dull brown in colour, with white underparts. The eyes are on the right side and the snout sticks out beyond the jaws, which are larger underneath than on top.

Ireland, the Bristol Channel, and the North Sea contain the main sole-fishing grounds. The fish are generally found over mud or sand, where they forage for marine worms, shrimps, and so on.

Baits The best bait is probably a bunch of small ragworms. Mussels, shrimps, lugworms, and razor-fish are also used.

Tackle and Fishing Methods Very light paternoster gear on monofilament line is effective, whether fished from boat, pier, or shore. Night fishing often produces the best bags.

General The British record is a 4 lb. fish taken from Clevedon Pier.

C. W.

Tope

The tope (*Eugaleus galeus*) is a member of the great class of requin sharks (Carcharimidae), the family which contains killers like the notorious tiger shark as well as such innocuous creatures as the smooth hound (*Mustelus mustelus*). In comparison with some of its relatives it is a small fish, with a possible maximum length of 7 or 8 ft, but, by virtue of its speed and sporting qualities and the fact that light tackle can be employed in its capture, it is held in high esteem by saltwater anglers. It is a long, slim, almost torpedo-shaped fish, varying in colour from grey to fawn.

The tope may conceivably be confused with its relative the blue SHARK, or even with spur DOG. The characteristic notched tail of the tope, however, apart from other zoological differences, should make identification simple here. More serious

Tope's tail

Jaws of female tope

difficulty arises with the smooth hound, which usually has a notched tail itself. The surest way to distinguish it from the tope is by examining its teeth, which are flattened, grinding teeth like those of the rays. I should stress, perhaps, that this examination should be done *after* the death of the fish.

No one, so far as I know, has made any detailed investigation into the growth rate of tope, since the species is not of commercial value (except to the Chinese, who utilize them for shark-fin soup). However, it may be stated that most tope caught around our coasts range between 20 and 40 lb. Small fish, of less than 20 lb. weight, are often reported from English Channel waters, sometimes in quantity, but I fancy that there is a strong possibility that many of these fish are smooth hound. Tope of between 40 and 50 lb. may be considered good fish, and a sprinkling of fish up to 60 lb. are reported each year. Tope of more than 60 lb. come into the category of fish-of-a-lifetime.

Tope are widely distributed throughout the oceans of the world. As far as British waters are concerned, they come inshore in April or early May, having spent the winter months in deep water (Dr Michael Kennedy* mentions specimens taken by trawlers in depths as great as 154 fathoms). June, July, August, and September are the months which provide the best of the tope fishing, but occasional fish are caught at odd times throughout the winter, usually in south-western districts and often in special circumstances. In Milford Haven, for example, large tope were taken in the January of 1962; these fish were plainly interested in the big shoals of herrings which had entered the Haven at that time. However, few specialist tope fishermen would consider serious fishing for the species once November is out.

While the tope are in the shallow, littoral water breeding takes place. Tope are viviparous, the young being born alive in numbers varying between twenty and forty. Tiny tope of a couple of pounds in weight are sometimes taken inshore in winter, which suggests that the young do not spend their first winter in deep water.

Tope are usually accounted demersal fish, that is, bottom swimming and bottom feeding. It is certainly true that tope feed a good deal on flatfish and other demersal species like whiting, but there are many occasions when they feed quite near the surface on such fish as mackerel and even sand-eels. Traditional tope-fishing methods are geared to the idea that they are bottom-feeding fish exclusively and, as we shall see, bottom fishing over clean ground, gravel or sand, is usually

* *The Sea Angler's Fishes* (Hutchinson).

adopted. But it is becoming increasingly clear that mid-water and surface fishing yields good dividends in the way of fish caught and enhanced interest in the fishing itself.

Baits It hardly needs saying that tope feed almost entirely on fish, though specimens have been found to contain such apparently indigestible creatures as large spider crabs. When tope are present in numbers, anglers out after other species often have their tackle smashed, even though the bait may be lug or ragworm. However, it is not suggested that such baits should be deliberately used in tope fishing, though it has always struck me that a very large soft crab might well prove attractive. In general, fresh fish baits – MACKEREL, herring, flatfish – will be taken, but in some years squid and cuttlefish come inshore in large quantities, and in these circumstances tope may very well become preoccupied with feeding on them, with the result that other fish baits are ignored. This was certainly my experience on one occasion, and is worth bearing in mind.

Tackle Tope are powerful, fast, hard-fighting fish, but because of the nature of the fight and the tactics they adopt there is fortunately no need to use the kind of heavy tackle that is necessary for CONGER and SKATE fishing. 15 lb. b.s. monofilament nylon is strong enough for the experienced angler, though it would be wise for the newcomer to tope fishing to use, say, 30 lb. line to begin with. Experience has shown that for all-round work (which includes shore fishing for tope involving long casting) a multiplier is the best reel to use. However, if only boat fishing is contemplated, a single-action centre-pin reel is perfectly adequate. One thing must be stressed: there should be *plenty* of line. I never go tope fishing with less than 300 yds of line on and even then there is a slight element of risk; on one occasion I had all my line run out by a tope when I was shore fishing.

For shore fishing, a light beach-caster is very suitable and indeed, although it is more than 11 ft long, it can be used for boat fishing as well, though many anglers would prefer a more conventional boat rod of 6 ft or so. The rod should be light, however, to match the line you are using. Just because tope are comparatively large fish, do not be tempted to buy one of those frightful, so-called 'heavy-duty', boat rods which are fitted only for dislodging congers from reefs and big skate from the bottom. Incidentally, hollow-glass is the best material for your rod. Split-cane is pleasant to use and to handle but it suffers badly from the effects of salt water even when carefully looked after. Make sure that you have stainless-steel rod rings and a reliable screw-up winch fitting. Having your reel fall off when you are playing a 50-pounder is no joke.

Because of the tope's sharp teeth, and also because of its rough skin, a wire trace is an absolute necessity. Cable-laid steel wire is by far the best to use. Alasticum is too liable to kink during the fight. A twisted wire covered in plastic is available, but this is most untrustworthy, and cannot be recommended. This kind of wire rusts from the inside, so that while there is no deterioration apparent from the outside, it will break like cotton at a small stress.

The trace should be not less than 4 ft in length. The reason for this is that tope often roll on the surface during play and a big one is capable of wrapping a good deal of trace around itself. Once the nylon main line rubs on its rough back there is every chance that it will part. Some boat anglers go much further than this and use traces as long as 20 ft. This possibly has the effect in the first place of allowing the bait a certain amount of presumably attractive play on the sea bed, and in the second place of keeping the lead as far away as possible from the tope. To use such a long trace, however, presents difficulties in landing the fish.

The lead should run freely above the trace, stopped by a swivel. Make sure that it *is* free to run, because tope are often very cautious fish and are liable to drop the bait if they feel the weight of the lead. How much weight you use will depend, of course, on the strength of the tide; but try not to use more than you have to.

The hook should suit the bait, that is to say it should be no bigger than the bait demands. If your bait is half a herring for example, a single No. 6/0 is adequate. Many newcomers to tope fishing seem to think it necessary to use what almost amounts to a shark hook, but although a big tope has a big mouth there is no advantage in this; the smaller hook gives much better penetration. Some experienced tope fishermen prefer to use a whole fish, in which case two hooks are very often used.

Fishing Methods

Baiting up: This is a matter of considerable importance in tope fishing. Most successful tope fishermen believe that the hook should be as inconspicuous as possible. I myself, having too often had the experience of wary tope dropping a carelessly mounted bait, am careful always to hide the hook altogether in normal tope-fishing – fishing over rocks being an exception, as we shall see.

Tope generally take the bait in this manner: there may be a

few nibblings and nudgings at the rod top to begin with, then several yards of line are stripped off very quickly. It is fatal to strike at this point. The tope has the bait between its jaws but it hasn't begun to swallow it yet. There will be a pause, during which the angler might think that the tope has dropped the bait, but then the line will race off again and the fish may be struck. Because of the way that line is often stripped from the reel by the bite, the reel must be free to run, yet not so free that the action of the tide or the wind will make the spool revolve. The reel is therefore left out of gear with the check on, or if the tide run is very fast, it is left in gear with a very light drag set. As soon as the presence of a tope is suspected the check should be knocked off, and if the reel is in gear it should be switched to free spool, the angler lightly checking it with his thumb to stop it over-running. When the moment to strike comes, the thumb can be used to brake the spool altogether. I write 'strike', but there should be no wild slashing of the rod over the shoulder. All that is necessary is to check the fish for a few seconds until the hook is set well home. The reel can then be flicked back into gear, the light drag having been pre-set, and the fight is on.

The tope must be allowed its first run against minimum drag. If it is checked too early on the light gear, either the line will go at once or the fish will roll to the surface and smash you that way. Eventually the fish will begin to slow down and by increasing thumb pressure you will be able to see if you can turn it. After a few encounters, your 'feeling' for what the fish is doing will increase in sensitivity and you will be able to handle it with increasing confidence.

No attempt should be made to land the tope until it is completely quiescent. A gaff may then be used, but it is perfectly easy to tail the fish, that is, grasp it firmly round the 'wrist' of its tail with both hands and haul it inboard or on shore. It can't bite you if it is held well out at arm's length. Don't attempt to recover your trace and hook until the fish is dead.

What I have described so far has been simple legering from shore or boat over clean ground, but, as I suggested earlier, tope are to be found also in quite different circumstances – over rocky ground where there may be a fast tide race and where POLLACK feed, the kind of place that is also attractive to shoaling MACKEREL and BASS. Obviously, bottom fishing is impossible here, and in any case the bait is much better for some movement since the tope are not shovelling up dabs from the bottom but chasing shoal fish. There is no need to bother with a running lead; a simple paternoster is rigged and the tackle lowered over the side of the boat until the lead taps bottom. The line is then taken up a fathom or two and a detachable float is set on the line. The boat is then allowed to drift over the reef. When a run comes the strike is made instantaneously.

It is better to use a very big lask of fish than a whole or a half one for this kind of fishing. Sand-eels are often a good bait for tope in these circumstances.

You'll notice that all the rules of tope fishing seem to be reversed in this reef fishing – no running lead, an instant strike, and an unconcealed hook – but these factors, which would almost certainly ruin all chance of success in conventional tope fishing, work the other way over the rocks. It is fair to say that all the fish I have caught in this manner have been of moderate size, though, as at Kilmore Quay, there is usually the chance of a good bag in the numerical sense.

General

The record tope was taken off Hayling Island in 1949 and weighed 73 lb. 3 oz. Perhaps the best fish since then was the 69½-pounder taken off Saundersfoot, Pembrokeshire, in July 1962.

Tope are widely distributed throughout British waters. Even in districts where no specialist tope fishing has been done the enterprising sea angler would almost certainly be rewarded if he fished consistently for them. As far as established centres for tope fishing are concerned, there are a number of stations on the English Channel which produce good tope annually, and where experienced boatmen may be found. One centre which every year yields its quota of specimen tope is Littlehampton in Sussex. The Thames estuary is noted for its tope fishing (the sport was practically born at Herne Bay), and the Solent, apart from producing the record fish, has always yielded consistently good fishing.

On the east coast, a good deal of tope fishing is done on the Wash, but few specimens over forty pounds have been reported from this district. At one time it was alleged that the rockier, south-western coast of England did not produce many tope, but I am sure that this misconception arose from the fact that the methods that had evolved in the 1920s for tope-fishing on the south-east coast were not applicable in, say, Cornwall. I have found that wherever rocky ground and reefs are present, the local tope may very well be found feeding on the pollack and mackerel of the reefs rather than on the adjacent clean ground.

In the last five years, the south coast of Pembrokeshire has come into prominence by producing some remarkable specimens, including two of over 60 lb. and a number of 50 lb. plus fish. Most of these were caught from the shore, from the rocks, in fact, of the Castlemartin peninsula, but recently boat fishing out of Saundersfoot harbour has proved very successful. These results have been achieved by no more than half a dozen fishermen. It would be interesting to discover whether more intensive fishing, such as is practised on the Channel coast, would produce proportionally more impressive results. The fishing potential of Cardigan Bay is unknown, but this might well be a classic tope area. Tope are caught consistently off the coast of north Wales, as well as in Morecambe Bay, but here, once again, as we move north the average weight of individual specimens seems to fall off.

In Ireland there are a number of places which can be rated as excellent from the tope fishing point of view. Amongst them I would give pride of place to Kilmore Quay in Co. Wexford, where very large bags of tope are made, though the average size of fish is small – somewhere around 25 lb. However, when bags of a couple of dozen fish in a day's fishing are commonplace, there is little to complain about in this. Without particularizing, it may be said that there is consistently good fishing for tope right along the south coast of Ireland, wherever a boat may be hired. On the west coast, very good results have been obtained in the last few years in the Shannon Estuary, while farther north there is reputed to be excellent tope fishing out of Moville, Co. Donegal. There is great and growing interest among sea anglers in tope fishing, and it may be asserted with confidence that this necessarily sketchy list of tope-fishing stations will be greatly added to in the next few years.

C. G.

Turbot

The turbot (*Scopthalmus maximus*) is one of the largest of the flatfishes. Its body is roughly diamond-shaped, scaleless, and covered with blunt, bony tubercles. The upper surface is a mottled and speckled brown, the underside white. The lateral line arches over the pectoral fins.

Turbot are found mainly around the south and west coasts, where they inhabit waters around banks, feeding on the fish which move across the shallow parts. There are several such banks along the south coast of England, the most notable being the Skerries off Dartmouth, the Shambles off Weymouth, and the Varne off Folkestone.

Baits

Undoubtedly the best bait of all is a live sand-eel, a favourite delicacy of the turbot. At low water when you can usually see the bottom, great shoals of these eels can often be seen on the tops of the banks. It is well worth while having a string of feathers with you. If they are jiggled up and down, it is often possible to hook a few eels, which will almost certainly attract the turbot once the tide begins to flow. The feathers must only be moved up and down a very short distance to get the eels, which, attracted by the bright colours, mill around the lures. Most of them will usually be foul-hooked, as the hooks are too large for them to take properly.

If live sand-eels are not available, the next best bait is MACKEREL or, if freshly caught, herring. Cut a long sliver of flesh from the belly and thread it on the hook so as to make it look like a sand-eel when placed in the water.

Tackle

Tackle should consist of a medium-sized boat rod, a reel with capacity for about 150 yds of line of up to 25 lb. b.s., a running boom with weight according to the strength of the tide, and a 4 yd nylon trace. Hook size should be 4/0.

Fishing Methods

The best method of fishing is to anchor above a bank where it falls off into deep water. It is most important to fish the side of the bank away from the tide. Therefore during the slack-water period it will be necessary to move from one end of the bank to the other.

Turbot invariably lie at the bottom of the shelving bank and come upwards to take the bait. An ideal depth at which to anchor is the eight-to-ten fathom mark, sufficiently far on to the bank to allow your bait to run out some 50 to 80 yds from the boat before it reaches the shelving area.

Normally the tide sweeps across the bank in a diagonal manner; it is therefore essential, when once the marks have been located, to take careful bearings at various stages of the tide, in order to know the exact location of the shelf for future fishing.

The slack-water period produces few, if any, fish. A strong flow of water is needed, as it allows the bait to work from side to side in the current.

When the bait is lowered to the bottom, allow the weight to work its way to the edge of the bank so that the trace will be flowing in the tide slightly out from the shelving face. The bait will now work in a life-like manner and should produce results if the fish are around.

Allow the turbot plenty of time to get the hook down before

striking. With a big fish in a heavy tide the strain will be severe and it is essential to get a firm hook-hold well inside the fish.

It requires a good deal of patience, particulary when fishing the Varne Bank, to get the fish near enough to the boat to gaff, for when the tide is very heavy once the fish is clear of the bank it invariably gets swept up to the surface by the force of the current. When this occurs, it is sometimes well worth while letting out extra cable on the anchor and reeling in at the same time. Then, when the fish has been boated, the boat can be hauled back to its original position.

Sometimes turbot will be seen to follow a bait through the water. They have been known to go for one on the surface. This indicates that these fish would, if given the opportunity, go for a moving bait such as a large silver spoon.

One attraction of turbot fishing is the fact that in addition to this species, WHITING, DOGFISH, TOPE, and DABS will be found on the shelving bottom, and even at slack water sport is normally brisk.

General The present record is held by R. Tochard of Dartmouth with a magnificent specimen of 28 lb. 8 drams. However, a new claim for a fish of 28 lb. 8 oz. has recently been submitted by W. T. B. Rodde of Ulverton, who landed his turbot when fishing the marks off Coverack. This fish has not as yet been accepted by the Record Fish Committee.

S. N.-B.

Whiting

As its name suggests, the whiting (*Gadus merlangus*) is a member of the cod family, although it lacks the barbule of the COD. It is easily recognizable by the dark spot behind its pectoral fin. It is a most prolific fish, which is to the sea angler what the ROACH is to the freshwater fisherman. During the autumn and winter months whiting can provide fair sport for the shore angler.

Judged against other sea fish whiting are not strong fighters. The good thing about them is that they often provide sport when other fish are inactive. They have often turned out to be face-savers in sea angling competitions from beach or pier and have made the bag for a number of prize-winners.

Whiting are at their largest and most numerous on the east coast, where they are caught in numbers by both beach and pier anglers. On the south and west coasts, inshore whiting are listed as small – up to 6 oz. – but I do not think this is correct. At times whiting are taken in the Bristol Channel well above the 1 lb. mark.

Baits

Baits vary according to locality, but the most generally used are worms, mussels, and strips of fish. Lugworm in particular will readily take fish at times. Sprats, whole if small, part if large, are a deadly bait particularly in the late part of the year.

Tackle

Use the lightest tackle possible depending on strength of tide and size of weight needed. Hooks should be on the small side, in the region of size 3 or 4. Some anglers use what one could term freshwater tackle – light rod, reel, and a 6–7 lb. line. This provides good sport; the only trouble with it is that at times something bigger comes along, more than the gear in use will handle, and bang goes the lot.

Fishing Methods

Paternoster gear is the one most commonly used, whether from boat, pier, or shore.

Whiting seem to come on all of a sudden. Often, for a time there is little doing and then all at once rod tips begin to jerk all along the line. Sport is often best around dusk, but it can continue after dark. Most bites seem to come near the top of the tide and continue for a time after the turn. But this varies with locality. In the Burnham-on-Sea area of the Bristol Channel, for instance, most bites occur on the out-going tide. So it is wise to check up locally.

Bites are sharp and whiting are noted for stripping the bait off the hook. I have seen anglers have dozens of bites and yet only hook the odd fish. Usually they have had the rod at rest, and by the time they get to it both bait and whiting have gone. It is safer to hold the rod, feel the bite, and strike quickly. As with roach fishing, you have to be quick, or it is too late.

General

The record whiting, of 6 lb., was caught in Loch Torridon, a deep-water sea loch on the west coast of Scotland. Any whiting that goes over the 1 lb. mark is a fair catch. Small ones are often used as bait for other fish.

Whiting are, of course, good eating, and a catch of fair-sized specimens is a most welcome addition to the larder.

R. P.

Wrasse

There are seven species of this fish and all are found round rocky coasts. Some of them are rare in British waters. The ballan wrasse (*Labrus bergylta*) and the cuckoo or striped wrasse (*Labrus mixtus*) are the main members of the tribe to interest the angler. The other better-known species are the corkwing (*Crenilabrus mixtus*) and the rainbow (*Coris julis*). All are beautifully coloured, with an almost tropical look. The rainbow is predominantly greenish with lighter diamond markings along its lateral line and an enormously long dorsal fin. The cuckoo is a splendid creature with yellow and blue stripes. The corkwing is greenish again, with rudimentary stripes on its upper half, and a stubby appearance. The ballan wrasse is a good thick fish with a long dorsal fin ending in an up-sweep at its rear end, and a rounded tail. The overall colouring is greeny blue and the fins have orange bands.

All wrasse have large scales, spiny dorsals, and thick lips.

Wrasse have a bad name with some anglers, because they are not good eating; they have a nasty habit of taking on the flavour of their current food. Their thick lips, too, are related to their diet, for they are great browsers and masticators of tough, rock-living molluscs. Thick and protruding lips enable them to suck these off rocks and out of crevices.

Although any rocky coast will produce wrasse, they are most plentiful and grow to specimen size mainly round the west coasts. South Devon, Cornwall, and west Wales are the places to look for big fish.

In these areas the ballan ranges from 1 lb. to 5 lb. A fish of 12¾ lb. was caught off Looe in 1912, together with several others of 10 lb. These, however, were exceptional, not only in their size, but also in being taken from a boat, for most wrasse, big ones included, are taken from the shore, usually from rocks running into deeper water.

Wrasse are warm-water fish, and are to be taken between April and the end of October. They are seldom seen in winter. The best time to look for them is on a sunny day, with a calm sea, and at low tide. On these days favourite spots such as deep coves and gullies can often produce a dozen or so of fish ranging up to 4 lb. or more. As the tide rises they move in and search for food among the weeds and rocks which were previously uncovered.

Baits The favourite bait is live prawn, but crab and ragworm can also account for many fish. Although the limpet is a major item of diet, it does not seem to work very well as a hook-bait.

Tackle and Fishing Methods

As the ground fished over is likely to be rough, float tackle is preferable to bottom gear. Paternoster gear does very well The float should be adjusted so that the bait hangs a foot or so off the bottom.

The most suitable tackle is that normally used for float-fishing for BASS, MACKEREL, POLLACK, etc. The rod should be of the light sea or salmon spinning type, 9 to 9½ ft in length. Glass rods, either solid or tubular, are now quite popular; they combine lightness with strength. The solid glass type are cheaper than either tubular glass or split-cane, and do very well for this kind of fishing.

Of the variety of line materials to choose from, monofilament and Terylene are now the most popular. Monofilament has the advantage of being cheap, but against this must be weighed its tendency to stretch. Terylene is expensive in comparison but it has all the other advantages without the drawbacks. It is very strong, does not stretch, is rot-proof, and, if greased, will float. At one time reels for this type of shore fishing were of the Nottingham type, but today the fixed-spool or the multiplier has taken its place. Terylene is by far the best line for use with a multiplier. For float-fishing, lines should be around 8–10 lb. b.s.

Unlike most sea fish, wrasse have small mouths, and a No. 1 or 2 hook is quite large enough for them.

General

Wrasse are not quite so easy to catch as many imagine. Their powerful dives down under a rock often mean a lost fish. Although poor to eat (this, by the way, is a judgement with which not all anglers would agree) they are certainly capable of giving good sport. The record ballan wrasse was caught at Looe in 1912 by F. A. Mitchell-Hedges. It weighed 12¾ lb.

R. P.

Appendix: *River Authorities and Licence Fees*

England and Wales

The Avon and Dorset River Authority
Rostherne, 3 St Stephen's Road, Bournemouth, Hampshire
S. £3 s., £2 m., £1 w., 7*s.* 6*d.* d.; T. 15*s.* s., 7*s.* 6*d.* m., 3*s.* 6*d.* w.; C. 2*s.* 6*d.* s. (no charge for juniors).

Bristol Avon River Authority
Green Park Road, Bath, Somerset
S. 20*s.* s., 8*s.* w.; T. 5*s.* s., 2*s.* w.; C. 2*s.* 6*d.* s., 1*s.* w.; (juniors 6*d.* s.).

Cheshire River Authority
County Hall, Chester
No licences required.

Cornwall River Authority
St Johns, Western Road, Launceston, Cornwall
S., S.T., and T. £3 s., 30*s.* w., 10*s.* d.; T. 15*s.* s., 7*s.* 6*d.* w., 2*s.* d.

Cumberland River Authority
256 London Road, Carlisle, Cumberland
S. £10 10*s.* s., £4 w.; T. and S.T. £2 w.

Dee and Clwyd River Authority
2 Vicar's Lane, Chester
S. £4 s., 30*s.* w., 10*s.* d.; S.T. £2 s., 15*s.* w., 5*s.* d.; T. 10*s.* s., 5*s.* w., 2*s.* d.; C. 5*s.* s., 3*s.* w., 1*s.* 6*d.* d.

Devon River Authority
County Hall, Topsham Road, Exeter
S. and T. Licence duties vary according to district.

East Suffolk and Norfolk River Authority
The Cedars, Albemarle Road, Norwich
T. 10*s.* y.; C. 5*s.* y., 1*s.* d.

East Sussex River Authority
1 Upper Lake, Battle, Sussex
S. and S.T. 10*s.* s.; T. 5*s.* s.; C. 2*s.* s. (1*s.* for juniors).

Essex River Authority
Rivers House, New Writtle Street, Chelmsford, Essex
S., T., and C. 10*s.* s.; C. 4*s.* s.

S. – Salmon
S.T. – Sea-trout
T. – Trout
C. – Coarse fish
s. – season
y. – year
m. – month
w. – week
d. – day
f. – fortnight

Glamorgan River Authority
Tremains House, Coychurch Road, Bridgend, Glamorgan
S., S.T., and T. 30*s*. s. (juniors 3*s*. 6*d*. s.); T. 7*s*. 6*d*. s.; C. 2*s*. 6*d*. s.

Great Ouse River Authority
Elmhurst, Brooklands Avenue, Cambridge
T. and C. 5*s*. y., 1*s*. 6*d*. d.

Gwynedd River Authority
Highfield, Caernarvon
S. and T. Licence duties vary according to river; C. No licence required.

Hampshire River Authority
The Castle, Winchester, Hampshire
S. £3 s., £2 m., £1 w. (half price for some rivers); T. 15*s*. s., 7*s*. 6*d*. m., 3*s*. 6*d*. w.; C. No licence required.

Kent River Authority
River Board House, London Road, Maidstone
T. and C. 7*s*. 6*d*. s., 1*s*. d.; C. 3*s*. s. (1*s*. for juniors.)

Lancashire River Authority
5 St Nicholas Street, Lancaster
Licence duties vary according to river.

Lee Conservancy Catchment Board
Brettenham House, Lancaster Place, Strand, London w c 2.
No licence required.

Lincolnshire River Authority
50 Wide Bargate, Boston, Lincolnshire
T. and C. 10*s*. y., 3*s*. w.; C. 5*s*. y., 1*s*. 6*d*. w. (No licence for juniors.)

Mersey River Authority
Liverpool Road, Great Sankey, Warrington, Lancashire
No licence required.

Northumbrian Authority
Dunira, Osborne Road, Newcastle upon Tyne 2
(For Northumberland) S. and S.T. £3 10*s*. (£1 10*s*. Tyne area) s., 30*s*. w.; T. £1 (juniors 5*s*.) s., 10*s*. w.; C. No licence required.
(For Durham) S. £1 s.; T. and C., 5*s*. s., 1*s*. w. (juniors 2*s*. 6*d*. s.).

Severn River Authority
Portland House, Church Street, Great Malvern, Worcestershire
S. (for Vyrnwy, Banwy) £2 2*s*. s. Elsewhere £3 3*s*. s.; £1 10*s*. f.; 7*s*. 6*d*. d.; T. and C. 5*s*. s.

Somerset River Authority
The Watergate, West Quay, Bridgwater, Somerset
T. 6*s*. 6*d*. s., 3*s*. 6*d*. m. (juniors 3*s*. 6*d*. s.); C. 3*s*. 6*d*. s., 2*s*. 6*d*. m. (juniors 6*d*. s.).

South West Wales River Authority
Penyfai House, Llanelly, Carmarthenshire
S., T., and S.T. £2 5*s*. s.; £1 w.

Sussex River Authority
57 Church Road, Burgess Hill, Sussex
S.T. 10*s*. s.; T. 5*s*. s.; C. 2*s*. s. (juniors 1*s*.)

Thames Conservancy
2/3 Norfolk Street, Strand, London WC2
No licence required. Weir season permits £1.

Trent River Authority
Meadow Lane, Nottingham
S. and S.T., 10*s*. s.; T. 2*s*. 6*d*. s.; C. 1*s*. (juniors under fourteen free).

Usk River Authority
The Croft, Goldcroft Common, Caerleon, Mon.
S. £6 10*s*. s., £3 m., £1 10*s*. w.; T. £1 s., 10*s*. w.
Reservoirs, 10*s*. s.

Welland and Nene River Authority
Oundle, nr Peterborough
T. and C. 7*s*. 6*d*. y.; C., 5*s*. y., C. 2*s*. w.

West Sussex River Authority
County Hall, Chichester, Sussex
S., S.T., and T. 10*s*. s.

Wye River Authority
4 St John Street, Hereford
S. £6 10*s*. s., £2 w., 13*s*. d. (Wye above Llanwrthwl Bridge or tributary above Builth Bridge £3 5*s*. s.); T., 10*s*. s., 3*s*. 6*d*. w.; C. 4*s*. 6*d*. s. (junior 1*s*. s.).

Yorkshire Ouse and Hull River Authority
21 Park Square South, Leeds 1, Yorkshire
S. and S.T., £4 s., £1 10*s*. w.; T. 5*s*. s., 1*s*. w.

Scotland

District River Boards certainly exist in Scotland for the preservation and administration of angling, but they issue no licences. Fees are invariably payable to riparian owners where salmon are concerned. Trout fishing, and certainly coarse fishing, can often be obtained free by tactful request.

Northern Ireland

There are overall rod licences, valid in each of the four fishery districts. These are: salmon and sea-trout, £1 10*s.* per season and 10*s.* per week except in the Foyle Fisheries Area where the fee is £2 per season; brown trout and coarse-fishing licences, 10*s.* per season. It pays to ask about close seasons; they vary slightly from district to district.

Eire

As might be expected, Eire has its own set of rules. No licence is required for brown trout or coarse fishing (indeed, there is no close season for coarse fish). Salmon and sea-trout licence fees are as follows: per season in all districts, £4; available in one district only for season, £3; the same, valid in district of issue only, £2.

Close Seasons – England and Wales
The following dates apply generally, though River Boards can make their own variations to suit local climatic and other conditions by by-law.
Salmon: 1 November to 31 January
Trout: 1 October to last day of February
Coarse Fish: 15 March to 15 June

Close Seasons – Scotland
Salmon: The close season varies widely from river to river. Some open as early as 10 January, others as late as 14 April. End of season dates are equally inconsistent. It pays to ask.
Trout: 7 October to 14 March, both dates inclusive.

Thames Conservancy By-laws

Editor's Note: By-laws imposed by various River Boards, of course, vary enormously. As far as fishery interests are concerned they are all aimed at preserving and improving sport for anglers. Some do it considerably more effectively than others.

It is plainly impossible to give all the by-laws of all the River Boards in Britian. Here, however, are those relating to the most important, and perhaps most heavily fished, river in Britain, the Thames.

As explained elsewhere in this book (see p. 14) the Thames is not entirely typical. It does not, for instance, charge licence fees. It also contains one of the few substantial **free** fisheries in Britain. Again, it imposes a minimum-size list on fish that may be taken and this 'Thames Standard' has an important effect in contests fished on Thames Conservancy waters. Nevertheless its rules give a fair idea of how the angler must cooperate to maintain his fishing.

Extracts from the Thames Conservancy By-laws

(A) No person shall, for the purpose of taking or attempting to take fish in the Thames, use or attempt to use any wheel, basket, instrument, net, hook, tackle, or other apparatus or device except the following, and then only in the places, at the times, and in the manner hereinafter prescribed, that is to say:

(1) Rod and line. Provided that:

(*a*) No person shall use a rod and line except with a natural or artificial bait, and only for the purpose of taking fish by hooking them in the mouth;

(*b*) No person shall fish with more than two rods and lines at the same time, and such rods when in use shall not be placed more than 15 feet distant the one from the other;

(*c*) No person shall fish with a rod and line having more than three separate baits attached thereto;

(*d*) No person shall leave a rod and line with the bait or hook thereof in the water unattended or out of sight or otherwise without having sufficient control thereof.

(2) A landing net with a diameter not exceeding two feet and a depth not exceeding three feet from the ring to the bottom of the net, and having not more rows of knots than seventy-two to the linear yard. Provided that no person shall use a landing net except a person angling with a rod and line, or an assistant to such person, for the purpose of landing a fish already hooked by means of a rod and line lawfully used.

(3) A minnow net with a diameter net exceeding three feet in any part thereof. Provided that no person shall fish with a minnow net except a person angling or about to angle in the river, or his servant or agent, for the purpose of obtaining minnows for bait to be used by persons angling in the Thames.

(4) A hand or well net.

(5) A grig wheel with a diameter not exceeding six inches. Provided that no person shall use a grig wheel in that part of the river which is situate above the City Stone at Staines, and provided also that no person shall place any grig wheel near any dam or weir.

(6) A gaff hook. Provided that no person shall use a gaff hook except a person angling with a rod and line, or an assistant to such person, for the purpose of landing a fish already hooked by means of a rod and line lawfully used.

(7) A casting or bait net. Provided that such net may only be used by assistant river-keepers, and then for the sole purpose of obtaining bait to be used by persons for angling in the Thames.

(B) The measurement of any net referred to in this By-law shall be made when the net is wet.

(C) Any person using or attempting to use for the purpose of taking or attempting to take fish in the Thames any wheel, basket, instrument, net, hook, tackle, or other apparatus or device, except as hereinbefore prescribed, shall be guilty of an offence against these By-laws.

No person on any vessel under way upon the Thames shall draw or cause or suffer to be drawn in the direction in which such vessel is proceeding any line with hook or bait attached thereto, whether such line be attached to a rod or otherwise.

No person shall use in the Thames any device or tackle that does not admit of the fish taken therewith being returned to the water without serious injury.

No person shall, with the intent or in such a manner as to take fish by means of foul hooking, snatching, or snaring in the Thames, use any line, rod and line, hook, wire, snare, or other similar device either alone or in conjunction with a rod and line.

No person shall fix or attach any net to the soil or make the same stationary in any way, and a net held by any person on any vessel or attached thereto when moored or anchored in the Thames, shall be deemed to be a fixed net for the purpose of this By-law. Provided that this By-law shall not apply to a keep-net used for the purpose of keeping fish alive by a person angling in the Thames.

No person shall place in the Thames at the mouth of any

river, creek, backwater, or brook communicating with or running into the Thames or at any mill sluice, race, or branch of the Thames, any net or device which might stop or catch fish or impede the free movement of the same into, out of, or up or down the Thames.

No person shall use or attempt to use any night hook, fixed hook, night line, handline, or fixed line in the Thames.

No person shall, between the expiration of the first hour after sunset and the commencement of the last hour before sunrise, fish for, take, or attempt to take any fish by any means whatever in that part of the Thames as lies above the City Stone at Staines nor when on any vessel on that part of the Thames which lies below the said City Stone.

(1) No person shall fish for, take, or attempt to take Salmon or Salmon Trout in the Thames during the period from the 1st day of September to the 31st day of March following (both inclusive), and no person shall fish for, take, or attempt to take Trout or Char in the Thames during the period from the 11th day of September to the 31st day of March following (both inclusive).

(2) No person shall fish for, take, or attempt to take Smelts in the Thames during the period from the 25th day of March to the 27th day of July following (both inclusive).

(3) No person shall fish for, take, or attempt to take Lampreys or Lamperns in the Thames during the period from the 1st day of April to the 24th day of August following (both inclusive).

(4) Except as hereinbefore provided, no person shall fish for, take, or attempt to take any fish in the Thames during the period from the 15th day of March to the 15th day of June following (both inclusive). Provided that during the period from the 1st day of April to the 15th day of June following (both inclusive) any person may (1) with a rod and line only, and by means of an artificial fly or spinning or live bait, fish for, take, or attempt to take Salmon, Salmon Trout, Trout, and Char, and (2) lawfully fish for, take, or attempt to take Bleak, Gudgeon, Dace, and Minnows, to be used only as spinning or live bait.

No person shall take in or out of the Thames, or have in his possession, or expose for sale on the river, or on the shore or banks thereof, or within one hundred yards on either side of the Thames, any fish of the species hereinafter mentioned of less than the sizes and dimensions hereinafter specified (that is to say):

Barbel	Extreme length,	16	inches
Bleak	,,	4	,,
Bream	,,	12	,,
Carp	,,	12	,,
Chub	,,	12	,,
Dace	,,	7	,,
Flounders	,,	7	,,
Grayling	,,	12	,,
Gudgeon	,,	5	,,
Lamperns or Lampreys	,,	7	,,
Perch	,,	9	,,
Pike or Jack	,,	18	,,
Roach	,,	8	,,
Rudd	,,	8	,,
Smelts	,,	6	,,
Tench..	,,	10	,,
Trout	,,	16	,,

Provided that this By-law shall not apply:

(*a*) To any person who takes any undersized fish unintentionally and at once returns such fish alive to the Thames with as little injury as possible.

(*b*) To any Roach, Dace, Gudgeon, Bleak, or Minnows taken from the Thames for use as bait, to be used by persons angling in the Thames. Provided that no person on the Thames, or on the banks or shores thereof, or within one hundred yards on either side of the Thames, shall be entitled to have in his possession, or under his control, at any one time more than fifty of such fish for use as bait, or to take from the Thames by himself, his servants or agents, more than fifty of such fish on any one day.

Any person who shall offend against any of these By-laws shall for every offence be liable to a penalty not exceeding £10, and in the case of a continuing offence to a further daily penalty not exceeding the like amount, which said penalties shall be recoverable, enforced, and applied according to the provisions of the Thames Conservancy Act 1894, as amended by the Port of London Act 1908.

Index

N.B. The main references are given in bold figures. An asterisk against a page number indicates an illustration on that page, and (G) indicates a reference to the Glossary definition.

Figures in italics indicate coloured illustration between these pages

Index

Index

Index

Index